Oracle Press™

Oracle Backup & Recovery 101

Oracle Press™

Oracle Backup & Recovery 101

Kenny Smith
Stephan Haisley

McGraw-Hill/Osborne

New York   Chicago   San Francisco
Lisbon   London   Madrid   Mexico City
Milan   New Delhi   San Juan
Seoul   Singapore   Sydney   Toronto

McGraw-Hill/Osborne
2600 Tenth Street
Berkeley, California 94710
U.S.A.

To arrange bulk purchase discounts for sales promotions, premiums, or fund-raisers, please contact **McGraw-Hill/**Osborne at the above address. For information on translations or book distributors outside the U.S.A., please see the International Contact Information page immediately following the index of this book.

Oracle Backup & Recovery 101

1234567890 FGR FGR 0198765432

ISBN 0-07-219461-8

Publisher Brandon A. Nordin	**Copy Editor** Sally Engelfried
Vice President & Associate Publisher Scott Rogers	**Proofreaders** Cheryl Abel, Susie Elkind, Stefany Otis
Acquisitions Editors Lisa McClain, Jeremy Judson	**Indexer** Valerie Perry
Project Editor Lisa Wolters-Broder	**Computer Designers** Michelle Galicia, Elizabeth Jang
Acquisitions Coordinator Athena Honore	**Illustrators** Michael Mueller, Lyssa Seiben
Technical Editor Roger Snowden	**Series Design** Jani Beckwith

This book was composed with Corel VENTURA ™ Publisher.

To Tina, my best friend. I love you with all my heart.
Kenny

To my family and friends who have provided motivation
and encouraged me to be me.
Stephan

About the Authors

Kenny Smith works for Pinnacle Data Technologies as the Director of Development. Pinnacle Data offers Oracle Consulting and EDI services. Kenny began working with Oracle technology in 1991 as an employee of the Southern Company. Over the years, he has designed and developed database applications and performed administrative duties for large and small clients around the country. He has published articles in *Oracle Magazine, Profit Magazine, Exploring Oracle* (Element K Journals), and *Oracle Professional* (Pinnacle Publishing), among others. He was a contributing author in *Ocp Training Guide: Oracle Dba* by New Riders Publishing. Kenny has presented at a number of Oracle conferences in the United States and Europe. He lives in Atlanta, Georgia, with his wife, Tina, and sons Tyler, Wesley, and Kevin.

Stephan Haisley has been with Oracle for a little more than five years, when he originally joined the UK RDBMS Worldwide Support Center. Throughout the years he has worked within various departments, including RDBMS Unix support, RDBMS NT support, Premium on-site support, and a year in consultancy. He now works as a Senior Technical Advisor for Oracle Worldwide Support Center of Expertise. This small group has the primary mandate of resolving the most complex of problems, leveraging the knowledge to the rest of the organization and training support with the internal workings and diagnostic methodologies of the RDBMS.

Contents

PART II
User Managed Recovery

PART III
Server Managed Recovery

PART IV
Appendixes

Acknowledgments

Kenny Smith

One of the biggest benefits of writing: you really have to learn your stuff. When I undertook this effort, I knew I had plenty to learn about Oracle backup and recovery. After meeting Stephan at the IOUG conference in Orlando in spring 2001, I asked him to take part in this book. Thankfully, he accepted. Stephan dramatically improved the quality of this book through his dedicated research, careful attention to the technical details, and expert guidance. Through e-mail, instant messages, chapter revisions, and phone calls, he tutored me in some important aspects of Oracle backup and recovery while we fine-tuned each chapter. Stephan, thanks for making this book the best.

Thanks to the wonderful folks at Oracle Press: Lisa McClain, Jeremy Judson, Athena Honore, and Lisa Wolters-Broder.

Thanks to Roger Snowden for technical editing and many helpful suggestions.

Many other people contributed to the success of this book. Mark Loftin helped with the RMAN media management layer discussion. Kathleen Woodard reviewed some of the chapters and gave us some helpful feedback. My brother, Jim Smith, works an instructor for Chubb Institute. His valuable insight into some of the chapters helped guide us from an instructor's perspective. Scott Phillips and David McConnell deserve thanks for their help and encouragement during the last stretch of book development.

Several individuals have provided inspiration to me throughout my career. Rick Goudeau inspired me to want to be a DBA. David Thomas taught me valuable programming and testing techniques. Garrett Suhm and David Wendelken encouraged me to write articles.

My family at the North Atlanta Church of Christ kept me focused on the important things during the long work hours. Thanks to Ron Swann and the many other close friends at the men's prayer breakfast.

Thanks to my wife's parents (Henry and Rubie Floyd) for their continued inspiration and support to me and my family. Henry had a vision for my writing before I did.

Even more thanks to:

My dad, James Sidney Smith, who taught me character and perseverance through his teaching and example.

My mom, Pat Smith, who has been my life's biggest fan.

My son, Tyler. Tyler helped me install Linux and gladly let me use "his" computer to develop many of the chapter's exercises. Thanks, buddy-boy.

My son, Wesley. Sometimes, Wesley would keep me company by doing his homework with me while I slogged through a chapter. I'm lovin' a Bundy.

My son, Kevin. Kevin asked me many times, "Is this book ever going to be finished?" Well, Kevin, it's finally finished.

While I was writing, she was cooking dinner. While I was scripting, she was putting three boys to bed. While I was reading, she was driving the boys to practice. While I was editing, she was loving and caring for our boys. And me. All this she did—after her own busy day at work. Tina—this is your book, too.

"I have chosen the way of truth, I have set my heart on your laws.
I run in the path of your commands, for you have set my heart free.
Your word is a lamp to my feet and a light for my path."
Psalm 119:30,32,105

Stephan Haisley

Writing my acknowledgements section for this book is a daunting task. I've had the opportunity to learn from so many great people that it is impossible to name them all.

My family deserves many thanks and much applause for supporting me in my great move across the Atlantic in 1999 from England to Colorado. I was never really sure if I was doing the right thing for the first year. After many positive family discussions and much upset, for which I am sorry, I have survived and made a success of it. Mum, Dad, Nicola, and Cheryl, please take a bow.

Since joining Oracle in 1996, I have had the pleasure to work with a number of extremely talented people. I would like to especially mention Jim Barlow, Joel Goodman, Richard Powell, Kevin Quinn, Mark Fulford, and Steve Flood. I have many fond memories of being beaten up technically and socially by these guys. I would of course like to thank the guys in the Center of Expertise (Steve, Roger, Frank, Hector, Roderick, GP, Kevin, Sunil, and Jose) for giving me the chance to learn more than I thought was possible. Team meetings have never been this much fun. Kenny Smith deserves a thank-you for giving me the opportunity to take part in this project.

Finally, I would like to say a very big thank-you to the love of my life, Theresa. Her support through the many additional hours of work after my normal "work all the time" schedule has been second to none. I am extremely lucky. My thanks also go to our puppy, Nessy, who has kept my feet warm on a number of late night sessions in front of the computer.

Introduction

ey, new DBA. Glad you picked up this book!

If you want to be a good DBA, then learn how to tune SQL, configure the database, write some good PL/SQL, and implement and test a sound backup and recovery strategy.

If you want to be a bad DBA, don't back up your database. Or back it up, but don't learn how to recover with your backup. Another bad thing to do: don't test that your backups can be used for recovery. Nothing gets you in hot water faster than a down system or lost data.

So here is yet another Oracle Press book. Perhaps your shelf is full of them by now. For some funny reason, you don't find many books on backup and recovery. You'll find plenty about general DBA functions. Tuning is a big topic. If you want to learn PL/SQL, you have your choice of many useful references. But backup and recovery doesn't have as many book choices available. I'd been watching the book store shelves for a simple guide that explains Oracle backup and recovery. I wanted simple examples. Most of all, I needed directions to practice what I'd read. I couldn't find a book like this on any of the Web sites or in the conference book stores.

So, I decided to write it.

How to use this book

You can take advantage of this book in one of three ways:

- Read this book to learn about Oracle database backup and recovery. Concepts and terminology pertaining to database protection get explained and defined in simple terms. This book contains elementary commands and scripts useful for protecting your database and its contents.

■ "Do" this book to comprehend Oracle database backup and recovery. The way to get the most of this book is to read the output of commands you've typed and compare them to the output of this book. Each of the chapters in Parts 2 and 3 contain an introduction and definition of task you'd accomplish. Then the bulk of the chapter talks you through the exercise that you perform at home. A simple PC will be adequate to perform the exercises in this book. You'll create a few databases on a Linux or Windows machine, load Oracle version 8.1.7, and get right to work. These hands-on chapters will guide you through the steps to accomplish each step and test the results. After you've performed all the steps, you will be ready to perform this function on your true Oracle database systems. If you need to, you can refer back to each chapter when you are called upon to accomplish a similar task.

■ Refer to this book when you must perform Oracle database backup and recovery tasks. I tried to write simple to follow "recipes" that can function as a guide for Oracle backup and recovery tasks. The simple commands and scripts can be built on for your production environment.

Hands-on practice instills the concepts and terms you've learned in that chapter. While this book is not an exam preparation guide, you can prepare yourself for the OCP exams by actually doing what you are studying. Most importantly, you'll gain confidence in your knowledge by putting your knowledge to work.

Oracle Backup and Recovery 101 is divided into three parts. The first part provides an overview of concepts and options that you can use to protect your Oracle databases. You'll also get instructions to set up practice databases used in the exercises contained in the chapters of parts two and three. The second part of the book covers user-managed backup and recovery subjects. The third part of this book covers server-managed backup and recovery topics. Many of the exercises in Part 3 accomplish a similar function as ones in Part 2. Therefore, you can contrast tasks perform with RMAN and without RMAN.

Part 1—Backup & Recovery Overview

The chapters in this part provide a conceptual backdrop for comprehending the interrelated aspects of Oracle database backup and recovery. The creative first chapter draws a unique analogy between everyday family life and an Oracle database. Once the first chapter lays a foundation, Chapters 2 and 3 prepare you to participate in the remainder of the book.

Chapter 1: Protect the Data

Oracle Backup and Recovery is a core skill and essential measure of system success. By drawing a lose analogy to a personal photo collection, you'll have a better grasp of the contents of an Oracle database. You'll also understand the interrelationship between the database structural components. This chapter covers the basic concepts and Oracle architecture important to backup and recovery.

Chapter 2: Backup & Recovery Options

Oracle offers plenty of options to backup your data and database structure. Each method has unique value and application in protecting your database. This chapter provides a quick overview of the different options, providing a preview for the remainder of the book.

Chapter 3: Hands-on Practice

Most Oracle database professionals have theoretical knowledge about recovery. Yet many have little practical experience recovery on real systems. Prepare yourself for your next critical recovery task. Expose yourself to recovery scenarios discussed in Parts 2 and 3 of this book. In this chapter, you'll create a database as a place practice and become comfortable as an Oracle Recovery Manager.

Part 2—User Managed Recovery

A database is comprised of files that can be protected. The chapters in this part provide how-to descriptions of Oracle database user-managed recovery operations. Physical backup and recovery operations involve using the database files to protect the database and fix it when it breaks. In Chapter 4, we discuss user-managed backup and recovery on a closed database. In Chapter 5, we describe user-managed backup and recovery on an open database. In Chapter 6, we clone a database while it is closed and open. In Chapter 7, we create a standby database. Chapter 8 covers the logical Oracle Export and Import utilities to extract and create data objects. In Chapter 9, we through how you might perform a user managed tablespace point in time recovery. The tablespace recoveries will be done using Oracle Export/Import and by transporting tablespaces between databases. Finally, in Chapter 10, we explore how you can use Log Miner to mine the redo log file SQL statements.

Chapter 4: Recovery from Closed Backup

An Oracle database is simply a collection of files that interact with each other. The Oracle Server interacts with these files to serve up the data used by applications and web pages. Protect your data by copying the files of the database while the database is stopped. In this chapter, I'll describe how you can backup the database files in a database. Then, using that backup, you can restore and recover the database when some part of the database breaks. By configuring database archiving of all redo files, you can recover the database completely or to a point in time.

Chapter 5: Recovery from Open Backup

As database availability becomes more important, many database maintenance operations must occur on the database while it is open and available for use. All user-managed backup operations and many recovery operations can occur while the database is open for business. In this chapter, I'll provide instructions for how you can backup your open database. Then you'll completely recover the database while it is open. Lastly, you'll incompletely recover the database while using an open database backup.

Chapter 6: Duplicate Database

Duplicating your database is the "acid test" of a full database recovery. You can duplicate your database on the same machine or on a different machine. By recreating the control file or using a control file copy, replacing the files from a backup, you confirm that your backup can be recovered from. In this chapter, I'll describe how you can duplicate a closed and open database on the same machine. You'll also learn other scenarios how you can put what you've learned in duplicating databases.

Chapter 7: Standby Database

A standby database remains ready for use if your source database should falter. A standby database is an identical copy of the original source database. The standby is constantly catching up with its source by applying redo log files. In this chapter, you'll configure a standby database with user-managed recovery techniques. You'll open the standby read-only and then activate it.

Chapter 8: Export & Import

Using Export, you can extract the data out of the database. You can then insert the data into the same database or another database with the Import utility. Use Oracle Export to generate the SQL commands that can be used to regenerate an identical logical data copy to a binary file. Use Oracle Import to regenerate some or all of the data using that binary file. In this chapter, you'll get to export data to a file and import data from the file. These sample operations will introduce you to the variety options you have with these handy utilities.

Chapter 9: Tablespace Recovery

An Oracle database can be partially recovered. You can recover a non-system tablespace to a previous state via a technique called Tablespace Point-in-Time Recovery. This chapter details how you'd perform this valuable option and when you might employ this backup and recovery technique. Tablespace Recovery makes use of datafile backups, redo application, Export and Import.

Chapter 10: LogMiner

All database transactions are logged to files. You can mine those files for the SQL commands contained within. LogMiner provides the means to extract the SQL commands within you log files. You can retrieve the transactional statements from the redo log files, which can then be re-applied to a database. In this chapter, you will analyze the contents of redo logs. Using the transactions retrieved, you'll be able to explore how to make use of the SQL by applying it to the database.

Part 3—Server Managed Recovery

Server managed recovery involves using Recovery Manager (RMAN) to perform backup and recovery operations. Because backup and recovery of database systems is so critical, Oracle provides a tool that will handle the details for you, the database administrator. This book devotes seven full chapters to the next generation of database protection. These chapters will help a new DBA gain experience with all the fundamentals for RMAN deployment and use. These seven chapters will also assist an old time DBA migrate to a new skill set from the old tried-and-true user managed techniques. Most of the tasks discussed in Part 2 can be accomplished quickly and easily by RMAN. Therefore, you can easily contrast how you perform a specific task via user-managed method with the equivalent server managed method.

Chapter 11: RMAN Configuration

Recovery Manager makes block level backups of some or all of your database files. You can use a recovery catalog to track RMAN backups and target database structure. In order to backup to tape, several steps are required to prepare your tape drives to accept RMAN backups. In this chapter, we'll cover how you can configure RMAN to backup to disk or tape, using a recovery catalog.

Chapter 12: RMAN Backup

Backups with RMAN can be accomplished with a few simple commands. You can back up datafiles, archive logs, and control files. You can backup all the data blocks or just the ones that have changed since the last backup. You can run backups using stored scripts. RMAN offers a number of features that enable you to minimize the time it takes to backup a database or to restore and recover it. We'll also discuss monitoring and parallel backups. You'll also find a basic RMAN backup strategy that can be built on within your RMAN deployment.

Chapter 13: RMAN Catalog Maintenance

After deploying a backup strategy with RMAN, that deployment will need some ongoing maintenance. You'll also need to verify that your database has sufficient backups for a quick and complete recovery. RMAN backups can stack up over time. You'll need to delete the obsolete backup files. In this chapter, you'll look at RMAN Catalog maintenance.

Chapter 14: RMAN Recovery

Recovery Manager earns its name when it comes time to fix a broken database. Provided that you have a good backup, recovery can be a snap. You can recover some or the entire database. Of course you can recover to a point in the past. You can recover in parallel. Just a few commands and you're back in business. RMAN will enable you to perform recovery from various categories of database failure. In this chapter, I'll discuss how you can perform various recoveries with RMAN.

Chapter 15: RMAN Duplicate Database

Recovery Manager allows you to duplicate a database from RMAN backups. In this chapter, you'll instruct RMAN to duplicate a database on the same machine. You'll also learn some tips and techniques for RMAN duplication operations. This chapter accomplishes the same tasks as described in Chapter 6 using RMAN.

Chapter 16: RMAN Standby Database

RMAN can create a standby database for you. In this chapter, you'll learn how. This chapter accomplishes the same tasks as described in Chapter 7 using RMAN.

Chapter 17: RMAN Tablespace Recovery

RMAN can perform a tablespace point in time recovery for you. During this chapter, you'll learn how. This chapter accomplishes the same tasks as described in Chapter 9 using RMAN.

Part 4—Appendixes

The two appendixes can be helpful in understanding the subject matter of this book:

- Appendix A provides a glossary of important backup and recovery terminology.

- Appendix B provides quick examples and explanations of how you might take what you've learned about RMAN in Part 3 and put it to use with RMAN on an Oracle 9i database.

This book contains numerous SQL files, Linux scripts, Windows scripts, and RMAN scripts. We've placed them on the Oracle Press Web site (www.oraclepressbooks.com); feel free to download them for use during these exercises. We've tried hard to write a useful, easy to follow and accurate book. If you find a problem or have a suggestion or comment, send us an e-mail at *OracleBackupRecovery@yahoo.com*. Any errors or clarifications will be periodically updated on the Oracle Press website in the Errata section.

PART
I

Backup and Recovery Overview

CHAPTER
1

Protect the Data

magine, after many days of torrential rains, the river near your house rises and overflows its banks. Local authorities issue an evacuation notice. You must evacuate your home in two hours because your single-story, three-bedroom house will be underwater by midnight. With only two hours, what do you take with you?

First you grab the kids. Then you gather up the pets. Maybe you pack up some jewelry, spare clothes, and the little bit of cash you have lying around the house. Finally, you gather up your family pictures. Two hours is up. Time to go.

Why would you collect your pictures? They represent the experiences of your life—your childhood, marriage, kids, friends, vacations, and so on. Good memories can be recalled and experienced through these photos. Though insurance may pay to replace your furniture and your tools, an insurance check cannot recover the pictures taken on your wedding day. Family and friends can lend a hand. Charities may make donations. Money can't replace the 8mm home movies of your first bicycle ride. The insurance adjuster doesn't have a video of your kids' first steps. These photos and movies cannot be replaced once they are gone. They are irreplaceable possessions.

Like a family, a company has important possessions. Companies possess buildings, equipment, brand names, intellectual property, and so on. Your company protects these assets. They lock the doors at night and post a security guard at the building entrance. They also purchase insurance against fire, flood, storm damage, and theft. Your company also protects its data. Like a family's pictures, company data may be irreplaceable. How do they protect their data? By hiring you, the database administrator.

Companies put their data on computers and computer tape. This data is managed by software called a database. If the database fails, a company might lose its data. Replacing the missing data may be impossible. Most times, replacing the data is possible but difficult and tedious. Lost productivity from a broken database can cost a company a lot of money.

As we begin this book about Oracle database backup and recovery, I want to explain the concepts and importance of protecting your company's most valuable electronic possession: the data. Your job is to protect the data against any loss *and* protect system availability. Company data can only be used when it is available and correct.

In this chapter, I'll provide you an overview of the Oracle Server with emphasis on data protection. A clear understanding of database architecture and mechanisms goes a long way toward helping you accomplish your ongoing task of database backup and recovery. You may have some DBA experience or may have been to some classes. Perhaps you have taken the Oracle certification test. You might even be an Oracle employee who is new to backup and recovery concepts. A strong fundamental conceptual grasp is critical to your success as a database administrator, especially in the area of data disaster protection.

Introducing the House of Sid

If you're like me, getting a mental handle on computer technology is slippery sometimes. I like to learn by association. I learn something new by comparing it to something I already understand. I want to draw you a mental picture by telling you about a fictitious family and their compulsive activities. As you read about the days and nights of this family, you might not understand what they are doing and why they do it. Afterwards, when you read about how an Oracle database works, I hope you will see some similarities.

Let's have some fun to start this chapter. Database administrators don't have a reputation of being real fun-loving people. We have a reputation of being overworked, terse, geeky, and often unpleasant. You may not have fun in the following discussion. But I did. (Any similarity between the family you are about to meet and your in-laws are purely coincidental.)

A man named Sid has a passion for taking, protecting, and organizing family pictures. Sid has a wife named Debbie and three sons named Logan, Archie, and Chuck. He has a large house with a live-in butler named Simon and a maid named Pam. I'd like to tell you about his family, his house and his passion: taking, collecting, and showing off his pictures.

Now, Sid enjoys his family, friends, and vacations. He is always taking pictures. In fact, he always has his camera with him. He does not want to miss a thing. Every breakfast, lunch, and dinner, pictures get captured. When the kids come home from school, they have to say hi to dad into the camera. While the kids do their homework, click, click, click goes the camera. At the ball games, when son Archie goes to bat, every pitch gets captured. At the school dance, Chuck's dad is recording footage of each slow dance and conversation by the soda machine. His dog, Sadie, is the most photographed dog in the world.

He and his family collect millions of pictures. Some photos get deleted. Some get changed. Sid has a fascinating system of processing pictures. Let me tell you about his family, his house, and the efforts he and his family go through to develop, organize, and protect all these pictures.

Sid takes his pictures with a special camera. His camera produces both a picture and a negative with each picture transaction. He does not have to change rolls of film in his camera (it is a fancy piece of technology). The photos get placed on the walls in the house and negatives get stored in a safe location.

Sid's House

Did I tell about Sid's house? Hmm. Well it's very big and full of—you guessed it—pictures. Because Sid has so many, he had to find a place to put them all. Some pictures get hung on the walls. Some get stashed in photo albums. Some are inserted into scrapbooks; some get stuck in a box and stored in a closet, never to be looked at again. All these pictures are placed somewhere in his house. He calls his places for pictures *Picture Spaces*. A Picture Space might be a room with many walls or a scrapbook with many pages. A room is a logical storage destination of pictures. The wall in the room is the physical structure that holds the pictures in the Picture Spaces.

Debbie's Chores

Because Sid is so busy taking and processing pictures, he is not able to manage the placement and storage of them all. That's his wife's job. Debbie's full name is Debra Wrider. Her shirts are monogrammed with DBWR—it's sort of a family tradition to label everything.

Keeping all these pictures organized is a big job, but Sid and Debbie have worked out a system. As Sid captures his photos, he places them on a special shelf in the kitchen. This special shelf is labeled "DB_BUFFER_CACHE." Every so often, Debbie checks that shelf to see if any newly developed pictures have arrived. During the day, she retrieves pictures from the shelf and distributes them to the Picture Spaces where they belong. In fact, during a baseball game or a school dance, Sid is cranking out the pictures so fast that Debbie can hardly keep up. It is quite a sight to see, Sid taking pictures, placing them on the special shelf, Debbie placing those pictures in the scrapbooks, framing them on the wall, putting them in the photo album.

When Sid comes into the kitchen with his pictures and negatives, he and his wife might have a conversation something like this:

Sid: "Honey, guess what I have for you?"

Debbie: "You have some more pictures, don't you? You know how much I love to organize pictures."

Sid: "Of course. Archie's baseball team won in the last inning. He won the game with a two-out double in the ninth inning. I caught it all on film."

Debbie: "Terrific. Those pictures will look great in Picture Space SPORTS on wall 9. I can't wait to put them there. I'll invite all the neighbors to come by and have a look."

Sid: "Archie was so happy about the game. OK. I'm going to take some more pictures. I'll be back in 23 milliseconds. Oh, and by the way, I just put those pictures on the DB Buffer Cache shelf. We are at Sid's Catalog Number 1,332,935 now."

Debbie: "Got it. Bye."

To keep up with pictures, frames and logs gets cataloged with a number called Sid's Catalog Number. He uses these unique, ever-increasing numbers as a means to track all the picture operations in the house. Sid and Debbie got tired of referring to Sid's Catalog Number. Sid would get writer's cramp from writing down the words "Sid's Catalog Number" on all the pictures, videos, and negatives, so nowadays, they just call Sid's Catalog Number the *SCN*. Remember SCN. Sid's life revolves around it.

Around the house, the family knows this number as the SCN. You find this SCN everywhere. Sid writes them on negatives. He writes the low and high number of the SCN on each pack of negatives. Debbie writes them on the places where she puts the pictures. This number is a very important number in Sid's compulsive household.

Debbie places pictures in frames. Every frame in the whole house is the same size. Some frames hold one picture. Some frames hold several pictures. A few really big pictures actually span more than one frame. Sid has a life-sized picture of a time when he went tandem skydiving. That picture takes two frames. When a picture spans frames, Sid calls this *picture chaining*.

Whenever Debbie changes the pictures in a frame and commits to the change, she writes the SCN of the picture on the frame. Each picture in the house has a unique number. They call this picture number the picture ID. These picture IDs help Sid keep up with all the pictures on a wall on all the walls in his house. If he needs a picture quickly, he finds it via the picture ID. From the picture ID, Sid can quickly find the wall and the frame containing the picture.

Sometimes, Sid will change a picture. If he wants to edit one, he gets Debbie to find his picture via the picture ID. Debbie brings him a copy of the whole frame containing the picture. Just in case Sid changes his mind and does not like the change made to the picture, they place a copy of the framed picture in a closet they call the *Rollback* closet. When Sid changes the picture and commits to his change, Debbie takes the changed picture back to the wall where it belongs and writes a new SCN on the frame. If Sid doesn't like his change, they take the frame from the Rollback closet and put it back on the wall. This way, the picture looks as it did before Sid accessed the picture frame.

Logan's Chores

Debbie is so incredibly busy dealing with Sid's pictures that she doesn't have the time or energy to handle Sid's negatives. Sid decided that his sons were spending too much time playing video games and eating potato chips. He decided to put them to work.

Sid's oldest son is named Logan William Randolph. Logan's shirts are all monogrammed with LGWR. Logan has a pretty simple but very important job. As Sid's camera produces pictures, it also produces negatives. Logan's job is to place the negatives into *notebooks*. The family erected another special shelf in the kitchen. Above the shelf, Sid placed a label for the negatives that he passes off to his oldest son. The label reads "LOG_BUFFER." Logan sits at the kitchen table and watches the special LOG_BUFFER shelf. As the negatives get placed on the shelf, he quickly places each negative on a sheet in the notebook. Sid calls these notebooks redo notebooks. He chose the name *redo notebook* so that he could redo a picture later using the negative. Logan checks his shelf work more often than Debbie does hers. Sid figures that as long as he has a negative, he can always reproduce a picture. Logan and his dad's conversations are short and sweet:

Sid: "Logan, negatives on the shelf!"

Logan: "Got it dad. Taking care of it right away."

Logan places these negatives in the redo notebook in the order that he receives them. When the current notebook he is filling gets full, he switches to another notebook. Every time he switches redo notebooks, he makes a note in the a*lert notebook* and calls his brothers to come do their chores.

Sad, isn't it, that dads can be so focused on negatives with their oldest child?

By the way, not every single negative is saved for every picture. Sid designates some pictures not be logged. These pictures do not have a corresponding negative saved to the redo notebook. Sid calls this *no logging*.

Archie's Chores

Sid's second son, Archibald, has a different job. His shirts are all monogrammed with ARCH. Archie takes the negative sheets in the redo notebooks and stores them away in a safe place.

When Archie finds that Logan has switched to a different redo notebook, he springs into action. Archie grabs the negatives and puts them in a safe location outside of the house. Sid built a climate-controlled underground storage shed in his backyard. That's where he keeps each negative for safekeeping. If a storm came through and damaged his house, he could use the negatives in the shed to replace the damaged pictures. Each copy of Logan's redo notebook is called an *archived redo notebook*.

On any day, you might hear this banter between Sid and his second son:

Sid: "Archie? Where are you?"

Archie: "Dad, I'm in my room. Is Logan switching notebooks now?"

Sid: "Yes. He has just now finished."

Archie: "OK, Dad. I'll copy the negative sheets and make a new notebook for the shed. Then I'll update the *control notebook* and write an entry in the alert notebook."

Sid: "You are a good boy. I know I can count on you."

Chuck's Chores

Sid's youngest boy, Chuck, makes sure that everything is in sync. His full name is Charles Kenneth Patrick Thomas. The monogram on his shirts is CKPT. Chuck's job is coordinating the picture numbers of each wall, album, and scrapbook with the numbers in the control notebook. He does this job each time Logan switches redo notebooks. When he gets the signal, he starts running around the house, writing down a number on every wall. He also writes that same number in the control notebook. This keeps every thing consistent. Here's how a conversation might go with Chuck:

Sid: "Hey, Chuck."

Chuck: "Dad, is Logan switching notebooks again?"

Sid: "Yes, son. You know the routine. Go through the whole house with catalog number 1,332,935. Write this number on the head of every wall of pictures, on the cover of scrapbook, and on the top of picture box."

Chuck: "OK, just give me a few microseconds."

Sid: "And don't forget to write 1,332,935 in the control notebook!"

Chuck: "Dad, I know already. I've done this hundreds of times today."

I bet you're getting tired just reading about Sid's crazy family, aren't you? By now you are probably beginning to figure out that Sid has a dysfunctional family. Dysfunctional, yes, but also efficient and reliable. Sid likes it that way.

The Control Notebook

How does the family keep up with all this activity? Sid, Debbie, Logan, Archie, and Chuck have figured out that to make this picture collecting operation run smoothly, they will have to take very copious, careful notes. Each of them writes all their stuff to a log they call the control notebook.

The control cotebook has a household inventory entry for every wall, scrapbook, and picture box in the whole house. If Sid adds on a room for more pictures, he makes notes in the control notebook. When Logan switches redo notebooks, he jots that down in the control notebook. Each time Archie creates an archived redo notebook in the shed, he writes the name and SCN number ranges to the control notebook. Each time Chuck finishes the rounds in the house, he logs the details in the control notebook also. This special notebook keeps a dynamic inventory of all the places and numerical progress in the house.

The Alert Log

Every so often something goes wrong. An error might occur. Debbie might have trouble putting a picture in a frame because there is no more room on a wall. Archie may not be able to tuck a strip of negative away because someone spilled soda on it. Because Sid thinks of everything, he bought a spiral notebook and put it in a kitchen drawer. On the front of the notebook, he wrote *"alert log"*. Everybody in the family has to write down any problems in this log. Not only do they have to write down the errors in this log, but they also write down progress of normal activities. This alert log is a handy place to keep up with all the comings and goings of Sid's family. If they have to explain extra details about a situation, they create a new *trace notebook* and write the information in it. This way, the *alert notebook* doesn't get more cluttered than it already is.

Morning Routine

This tightly knit family wakes up all together in the morning. They also always go to bed at the same time. They call these times of the day *startup* and *shutdown*. Here is the morning startup routine:

Sid starts his day by rising out of bed and getting a cup of coffee. Right by the coffeemaker, he keeps a list of instructions in a notebook called the *initialization parameter file.* Reading this list helps him start his day. As he sips his coffee, he walks over to the control notebook to confirm it is there. He walks around the house and wakes up Debbie, Chuck, Logan, and Archie, Simon, and Pamela (you'll meet them in a moment).

Once everyone is awake, he opens the control notebook. He confirms all the picture walls are OK based on the contents of the control notebook. Once everything checks out, he opens his house to guests and starts taking pictures.

Sid hired a butler named Simon to help him in the mornings. His tuxedo is monogrammed with SMON. (The monogram is missing a letter in his name.) Some mornings the house is especially messy. The bedtime before, everybody in the family didn't get to clean up after him or herself. Once Simon is done, Sid opens the shades, turns on the phones and unlocks the doors. His house is open and ready for guests. Sid and Simon might start the day like this:

Simon: "Good morning, sir. How can I assist you today?"

Sid: "Yes, Simon. Good morning. Looks like we have a mess here. We crashed last night. Can you take care of all these uncompleted pictures and rollback please?"

Simon: "But of course. These negatives in the redo notebook will be reproduced and placed in the correct frame in short order."

Sid: "When you are done, you'll rollback, won't you?"

Simon: "Why, certainly, sir. I'll take these picture frames from the Rollback closet and place the old copy back where they belong."

Sid: "Excellent. Once you are done, I'll open the house."

Bedtime Routine

The bedtime routine at Sid's house is also interesting. By the time Sid's head hits the pillow, he likes everything in his house closed up, put up, and shut down. The first bedtime activity is to tell all the guests at the house to go home. Sid's evening mood may take one of four options. First, sometimes Sid is patient,and he waits for guests to leave on his or her own. Once everyone leaves, he starts the bedtime activities. Second option, Sid is impatient. He watches each houseguest. When each guest finishes whatever they are doing (looking at pictures, and so on), he shows them the door. Third option, Sid can be very impatient at bedtime. At these times, Sid grabs guests and escorts them to the door and doesn't let them finish what they are doing. Fourth option, Sid pulls the circuit breaker on the house. "Time to crash!" he screams. The house is left in disarray. Simon will have to clean up the mess in the morning after they wake up.

When a guest exits the home and leaves a mess, Sid calls his maid, Pamela Monica. She monitors guest activities and cleans up for them after they leave the house. Her cleaning equipment is labeled PMON.

If Sid doesn't crash the house, everybody cleans up, turns out the lights, synchronizes the notebooks and performs all their individual duties to completion. Debbie gets every picture off the DB Buffer Cache shelf and puts them on the appropriate wall. Logan ensures the LOG_BUFFER shelf is empty and puts all negatives in the current redo notebook. Chuck makes his rounds in the house and updates the walls and notebooks with the highest and latest Catalog Number (SCN). Archie puts the latest strip of negatives into archived redo notebooks, puts them in the backyard shed then updates the control and alert notebooks. Once everyone is done, Sid turns out the light and crawls into bed.

Sid's Problems

Sometimes, things go wrong at Sid's house. When any of these events happen, activity stops around the house:

- When Sid wakes up and he can't find the *initialization file*, he can't start his day.

- On occasion, Sid needs to recover lost pictures using negatives stored by Archie in the backyard shed. If he is missing a sheet of negatives or the negatives get damaged during recovery, he can't recover any more pictures taken after the unavailable negatives.

- Sid lost several negatives once. He accidentally opened the camera and exposed the film. This drove him bonkers. His world virtually came to an end. He contacted the camera manufacturer, and they made him a special camera with two film chambers. This way, if film is damaged, he can depend on the film in the other chamber. Sid calls this *mirroring*.

- If the backyard shed is full and Archie doesn't have room to put the package of negatives, Archie just waits for room in the shed. This makes Sid and Debbie wait. The whole Sid household comes to a grinding halt.

- Once Debbie caught the flu and had to stay in bed. You guessed it: Sid shut down the house in a panic.

Despite these and other family setbacks and dysfunctions, Sid's family can handle billions of pictures and thousands of concurrent houseguests.

You might wonder, as I did, how Sid has the time and energy for all these picture-collecting activities. Doesn't he have job? Actually, no. Money is not an object for Sid. He doesn't have to work. He made a smart investment several years ago. He bought bunches of shares of computer companies stock back in 1984 back when it first went public. The company he invested in has its corporate headquarters in Redwood Shores in California.

After being introduced to Sid's family house, you can see that he has structures for all family procedures. Like this family operation, an Oracle database has places, processes, and procedures. With this family analogy in mind, I'll now briefly describe Oracle database structures, processes, and operations that pertain to Oracle Backup and Recovery. Maybe you'll recognize some similarities to Sid's family.

The Oracle Server

The Oracle Server consists of an Oracle database and an Oracle instance. An Oracle database is a collection of data stored in files treated as a unit. An Oracle instance is the combination background processes and memory structures. The system identifier of an Oracle instance is referred to as its *SID*.

Database Contents

When considering your duty to protect the database data, you want to know what you are protecting. Though an Oracle server is complex software, I'll speak of it in simple terms here as we get started. When you protect the database, you are interested in protecting the information contained within the files. The data in the database exists in various forms: tables, indexes, views, PL/SQL code, Java code, and so on. Backing up a database protects these database objects and allows you to replace them if necessary.

Memory Structures

One of the first things a DBA learns when he or she joins the mass of Oracle administrators is the components of the System Global Area (SGA). This area of memory that is allocated when the instance is started is split up into three main sections:

1. **Shared Pool** Split into the library cache (contains shared SQL areas) and the dictionary or row cache (contains data dictionary content data). There are also two other pools called the Large Pool and the Java Pool. The large pool is used for RMAN operations, parallel executions (parallel query), and session memory when using Multi Threaded Server. The Java pool is used by java code and its data.

2. **Buffer Cache** Stores the most recently used data blocks that have been read from the datafiles on disk. When a data block gets updated (for example, inserting new rows into a table), the block must be placed in the buffer cache, and then it will be updated. At some later time, the data block will be written back to disk, reflecting the new updates.

3. **Redo Log Buffer** When data blocks are being updated, the changes made to them are recorded in the redo log buffer. The changes are logged so that they can be reapplied in the event of a failure. The redo entries are created before the changes are made to the actual data block, and the log buffer contents are copied to the online redo log when a transaction commits, when the log buffer is 1/3 full or when 1Mb of redo entries have been created.

These are all equally important to database operations, but the two that have direct relevance to backup and recovery are the buffer cache and the log buffer. All will become clear as we move through the rest of this chapter.

Database Structures

Where does an Oracle database store tables, indexes, and code? These objects are stored in structures within the database. Listed here is a brief description of key logical structures for backup and recovery:

■ **Tablespace**   A tablespace is a logical storage area for related objects. Every database object is stored in a tablespace. You can specify the tablespace where tables and indexes will reside at creation time. You can also change the tablespace location of tables and indexes once they have been created. An *online* tablespace is available for users, while an *offline* tablespace is not accessible to users. You can specify a tablespace as *read-only* to eliminate the need to perform continual backups of large, static portions of a database. A *temporary* tablespace efficiently manages space for sort operations. A *transportable* tablespace can be moved between databases.

■ **Segment**   A segment can be a data, index, temporary, or rollback segment. An Oracle *data segment* holds all of the data for either a table, a cluster of tables, or a partition of a table. Similarly, index data is stored in an *index segment*. During certain query processing, *temporary segments* provide a temporary workspace for intermediate stages of SQL statement parsing and execution. A *rollback segment* (sometimes referred to as an *undo segment*) stores the old values of data that was changed by each transaction (whether or not it was committed). Rollback segments are used to provide read consistency, to roll back transactions, and to recover the database from uncommitted transactions. A segment can reside in only one tablespace, but a tablespace can store many different segments.

■ **Extents**   An extent is a logical unit of database storage space allocation made up of a number of contiguous data blocks. Once an extent fills with data, Oracle allocates a new extent for the segment. A segment contains an initial extent and allocates additional extents on request or as needed.

■ **Data Block**   A block is the lowest level storage container within a database and the smallest unit of input/output (I/O) according to Oracle. Typically a database block is 2, 4, 8, or 16 kilobytes in size. When you create a database, you define the data block size for all tablespaces in the database. In Oracle 9*i*, a database can have multiple block sizes, making the transporting of tablespaces between databases easier.

■ **Row**   Table and index data is stored in rows. A row will be contained in one or more data blocks.

■ **Rowid**   Oracle uses a rowid to locate of every row in the database. The rowid identifies a row in a data block within a datafile.

- **System Change Number**   Each database transaction is assigned a unique system change number (SCN) when it commits. This ever-increasing number is used throughout the database to control concurrency and consistency, to order redo, and for recovery. It represents a consistent comitted version of the database and can be thought of as the database equivalent to a clock.

- **Change Vector**   As changes are made to the database, the details of the change are recorded as change vectors. From these, database transactions can be reproduced. Simply speaking, a change vector records a change to a single data block to take it from one state to another.

NOTE
*Every Oracle database has a SYSTEM tablespace.
The SYSTEM tablespace contains the data dictionary
tables for the entire database. All information stored
on behalf of stored PL/SQL program units (procedures,
functions, packages, and triggers) resides in the
SYSTEM tablespace.*

Oracle Contents at Sid's House

Like Sid's house stores pictures, an Oracle database stores data. Here are the specifics of the parallels:

- **Oracle Instance**   *Sid operates his home-base picture collecting operation.* An Oracle instance contains memory structures and background processes.

- **Oracle Database**   *Sid's house contains pictures and related notebooks, walls, and sheds.* An Oracle database consists of data in files.

- **Row**   *Sid takes pictures for viewing, changing, and removing.* A database row stores data which can be viewed, changed, removed, or added.

- **Rowid**   *Each picture in Sid's house has a unique picture identifier. This identifier specifies the picture location, the frame, and the wall containing the picture.* Every database row has a unique row identifier. The row id specifies the object identifier, datafile, data block, and row.

- **Block**   *Frames hold pictures on the walls of Sid's house.* Database blocks contain rows and are stored in datafiles.

- **Tablespace**   *Sid stores the pictures in rooms called Picture Spaces.* Data is collected in logical groupings called tablespaces.

- **System Change Number** *When Sid places a picture in a frame, he writes an ever-increasing catalog number on the frame. Logan and Archie write a catalog number on each notebook of negatives. Chuck updates walls with the current catalog number.* The system change number can identify when each change was made within the database.

- **Rollback** *If Sid changes a picture, he copies the contents of the frame and puts it in the Rollback closet.* When a data block is changed, undo information is recorded in the rollback segments.

- **Change Vector** *Sid creates negatives for his pictures so that pictures can be reproduced.* Database transactions generate change vectors stored in redo files for database recovery.

This very simplified and abbreviated overview of database contents serves as a basic introduction to the contents of a database. Managing database object sizes and parameters relates to database tuning. Building database code relates to application development. Protecting the contents of your database data, structures, and code is the purpose of this book. Now I'll zoom in on the really important files that compose your Oracle databases.

Oracle Database Files

When you work on a computer, software permanently stores the computer information on disk. For example, when you create a letter or a document in a word processing program, the document contents are saved to your hard disk when you click the Save button. An Oracle database consists of several files on computer disks. These files contain the database information and structures needed for accurate operation. Let's look at each file and describe its function and the relationships between them.

NOTE
An Oracle database is simply a collection of files. The three key file types are datafiles, redo log files, and control files.

Datafiles

All data within the database is stored in datafiles. All the tables, indexes, triggers, sequences, PL/SQL code, views—everything lives in datafiles. Though these and other database objects are contained logically in tablespaces, they are actually stored in files on your computer hard disk.

Every datafile has special formatting internal to Oracle software. Something important to be aware of is that the datafile has a header and a range of blocks. The header of an Oracle datafile contains a number of structures including the database ID (a number assigned when the database was created), the file number and its name, the file type, the creation SCN, and the file status. The file header is used by Oracle to make sure the file is as expected (e.g., it is up-to-date with the rest of the database). A datafile can belong to only one tablespace, but a tablespace can be comprised of many datafiles.

Online Redo Log Files

As operations are performed against the database, most of them are recorded in the online redo log files, once the redo entries have passed through the redo log buffer. By looking at each word in the name of this file type, you can figure out its purpose:

- **Online**   The database can use this file as a place for storing data transactions. They are called online because they must be online and available fo the database to use.

- **Redo**   Denotes that something can be redone. Redoing a task means to perform the task again. With computers, redoing a task means to accomplish a task exactly as it was previously performed. Therefore, the purpose of an online redo log file is to store information about database changes so that they can be redone later.

- **Log**   Most database changes get logged. I am not talking about a large section of a trunk or limb of a fallen tree. The term *log* is more like the record kept by a ship or an aircraft that details actions taken by the commander.

- **File**   It is just like any other operating system file, and can be seen when listing the directory contents for its location.

The name *online redo log files* is a good, descriptive name. It is also very long and takes a while to say and write. You'll hear and see these files referred to as the redo logs, the redo files, and the log files.

Every database must have at least two online redo log files. Why? As the database is operating, each database change is being recorded to one redo log file. This redo log file is referred to as the current redo log file. Once that file becomes full of redo information, the Oracle database needs somewhere to write more redo. To prevent overwriting the current redo log file immediately, the Oracle server software begins writing information to the next redo log file. This change is called a *log switch*.

Because redo files are critical to complete database recovery, Oracle provides a means to mirror the files. Online redo log files exist in groups. Instead of writing redo information to one online redo log file within each group, the Oracle server can write to two (or more) online redo log files simultaneously. Each file is a member of the group.

Redo files contain change vectors (which are collected together into redo records) and other important information used in recovery. These redo records are copies of data that was recorded in the redo log buffer. Each redo log file header contains such information as the Database ID, the file number, file type, the lowest SCN numbers contained in the log, and the lowest SCN number contained in the next redo log.

NOTE
By setting the No-logging attribute for a table, partition, index, or tablespace. By setting this attribute for a database structure or object, you designate that data changes to this can be made without generating redo. Normal SQL will create redo on a NOLOGGING table. SQL with specific options will not generate redo information. The combination of NOLOGGING on the object and special SQL options prevents redo entries for that SQL statement. When you prevent redo from being written, you trade better performance for data recoverability via redo entries.

Archived Redo Logs Files

Once an online redo log file has been filled, the Oracle server software begins writing to another of the existing redo log file groups. Once this log switch occurs, Oracle can copy the contents of the recently filled redo log file(s) to a different location. Once the online redo log file is copied, you refer to the copied file as an *archived redo log file*. Archived redo log files contain a running history of database transactions. Online redo log files must be copied (archived) if you want to retain this database change history. Why? Because the online redo log files are constantly being reused. The information in the online redo log files is written over repeatedly. Therefore, the archived redo log files contain a copy of change vector information needed to reapply the database transactions (thus the name archived redo log files). You might hear them called archive files, archive log files, or archive logs.

These archived redo log files are your lifelines to successful recovery. If part of your database is lost or damaged, you'll usually need several archive logs to fix the database. The archive log files must be reapplied to the database in sequential order. If one of the archive log files is missing, remaining archive log files cannot be used. Therefore, keep all your archive log files since the last backup was taken and guard them carefully.

Control Files

Because an Oracle database is a physical collection of related datafiles, some method is necessary for synchronizing and controlling them. Therefore, an Oracle database has a *control file*. The control file contains an inventory of all files comprising an Oracle database.

A control file is a file on the database server hard disk. This file contains key database information about the database and the database files. For example, the control file stores the database name, all datafile names, all datafile numbers, the database block size, the online redo log file locations, the online redo log group definitions, the current database system change number, archived log file locations, archived log file information, and backup history.

Because the control file is critical to the operation of the database, Oracle software allows you to multiplex these files. You can have several copies of the control file. This protects you if you lose a control file on your hard disk.

The key required files needed for operation of an Oracle database are the datafiles, online redo log files, and the control file(s). The archive log files are not required but are necessary to completely recover your database in the event of a failure.

Initialization Parameter File

Another required file for an Oracle database is the database *parameter file*. This singular file is used only when the database instance is started. When you start your database instance, this file must exist and will be read by the Oracle software. The parameter file contains important information needed to initialize the database. This file contains the location of your database control file(s), the database name, archived redo log file information and other memory and functional parameters. Once the database starts, this file is not used again until the next database startup. The database parameter file might be called the PFILE, the initialization file or the init.ora.

In Oracle 9*i*, a Server Parameter File (SPFile) is a binary image of the text parameter file. Oracle 9*i* software stores system dynamic parameters in the server parameter file. This means that you don't have to change the init.ora file each time you alter system parameters while the database is running.

Alert Log File and Trace Files

As the database operates, events and errors get logged to text files on the database server. The *alert log file* is helpful for the database administrator to track significant database activities like a database startup and shutdown, the parameter settings used when the database is started, and online redo log switches. Also, many database errors are written to this file for investigation. Any database structural changes made to the database (adding log files, adding a tablespace, dropping datafiles, and so on) are also logged in the alert log file.

When a database error occurs, a *trace file* may be generated. This trace file contains detailed information about an error event. Oracle Worldwide Support may ask for a copy of these files when you contact them for help.

Password File

An optional *password file* provides database operational security. You don't want anyone to have the privilege to shut down or start up your database from client machines on the network unless you grant it to them. This encrypted password file serves to validate users (including yourself) who need to perform specific database operations from machines other than the database server machine.

Oracle Files at Sid's House

The files in an Oracle database compare to the notebooks and walls used by Sid and his family to store pictures, note changes, store progress, and take inventory.

- **Datafile** Sid's wife places pictures in frames on walls in the house. Each wall is like a datafile. A datafile stores data within data blocks.

- **Online Redo Log File** As picture negatives are produced from Sid's camera, Sid places the negatives on a shelf. Logan inserts the negatives in a notebook to protect them for future reuse. The online redo log file stores database transactions as change vectors. The log writer process flushes the contents of the LOG_BUFFER to the current online redo log file.

- **Control File** Sid and his family use the control notebook as a master inventory for location of all picture wall locations, online notebooks for negatives, and archived negatives placed in the shed. This notebook also tracks the catalog numbers for each of these locations. A database control file tracks the location of all datafiles, online redo logs, and archived redo logs. Using the database system change number, the control file confirms that all database files are synchronized.

- **Archived Redo Log File** When Logan fills a notebook with negatives, he begins placing his negatives in a new notebook. When this notebook switch occurred, Archie copies the negatives in the full notebook and places them in a notebook in the backyard shed. An archived redo log file is created by the ARCH process as a copy of the contents of an online redo log file.

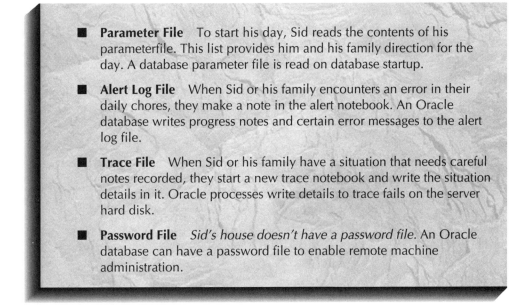

- **Parameter File**   To start his day, Sid reads the contents of his parameterfile. This list provides him and his family direction for the day. A database parameter file is read on database startup.

- **Alert Log File**   When Sid or his family encounters an error in their daily chores, they make a note in the alert notebook. An Oracle database writes progress notes and certain error messages to the alert log file.

- **Trace File**   When Sid or his family have a situation that needs careful notes recorded, they start a new trace notebook and write the situation details in it. Oracle processes write details to trace fails on the server hard disk.

- **Password File**   *Sid's house doesn't have a password file.* An Oracle database can have a password file to enable remote machine administration.

These are the important files that make up an Oracle database and the Oracle database environment. Next, let's look at the database processes that perform operations on these files. We'll also look at key memory locations involved in database structure activity.

Oracle Database Processes

An Oracle database is the files of the database. The Oracle processes and memory comprise the instance of the database. These processes continuously run and perform database tasks. The memory areas hold data and information used by the database processes.

Processes Defined

Though many processes comprise an Oracle database, in this book I will focus on the processes responsible for backup and recovery activities. Some processes perform several functions. I will highlight the functions that pertain to database backup and recovery.

- **Database Writer**   The database writer process writes data from memory to the datafiles. Because the fundamental storage unit of the database is data blocks, database writer writes blocks. The database writer does not have to write transactions to blocks immediately when those transactions are committed. The data block can remain in memory as changed blocks, sometimes referred to as *dirty blocks.* When memory is needed or at a checkpoint, the database writer will clean out dirty blocks by physically writing them to disk in the datafiles. You can have multiple database writers in the database. The abbreviation for this background process is DBWn, where *n* is the number of the database writer process. Database writer also performs functions during a database checkpoint.

■ **Log Writer**   Log Writer writes information from the database log buffer to the current online redo log file. Refer to this redo information written as redo entries, redo records, or change vectors. Redo entries are written sequentially and contain information required to re-apply data block changes needed for recovery. If you have multiplexed redo log files into groups, log writer fills each redo log file in the group simultaneously. Abbreviate log writer as LGWR.

■ **Archiver**   Archiver copies the contents of a redo log file to another destination for safekeeping. When the current online redo log file fills up, the Oracle software switches its logging efforts to the next online redo log file. Once this switch occurs, the archiver process copies this file to a destination directory or to another database connection. Because a redo log switch can be initiated manually, the archiver will copy the current redo log file once the switch occurs. Each and every redo log file is copied. The redo records contained in these archived redo log files contain every database change made. They are vital for complete database recovery. If the redo log switches are occurring faster than the current archive processes can copy, then the log writer process can spawn another archiver process. The archiver will be abbreviated as ARCH, where H is number of the process.

■ **Checkpoint**   The checkpoint process notifies the database writer that it is time to write all changed blocks in memory. A checkpoint also updates all the datafile headers and control files with the most recent checkpoint information. A checkpoint synchronizes all the database files with each other. Checkpoints occur when a redo log switch occurs at a specified interval, when databases are offlined, when a tablespace is put into hot backup mode, or at database shutdown. The checkpoint process will be abbreviated as CKPT.

■ **System Monitor**   System Monitor provides several functions in an Oracle database. For recovery purposes, System Monitor performs instance recovery if the database fails to close normally and cleanly. When a database shuts down normally, Oracle software is able to clean up after itself by synchronizing files, updating information, and cleaning up user transactions. When a clean shutdown does not happen, the System Monitor performs database crash recovery the next time the database starts up again. A database instance has only one System Monitor process, and it is abbreviated as SMON.

■ **Process Monitor**   Process Monitor cleans up after failed user processes. When a user connection is cut off, Process Monitor rolls back uncommitted transactions and frees resources and locks used by the user session. Abbreviate Process Monitor as PMON. You'll only have one PMON process in a database instance.

These processes accomplish more than listed here, but this overview of functionality covers the important features related to database backup and recovery.

Oracle Processes at Sid's House

Processes in an Oracle database are similar to Sid's family members and house employees.

■ **Database Writer**   *Debbie takes pictures off the special shelf and places them in frames on walls.* The database writer processes reads changed blocks in the buffer cache and writes them to datafiles.

■ **Log Writer**   *Logan places picture negatives in a redo notebook.* The log writer process records database transactions in the online redo files.

■ **Checkpoint**   *Chuck scurries through the house and writes the latest catalog number on every picture-covered wall. Chuck also updates the control notebook with this number. Typically, this occurs every time Logan changes notebooks for picture negatives deposits.* The checkpoint process updates datafiles and control files with a checkpoint SCN.

■ **Archiver**   *Archie copies the contents of Logan's notebook of picture negatives. He places the copy in a shed in the backyard.* The archive process copies recent noncurrent online redo log files to destination specified in the parameter file.

■ **System Monitor**   *Simon the butler picks up the house and puts everything in order the morning after Sid crashes the house by pulling the circuit breaker.* System Monitor performs crash recovery on instance startup.

■ **Process Monitor**   *Pam the maid cleans up after houseguests that leave abruptly.* Process Monitor cleans up after failed or disconnected user processes.

Oracle Database Operations

Now that you've read about files and processes, let's talk briefly about the database operations that initiate activities on the database files. During typical database operations, activity is abundant. An Oracle database has a plethora of commands and events. I want to highlight some typical key events that affect specific database files and act as important milestones in the operation of a database, specifically in backup and recovery.

When a database is started, the processes are started and the memory areas are allocated. When a database is shut down, the processes have stopped and the memory areas are freed. A started database is called an *open* database. A shutdown database is called a *closed* database.

Transaction

Database changes occur in *transactions*. A transaction is a logical unit of work that contains one or more SQL statements. All statements in a transaction are committed or rolled back together. Understanding the database activities that occur during a transaction will help you understand backup and recovery mechanisms. A transaction may contain one or more insert, update, or delete statements. These statements are *data manipulation language* (DML) commands. During a transaction, redo and rollback information gets created and tracked. Rollback information is written as undo entries to a rollback segment. Rollback segment undo entries allow a user to undo a transaction if the change is rolled back. Because rollback segments contain data blocks in the same way a table object does, when undo blocks are updated, they also generate redo information. This could be called *redo for the undo*. Redo information for a transaction is written as the transaction progresses. Once a transaction has been committed, it can't be undone very easily.

All transaction information gets recorded to the current redo log file as change vectors. One transaction can create many redo records. A redo records is a collection of change vectors that describe a single atomic change to the database. A change vector (also known as a redo vector) describes the database change to one data block. Either all vectors in the redo record are applied, or none of them are. A single transaction may generate one or more redo records containing one or more redo vectors.

Each database transaction that changes data performs several tasks. A specific transaction may change many blocks. To simplify the discussion, take a committed transaction that changes only one data block. During the transaction, the Oracle Server:

- ■ Checks the buffer cache to see if the target data block is in memory.
- ■ Fetches the target data block from disk if not found in memory.
- ■ Records the redo records to the redo log buffer.

- Creates operation codes and data required to undo the block change into an undo segment (rollback segment).

- Changes the data block in memory to the new value.

- Generates a redo commit entry in the log buffer and provides the transaction a commit SCN.

- Flushes the redo log buffer to the online redo logs.

- Releases the blocks in the rollback segment holding the undo for this transaction. The transaction table entry is released and therefore releases the undo records in the rollback segment.

- Eventually, DBWR writes the changed block to a datafile *after* the redo records have been written out of the log buffer to the log file.

If a user process fails during these tasks, PMON will clean up the mess.

The Life of a Database Transaction

A user named Jim changes his home phone in the Employee Application from 111-222-3333 to 111-222-4444. He makes his change via a form in a browser. What happens to his phone number information? Say the employee table has a column named phone, and the employee table is in a tablespace named Users. The Users tablespace is made up of a file named user.dbf.

When Jim submits his change, the block containing his employee row is fetched from datafile user.dbf and read into the buffer cache. Before the changed phone number is placed in the data block in memory, a redo record gets written to the log buffer. The redo record notes the block change from the old state to the new state. When Jim commits his change, the block in the rollback segment is freed and the current redo log group receives a commit on Jim's transaction. While Jim clicks on his sports web page to check the scores, the online redo log fills up. The database begins writing to the next empty redo log. The data block containing Jim's phone number change gets written to user.dbf during the checkpoint. The archiver begins to copy the online redo log containing Jim's transaction details. Once the archiver is finished, Jim's new phone number exists in two locations: a database block in a file called user.dbf and an archive log file in the archive destination.

Startup

Before a database is available for applications and users, you start up the database. The database startup proceeds through several activities. Database startup goes through three phases named Nomount, Mount, and Open.

- **Nomount** You can think of this phase of startup as starting up the Oracle instance. This startup command:

  - Reads the database parameter file

  - Starts the required background processes and allocates memory as defined in the parameter file

  - Writes progress to the alert log file

- **Mount** During the mount phase of instance startup, the control file(s) specified in the database parameter file are read. Remember that the control file is like the glue that holds the database together. From the control file, the instance finds out the following and then writes progress to the alert log file:

  - The names and file locations of all the datafiles and redo log files

  - The database name

  - The latest system change number

- **Open** Every online datafile comprising the database must be synchronized before the database will open. During the open phase:

  - All the online datafile headers are compared to the control file information.

  - If all the files are synchronized, the database can open.

When a database closes abnormally, the next time it opens, Oracle software automatically performs *crash recovery*. During this recovery, SMON rolls forward transactions written to the online redo logs that had not been recorded in datafiles. Then SMON rolls back any uncommitted transactions. The undo information stored in the rollback segments gets processed to undo uncommitted changes to data blocks in datafiles. Before the database opens, all datafiles must be consistent with the control files and the redo logs. Crash recovery activities get recorded in the alert log file during startup.

CAUTION
Try not to confuse roll forward with roll back. Roll-forward operations read and apply redo entries in redo files to make data blocks contain data as they were originally changed. Roll-back operations read undo information in rollback segments to put data blocks back to the state they used to be.

Log Switch

Oracle software changes the current online redo log file receiving redo entries at a log switch. Typically, a log switch occurs when the current online redo log has no more room to hold more changes. An administrator can also initiate the log switch. The log switch encompasses several tasks:

- The Oracle server marks the latest online redo log group as active.

- A checkpoint occurs for the database.

- The Oracle server begins writing to the next online redo log group.

Once the switch is complete, ARCn begins to copy the last online redo log file to the archive destination.

Checkpoint

At specified intervals or a redo log switch, the database undergoes a checkpoint. The current state of the data in memory is saved to disk. The checkpoint makes sure that any redo before this is not required for the current datafiles, as all of the changed data blocks have been written to disk.

- CKPT process notifies the DBWn to write all changed blocks in the buffer cache to disk.

- CKPT updates the control files and datafiles header with checkpoint details.

- The checkpoint gets logged in the alert log file.

Shutdown

When the database is shut down, various tasks occur depending on the method:

■ **Normal**   A normal shutdown waits until all users disconnect before the shutdown occurs.

■ **Transactional**   A transactional shutdown removes all current users from the database after they commit their current transaction.

■ **Immediate**   An immediate shutdown removes all current users from the database and rolls back any uncommitted transactions.

■ **Abort**   An aborted shutdown does not provide any opportunity for the database to clean up. Crash recovery is required after this method of shutdown.

Each of the first three shutdown methods lets the database clean up all transactions, write any changed data blocks to datafiles, and synchronize the control files to all the datafiles with the latest database SCN. When the database is restarted, no crash recovery is required. During a clean shutdown, uncommitted database changes are rolled back.

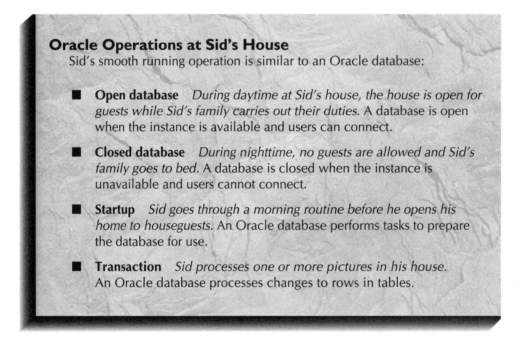

Oracle Operations at Sid's House
Sid's smooth running operation is similar to an Oracle database:

■ **Open database**   *During daytime at Sid's house, the house is open for guests while Sid's family carries out their duties.* A database is open when the instance is available and users can connect.

■ **Closed database**   *During nighttime, no guests are allowed and Sid's family goes to bed.* A database is closed when the instance is unavailable and users cannot connect.

■ **Startup**   *Sid goes through a morning routine before he opens his home to houseguests.* An Oracle database performs tasks to prepare the database for use.

■ **Transaction**   *Sid processes one or more pictures in his house.* An Oracle database processes changes to rows in tables.

- **Log switch** *Logan switches notebooks to hold picture negatives.* An Oracle database stops write to an online redo log file and begins writing to another.

- **Checkpoint** *Chuck synchronizes walls and the control notebook.* An Oracle database synchronizes datafiles and control files.

- **Shutdown** *Sid's family prepares for bedtime according to established routines.* An Oracle database closes and cleans up files.

Summary

This chapter defines Oracle database terms as foundation for the rest of the book. A database has files, processes, and operational procedures to hold and protect data. I chose to describe the terms by drawing an analogy to things you are already familiar with. A family taking and storing photos can be compared to a database that stores data. As you move forward through this book, feel free to return to this chapter and review information about structures, processes, and operations of an Oracle database.

Chapter Questions

Check your comprehension of terms and files by answering these questions. Unless otherwise noted, the question will only have one correct answer.

1. An Oracle database contains datafiles. Datafiles contain

   A. Rows of data organized in database blocks

   B. Redo records from database transactions

   C. Archived transactions for database recovery

   D. Session trace information

2. What purpose does an online redo log file serve in a database?

   A. Posts database content to web pages

   B. Lets users undo database change while connected

   C. Holds change vectors from database transactions

   D. Stores parameters for database startup

3. Which method of database shutdown occurs without performing memory and file cleanup operations?

   A. Shutdown normal

   B. Shutdown transactional

   C. Shutdown immediate

   D. Shutdown abort

4. What database events does a log switch trigger? (Pick the best answers.)

   A. A database checkpoint

   B. Archiver will copy a redo log to the archive directory

   C. A refresh of the parameter file

   D. A log entry to the alert log file

5. Which database file serves to locate and synchronize other files in the database?

   A. Archive redo log file

   B. Control file

   C. Parameter file

   D. Alert log file

Answers to Chapter Questions

1. A.   Datafiles hold the data in the database. Tables, indexes, stored code, and so on are stored in the datafiles.

2. C.   The online redo log file keeps ongoing records of all transactions made to the database.

3. D.   When a database is aborted, the Oracle instance does not perform cleanup and synchronization operations.

4. A, B, D.   A log switch starts the checkpoint operation. After the log switch, the most recent redo log file can be archived. The log switch is recorded in the alert log file.

5. B.   The control file keeps track of every datafile, redo log file, and archived log file.

CHAPTER
2

Backup and
Recovery Options

our primary goal as a database administrator: protect the data. You have other responsibilities—tuning, configuration, maybe some coding. Still, job one is keeping the system running with all of the data. Oracle provides different protection options to keep the data available. In this chapter, we'll look at your options and provide a preview to the rest of the book.

Sometimes a database will break and need to be fixed. If a database failure occurs, management and users would look to you, the DBA, to make the system available again. Protecting your data and keeping the database available means that you will be able return the database to the way it was in the past, or to the way it was until the exact time before the failure. After restoring some or all the database to a previous state, it can be moved forward in time. Returning the database back to working order in this way is called *restoration* and *recovery*. To recover a database, you must make a copy of the database contents. This copy is called *backup*. Database backup and recovery fall into two categories: user-managed and server-managed.

NOTE
Don't worry if you don't catch on at first to all the backup and recovery methods that can be performed in an Oracle database. Each of the items I discuss in this chapter are covered in greater depth with examples later in the book.

User-Managed Backup and Recovery

A *user-managed* backup strategy for an Oracle database means that you manage the backup and recovery operations. You can back up and restore database files using operating system utilities and recover using the SQL*Plus RECOVER statement or the SQL ALTER DATABASE RECOVER statement.

Data is actually stored in files on a computer server's hard disk. As I covered in the last chapter, a database consists of datafiles, control files, online redo log files, archived redo log files, an initialization file, and a password file. Making copies of these files is called a physical backup. During a physical backup, operating system copy commands copy database files to a different location. At the conclusion of a physical backup operation, you'll have copies of database files in your Oracle database. Physical backups may also be referred to as file-level copies or structural copies. In this book, I will refer to backup of database files as a physical backup. *Physical recovery* operations use these file copies to restore and recover the database. Backups and recovery use files copied to and from *media*. Media can be a computer hard disk, magnetic tape, or optical disks.

Physical Backup Options

Physical backups of a database can be executed in a variety of methods. During a backup, the files can be copied to media for safekeeping. Alternatively, a physical backup can be a copy of database files from the existing location to another hard disk on the database server. Or the backup might be a file copy of database files to the hard disk of a different server. You might even e-mail database files as an attachment. Simply put, a physical database backup is the process of copying some or all of the files in the Oracle database.

The actual file copy command can be executed any number of ways. The copy command can be invoked at an operating command prompt. You may want to automate the physical backup process by using a vendor's backup tool or by scripting the file copy commands in a script. Automating the physical backup procedure means that you don't have to type each and every copy command. Whether you build your own set of backup commands or you employ a vendor tool to perform the backup commands for you, the backup is just an operating system copy of the files in your database.

Remember, the files comprising an Oracle database are *all* interrelated. The datafiles are synchronized with the control files. All the redo log files contain a running log of the contents in the datafiles and are consistent with the state of the control file. This means that you have to perform your physical backup in a certain way to be able to recover your database. Wouldn't it be nice if a database backup were as simple as copying a file? Unfortunately, it is not. Maintaining the synchronization and coordination of database files makes taking a physical backup a little more complicated.

Physical backups can be done when the database is in two states: closed or open. A closed backup means that the database has been shut down prior to the file copy. This is called a *consistent* backup. An open backup means that the database is available to users during the backup. This is called an *inconsistent* backup.

Closed Physical Backups

Closed backups are the simplest method of physically backing up a database. Once a database has been shut down, it is referred to as a closed database. During the shutdown operation, the Oracle software has the chance to synchronize the datafiles and control files. Any information in the database buffer cache is flushed to the database files. The complete set of database files can now be copied to a new location to preserve the entire database structure. All the database files as a group can be used to restore the complete database. All running transactions have been either committed or rolled back; hence, the term *consistent backup.*

NOTE
A closed database physical backup is also known as a cold backup or a consistent backup.

The means of database shutdown has consequences on the quality of your database physical backup. The database shutdown command has four different options, as discussed in Chapter 1. These options complete tasks on the database files during the time that the database is being "turned off." Understanding the file states of each of the shutdown options is critical to avoiding foul-ups when you recover from a database backup.

NOTE
Get comfortable with the results of the four shutdown options. Grasp these concepts and you will avoid much confusion later on during a database restore and recovery.

Open Physical Backups

Many databases must remain available most of the time. Yet they still need to be protected. Therefore, Oracle provides a means to physically back up the database while the database is open and available to users. An open database backup is done at the tablespace level. You begin backing up the datafiles in a tablespace by placing the tablespace in backup mode. Then each tablespace datafile is copied using an operating system command. Once all the datafiles are copied, the tablespace is taken out of backup mode. To complete an open backup of

L ike me, you may have kids. When their mother and I tell them that it is time to go out to dinner, each son has to shut down what they are doing before we can all walk out the door. Ideally, when Dad says it's time to go, my son will stop playing with his toys, place the toys neatly in the toy box, turn off the television, tell his friends that they have to go home, and pick up after his friends. We'd like him to then return his dishes to the sink, rinse them off, and put his dishes in the dishwasher. He should turn off the light in the rooms where he was playing, put on his clothes, and wait at the door with a smile on his face. This would be comparable to a normal database shutdown or a clean shutdown. (In our home, this would be an abnormal experience.) Usually, when we tell our son that it is time to go out to dinner, he will complain for a while and then walk to the door to leave. No toy cleanup. Lights left on. Television blaring. Sometimes, Dad has to march up to his room, grab him by the arm and yank him out the door. This process is comparable to a database shutdown abort (*not* a clean shutdown). The state of their toys and room require cleanup when we get home and start things up again.

the whole database, the above process is completed for every tablespace in the database. Oracle's Recovery Manager handles open database backup differently, as you'll see later in the book.

NOTE
An open database physical backup is also known as a hot backup or an inconsistent backup.

NOTE
If the database files are consistent during backup, you can open the database without recovery. If the database files are not consistent, you have to perform recovery to make all files consistent. Then you can open the database.

Physical Recovery Methods

Physical recovery, like physical backup, brings the database back to a previous state by performing database file operations. Physical recovery has two parts: restoration of previous file copies and recovery of transactions contained in redo log files. When you recover all the database files, this is called whole database recovery. You can repair broken database parts. *Tablespace recovery* is the recovery of one or more broken tablespaces. *Datafile recovery* is the recovery of one or more broken datafiles. If you lose your control files, you can recreate them. Archive redo log files are used to roll forward changes in your data files. If you lose a redo log file needed for recovery, the data in that redo cannot be replaced. You can completely recover a database by restoring backup datafiles and applying redo logs in the sequence the log files were created.

Consistent versus Inconsistent Backup

You are in your home and hear the sound of a broken window. Heading to the back of the house, you see a group of kids, dazed and scared. As you ask all seven kids what happened, you get answers from each one. If they all give you the same answer, then you are ready to proceed forward with your plan of action. In this case, they all give you a consistent answer. If you ask all the kids what happened and you get some different answers, you can say that their answers are inconsistent. Before you proceed with your plan of action, you may have to apply some redo. You will have to ask more detailed questions until you get consistent answers. Once the picture of events becomes clear, you are ready to proceed with the remedy.

Crash Recovery

The database instance is aborted if the instance stops abruptly without performing synchronization operations. An instance can be crashed via the shutdown abort command. Unexpected hardware and software events can crash the instance: OS failure, hardware CPU, memory or disk failure. An unexpected bug in Oracle software might crash the instance. Pull the power plug on your database server and the instance will crash then, too.

When the database starts after an instance crash, Oracle performs crash recovery. This is sometimes referred to as Instance Recovery, due to the fact that on a parallel server (OPS) environment, the failed instance is recovered by one of the surviving instances. First, the database is rolled forward using the current redo log file. Once the redo log changes are applied, any uncommitted transactions contained in rollback segments have to be rolled back. Once these two steps are completed, the database can be opened for use. Crash recovery occurs automatically at database startup if necessary.

Restore

When you repair a broken database via physical operations, sometimes you must copy one or more database files from the backup location to the database location. A *physical database restore* is the replacement of all database files from a backup. A restore replaces the files back to the way they all used to be when the database files were copied during backup.

Replacing a tablespace from backup is called a *tablespace physical restore*. Replacing a datafile from backup is called a *datafile physical restore*. If you restore all files from a closed database backup, you can open the database without recovery. If you restore one of the datafiles into an existing database, this restored file will not be consistent with the other datafiles. Attempts to access that file will produce database errors until it is recovered.

CAUTION
Many database recovery foul-ups occur when the files used for restore are not consistent with each other. This happens if files used for the restore are from different backup operations at different times and you do not have enough redo logs to make them all consistent. This also happens when the database is not shut down cleanly prior to database backup or when the tablespace datafiles are backed up without the tablespace being placed in backup mode first.

Recovery

To bring the database back to working order, you may need to recover the datafiles completely or to a specific point in time. During recovery, Oracle reads transactions in the redo log files and applies them to the datafiles. Since each transaction is recorded in the database redo logs, you can use these files to apply previous transactions to a restored copy of datafiles. The scope of the restore and recovery can be one or more datafiles, one or more tablespaces, or the whole database. You can restore and recover some or your entire database, provided that you have copies of your redo log files. When all consistent database files reach the same database state, recovery is complete.

NOTE
The term recovery *can mean two things: reapplying redo log transactions or the complete process of fixing a broken database via restoration and recovery. Restore and recovery work together to bring the Oracle system back to working order.*

Physical database recovery can be accomplished in a variety of ways, including complete database recovery, incomplete database recovery, and tablespace point-in-time recovery.

Complete Database Physical Recovery   Typically, you will recover the whole database completely. This means that you will replace all damaged datafiles from a recent physical backup. This restore can be a restoration of every datafile in the database. Once you restore the datafile(s), you issue the recover command. The Oracle software reads header information from all of the online datafiles in order to discover how up to date they are. The restored file(s) will have a lower SCN (system change number) value because they are older. Then, the appropriate redo log files are found, read, and applied. Redo log files are applied this way until every database transaction is applied. When the database is opened after this type of recovery, you have completely recovered the database and have not lost any data. To apply complete recovery, you will need any archive redo logs, the most current online redo log, and any online redo logs that have not been archived.

Incomplete Database Physical Recovery   Bringing the database back to working order might mean that you restore and recover the database without reapplying every transaction in every redo log file. This type of recovery might be necessary if a database operation occurred that you didn't want to happen again, like dropping a large important production table. To perform an incomplete whole database recovery, you restore all datafiles from a recent physical backup. Once you restore the datafiles, you issue the recover command and specify the point in time that you want the database recovery to stop. I'll refer to the point that you specify a recovery to halt at as the *stop parameter.* You define the recovery stop parameter by providing the RECOVER DATABASE command with a specific date and time (time-based recovery), a specific redo log file (cancel-based recovery), or a specific database SCN (change-based recovery). Oracle software tries to find the appropriate redo log files to read and apply them. Redo log files are applied this way until the stop parameter you specified is reached. When the database is opened after this type of recovery, you have incompletely recovered the database. You have also lost any data or changes made after the stop parameter.

When you perform an incomplete recovery, you create a new database *incarnation*. After incomplete recovery, you must reset the logs when you open the database. This must be done because after an incomplete recovery, you do not need any of the redo. Whenever you open the database with the RESETLOGS, information in the datafiles and the redo log files get changed. All datafiles headers get a new RESETLOGS SCN and time stamp. The online redo log sequence number resets to 1. The control file is updated to reflect the new database incarnation.

The three methods of point-in-time recovery are:

- **Time-based recovery** You can specify the moment in time that you want the database recovered to. When you tell the Oracle software to recover until a specific moment in time, the software will apply any and all changes to the database made up to the specified time. This process works because each database change is given a specific date and time stamp. Those date and time stamps are contained for each transaction in each redo log file. At the conclusion of time-based recovery, your database will contain all the data as it did at the time you define. When the database is opened, all uncommitted transactions are rolled back.

- **Cancel-based recovery** You can continue recovery until a specific redo log file is reached. At the end of this recovery option, all database changes made will be reapplied to the database via the redo logs, including the last redo log that existed before you cancelled. At the conclusion of successful cancel-based recovery, your database will contain all data as it did when the last redo log applied was filled. When the database is opened, all uncommitted transactions are rolled back.

- **Change-based recovery** You can specify the Oracle database SCN that you want to recover to. When you tell the Oracle software to recover until a specific SCN is reached, changes are applied up to the specified SCN. At the conclusion of change-based recovery, your database will contain all the data when the database reaches the change number you specify. When the database is opened, all uncommitted transactions are rolled back.

Tablespace Point-in-Time Physical Recovery Fixing a broken database might mean that you restore and recover a specific tablespace to a previous point in time that is different from the other tablespaces in the database. Tablespace point-in-time recovery (TSPITR) enables you to quickly recover one or more non-SYSTEM tablespaces to a time that is different from that of the rest of the database. TSPITR enables you to recover a consistent data set; however, the data set is the entire tablespace rather than just one object. TSPITR is most useful for recovering when a table is mistakenly dropped or truncated or a table gets logically corrupted. A table can be logically corrupt when some erroneous DML statements are applied to it and not reflected in other related objects. To perform TSPITR, you restore a cloned database consisting of the system, rollback, and needed tablespaces (sometimes you must also include a temporary tablespace). You then do incomplete recovery on this database to recover the tablespace to a point before failure. The recovered tablespace objects can then be made available to the original database. Those objects can be either exported from the clone to the production database or the teblespaces can be transported from the clone database to the production database.

Duplicate Database

Some backup and recovery activities are not always a result of a crisis or a database failure. A database administrator might need to create a copy of an existing database. This copy process is called cloning or duplicating a database. Creating a duplicate database is a backup and recovery operation. Instead of restoring a database to its

Database Restore versus Recovery

To help distinguish the difference between restore and recovery, think about a broken piece of furniture versus a broken bone in your arm.

When you restore a furniture piece, you bring the furniture back to an original condition as it existed years ago when it was originally built. Typically, you restore an entire piece of furniture, because if you restored just part of it, the restored part would look different from the remainder of the furniture piece. Restoring a database means to bring the database back to the way it existed at the time it was backed up. When you restore a part of the database, you restore that part to the way it existed when it was backed up.

You might think of recovery as the process of healing from a broken bone. When you arm breaks, the doctor will first restore the bones in your arm to their correct location. Then your body recovers your broken bone by applying bone cells to the fracture. Recovery begins with restoration. After you restore parts or the entire database, you apply redo log information to recover the database to a point that you specify.

When you recover a database, the recovery might be complete or incomplete. When you have a complete recovery from a broken arm, you have complete use of your arm as if it were never broken. Incomplete recovery means that your arm healed but doesn't have all the use that it did before. A complete recovery means that the database has all data as it did prior to the moment it broke. An incomplete database recovery brings back most of the data, but not all.

original location, you are restoring that database to a new location. That location might be on the same machine, although most times, you will duplicate a database to a different machine. You might duplicate a production database as a testing or development database. You might move a database from one machine to another for performance or maintenance reasons. Creating a duplicate database also serves to verify that an existing backup works as expected.

Standby Database

Some Oracle installations require that a database failure must be fixed in a matter of minutes or seconds. In this high availability scenario, you might choose to set up a standby database. A standby database is a duplicate of an original database that is constantly being updated using the original database's archived redo log files. The standby database stays in recovery mode when applying the archived redo log files from the original database. The standby database can be opened in a read-only mode. While in read-only mode, the standby database can be queried but not updated or changed. In the event of a database failure on the original database, the standby database can be opened quickly and used in place of the original database. In Oracle 9*i*, the standby database feature is now called Data Guard. The Data Guard feature was available in 8.1.6 and 8.1.7 on certain hardware platforms.

Logical Operations

You can protect the data content of your database by copying only the data within it. When you protect database data by copying the data, you perform a *logical backup*. The data can be copied to a file or another database table. You can use the data copied to restore the data to the original database or to a different database altogether. You cannot create or restore a whole database from a logical copy. The database must exist before the data can be restored in it (a data dictionary must exist before you restore the data).

Oracle Export

Oracle provides a utility named Export that copies database data. An Oracle Export creates a file containing a copy of user schemas and the data in the schemas. *Schemas* are the collection of database objects owned by a database user: tables, views, database links, triggers, procedures, functions, packages, and so on. An Export file contains all the commands necessary to recreate everything owned by one or more users in a database. To restore a users schema and data from an export to an Oracle database, you'd use the Oracle companion utility named Import.

Oracle Import

Oracle Import restores data from an Export file by reading an Export file and recreating user schema and user data in the target database. You can import part or all of the contents of an Oracle Export file. You can import the file contents into the original database where the schema was originally created, or import the file contents into a different user on the original database or to a different database. The data recreated will be the same data that was created from the original export.

NOTE
The term export *may mean the process of running the Export utility. When referring to the utility, the name will be capitalized. The term* import *may mean the process of running the Import utility. When referring to the utility, the name will be capitalized.*

Oracle LogMiner

Each Oracle database transaction is written to a redo log file. The redo log file can be archived and saved for recovery later. Oracle's LogMiner utility reads log files and rebuilds the SQL statements contained within them. You can use the SQL that LogMiner provides to regenerate or undo SQL statements made in previous database transactions. Since the redo log files are formatted in a proprietary Oracle structure and can't be opened and read, LogMiner can help you to recover SQL statements for reprocessing. This is far easier than dumping the redo contents and trying to decode it.

Server-Managed Backup and Recovery

A *server-managed* backup and recovery strategy for an Oracle database means that Recovery Manager (RMAN) handles the backup and recovery operations. You instruct RMAN to make backups, perform restores, and complete recoveries. This was introduced in Oracle 8.0.

Oracle's RMAN provides a mechanism for database backup, restoration, and recovery that is flexible, efficient, and intelligent. RMAN performs block-level database backup and recovery. The smallest atomic unit of an Oracle database is a data block. Datafiles, redo log files, and control files are comprised of data blocks. RMAN reads and writes these data blocks to a backup location. During recovery, RMAN reads the database block copies from the backup location and rebuilds the database. Though RMAN can also make image copies of datafiles and control files, its most valuable trait is its ability to work with database blocks.

Recovery Manager Features

If you are new to Oracle database administration, you may not appreciate fully all the benefits and features of RMAN. This tool will take care of much of the work for you in protecting the database. What used to be difficult and take detailed effort can now be accomplished with just a few commands with RMAN.

Oracle's Recovery Manager has various features at your disposal you'll find useful as you protect your database:

■ **Intelligence** As a DBA, you've got a lot of work to do. When you create a physical backup, you must create commands to perform the backup. When recovery is necessary, you must find the appropriate backup files, restore them, locate the archive log files, restore them, and perform recovery. All these details can be tedious and difficult to keep up with. Yet it is very critical that you don't miss a thing. Though many database administrators create scripts to automate backups, I've seen few scripts to perform recoveries. And recoveries often need to happen fast. Wouldn't it be nice to have a program that would handle all the tedium of backup and recovery for you? And get it right every time? Wouldn't it be nice to simply be able to back up a database with a backup database command? Or restore a database with a restore database command? Or recover a database with a recover database command? Well, now you do. Using RMAN, you can issue the backup database command. RMAN figures out what files comprise your database and copies all the blocks in those files to the location you specify. When you need to restore a broken database, simply issue the restore database command. RMAN reads the target database control file or its own catalog, finds the backup files, and restores needed files from the correct database backup. RMAN performs recoveries, finds redo backup files, and applies redo to the datafiles. RMAN is intelligent software that can figure out what operations on which files must be performed to accomplish the results that you, as an RMAN user, dictate.

■ **Block-level operations** RMAN database backup occurs at the block level. When you perform backups, you only copy blocks that have been used by the database. You can specify incremental backups. With incremental backups, you backup only changed blocks. By specifying what you want to back up and at what level you want to back up, you can significantly speed up backups and reduce the server workload. RMAN reduces the size of your backup and the time to create it. For example, if your 20GB database has 5GB of data, RMAN will back up only blocks containing the 5GB of data. It will not store 15GB of empty datafile space.

■ **Backup scope** When running backups and recoveries, you can specify what part of the database you want to work on. You can back up a control file only, one or more datafiles, one or more tablespaces, the whole database, and some or all archive log files. The same is true with recovery. You can recover only the broken portion of the database.

■ **Catalog** One of the big hassles of database backup and recovery is recording the occurrences and details of database backups. As database administrator, you will make backups regularly and automatically. When a recovery is needed, you may find yourself scrambling to find out the details of your recent backups. Most DBAs (like me) are too lazy or busy to make careful notes about backup details. As RMAN operates on a database, backup information gets written in the backup database's control file. Details about backup times, files, and levels are stored in the control file of the database you are backing up. If you lose that control file, you've lost your backup record details. More importantly, RMAN has lost its backup information for the recovery process. RMAN can also use a catalog to store database backup and recovery details. This catalog is a schema of tables, views, and sequences that contains a history of all database backups for one or more databases. You can place this catalog on any Oracle database within your network. When recovery is needed, RMAN can use the catalog information to restore and recover the broken database.

■ **Media management layer**   During backup operations, you'll often want to write backups to tape devices. You configure a media management layer that facilitates the communication of commands and data between RMAN and your server's tape device. Once you've configured your media management layer, you can issue RMAN backup and recovery commands that will read and write to your tape device. That tape device might have a single tape or an array of tapes. From RMAN's perspective, it does not matter. The complexities of interfacing with the tape device are handled in the media management layer and in the tape vendor's software.

■ **Stored scripts**   When you issue RMAN commands, you can start up this program and enter commands at the RMAN prompt. You can automate repeating tasks by typing commands into a file and invoking that file with RMAN. You can also create a script of commands and store that script in the Recovery Manager catalog. This stored script can be called from the RMAN command line similar to the way in which a stored procedure can be called from the SQL*Plus prompt.

■ **SQL interpreter**   From the RMAN prompt, you can issue SQL commands that perform database operations. For example, you can shut down a database, start one up, or change the database archive log mode. These commands and others let you automate functions and perform database maintenance, all from the RMAN prompt.

■ **Performance**   For a very large database, performing large backups may be time consuming and resource intensive. RMAN provides various parameters to control the number and size of files created during backup the number of files being read at one time, and the maximum amount of data to be read each second. RMAN uses channels to perform backups and recoveries. A channel is a connection to the database or stream connection to your backup media. You can specify the number of channels for backup to increase the throughput when speed is important. In environments where database availability is important, you can back up a database while it is open and available to users and applications. Due to the way in which RMAN handles open database backups, there is no need to put a tablespace into hot backup mode. Because of this, no extra redo is generated and it will therefore perform better than user-managed hot backups due to less redo contention.

If you have been a database administrator for a while, you've probably become accustomed to your current backup and recovery tool set. Many veteran DBAs I talk to say that they intend to learn RMAN but haven't yet. Perhaps the features and capabilities provided by RMAN will prompt you to take the time to learn and deploy RMAN in your database environment.

RMAN has many other benefits in addition to these. I'll explain and demonstrate these capabilities carefully in the Recovery Manager chapters in Part III of this book.

Recovery Manager Capabilities

You can use Recovery Manager to perform a myriad of useful database duties. These tasks are the same as those available when you use physical database recovery operations. Using RMAN, the execution of each is much easier.

- **Database file copies** If you want to make image copies of datafiles or control files, you can use RMAN to perform these tasks. This is the same as a hot backup of a datafile described earlier.

- **Duplicate database** Using RMAN, you can create an identical copy of a whole database. This database duplicate can be on the same machine or on an entirely different machine. The cloning command in RMAN is the duplicate database command. That's right: with RMAN, you can copy a whole database with just two words, *duplicate database* (you still have to configure your communication channels and possibly use extra recoery commands). The database can have same name as the current database or it can be changed during the duplication process.

- **Standby database** RMAN will also let you create a standby database. This standby database can be used as a failover database in the event that the master database breaks. Once again, RMAN makes something that is quite complicated a simple and straightforward operation.

- **Tablespace point-in-time recovery** Tablespace point-in-time recovery can be accomplished with RMAN commands. Using RMAN, you can keep all the parts of your database current except one or more specific tablespaces. This way, you minimize the database loss of data but bring a tablespace's contents up to the point where a failure or an error occurred.

Oracle Backup and Recovery (Other Options)

In this book, you'll learn about Oracle user-managed and server-managed backup and recovery for Oracle 8*i*, but keep in mind that you do have some options to consider when protecting your database. Oracle has released version 9*i* containing some new features and options. You can also use Oracle's Enterprise Manager to perform many database backup and recovery options. Finally, vendor software solutions can help you protect your database.

Oracle 9*i* Enhancements

During this book, I will be discussing Oracle backup and recovery in release Oracle 8*i* (8.1.7). However, some new and useful features have become available with Oracle 9*i*. For example, standby database functionality in Oracle 8*i* was significantly enhanced and repackaged in Oracle 9*i* as Oracle Data Guard. This feature was offered on a small number of hardware platforms in 8.1.6 and 8.1.7. Data Guard automates complex tasks and provides enhanced monitoring, alert, and control mechanisms. New modules now help you to survive mistakes, corruptions, and other disasters that might otherwise destroy your standby database. Also, the downtime required for upgrades, such as hardware and operating system maintenance, can be significantly reduced using Oracle 9*i* standby databases.

Recovery Manager has also been improved. RMAN now allows the DBA to specify certain data blocks that may have become corrupt to be restored and recovered. When RMAN first detects missing or corrupt redo during block media recovery, it does not immediately stop recovery; it will signal an error, though. It does this because the block may become a *newed* block later in the redo stream. When a block is newed, all previous redo for that block becomes irrelevant because the redo applies to an old incarnation of the block. For example, Oracle can new a block if the extents in a table are deallocated and the block is used again. Another notable RMAN enhancement is the ability to configure a backup copy retention policy. When a retention policy is in effect, RMAN considers backups and copies of datafiles and control files as obsolete, thus unneeded for future recovery. You can then periodically or regularly issue the report on obsolete backups and delete those backups via the configured retention policy.

These Oracle 9*i* enhancements are not a complete list of improvements. To see an exhaustive listing of enhancements, see the Oracle manual *Oracle 9*i *Database New Features*.

Oracle Enterprise Manager

Each of the Oracle native backup and recovery solutions can be invoked from an operating system prompt. You can perform the steps to accomplish physical backup and recovery from an operating system prompt and with SQL*Plus. When performing operating system commands like file copy, you issue those commands from the operating system prompt. When you execute database commands, you execute them from an Oracle SQL*Plus prompt. Logical backup and recovery operation are invoked from the operating system prompt or from Oracle's SQL*Plus. Oracle Export and Import can be invoked from the operating system prompt. Finally, Recovery Manager is invoked from the operating system prompt.

To assist you with database administration tasks, Oracle developed Oracle Enterprise Manager (OEM). Written in Java, OEM provides a graphical user interface for executing most database administration tasks. If you want to perform a physical database backup, you can control the startup of the database with OEM in tandem with operating system commands to copy files. You can use OEM to perform physical database recovery. You can generate logical backup solutions with OEM. You can invoke Export and Import data copies. Finally, you can create and execute RMAN scripts from the OEM graphical user interface.

Oracle Enterprise Manager also allows you to create scripts for many of the backup and recovery operations you will perform. You can create the script in OEM and run those scripts at scheduled times. You may also create scripts outside of OEM, but use OEM to control the execution of those scripts via OEM's job scheduling capability. In this book, I will discuss backup and recovery operations from the command prompt rather than from Oracle Enterprise Manager.

Vendor Solutions

When you purchase and deploy an Oracle database solution, all the backup and recovery facilities you need to protect your data are available to you with your Oracle software purchase. For example, the SQL*Plus, Export, and Import utilities do not require any additional licensing for your use. Neither does Recovery Manager. There are also other options available for purchase from vendor software companies that you might like to investigate.

An Oracle database can be quite complicated, with its many advanced features and configurable components. Your company may place critical company data assets in the database. Your organization may become completely dependent on the availability of your Oracle system. Because of these crucial demands and complications, vendor software companies have solutions to help you with your backup and recovery chores. The vendor software solutions have costs for licensing fees. You might find one or more vendor solutions that augment the Oracle recovery solutions and make your work life much easier.

Hardware Solutions

There are hardware options for high availability in the event of hardware failure. A standard hardware solution is the use of Redundant Array of Independent Disks (RAID). Hardware that Oracle database software runs on fails at some point. The disks will fail that contain Oracle database files. To safeguard against file loss when a hard disk breaks, RAID offers a wide variety of protective storage options. The most commonly used is RAID 0+1 and RAID 5. RAID 0+1 provides mirroring and striping of your disk contents. If you require five disks to store your database, then you will need a second set of five disks to mirror the data. The data is striped over the mirrored five disks. If a disk is lost, the mirrored copy can be used. RAID 5 stripes the data across multiple disks adding parity check data. If a disk is lost, it is possible to recreate the lost disk contents using the parity data stored on the other disks.

Many hardware vendors now offer different combinations of data mirroring, striping, and adding parity data. This technology, combined with large, battery backed up disk caches, can provide a bit more reassurance to a DBA that the data they are protecting does not have a single point of failure if a disk were to crash.

CAUTION
Using RAID or mirrored disk solutions is a high availability solution and not a backup solution. If a corruption occurs in a disk or a user makes an error that mirrored on other disks, what happens? The corruption and error is reproduced on mirrored disks. You still need a good, robust backup and recovery strategy in place. Hardware failover and availability is not backup and recovery; it's high availability in the event of hardware failure.

Software Solutions

A number of software vendors have developed powerful and easy-to-use backup and recovery solutions. Some solutions assist with physical backup and recovery. Some vendors offer logical backup solutions. Some vendors offer software that coordinates backup solutions with Oracle Recovery Manager. Following is a short list of companies and their solutions that I know of. This list is not inclusive, and I don't endorse any vendor over another in this book, but you can investigate these products. You might find one or more of these solutions very helpful, as have other companies around the world.

- **BMC**   SQL-BackTrack™ for Oracle product is a backup and recovery product. **www.bmc.com**

- **Computer Associates**   ArcServe provides file system backup, specializing in Windows operating systems. **www.ca.com**

- **Hewlett-Packard**   OmniBack offers file system and online database backups. **www.hp.com**

- **Legato**   NetWorker® and NetWorker BusinesSuite™ provide file system and Oracle database backup protection. **www.legato.com**

- **Veritas**   NetBackup™ provides file backup and online database backup. **www.veritas.com**

Many of these companies provide configurable modules. You can purchase their base product and an add-on module that integrates online backups with Oracle's Recovery Manager. Some products are available on specific operating systems and others are available on most popular Oracle operating systems. Each product provides backup and restoration of Oracle data and files to tape backup devices. These companies are just a few of the options available to you. To find out more about each product and company, check out their web page or contact them directly. In this book, I'll stick to discussing the Oracle backup and recovery solutions provided with your Oracle software. You can also find tape vendors with media management layer compatibility from Oracle's website.

Summary

In this chapter, you read a quick overview of the backup and recovery options for use as an Oracle DBA. You can manage backup and recovery options yourself via physical file operations or logical data operations. You instruct the server to manage backup and recovery operations via Recovery Manager. The RMAN utility allows you to back up and recover your database at the smallest database atomic unit, the database block.

These solutions aren't mutually exclusive of one another. In a real system, you may choose to back up your database using a combination of the methods described here. When you repair a broken database, you may want to have more than one option available to you for recovery.

This chapter is a preview to the rest of this book. The second part of this book exposes you to basic user-managed backup and recovery operations. The third part of this book covers server-based operations via Recovery Manager. The concepts and details you learn in Part II will be an important foundation for operations performed by RMAN in Part III. In the next chapter, I'll talk about a small sample database that you can set up to try the things you read throughout the remainder of the book.

Chapter Questions

Check your comprehension of terms, backup options, and recovery operations by answering these questions. Unless otherwise noted, the question will only have one correct answer.

1. You can back up a database using a physical backup. A physical backup is performed by doing what?

   A. Shutting the database down

   B. Extracting the data from the database

    C. Making a copy of database files in a database

    D. Running the Export utility while doing an aerobic workout

2. The Oracle Export utility can copy the data within a database to a file outside of the set of database files. Export is an example of which type of backup?

    A. Physical backup

    B. Cold backup

    C. Logical backup

    D. Recovery Manager backup

3. When you recover a database, you apply previous database transactions stored in redo log files to an existing database. Restoring a database file means to replace files to a database from a previous physical backup. Why might recovery be needed on a restored datafile?

    A. The datafile might be from a different database.

    B. Changes must be applied to the restored file to bring it current with the rest of the database.

    C. The restored datafile is an Export file.

    D. Databases don't have datafiles.

4. Which tasks can Recovery Manager not accomplish? (Pick any that apply.)

    A. Perform full database recovery

    B. Create a duplicate and standby database

    C. Perform tablespace point-in-time recovery

    D. Cook a scrambled egg

5. Recovery Manager can use a catalog to track backups and database information. Why would you want to use the RMAN's recovery catalog?

    A. As a contingency if the target control file is lost

    B. To order socks from the store

    C. So that RMAN will run more efficiently

    D. Because Oracle said so

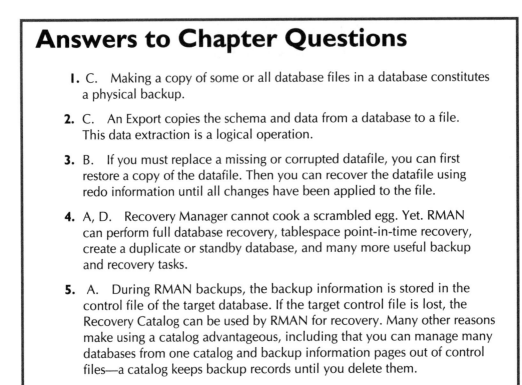

Answers to Chapter Questions

1. C. Making a copy of some or all database files in a database constitutes a physical backup.

2. C. An Export copies the schema and data from a database to a file. This data extraction is a logical operation.

3. B. If you must replace a missing or corrupted datafile, you can first restore a copy of the datafile. Then you can recover the datafile using redo information until all changes have been applied to the file.

4. A, D. Recovery Manager cannot cook a scrambled egg. Yet. RMAN can perform full database recovery, tablespace point-in-time recovery, create a duplicate or standby database, and many more useful backup and recovery tasks.

5. A. During RMAN backups, the backup information is stored in the control file of the target database. If the target control file is lost, the Recovery Catalog can be used by RMAN for recovery. Many other reasons make using a catalog advantageous, including that you can manage many databases from one catalog and backup information pages out of control files—a catalog keeps backup records until you delete them.

CHAPTER
3

Hands-on Practice

f you look on the bookshelves of your local mega-bookstore or search a book shopping website, you find many books about Oracle software. Most of the books give you an overview of SQL or a how-to guide to get started with Oracle. Many of the books discuss Oracle tuning. Some cover specifics for a particular operating system. Still others discuss Oracle development using Oracle tools and languages. But you will not find many books specifically covering Oracle backup and recovery. Why aren't there more books on backup and recovery? Well, I have a theory, which goes like this: most DBAs are very busy. They are busy installing software, applying patches, moving data, configuring software, tuning databases, streamlining SQL (and on and on). They do not have the time or opportunity to perform recovery operations. They intend to test their database backups. Many DBAs might actually be successful in budgeting time and resources for recovery practice but this is quite rare. Despite the everyday demands of the DBA, however, recovery and backup is one of the most important practices you can engage in. Therefore, in this book, I'll explain backup and recovery *and* provide you with opportunities to practice what you are learning.

Exposure Therapy

I watched a news program recently that discussed a particular obsessive-compulsive disorder of individuals who have a unique phobia: they are afraid to drive a car. They fear that if they drive, they will run over someone with their automobile. This news show profiled individuals that would leave their driveway carefully and pull out into the street. Before proceeding out of their neighborhood, the driver would stop the car, get out, and search the surrounding area for the body of a person that he might have run over. Once the driver did not find a body, he proceeded down the street, careful not to run over someone. Many times during his drive, he stopped the car, got out, and checked for bodies. This extreme phobia is debilitating and confining to those that suffer from it.

The news anchor described how people get therapy for this particular condition. An expert psychologist discussed how he helps victims of obsessive-compulsive disorders with a treatment known as exposure therapy. They showed footage of this psychologist riding in the passenger seat as the patient drove a car in a large empty parking lot. The doctor placed a sandbag on the parking lot pavement. The patient was given instructions to drive the car over the sandbag. With all the courage she could muster, the patient was able to steer her vehicle over the sandbag. The psychologist explained to the patient that if her car were to run over a person's body, she would experience physical sensations as she had when she steered her car over the sandbag. After a series of exposure therapy treatments with the doctor, she was able to face and overcome her fears.

What does overcoming the fear of driving have to do with Oracle database protection? Good question. The answer is exposure therapy. Database administrators are charged with the responsibility of protecting a critical company asset: the company data. DBAs have the responsibility of keeping database systems available for vital company applications. Though this responsibility falls squarely on the DBA's shoulders, many have very little practice with database recoveries in the event of various failure scenarios. Providing yourself the opportunity to perform multiple database recoveries in a variety of situations can help you face this concern. You can practice recoveries from backups on a small scale first to build up your confidence and knowledge. Once you've succeeded on a practice database, you'll be equipped to schedule and perform a practice database recovery on your actual Oracle system.

This concept of recovery practice is the thrust of this book. You can expose yourself to various backup and recovery exercises as described herein. You'll make mistakes. You'll get things out of order. You'll also learn and eventually succeed. A database administrator with skills in backup and recovery is worth their weight in gold. Don't be lazy as you read this book; follow along at home. When I wrote this book, I performed every activity described here. The errors I list are actual errors I've encountered. These chapters will guide you through specific backup and recovery operations and serve as a cookbook recipe for real database operations. You can refer back to relevant chapters later when you must perform a similar task.

Experts say that you remember some of what you read, more of what you hear, and most of what you do. Though you can make use of this book without actually performing exercises along with the text, it will be much more valuable to you if you perform the exercises. This chapter describes how to set up databases for these exercises.

During this chapter, you will install Oracle software, create three databases, and add two users to one of the databases. Examine Figure 3-1 to see the directory structure you will create. To run a database, you first need to install the Oracle software.

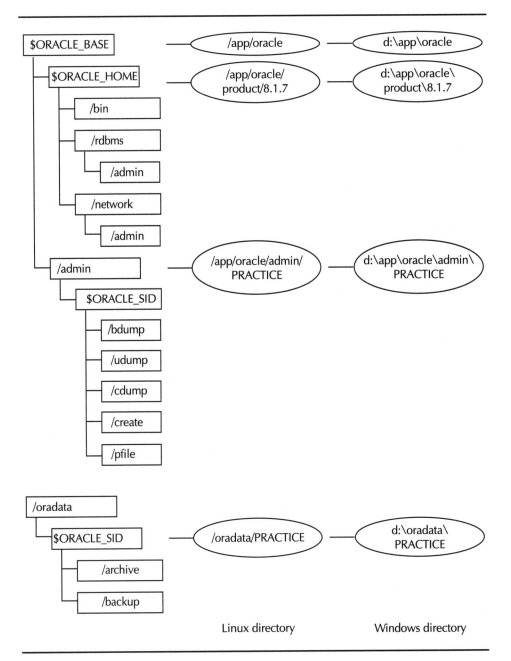

Linux directory   Windows directory

FIGURE 3-1. *Directory structure for Oracle software, databases and backup/recovery exercises in this book*

Machines for Activities

You will need a computer to install some databases. You probably have access to a machine at work or home for this purpose. If you don't have access to a more powerful computer like a Sun or HP box, you can use your primary PC (personal computer), a spare PC at work or a PC at home. You'll need a PC with enough hard disk space to hold the Oracle software and several Oracle databases.

Oracle8*i* Enterprise Edition Release 3 (8.1.7) will be used throughout this book. This version requires about 1GB of hard disk space when installed. The databases you'll install will be about 200MB each. If you've got a machine with at least 2GB of free space, you'll have just enough disk space to work through all the activities in this book. The machine will also need plenty of memory because databases use lots of it. I recommend at least 128MB of RAM. During some of the operations in the chapters, you'll be running three databases on your computer at once. The central processing unit (CPU) of the computer will perform the database calculations and other computer tasks. A fast CPU on your computer will be helpful but is not necessary.

Each chapter will contain exercises and tasks, including instructions, commands, output and results. You can complete the tasks on your computer as you read the book. At the end of each chapter you'll find some simple troubleshooting tips and some questions to test your understanding. The chapter summary has references to Oracle manuals where you can find further information.

Environment Variables and Oracle Software

Oracle uses operating system *environment variables* heavily in the management of its software. An environment variable is a value assigned to a name in the operating system. Software can fetch the value of the variable by using its name.

Though Oracle software uses many environment variables, three very important variables are ORACLE_HOME, ORACLE_BASE, and ORACLE_SID. The ORACLE_HOME defines the directory location of the Oracle executables that you want to run. A computer may have several versions of Oracle software installed. Most Oracle programs look to the ORACLE_HOME environment variable to determine which software version to run. The ORACLE_BASE defines the base directory where the database management files are installed. The ORACLE_SID defines the Oracle database name that you want to work on locally. On Linux, they must be set at the command prompt. On Windows, environment variables can be set at the command prompt or in the registry.

When you pick a machine for your personal training, you will also need to pick an operating system that will run the databases on this machine. The two operating systems I used while performing the exercises are Linux and Microsoft Windows NT.

Oracle Server on Linux

You can install the Linux operating system on a machine easily and cheaply. Linux runs on Intel-based personal computers and can be downloaded from the Internet or purchased from a computer store. Linux is a cousin to the Unix operating system. Therefore, many of the configuration aspects to installing Oracle will be similar on Linux to Sun Solaris, HP UNIX, IBM AIX, and any other Unix-based servers. You will find that installing Oracle on Linux will provide you with an inexpensive and valuable Unix-like environment for learning and practicing Oracle database recoveries.

You can choose any Linux version that you find to be compatible with Oracle version 8.1.7. I chose SuSE Linux 7.2 Personal for my test machine. I installed a second hard disk in the computer my kids use to play computer games. Then my son and I installed Linux on the new hard disk.

If you choose Linux for your Oracle installation, the installed directories will look like Table 3-1, which shows the file content, the full directory path location, and the abbreviated method of accessing that directory via Linux environment variables.

Oracle Server on Windows NT

I chose Windows NT Service Pack 6 for practicing Oracle database recovery operations because most organizations have Windows NT available and many PCs come with Windows NT preinstalled. Because Oracle software operates on Windows 2000 similarly to the way it does on Windows NT, you can also use Windows 2000 to accomplish chapter exercises. When you install Oracle on your Windows computer, you create directories, which are listed in Table 3-2. Several databases can be run from one software installation. Each database has its own administration and database file directories.

Directory Contents	Linux Directory	Directory via Environment Variables
Oracle base directory	/app/oracle	$ORACLE_BASE
Oracle software	/app/oracle/product/8.1.7	$ORACLE_HOME
Database administration files	/app/oracle/admin/ $ORACLE_SID	$ORACLE_BASE/admin/ $ORACLE_SID
Database files	/oradata/$ORACLE_SID	/oradata/$ORACLE_SID

TABLE 3-1. *Directories on Linux*

Directory Contents	Windows NT Directory	Directory via Environment Variables
Oracle base directory	D:\app\oracle	%ORACLE_BASE%
Oracle Software	D:\app\oracle\product\8.1.7	%ORACLE_HOME%
Database Administration Files	D:\app\oracle\admin\%ORACLE_SID%	%ORACLE_BASE%\admin\%ORACLE_SID%
Database Files	D:\oradata\%ORACLE_SID%	D:\oradata\%ORACLE_SID%

TABLE 3-2. *Directories on Windows NT*

Oracle Server on Unix

Most production installations of Oracle run on a flavor of the Unix operating system. If you are reading this book and have access to a UNIX machine at home or at work, you can use that machine to work through the exercises in this book. The UNIX commands and directory structure will be identical to the Linux structure previously discussed.

During this book, examples will typically be described in Linux first. Most commands available in Linux are also available in Windows NT. If the database operation can be performed differently in Windows NT, I'll note the difference. I chose Linux as the default operating system in this book.

Oracle Software Installation

Now that you have a machine to work on, you need to install the Oracle software. Your first exercise of this chapter is to install the Oracle software on your Linux or Windows NT machine.

Exercise 3.1: Load the Oracle Software

Installing the software involves three primary tasks. In each chapter, I will include time estimates as follows for the exercise tasks to give you an idea how much time is involved.

Task Description	Minutes
1. Find Oracle Software	-
2. Install Oracle Software	30
3. Confirm Software Install	10
Total Time	40

The installation instructions I'll provide you here are concise and specific to the scope of this book. Consult Oracle's documentation for a full explanation if you want to learn more or if you run into problems. Check out the *Oracle8i Installation Guide for Linux* or *Oracle8i Installation Guide for Windows NT* for all the details. You can find these documents online at docs.oracle.com or on your installation media.

Task 1: Find Oracle Software

To install Oracle on your machine, you'll need to get a copy of the software. You can install the Oracle software from a CD-ROM or download it from http://technet.oracle.com. As an Oracle Technology Network (OTN) registered user, you can download Oracle software for trial purposes. Choose Oracle Server 8.1.7 Enterprise Edition for either Linux or Windows NT. You can install a different version, but you may not be able follow some of the exercises in this book exactly as I've described.

CAUTION
As you install the software, be sure to read and agree to the Oracle licensing terms.

Task 2: Install Oracle Software

When you install Oracle software, a Java-based graphical interface guides you through the installation process. This Java program is named the Universal Oracle Installer. You'll be presented with several screens during the software installation process. As you answer the questions on the screen, install the software as noted here. Make sure to install the Oracle software in a specific directory on your computer so you can follow my examples throughout the book. When you install your software, follow these guidelines:

1. Install Oracle Enterprise Version 8.1.7. Your software version option may have different numbers in the last two digits, but make sure the first three digits are 8.1.7.

2. For a Linux install, enter **/app/product/oracle/8.1.7** in the Path field for the ORACLE_HOME directory.

3. For a Windows NT in the Oracle Home Name field, type **817**. In the Path field, type **D:\app\product\oracle\8.1.7**. Oracle on Windows NT has named Oracle Homes; Linux does not.

4. On the Installation Types screen, choose a minimal install. You'll create your own customized database after the installation of the software.

On any remaining screens, accept the default values but do not choose to create a database. You'll do that in the next exercise.

Task 3: Confirm Software Install

Once you install the software, you can find it on your hard disk. Open a command prompt or a file manager and look at the Oracle software directories. You'll see directories like bin, network, and rdbms underneath the $ORACLE_HOME directory. For a Windows install, you can also now see new entries on your Windows Start menu.

You can set environment variables to help you when you administrate your software and databases. Set your environment variables at your Linux operating system command prompt with the export command:

```
LINUX> export ORACLE_BASE=/app/oracle
LINUX> export ORACLE_HOME=/app/oracle/product/8.1.7
LINUX> export ORACLE_SID=PRACTICE
LINUX> export PATH=PATH:$ORACLE_HOME/bin
```

You can add these lines to your logon script (e.g., profile) so that the environment variables are set each time you logon.

On Windows NT, you can use the set command to define your environment variables:

```
WINNT> set ORACLE_BASE=d:\app\oracle
WINNT> set ORACLE_HOME=d:\app\oracle\product\8.1.7
WINNT> set ORACLE_SID=PRACTICE
WINNT> set PATH=%PATH%;%ORACLE_HOME%\bin
```

Or you can modify your registry as described in the *Oracle8i Administrator's Guide for Windows NT*. Throughout the book, I'll refer to directories by using environment variables as I've described here.

Databases for Practice

Each chapter contains backup and recovery database exercises using Oracle's tools and commands. You will work with three databases in the course of the book in a variety of ways. You'll be using the same databases, tablespaces, tables, and users over and over throughout the book.

1. **Database named PRACTICE**   The primary database used during this book is a database named PRACTICE. This database will consist of exactly 200MB of datafiles and 3MB in three redo log files. This database will get backed up, broken, repaired, and duplicated.

2. **Database named RCAT**   Recovery Manager makes use of a catalog. The catalog is a schema stored on a database. Oracle documentation for Oracle8*i* uses a database named RCAT (short for recovery catalog)

in their examples. We'll use the same name in this book also. You'll create a database named RCAT and maintain a recovery catalog user named RMAN817 on this database. This database will be needed in the Recovery Manager chapters in this book.

3. **Database named CLNE** In several chapters of this book, you will create a duplicate database of the PRACTICE database. This duplicate database will be named CLNE.

Before you begin working on these databases, you need to create them. I'll describe how you might create the databases and their supporting services in the next exercise using Oracle's Database Configuration Assistant.

Exercise 3.2: Create PRACTICE Database

An easy way for a beginner to create a database is to use Oracle's Database Configuration Assistant. This Java utility accepts your parameters and creates all the database files and supporting directory structures needed for your database. Once you progress through the series of screens, the tool will create the database for you. You can also instruct the tool to save the database creation commands to a script file. You can run this script later from the SQL*Plus prompt.

NOTE
If you want to create your database using your own database creation scripts, create a PRACTICE database according to the specifications defined in this exercise. Use Table 3-3 and Table 3-4 as a guide to create your database.

Your first exercise is to create a database named PRACTICE. The steps to accomplish this task are listed next.

Task Description	Minutes
1. Launch Database Configuration Assistant	5
2. Configure Database Configuration Assistant	10
3. Create the Database	30
Total Time	45

I want you to create the PRACTICE database in a specific way. In each chapter of the book, I'll detail operations on specific files and locations. You can follow the exercises better if you have identical files when you try to compare your steps and results with mine. Create a database that has tablespaces as defined in Table 3-3.

Tablespace	Size MB	Datafile Linux	Datafile Windows NT	Auto Extend	% Increase	Storage: Initial KB	Next KB	Min	Max
SYSTEM	100	/oradata/PRACTICE/system01.dbf	d:\oradata\PRACTICE\system01.dbf	Off	50	64	64	1	4096
TOOLS	20	/oradata/PRACTICE/tools01.dbf	d:\oradata\PRACTICE\tools01.dbf	Off	0	64	64	1	4096
USERS	10	/oradata/PRACTICE/users01.dbf	d:\oradata\PRACTICE\users01.dbf	Off	0	64	64	1	4096
RBS	20	/oradata/PRACTICE/rbs01.dbf	d:\oradata\PRACTICE\rbs01.dbf	Off	0	64	64	4	4096
INDX	20	/oradata/PRACTICE/indx01.dbf	d:\oradata\PRACTICE\indx01.dbf	Off	0	64	64	1	4096
TEMP	20	/oradata/PRACTICE/temp01.dbf	d:\oradata\PRACTICE\temp01.dbf	Off	0	64	64	1	4096

TABLE 3-3. *Use these PRACTICE Tablespace Parameters*

Task 1: Launch Database Configuration Assistant

Launch the Database Configuration Assistant from either Linux or Windows NT like this:

```
LINUX> /oracle/8.1.7/bin/dbassist &
WINNT> D:\Oracle\8.1.7\bin\launch.exe D:\oracle\8.1.7\assistants\dbca DBAssist.cl
```

On a Windows installation, you'll find a shortcut on the Windows Start menu for this tool also. The Database Configuration Assistant will ask you a variety of questions to help you customize your database.

Task 2: Configure Database Configuration Assistant

When you run the Database Configuration Assistant, you'll encounter a number of self-explanatory screens. Create a customized (not typical) database, pay attention to these points:

1. Do not select any optional database features for your database (Oracle Time Series, Spatial, JServer, Intermedia and so on). These options make the SYSTEM tablespace unnecessarily large for the exercises in this book.

2. Set the Global database name to PRACTICE in all uppercase. Set the SID to PRACTICE in all uppercase. Set the compatibility parameter to 8.1.0. The initialization file location will be filled in for you as you type the database name.

3. Set the values for each of the tablespaces in the database to the values listed in Table 3-3. Figure 3-2 shows the configuration screen where you set the tablespace files and parameters.

4. Create three 1MB redo log files in the /oradata/PRACTICE directory on Linux or the d:\oradata\PRACTICE directory on Windows NT. Name the redo log files redo01.log, redo02.log, and redo03.log.

Task 3: Create the Database

When prompted, let the Database Configuration Assistant create the database now for you. You could also save the scripts that it has created to be used again or in another environment.

Once the database build is complete, you have an Oracle database named PRACTICE. On Linux and Windows, the database directories and files have been

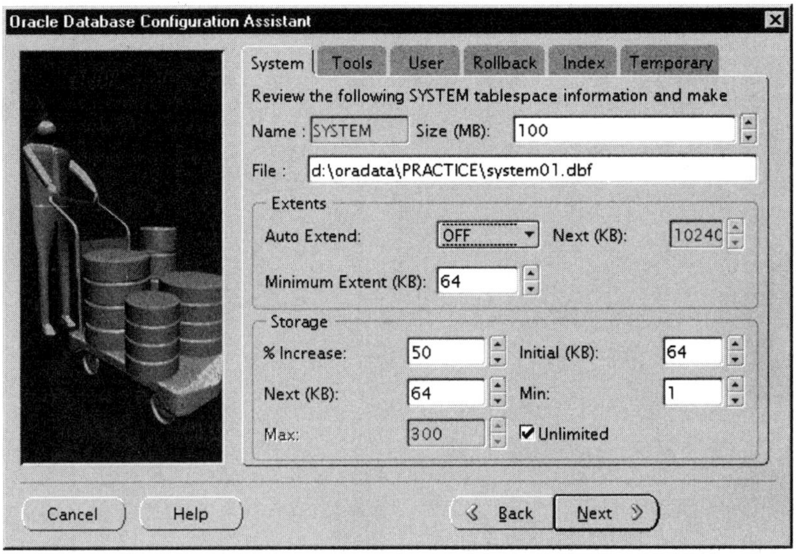

FIGURE 3-2.   *Configure the tablespace datafiles in Database Configuration Assistant*

created for you. On a Windows installation, services have been added and started for this Oracle database. To see this Windows service, browse the services in the Control Panel for the database service necessary to start and run your new PRACTICE database. You'll see a new service named Oracle817PRACTICE.

The database files and directories created are listed in Table 3-4. The administration directories are listed there as well. Once you've created this database, you're ready to get connected and have a look around.

CAUTION
This database is not set up optimally and these settings do not constitute best practices for database creation. You want a database that will help facilitate backup and recovery exercises. On a production database, place control files on separate disks and mirror your redo logs. Place members of each redo log group on separate disks.

Directory, File or Service Name	Linux Location	Windows NT Location	Notes
Data Files	/oradata/PRACTICE/	d:\oradata\PRACTICE\	Datafiles of the PRACTICE database are in this directory
Control Files	/oradata/PRACTICE/control01.ctl /oradata/PRACTICE/control02.ctl /oradata/PRACTICE/control03.ctl	d:\oradata\PRACTICE\control01.ctl d:\oradata\PRACTICE\control02.ctl d:\oradata\PRACTICE\control03.ctl	Three control files are in the same directory as the datafiles and redo logs
Redo Log Files	/oradata/PRACTICE/redo01.log /oradata/PRACTICE/redo02.log /oradata/PRACTICE/redo03.log	d:\oradata\PRACTICE\redo01.log d:\oradata\PRACTICE\redo02.log d:\oradata\PRACTICE\redo03.log	Three online redo log files are in the same directory as the datafiles and control files
User Dump Destination	$ORACLE_BASE/admin/ PRACTICE/udump	%ORACLE_BASE%\admin\ PRACTICE\udump	All trace files for server processes are written to this directory
Background Dump Destination	$ORACLE_BASE/admin/ PRACTICE/bdump	%ORACLE_BASE%\admin\ PRACTICE\bdump	All trace files for background processes and the alert log are written to this directory
Core Dump Destination	$ORACLE_BASE/admin/ PRACTICE/cdump	%ORACLE_BASE%\admin\ PRACTICE\cdump	Oracle dumps core files to this directory.
Parameter File Destination	$ORACLE_BASE/admin/ PRACTICE/pfile	%ORACLE_BASE%\admin\ PRACTICE\pfile	Database initialization parameter file is found in this directory.
Archive Log Destination	/oradata/PRACTICE/archive	d:\oradata\PRACTICE\archive	Archived redo logs will be stored in this directory.
Database Service	–	Oracle817PRACTICE	Windows NT database service necessary to start and run your new PRACTICE database.

TABLE 3-4.   *Important Files, Directories, and Services for Your PRACTICE Database*

Exercise 3.3: Tour the PRACTICE Database

Now that you have created a database, you can connect to it, view the database files and directories, start and stop the database. You might think of this as a getting acquainted exercise. Take a quick tour of your new PRACTICE by performing the following tasks:

Task Description	Minutes
1. Get Connected	15
2. Query the Data Dictionary	10
3. View Database Administration Files	10
4. Shut Down the Database	5
5. Start Up the Database	5
6. Examine DBA Studio	10
Total Time	50

Some tasks you perform now will be repeated throughout the rest of the book.

Task 1: Get Connected

When you installed your Oracle software, you installed all the database executables, support files and a number of utilities. One utility you'll use a lot is SQL*Plus. SQL*Plus is like the command prompt of an Oracle database. You can control database operations and query and change data with this utility. SQL*Plus has its own manual in the Oracle documentation set. In Oracle 9*i*, the server manager utility is not available. All server management commands are now supported in SQL*Plus. In this book, we'll use SQL*Plus exclusively for database access and control.

NOTE
*In this book, when commands are entered at the SQL*Plus prompt, you will see a SQL> prompt at the beginning of the command. For operating system commands, the prompt will be WINNT> or LINUX>.*

Start SQL*Plus from the OS command line and try to log in to the PRACTICE database as two different users: SYS and SYSTEM. Try to execute these commands to connect to the database.

```
LINUX> sqlplus /nolog
SQL> connect sys/change_on_install
Connected.
SQL> connect system/manager
Connected.
```

Congratulations! You have connected to your database.

When a user connects to a database, that user has *privileges* and *roles*. A privilege is granted to a database user or role allowing that user or role to perform tasks. A role is a named collection of privileges. Most administration operations in a database can be accomplished when you are connected as SYS or SYSTEM. However, you cannot start up or shut down a database as SYS or SYSTEM unless you are connected as these users using the SYSDBA or SYSOPER role. Try these connections to confirm that SYS and SYSTEM have the SYSDBA role.

TIP
The INTERNAL user is a shortcut means of connecting to a database as the SYS user with the SYSDBA role. In Oracle 9i, the INTERNAL username is no longer available.

```
SQL> connect sys/change_on_install as sysdba
Connected.
SQL> connect system/manager as sysdba
Connected.
```

The SYS user has the SYSOPER role by default, but SYSTEM does not. Throughout this book you will perform most operations as SYS with the SYSDBA role.

So far, you have connected to the PRACTICE database using a local connection without using Net8 as a local connection. The database must have a listener process running to accept Net8 connections. Test your Net8 connectivity to your PRACTICE database with these connection commands:

```
SQL> connect sys/change_on_install@practice as sysdba
Connected.
SQL> connect system/manager@practice as sysdba
Connected.
```

The @ sign in the connect command instructs the command to use Net8 when connecting to the database. If you do not specify the Net8 connect string, the connect command will connect to the database defined by the ORACLE_SID environment parameter. Refer to the Net8 Administrators Guide for a detailed explanation of the use and configuration of Net8. In this book all connections will be local to the database server.

Task 2: Query the Data Dictionary

The Oracle database you created contains a data dictionary. As an English dictionary defines English words, the data dictionary defines details about your database. Select some information from your data dictionary to confirm you have created the database as described earlier. Run the following query to check the name and archive log mode of the database you are connected to:

```
SQL> SELECT name, log_mode FROM v$database;
```

Run this query to see the version of the database:

```
SQL> SELECT * FROM v$version;
```

Your new PRACTICE database has many dynamic data dictionary views that you can use to manage your backup and recovery operations. Table 3-5 lists some of those we'll be using in this book. From SQL*Plus, query your PRACTICE database with each view listed. For example, if you want to see the datafiles in your database, you can query the data dictionary like this:

```
SQL> SELECT name, bytes FROM v$datafile;
SQL> SELECT file_name, bytes FROM dba_data_files;
```

Either of these two queries provides datafile information on the database. During some backup and recovery operations, you'll only be able to use the dynamic views. Many of the v$ dynamic views are available to you when the database control files are mounted but the database is not opened. The data dictionary views are available only when the database is open. This is because the data dictionary tables contain information in the SYSTEM tablespace, and the v$ dynamic views contain information from the database control file.

Database Object or Structure	Dynamic or Dictionary View
Database Information	V$DATABASE, V$INSTANCE
Database Parameter Information	V$PARAMETER
Tablespace Information	V$TABLESPACE, DBA_TABLESPACES
Datafile Information	V$DATAFILE, V$TEMPFILE, V$DATAFILE_HEADER, DBA_DATA_FILES, DBA_TEMP_FILES
Redo Log File Information	VLOG, VLOGFILE, V$LOG_HISTORY
Control File Information	V$CONTROLFILE
Database Recovery Information	V$RECOVERY_FILE_STATUS, V$RECOVERY_LOG, V$RECOVERY_PROGRESS, V$RECOVERY_STATUS, V$RECOVER_FILE

TABLE 3-5. *Dynamic and Dictionary Views Used for Backup and Recovery*

If you type the following query, you'll see the location and size of the online redo log files for the PRACTICE database:

```
SQL> SELECT member, bytes
  2    FROM v$logfile lf, v$log l
  3    WHERE lf.group# = l.group#;
```

Confirm the location of the control files for your database by looking at the v$controlfile view.

```
SQL> SELECT name FROM v$controlfile;
```

The results of the datafile, redo log, and control file queries shown in this task should yield the same files as an operating system file listing of the directory contents in the /oradata/PRACTICE/ directory.

TIP
The dynamic view names are almost never plural.
The data dictionary view names are usually plural.

You'll learn how to use these dynamic and dictionary views later in this book. These are just a few basic queries to give you a taste of selecting information from the database about the database.

Task 3: View Database Administration Files
During database creation, several important files that do not contain database data get created. Take a moment to locate these files on your computer for your new database. Open them in an editor and look at their contents.

- **The parameter file**   When the database instance starts, Oracle will read the database parameter file. The PRACTICE database parameter file is named initPRACTICE.ora in the $ORACLE_BASE/admin/PRACTICE/pfile directory. When you answered questions in the Database Configuration Manager, those answers have been recorded in this file. If your database block size choice was 8192 bytes, you'll see the db_block_size parameter set to 8192 in the parameter file.

- **The alert log**   Major database events and errors are written to the database alert log. The alert log can be found in the $ORACLE_BASE/admin/ PRACTICE/bdump directory. Open the file named alert_PRACTICE.log or practiceALRT.log with an editor. Look in the file for a record of database startups, shutdowns, and redo log switches.

- **The password file**   A password file has been created so that you can administrate this database from another machine than the one the database is located on. This file can be found at $ORACLE_HOME/dbs/ pwdPRACTICE.ora on Linux and %ORACLE_HOME%\database\ PWDPRACTICE.ora on Windows NT. You will not be able to view the contents of this file.

Task 4: Shut Down the Database

To shut down an Oracle database, you use the shutdown command from the SQL*Plus prompt. You have four options on the shutdown command (normal, immediate, transactional and abort); use the immediate option now.

```
SQL> connect sys/change_on_install as sysdba
Connected.
SQL> shutdown immediate
Database closed.
Database dismounted.
ORACLE instance shut down.
```

When the database closes, it writes information to the alert log and closes the database files in a clean, consistent manner.

Remember, when you shut down a database, the Oracle Server does a lot of work, including writing the current SCN number to all database files, flushing the dirty blocks on the buffer cache to datafiles, and rolling back uncommitted transactions. The control files have to be updated also. A *clean* shutdown allows the database to clean up all the memory and files. You can be assured that the database files are in a consistent state. If you abort the database like this:

```
SQL> Shutdown abort;
```

Oracle does not perform the cleanup operations. Because of this you'll notice that a shutdown abort completes more quickly than the other shutdown options.

Task 5: Start Up the Database

To start up an Oracle database, issue the startup command:

```
SQL> connect sys/change_on_install as sysdba
Connected.
SQL> startup
ORACLE instance started.
Total System Global Area    30484508 bytes
Fixed Size                     75804 bytes
Variable Size               13553664 bytes
Database Buffers            16777216 bytes
Redo Buffers                   77824 bytes
Database mounted.
Database opened.
```

During database startup, the initialization file is read, the memory structures are allocated and the background processes start. The database files are mounted and the database is opened. When a database is started, it goes through three stages that you can see in the output from the command: NOMOUNT, MOUNT, and OPEN. You can open the database one stage at a time; try starting your PRACTICE database in stages:

```
SQL> startup nomount
ORACLE instance started.
...
SQL> alter database mount;
Database altered.
SQL> alter database open;
Database altered.
```

Task 6: Examine DBA Studio

Oracle provides a graphical user interface tool you'll find very handy in administrating databases. Oracle Enterprise Manager's DBA Studio combines multiple database administration tools into one Java application. Use DBA Studio to administer:

- Instances, including startup, shutdown, and database parameters

- Schemas, including tables, indexes, and views

- Security, including database users, roles, and privileges

- Storage, including tablespaces, datafiles, rollback segments, redo logs, control files, and archive logs

DBA Studio behaves identically on Linux and Window NT. You can start this tool from the OS command prompt like this:

```
LINUX> oemapp dbastudio
WINNT> oemapp dbastudio
```

On a Windows installation, the Oracle installation creates a menu selection for DBA Studio on the Start menu.

Open DBA Studio and connect to your PRACTICE database. Connect as the SYS user. If you have problems, consult the online help within the tool. Figure 3-3 shows the DBA Studio navigation screen. Open your PRACTICE database and have a look around. Explore the four primary areas of your database:

- **Storage**   Expand the Storage node on the navigator tree. Look at your control files, tablespaces, datafiles, rollback segments, redo log groups, and archive logs.

- **Instance**   On the instance node, examine your database and all the initialization parameters.

- **Schema**   Open the schema node. See if you can find v$datafile view owned by SYS.

- **Security**   Navigate to the security node and see which roles have been granted to SYSTEM.

You'll find that DBA Studio provides a convenient means to examine and administer your database. The information in many dynamic and dictionary views is graphically presented in this tool. Though you can perform many administration duties from this tool, you will perform backup and recovery operations only from the command prompt during the course of this book.

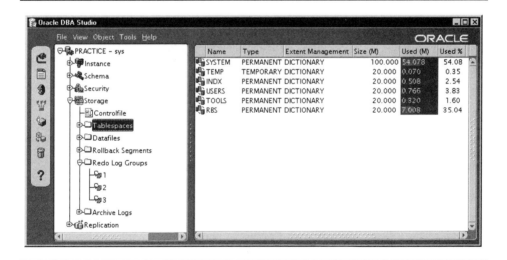

FIGURE 3-3.   *Use DBA Studio to administer your PRACTICE database*

Exercise 3.4: Modify PRACTICE Database

You need to modify the PRACTICE database so you can use it in the exercises throughout this book. Complete the following tasks to prepare the database for use in subsequent chapters.

Task Description	Minutes
1. Change Passwords	10
2. Add a Datafile	10
3. Create User SCOTT	10
4. Create User TINA	10
5. Create TINA'S Objects	10
6. Generate Database Activity	15
Total Time	65

The activities in this exercise prepare the PRACTICE database by creating structures, adding users, and generating data.

Task 1: Change Passwords

Two users are automatically created in your database with default passwords. Those users are SYS and SYSTEM. The SYS initial password is change_on_install. The SYSTEM initial password is manager. The default passwords for SYS and SYSTEM need to be changed for security reasons on a real-world database. Change the password for these users to PRACTICE with ALTER USER command:

```
SQL> connect sys/change_on_install
Connected.
SQL> alter user sys identified by practice;
User altered.
SQL> alter user system identified by practice;
User altered.
```

There, that's better. I get very tired of typing change_on_install, don't you? You could of course change these passwords to anything that you desire.

Task 2: Add a Datafile

The reason you created the users tablespace with a 10MB datafile instead of a 20MB file like the other nonsystem tablespaces is because you need one tablespace with two datafiles for the upcoming backup and recovery exercises. Create a second datafile for the users tablespace with the ALTER TABLESPACE command:

```
SQL> ALTER TABLESPACE users ADD DATAFILE
'/oradata/PRACTICE/user02.dbf' SIZE 10M;
Tablespace altered.
```

The USERS tablespace is now 20MB and consists of two datafiles.

Task 3: Create User SCOTT

A sample user schema has been available for illustration purposes for many versions of Oracle software. User SCOTT owns four tables. You can create user SCOTT by executing a script named utlsampl.sql located in the $ORACLE_HOME/rdbms/ admin directory. You can run a script from SQL*Plus with the @ symbol or the start command:

```
SQL>@/app/oracle/product/8.1.7/rdbms/admin/utlsampl
```

This user will be used for logical backup and recovery exercises in later chapters.

Task 4: Create User TINA

You need to create another user, TINA, to help illustrate point in time recovery throughout this book. TINA will own one table that contains rows that track activity over a time period. You will create and schedule an Oracle job to populate this table with data. As you perform database recoveries, we will examine this table to help illustrate the result of recovery principles. Create TINA and grant her roles and privileges like this:

```
SQL> GRANT CONNECT, RESOURCE, UNLIMITED TABLESPACE TO tina
  IDENTIFIED BY panda;
SQL> ALTER USER tina DEFAULT   TABLESPACE tools;
SQL> ALTER USER tina TEMPORARY TABLESPACE temp;
```

Task 5: Create TINA's Objects

TINA's only purpose in the PRACTICE database is to track time. The rows added to her one table will provide you the means to confirm that your recoveries perform as expected. TINA owns one table, one procedure, and one job. Her table is named DATE_LOG, her procedure is named CREATE_DATE_LOG_ROW, and her job will be added in the next task.

```
SQL> CONNECT tina/PANDA
SQL> DROP TABLE DATE_LOG;
SQL> CREATE TABLE DATE_LOG
   (create_date     DATE CONSTRAINT create_date_pk PRIMARY KEY);
SQL> CREATE OR REPLACE PROCEDURE create_date_log_row
IS
-- Purpose: Insert a row with the current date/time into DATE_LOG.
```

```
BEGIN
  INSERT INTO date_log (create_date) VALUES (SYSDATE);
END;
/
```

This code creates a table, and a procedure. Take the time to run these commands on your PRACTICE database.

Task 6: Generate Database Activity

During your backup and recovery exercises, you need some ongoing database activity to verify that your recovery has completed correctly. Activity can be generated by inserting rows into the TINA.DATE_LOG table. You can insert rows into this table with an insert statement, a procedure call, or a database job.

Insert the current date and time into the table with a simple INSERT command:

```
SQL> INSERT INTO tina.date_log VALUES (SYSDATE);
```

You can perform the same insert by executing the procedure you just created.

```
SQL> execute tina.create_date_log_row;
```

Either method places a new row into this table.

Now you need to create the job that will continuously insert rows into the TINA.DATE_LOG table. Use this command to create and schedule the job:

```
SQL> VARIABLE jobno number;
SQL> BEGIN
-- Run the job every 10 minutes
    DBMS_JOB.SUBMIT(:jobno, 'create_date_log_row;', SYSDATE, '(SYSDATE +
1/(24*6))');
    commit;
END;
/
SQL> print jobno
```

Make the row inserts automatic by submitting the job you just created to the Oracle job scheduler. This scheduler executes jobs at regular intervals as defined by the job. The job scheduler can be turned on at database startup or dynamically while the database is open. Set two parameters in the PRACTICE database parameter file so that the job scheduler starts automatically.

```
job_queue_processes = 2
job_queue_interval  = 30
```

The job_queue_processes parameter starts two Oracle scheduler processes. The job_queue_interval says that the job scheduler process will wake up every 30 seconds to see if any jobs need to be run.

To start the job scheduler once the database is open, use the ALTER
SYSTEM command:

```
SQL> ALTER SYSTEM SET job_queue_processes = 2;
```

This starts two background processes that run scheduled database jobs. You cannot
specify the job interval once the database is open. The default interval is 60 seconds.

Try starting the job processes via the database parameter file or the dynamic
command. After a few minutes, you can select data from the table TINA.DATE_LOG.
You will see rows in this table that have been inserted by the job you submitted.

```
SQL> SELECT * FROM TINA.DATE_LOG;
```

You may decide to change the interval that the database job will run. You can find
out the job number of the job by querying the USER_JOBS table as user TINA.

```
SQL> SELECT job, what FROM USER_JOBS;
```

Then you can change the interval using this procedure and some date arithmetic,
where 1 is the job number.

```
SQL> execute DBMS_JOB.INTERVAL(1, null, null, 'sysdate+1');    -- Every Day
SQL> execute DBMS_JOB.INTERVAL(1, null, null, 'sysdate+1/24');-- Every Hour
SQL> execute DBMS_JOB.INTERVAL(1, null, null, 'sysdate+1/(24*60)');    -- Every
Minute
```

You can turn off the job by making it appear as broken. To do this you need
to retrieve the job number, which is shown above. Then execute the following
command as the TINA user to stop the job (I am using job number 1234 in
this example):

```
SQL> execute DBMS_JOB.BROKEN(1234, TRUE);
```

Oracle will not run this job now until you change it to not broken using the
following code:

```
SQL> execute DBMS_JOB.BROKEN(1234, FALSE, SYSDATE);
```

The job will run straight away and then return back to the scheduled interval you
defined when you first created the job.

User TINA now has a table, a procedure, and a job that calls the procedure
to insert a row into the DATE_LOG table at intervals of your choosing. For your
exercises, set the parameters in the parameter file and let the job scheduler take
care of the rest.

Create RCAT Database

One of the tools you will use for backup and recovery is Recovery Manager. The Recovery Manager catalog is stored in an Oracle database and stores important for backup information that RMAN can use. The database you will use for the Recovery Manager database will be RCAT (short for Recovery Catalog). Create a database named RCAT as you created the PRACTICE database earlier. You can do this using your own creation scripts or using Database Configuration Assistant. For the purposes of this book, the locations of database files for the RCAT database don't matter.

When I created the RCAT database using the Database Configuration Assistant, I instructed the tool to copy existing database files. Doing this can be faster than creating and running all the create database scripts. Upon completion, your computer will contain database files, directories, and services for the RCAT database. These files will be in locations in the RCAT directories rather than the PRACTICE directories. Be sure to change the SYS and SYSTEM password.

Troubleshooting

While performing the exercises in this chapter, you may run across some result or error you aren't expecting. Look over this list for troubleshooting ideas. If you need further help in this or other chapters, find it at http://metalink.oracle.com. Once you register, you'll be able to find plenty of troubleshooting hints and advice.

Connect Command

During the connection examples in the chapter, you may have some problems.

1. **File not found.** If you type SQL*Plus and the OS does not find the program, check that your PATH environment variable has been set correctly.

2. **ORA-01031: insufficient privileges.** You may be connecting to a database using the SYSDBA or SYSOPER role that you don't have granted to you. Either log on as a different user with these privileges or grant them to the failing user.

3. **ORA-01034: ORACLE not available.** When you connect in SQL*Plus using a local connection (without Net8), the database must be started for the connection to work. Connect as SYSDBA and start the database. Also make sure that the ORACLE_SID is set correctly.

4. **ORA-12500 (TNS-12500) TNS: listener failed to start a dedicated server process.** When you connect in SQL*Plus via Net8, the database service, listener, and database must be started for the connection to work. Make sure all of these components are currently running and try your connection again.

5. **ORA-12560 (TNS-12560) TNS: protocol adapter error.** Your Oracle connection is not valid because the instance was aborted while you were still connected to it. Exit SQL*Plus and launch it again starting a new connection. On Windows NT, the database service may not be running.

6. **ORA-24314: service handle not initialized.** You may be connecting to a database without Net8 and do not have your ORACLE_SID environment variable set. Change the ORACLE_SID value and try the connection again.

7. **ORA-24323 value not allowed.** Your Oracle connection is not valid because the instance was aborted while you were still connected to the database. Exit SQL*Plus and launch it again starting a new database connection.

Select Command

When you select from the data dictionary, you might get an error.

■ **ORA-00942 table: or view does not exist.** When you select from the database view, you may get this message. If it isn't a typing error, then the view may exist but your connected user may not have select privilege on it. Grant the correct privileges to the selecting user. You may also need to specify the table owner before the table name.

■ **ORA-01219: database not open: queries allowed on fixed tables/views only.** You may be connected to a database that is mounted but not open and you are trying to select from a view or table that is not accessing the control file. Either open database or select information from the v$ dynamic views.

Shutdown Command

You may see some messages or experience some odd behavior when you shut down your database.

■ **Shutdown hangs for seconds.** Be patient. Oracle software has some cleaning up to do.

■ **Shutdown hangs for minutes.** If you issue a shutdown normal and a user is connected to the database, the shutdown command will wait until the user disconnects. You may be connected to your own database several times. To demonstrate the shutdown options on user connections, connect to the database via SQL*Plus. Open another SQL*Plus session (from a different command prompt) and shut down the database. A normal shutdown waits for the first connection to disconnect before the shutdown can proceed.

- **ORA-01109: database not open.** While shutting down a database, the database was not open. Disregard this message.

- **ORA-01507 database not mounted.** While shutting down a database, the database was not mounted. Disregard this message.

Summary

By now you have chosen a computer on which to practice database recovery operations. You have installed either Linux or Windows NT on this machine as well as Oracle 8.1.7 Enterprise edition, and you have built two databases. You have then been shown how to see data within the data dictionary. With this foundational work completed, you will be able to accomplish each exercise in all the chapters of this book.

During the following chapters of this book, I'll instruct you in each step of performing backups and recoveries. If you follow along and perform these database operations at home, you will learn more than by simply reading along. Make this book a hands-on training tool and you will be further ahead in your understanding and skill of Oracle backup and recovery.

I covered Oracle installation and database creation briefly in this chapter. To learn more about installing Oracle on Linux or Windows NT, refer to the *Oracle8i Installation Guide for Linux* or *Oracle8i Installation Guide for Windows NT* for all the details. You can find these documents online at docs.oracle.com or on your installation media. Consult *Oracle8i Administrator's Guide for Windows NT* or *Oracle8i Administrator's Guide for Linux* to learn more about database creation using the Database Configuration Assistant. If you want to learn more about managing the job system, look in Chapter 17 (DBMS_JOB) in the *Oracle8i Supplied PL/SQL Packages Reference* manual.

Chapter Questions

Try to answer these questions that review important concepts covered in this chapter.

 1. What purpose does the environment variable ORACLE_SID serve?

   A. Defines the location of the Oracle software files.

   B. Defines the location of the Oracle database and administration files.

   C. Defines the database instance name for the current OS session.

   D. Defines the serial number for your Oracle installation.

2. What tool can you use to create and delete an Oracle database?

   A. Oracle Universal Installer

   B. Oracle Database Configuration Assistant

   C. Oracle DBA Studio

   D. A monkey wrench

3. What are some differences between dynamic views and data dictionary views? (Pick any that apply.)

   A. Most dynamic views are available when the database is mounted but not open; dictionary views are not.

   B. Dynamic views display information from the current control file or memory structures; dictionary views display information from the SYSTEM tablespace.

   C. All dynamic views begin with the letters v$; most dictionary views begin with either DBA_, ALL_ or USER_.

   D. Dynamic views have a singular name; most dictionary views have a plural name.

4. What command starts the database instance and mounts the control files but does not open the database for user access?

   A. STARTUP

   B. STARTUP NOMOUNT

   C. ALTER DATABASE MOUNT

   D. STARTUP MOUNT

5. What views might you query to see the current datafiles in your database?

   A. VLOG, VLOG_HISTORY

   B. V$CONTROLFILE

   C. V$DATAFILE, V$TEMPFILE, DBA_DATA_FILES

   D. V$PARAMETER

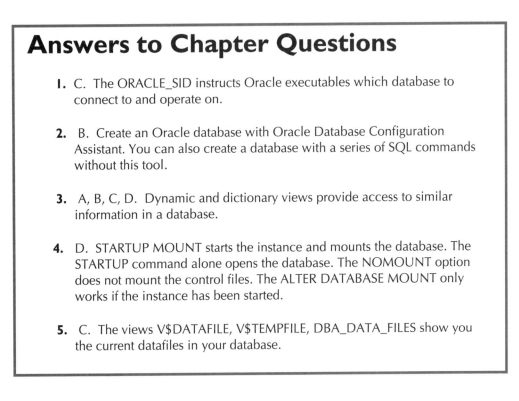

Answers to Chapter Questions

1. C. The ORACLE_SID instructs Oracle executables which database to connect to and operate on.

2. B. Create an Oracle database with Oracle Database Configuration Assistant. You can also create a database with a series of SQL commands without this tool.

3. A, B, C, D. Dynamic and dictionary views provide access to similar information in a database.

4. D. STARTUP MOUNT starts the instance and mounts the database. The STARTUP command alone opens the database. The NOMOUNT option does not mount the control files. The ALTER DATABASE MOUNT only works if the instance has been started.

5. C. The views V$DATAFILE, V$TEMPFILE, DBA_DATA_FILES show you the current datafiles in your database.

PART
II

User Managed
Recovery

CHAPTER
4

Closed Backup
and Recovery

he simplest method of database protection is copying all the database files to another location. In the event of a failure, you can restore the copies of all the files back to the original location, start up the database, and you are back in business. This operation is called a full (or whole) consistent database backup and restore.

When you perform restoration or recovery, you use a backup that was made on a consistent or an inconsistent database. A consistent database has been shut down cleanly and has synchronized files. The datafiles, redo logs and control files, shown in Figure 4-1, reflect a consistent database state. Because the database closed cleanly before backup, all these files have been "stamped" with the same database SCN (known as the Stop SCN). As a group of files, they represent a consistent database. During this chapter, you will perform consistent backups and then restore and recover the PRACTICE database. In the next chapter, I'll guide you through inconsistent backup and recovery.

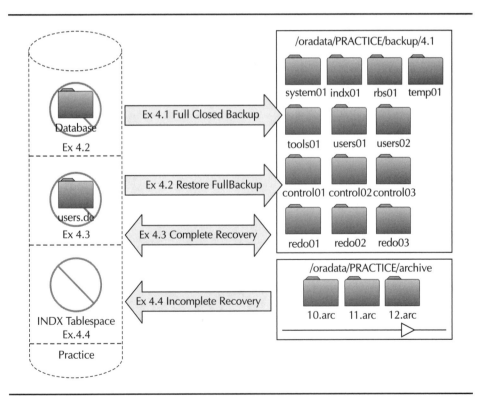

FIGURE 4-1.   *Closed backup, restore, and recovery operations*

NOTE
A consistent database backup is often referred to as a cold backup. The term originates for the notion that the database files are not experiencing activity and transition. When database is shutdown, the database files are frozen: cold.

In this chapter, you will perform several types of complete physical recoveries. The first scenario will be a complete closed backup and restore with no recovery. The second is a complete closed backup and recovery. The last scenario is an incomplete recovery. All the operations during this chapter will be performed on the PRACTICE database. You will also configure your PRACTICE database to use archive logging.

Closed Backup and Complete Restore

Make a full backup of the database by copying every file in the database. Before copying the datafiles, control files, and redo log files, close your database. A closed (clean shutdown) database will have consistent files. Remember: while the database is open, transactions are being written to memory, redo log files, and datafiles, and the control files are being updated. If you make a physical copy of the files while the database is open, the resulting copies of the files will be inconsistent with each other, and you will not likely be able to restore your database from those files. It is possible to back up a database when the database is open, but this is done at tablespace level and is discussed in Chapter 5.

CAUTION
Copying the redo logs on a cold backup can create problems if you mistakenly restore them over the production redo log files. This mistake removes the prospect of complete recovery of your production database. Therefore, many DBAs choose not to copy the online redo log files during backups. If the database has been closed cleanly before the backup, the online redo logs are not necessary for the complete recovery.

Exercise 4.1: Back Up a Closed Database

In this exercise, you will back up all the files in the PRACTICE database. Next, you will remove all database files to simulate a massive computer failure, and then you'll restore all database files from the backup and open the database.

Task Description	Minutes
1. Generate Database Activity	5
2. Create Backup Script	10
3. Run Backup Script	10
Total Time	25

This exercise is the simplest form of database backup: a full copy of the database files to a backup location.

Task 1: Generate Database Activity

During many of the exercises in this book, you want the database to be changing. You also want to confirm that your operations produce the result you expect. To accomplish these two goals, begin inserting rows into Tina's DATE_LOG table, as discussed in Chapter 3. Have a look at the table to see that new rows have been created. Finally, make a note of the latest row entered in the TINA.DATE_LOG table.

```
SQL> SELECT TO_DATE(max(create_date),'HH24:MI:SS') latest_time
  2    FROM tina.date_log;
```

When you restore the database, you can check the maximum time then and compare that time with this time.

Task 2: Create Backup Script

Scripts are a useful method to perform database tasks. You can use a script like the following to back up all the files in your database. Throughout this book, I'll provide some very basic scripts like this one that you can learn from and then build upon. This script will work on your Linux database. Modify the copy command and the directory names so that it will work for a Windows database.

```
1.    Remark Set SQL*Plus variables to manipulate output
2.    set feedback off heading off verify off trimspool off
3.    set pagesize 0 linesize 200
4.    Remark Set SQL*Plus user variables used in this script
5.    define dir = '/oradata/PRACTICE/backup/ch04'
6.    define fil = '/tmp/closed_backup_commands.sql'
```

```
7.   prompt *** Spooling to &fil
8.   Remark Create a command file with file backup commands
9.   spool &fil
10.  select 'host cp '|| name    ||' &dir' from v$datafile     order by 1;
11.  select 'host cp '|| member ||' &dir' from v$logfile      order by 1;
12.  select 'host cp '|| name    ||' &dir' from v$controlfile order by 1;
13.  select 'host cp '|| name    ||' &dir' from v$tempfile     order by 1;
14.  spool off;
15.  Remark Shutdown the database cleanly
16.  shutdown immediate;
17.  Remark Run the copy file commands from the operating system
18.  @fil
19.  Remark Start the database again
20.  startup;
```

You can see from this script above all the commands necessary to run a complete backup of all database files.

■ Lines 2–3 set SQL*Plus variables that prevent the output of the selections from the database from displaying information you don't want in the command file. In these lines, you set system variables that control the operation of your current SQL*Plus session.

■ Lines 5–6 specify SQL*Plus user variables for your commands within the script. A user variable saves you keystrokes. You define a variable named dir to be a text string. Later in the script you can refer to the user variable value by preceding the variable name with an ampersand. The dir value in this script specifies the directory location to copy the backup files, too. The fil specifies the name of the file containing the backup commands.

■ Line 7 demonstrates how you can display output using the SQL*Plus prompt command.

■ Line 9 instructs SQL*Plus to begin writing all screen output to a file. The file name is the value held in a variable named fil. In this script, the output of subsequent lines are written to /tmp/closed_backup_commands.sql.

■ Lines 10–13 create several OS commands to perform a file copy of each database file in the PRACTICE database. These lines select information from the data dictionary and create OS commands. The || symbol performs string concatenation in a SQL command. You use v$ dynamic views to copy each datafile, online redo log file, control file, and temporary file. The word host precedes each copy command. From a SQL*Plus prompt, you can run an OS command by beginning the line with the word host (or the exclamation mark on Linux). The PRACTICE database does not have any temporary files, but I added line 13 to be complete.

- Line 14 turns off writing to file /tmp/closed_backup_commands.sql.

- Line 16 shuts down the database cleanly.

- Line 18 executes all the commands in the script you just created. This step will take the most time because the database files are being copied. If you open closed_backup_commands.sql after you run closed_copy.sql, you'll see the copy commands following the host keyword. Be sure to look over the commands in the command file script.

- Line 20 starts the database again.

To run this script, connect as SYS or SYSTEM using the SYSDBA role.

TIP
Learn to create scripts by selecting information from the data dictionary. Not only do you save typing time, you also insure that the script is accurate at the time it runs. Selecting from the data dictionary guarantees that the command will produce all the output you need.

Task 3: Run Backup Script

The backup script just shown can be run as is or in pieces. You can create a file with the script commands and execute that file from SQL*Plus. If you create a file named closed_backup.sql, you can run this file using the start command or the @ symbol:

```
SQL> @closed_backup.sql
```

or

```
SQL> start closed_backup.sql
```

CAUTION
Scripts in this book are intentionally simple and not ready for production database usage. When you deploy backup on production machines, you'll add error handling, notification, verification, and other required elements.

Exercise 4.2: Restore the Whole Database

In this exercise, you will restore all the copied files in the PRACTICE database taken in the previous exercise. Once the files are restored, you'll be able to open the database without recovery because the files were consistent when backed up in the previous exercise. (The PRACTICE database is not running in archive log mode yet. Therefore, recovery using archived log files after a restore is not possible.)

Task Description	Minutes
1. Remove Database Files	5
2. Run Restore Script	10
3. Open Database	5
4. Confirm Database Restore	5
Total Time	25

If a machine had a massive failure, you might lose all your database files. Backup copies typically get copied to tape and moved offsite to secure storage. When you restore the whole database, you copy all the files as a group to the original location from the tape backup. The locations of the database files can be changed, as you'll see later in the book. For now, let's keep it very simple.

Task 1: Remove Database Files

Let's say that a new system administrator accidentally removed all the files in your database while the database was shut down. To simulate this failure, shut down your database and remove all database files in the PRACTICE database like this:

```
rm /oradata/PRACTICE/*
```

You can try to open the database without the database files, and the startup command will fail. Try it and see what message you get.

Task 2: Run Restore Script

The restore operation is very simple on the PRACTICE database because all the backup files are in one directory. You can restore all the database files like this:

```
cp /oradata/PRACTICE/backup/ch04/* /oradata/PRACTICE
```

You are simply copying the backup files from the backup destination to the original location. In a real world system, files usually get restored from tape to many different file systems.

Task 3: Open Database

Before you open this restored database, mount control files and get familiar with some important dynamic views. The remaining discussion in this task is not a necessary part of the database restore, but will help familiarize you with important database restore and recovery information. Mount the database first before you open it:

```
SQL> startup mount
```

From a separate OS prompt, open the alert log with an editor and find the time of database shutdown before the backup was taken in Exercise 4.1. (Throughout the exercises in this book, you will often have more than one OS prompt or SQL session open simultaneously.)

```
ALTER DATABASE CLOSE NORMAL
Tue Jan 1 11:40:35 2002
SMON: disabling tx recovery
SMON: disabling cache recovery
Tue Jan 1 11:40:37 2002
Thread 1 closed at log sequence 212
Tue Jan 1 11:40:37 2002
Completed: ALTER DATABASE CLOSE NORMAL
```

The alert log listing shows the time and log sequence when the database was closed. With the database mounted, look at the last change and checkpoint change columns in the v$datafile view. During a clean shutdown, the Oracle Server performs a checkpoint and updates all online datafile headers. Does the time of the last checkpoint agree with the time of the shutdown prior to backup?

```
SQL> alter session set NLS_DATE_FORMAT='HH24:MI:SS';
SQL> SELECT file#,
  2         status,
  3         checkpoint_change#,
  4         checkpoint_time,
  5         last_change#,
  6         last_time
  7    FROM v$datafile;
```

Note that the time of the shutdown is the same time the datafile checkpoint occurred.

```
FILE# STATUS  CHECKPOINT_CHANGE# CHECKPOI LAST_CHANGE# LASTTIME
----- ------- ------------------ -------- ------------ --------
    1 SYSTEM               43857 11:40:36        43857 11:40:36
    2 ONLINE               43857 11:40:36        43857 11:40:36
    3 ONLINE               43857 11:40:36        43857 11:40:36
    4 ONLINE               43857 11:40:36        43857 11:40:36
    5 ONLINE               43857 11:40:36        43857 11:40:36
    6 ONLINE               43857 11:40:36        43857 11:40:36
```

Confirm that the change time of the datafiles concurs with the database shutdown time; the checkpoint and last change numbers are the SCN values for the datafile when the database closes.

When the datafiles undergo a checkpoint, an SCN will be stamped on the file. Actually, the SCN is written in the header of the files and to the control file. Compare the change number of the datafile checkpoint with the online redo log first change number. The change number in the datafile will be greater than the first change number of the current redo log in our example.

```
SQL> SELECT group#, sequence#, status, first_change#, first_time
  2     FROM v$log
  3     ORDER BY first_change#;

GROUP#   SEQUENCE# STATUS     FIRST_CHANGE# FIRST_TI
------   --------- ---------  ------------- --------
     3         210 INACTIVE           43372 11:32:30
     1         211 INACTIVE           43470 11:32:32
     2         212 CURRENT            43538 11:32:35
```

In the previous output, the SCN for the datafile checkpoint is 43857. The first change number in the current redo log is 43538. Therefore, the database backup occurred on the database while redo log group 2 was current.

NOTE
When you select from the v$ views, you are often exploring the contents of the mounted control file. You are not looking at the datafile or the redo file contents, you are looking at what the control file thinks the datafiles and redo logs contain.

After exploring these views with the control file mounted, you can open your database with the ALTER DATABASE OPEN command. During the open command, the Oracle Server compares the SCN in the datafile headers with those in the control file. If all values are consistent, the database can be opened.

Task 4: Confirm Database Restore

When a database opens, Oracle automatically confirms that the database files are consistent. An Oracle database will not open unless the datafiles, control files, and online redo logs are consistent. To test that the data in the database is what it was at the time of the backup, you can select the maximum date/time from the TINA.DATE_LOG. This was shown in the previous exercise. This time should be the same time as it was when the database was backed up.

This exercise illustrates a cold backup and a complete restore of all database files. Your next exercise will be to turn on archiving for the database, take a cold backup, and then carry out complete recovery.

TIP
Make a file copy of the contents of all the files in the /oradata/PRACTICE/backup/ch04 to a different location. You can use this copy as a base backup for your database in the event that something goes wrong with your future database backups and recoveries.

Complete and Incomplete Recovery

Backup and restore works well if you want to be able to restore the database as it was during a backup. However, database restoration by itself has a big deficiency: you lose transactions that occur between backups. If you back up your database every night and you have a database failure at lunchtime, you can restore the database to the state it was the night before. Then you call your users and tell them they will have to redo all the work they did in the morning.

Users don't like to do their work over again.

Oracle recovery allows you to apply redo to a restored database. The database redoes the work accomplished rather than the users or the database application having to do it. The information necessary to redo the work is all contained in the redo log files.

Exercise 4.3: Complete Database Recovery

In this exercise, you will remove one datafile and recover that datafile so that it is consistent with the rest of the database. Before you do this, you must put the database into archive log mode, therefore saving the redo information that gets generated.

Task Description	Minutes
1. Configure Database Archiving	15
2. Run Backup Script	10
3. Advance the Redo Logs	10
4. Remove One DataFile	5
5. Restore Missing DataFile	5
6. Recover Restored DataFile	10
7. Confirm Database Recovery	5
Total Time	60

Like many exercises in this book, this exercise builds on the previous one. You may need to refer back to previous tasks as you proceed.

Task 1: Configure Database Archiving

You can instruct Oracle to copy the online redo log files to one or more offline destinations. The process of copying online redo log files into archived redo log files is called *archiving*. Archiving must be enabled in order to recover your database. Archiving occurs only if the database is in *ARCHIVELOG mode*. When the database is in ARCHIVELOG mode, you'll want the archiving to occur automatically so that you don't have to worry about managing it yourself. This task contains instructions to configure archiving parameters and set the database into archiving mode.

First, determine if the PRACTICE database is in ARCHIVELOG mode by looking at the v$database view:

```
SQL> select dbid, name, log_mode from v$database;
      DBID NAME        LOG_MODE
---------- --------- ------------
2629144163 PRACTICE  NOARCHIVELOG
```

The *database id* (dbid) is a unique number assigned by Oracle when the database is created. These results show that the PRACTICE database is not in ARCHIVELOG mode. Therefore, each time the database switches to the next redo log for recording database changes, Oracle writes over transactions in a previous redo log. The redo change information in the online redo files cannot be applied once they are overwritten.

Before you place the database in ARCHIVELOG mode, you'll want to configure the archiving process via database parameters in the parameter file. The *archiver*, Oracle's archiving background process, needs to know where to put the redo log file copies, what to name them, and whether to do the archiving automatically.

- **Archive Destination**   Instruct the database where to put archived redo log files by adding this line to the parameter file:

  ```
  log_archive_dest_1 = "location=/oradata/PRACTICE/archive"
  ```

  Archive files will be placed in this directory as they are copied. The location keyword in quotes means to copy files to a directory on the local hard disk. Archive files can be copied to multiple locations (up to five different locations). For your exercise, one location is all you need.

- **Archive Format**   Specify the naming convention of the archive files in the parameter file. Add this line to your file:

  ```
  log_archive_format = %s.arc
  ```

Archive files will be named in sequential order, where %s is the log sequence number. You have a few options available in defining the format of your archive log names, but for these exercises, keep them simple. Each time the online redo logs switch, a new sequence number is generated. That sequence number can be seen in the alert log and in the SEQUENCE# of the v$log view.

■ **Archive Start** Make sure the PRACTICE database automatically archives redo log files by setting LOG_ARCHIVE_START:

```
LOG_ARCHIVE_START=TRUE
```

The value takes effect the next time you start the database. Why? The parameter file is read when the instance is started.

After you have changed your parameter file, place your database in ARCHIVELOG mode. To make this change, shut down your database and then mount it. Restarting your instance causes the parameter changes you've made in the initPRACTICE.ora file to be read.

While the database is mounted but not open, change the archiving mode of your database like this:

```
SQL> SHUTDOWN IMMEDIATE;
SQL> STARTUP MOUNT;
SQL> ALTER DATABASE ARCHIVELOG;
```

When you open the database, every time the current log file switches, a file will be created in your archive destination directory. These files keep a running record of changes made to your PRACTICE database.

Before you move on to the next task, I want to mention a note on database parameters. Some database parameters, called *static parameters*, can only be defined in the parameter file. Other parameters, *dynamic parameters*, can also be changed when the database is open. If you set a dynamic database parameter, that value remains until you set it again or until the database is restarted. When the database is restarted, the value will be set to the value in the initialization file or take on a default value. The LOG_ARCHIVE_DEST_1 is a dynamic parameter; the LOG_ARCHIVE_START and the LOG_ARCHIVE_FORMAT are static parameters and cannot be changed on the fly. Dynamic parameters can have persistence through database restarts in 9*i* using the SPFile feature.

To set an archiving location on an open instance, use the alter system command:

```
ALTER SYSTEM SET log_archive_dest_1 = "location=/oradata/PRACTICE/archive";
```

Though you can't set the LOG_ARCHIVE_START parameter dynamically, you can enable automatic archiving on an open instance with either of these commands from a SQL*Plus prompt:

```
ALTER SYSTEM ARCHIVE LOG START;
ARCHIVE LOG START;
```

With all parameters in place and the archiving mode set, run some commands to verify your parameter settings are now in effect. Have a look at the contents of the v$archive_dest view. Check that the directory for archiving is correct.

```
SQL> SELECT dest_id, status, destination
  2     FROM v$archive_dest
  3     WHERE dest_id = 1
DEST_ID STATUS DESTINATION
------- ------ ------------------------------------
      1 VALID  /oradata/PRACTICE/archive
```

A valid status means that you have properly initialized the destination and this directory is available for archiving.

You can check each archiving parameter to confirm each setting. You can check any parameter setting by selecting from the v$parameter view or by using the SQL*Plus show parameter command:

```
SQL> show parameter log_archive_start
SQL> show parameter log_archive_dest_1
SQL> show parameter log_archive_format
```

Another useful SQL*Plus command for examining archive information is the archive log list command:

```
SQL> ARCHIVE LOG LIST
Database log mode              Archive Mode
Automatic archival             Enabled
Archive destination            /oradata/PRACTICE/archive
Oldest online log sequence     200
Next log sequence to archive   202
Current log sequence           202
```

The output of this command shows you the important details about your current archive settings and status. From the output above, you see that

■   The database is operating in ARCHIVELOG mode.

■   The database will automatically archive redo log files.

■ The archived redo log's destination is /oradata/PRACTICE/archive.

■ The oldest online redo log group has a sequence number of 200.

■ The next filled online redo log group to archive has a sequence number of 202.

■ The current online redo log file has a sequence number of 202.

Once you've checked that your settings from the parameter file have taken effect, open the database and generate some archive log files.

```
SQL> ALTER DATABASE OPEN;
```

Your PRACTICE database has now been configured to archive the redo log files. On your small PRACTICE database with little transaction activity, the 1MB redo logs won't fill very often. A log switch occurs when LGWR stops writing to one online redo log group and starts writing to another. By default, a log switch occurs automatically when the current online redo log group fills. You can also manually switch the log files with the ALTER SYSTEM command.

```
SQL> ALTER SYSTEM SWITCH LOGFILE;
```

Force log switches by running this command several times, and review the v$log and v$log_history views. Note that the sequence number of the log files is increasing. Each time you switch log files, the log file sequence increases by 1. Also, check that your archive destination directory now contains some files. The files will contain the sequence number of the log file if you defined the format of the file with the wildcard %s or %S. You will see that the sequence number in the filename matches the sequence number in the views. Follow the trail of log file numbers. Note that the archived redo log files are different sizes and are most likely smaller than the 1MB online redo log file size. The archiver process creates a copy of the redo contents of the most recent online redo log file. Since you forced a log switch, the online redo log was not full. Therefore, your archive log files will not be the full 1MB size.

Task 2: Run Backup Script

After placing your PRACTICE database in ARCHIVELOG mode and setting the necessary parameters, you are ready to make another closed backup of the database. The previous backup made in Exercise 4.1 will not allow you to recover your database to the current point in time. Why? Because database changes have occurred since the first backup until now. The redo information has been lost in the overwriting of the online redo log files. For this reason, Oracle recommends that you perform a full backup after you place your database in ARCHIVELOG mode.

With a whole database-consistent backup and a copy of all archive log files, you'll be able to recover your database to any point in time after the backup. This backup will overwrite the backup created in Exercise 4.1.

Task 3: Advance the Redo Logs

With the full database backup complete, generate some frequent activity on the database by inserting rows into TINA.DATE_LOG, and then force a log switch. When you break the database in the next task, the recovery process should need at least one archive log file to complete the full recovery. When you perform the forced log switch, you will see a line like this in your alert log file:

```
Thread 1 advanced to log sequence 219
   Current log# 3 seq# 219 mem# 0: /oradata/PRACTICE/redo03.log
```

This entry in the redo log verifies that the log switch occurred. You can also query the v$log or v$log_history views, or issue the ARCHIVE LOG LIST command to confirm that the log sequence advanced.

Task 4: Remove One DataFile

To perform recovery on your PRACTICE database, break it first: remove the users01.dbf file using an OS delete command. In Linux, you can remove this file while the database is open. After the file is removed, shut down the database and note the error you see. During the shutdown, the database attempts to update the headers of all the datafiles. When it tries to update the header of the users01.dbf, it can't find it. This error will be reported to your SQL*Plus session and to the alert log file. (In Windows, you must shut down the database first to remove the file. Windows locks the files, thus preventing deletion. When you attempt to open the database, you'll see the same errors described below):

```
ORA-01157: cannot identify/lock data file 3 - see DBWR trace file
ORA-01110: data file 3: '/oradata/PRACTICE/users01.dbf'
ORA-27041: unable to open file
OSD-04002: unable to open file
O/S-Error: (OS 2) The system cannot find the file specified.
```

Oracle is now unable to open the missing file. A DBWR trace file will be created in the $ORACLE_BASE/admin/PRACTICE/bdump with additional details about the error.

Task 5: Restore Missing DataFile

Though you can recover the missing datafile while the database is open, shut down your Linux database by aborting the instance (SHUTDOWN ABORT). Once the database is shut down, you can try to perform a normal startup. When you attempt to open the database, you face the same error that tells you that the users01.dbf file cannot be found. With the database mounted, take a look at the contents of v$recover_file. This view lists all files that require recovery and provides an error that explains why each file must be recovered.

TIP

Since you have only lost one nonsystem datafile, you would typically recover the one datafile after taking its tablespace offline. The database remains open for users while you perform recovery. I will first illustrate recovery from a mounted database. In the next chapter, you'll recover a lost datafile while the database is open.

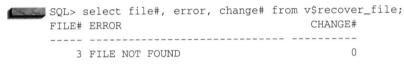

```
SQL> select file#, error, change# from v$recover_file;
FILE# ERROR                               CHANGE#
----- ------------------------------- ----------
    3 FILE NOT FOUND                          0
```

File number 3 must be recovered because the file was not found when the database open operation attempted to open the datafile. Copy the users01.dbf from the backup directory from your consistent backup in Task 2. With this datafile in place, v$recover_file will show you something different: the error will be blank and the change# column will have a number. Compare that number with the checkpoint change number for all the files in the v$datafile view. You should see the SCN from the v$datafile view is a higher number than the number in v$recover_file. The v$datafile reads information from the control file about the datafiles in the PRACTICE database, while the v$recover_file displays the change number from the header of the file that you just restored. Therefore, the database cannot be opened until the SCNs for all online datafiles are the same in the header of the datafile and in the control file. They must also have the same value as each other. To achieve this consistency prior to opening the database, you must perform recovery.

Task 6: Recover Restored DataFile

Bringing all datafiles to a consistent change number requires redo information from the redo logs. Every change needed is contained in one or more archive logs and the current online redo log. See if you can figure out what redo files must be applied to the users01.dbf file for a complete recovery. Note the change numbers in v$recover_file and v$datafile for this file. Find out which redo log files must be applied by looking at v$log_history and v$log. You'll need the redo log files that span the range of sequence numbers from the time when the database backup occurred through the current redo log file.

```
SQL> SELECT * FROM v$log_history WHERE ROWNUM < 10
  2   ORDER BY sequence# DESC;
SQL> SELECT * FROM v$log;
```

Your output might look like the results in Table 4-1. For example, if the v$recover_file says that the change# of the users01.dbf file is 64300, and the v$datafile view says the checkpoint change of the file ought to be 64440, which redo logs contain the changes to get this file current with the control file? Complete recovery requires redo from archived redo file sequence 218 and from the online redo log file 219.
Recover the database with the recover database command.

```
SQL> RECOVER DATABASE;
```

With this command, Oracle determines which datafiles need recovery and which redo files are needed for recovery. When media recovery is complete, you'll get a message:

```
Media recovery complete.
```

v$log_history

Sequence	First Change#	Next Change#
218	64160	64349
217	44155	64160
216	44154	44155

v$log

Sequence	First Change#	Archived
219	64349	NO
218	64160	YES
217	44155	YES

TABLE 4-1.   *Change Numbers in Redo Files*

After recovery, check the contents of v$recover_file. You should find that no rows are returned. This indicates that all the redo needed for users01.dbf was applied to it. Take a look at the alert log to see what actions took place during recovery.

```
ALTER DATABASE RECOVER  database
Sun Jan 2 08:20:28 2002
Media Recovery Start
Media Recovery Log
Recovery of Online Redo Log: Thread 1 Group 2 Seq 218 Reading mem 0
  Mem# 0 errs 0: /ORADATA/PRACTICE/redo02.log
Recovery of Online Redo Log: Thread 1 Group 3 Seq 219 Reading mem 0
  Mem# 0 errs 0: /ORADATA/PRACTICE/redo03.log
Media Recovery Complete
Completed: ALTER DATABASE RECOVER  database
```

Did you estimate correctly which redo files would be needed for recovery?

Task 7: Confirm Database Recovery

Before we move on to the final exercise in this chapter, check the latest database date/time in TINA.DATE_LOG. This time will be the latest time taken from this table just before you broke your database by removing the datafile in Task 4.

Congratulations. You have finished a successful complete database recovery.

Exercise 4.4: Incomplete Database Recovery

You have by now completed a successful database restore and a database complete recovery. Incomplete recovery uses a backup and then rolls it forward to a point in time before now. Instead of applying all of the redo records generated after the most recent backup, you apply redo up to a specific point. Incomplete recovery of the whole database may be needed when

- You lose a database object by mistake

- You lose some or all of the online redo logs

- You lose an archived redo log needed during recovery

- You drop the wrong tablespace by mistake

Incomplete media recovery begins by restoring all datafiles from backups created prior to the moment you'd like to recover to. You issue the recover command defining the point you want recovery to cease. When you open the database, you'll have to disregard the remaining redo for the database. This is done because you are choosing to stop redo application before all of it has been applied. Once the database is open, the disregarded redo cannot be used. The way in which you disregard the remaining redo is by opening the database with the RESETLOGS option. Resetting the log files creates a new *incarnation* of the database. The sequence numbering of the recovered database begins with a new stream of log sequence numbers starting with log sequence number 1.

To illustrate backup and incomplete recovery, in the next exercise you'll perform similar tasks to those in Exercise 4.3. In this exercise , you will drop the INDX tablespace and recover the database to the point just before this "mistake" occurred.

Task Description	Minutes
1. Drop Tablespace	10
2. Investigate Recovery	10
3. Restore Datafiles and Control Files	10
4. Recover Database Incompletely	10
5. Open with Reset Logs	5
6. Confirm Database Recovery	5
Total Time	50

When you perform Task 4, you'll have the option of performing the recovery one of three ways. If you want to try each recovery, you'll have to rework all the earlier tasks of this exercise.

Task 1: Drop Tablespace

The first task in this exercise is to create a condition where incomplete recovery would be valuable, so drop the INDX tablespace on the PRACTICE database. Before you do this, insure that new rows are being inserted into TINA.DATE_LOG. At the end of this exercise, you will check the latest entry into this table. Also, force at least three log switches. This recovery should use archived logs, not just the online logs.

I chose to drop a tablespace in this exercise because the drop tablespace command writes a message to the alert log, while a drop or truncate table does not. You'll use the alert log information in your recovery investigation.

Before you drop the tablespace, note the maximum time in the TINA.DATE_LOG table prior to the drop command:

```
SQL> SELECT TO_DATE(max(create_date),'HH24:MI:SS') latest_time
  2    FROM tina.date_log;
```

To drop the INDX tablespace use this command:

```
SQL> drop tablespace indx including contents;
Tablespace dropped.
SQL> ALTER SYSTEM SWITCH LOGFILE;
```

After you execute this command, look at the v$tablespace or the dba_tablespace views. Note that the INDX tablespace is not listed anymore. Before you perform incomplete recovery, be sure some more rows are inserted into TINA.DATE_LOG.

CAUTION
The drop tablespace command is an irrevocable operation. Be absolutely sure you are connected to the PRACTICE database prior to issuing this command.

Task 2: Investigate Recovery

When a mistake occurs, you might get a phone call describing the problem. A user or developer may not know the exact time of the accident. They certainly won't know the log file sequence number or the SCN values when the mistake occurred. Depending on the mistake that was made, you can sometimes get a definite time when it occurred. For changes to the database structure (for example dropping a tablespace) there will be an entry in the alert.log. For object changes, like dropping a table, you must use approximate times supplied by the people involved. Alternatively, you could use LogMiner to try and figure out a more accurate time (this is covered in Chapter 10). Before you restore and recover your database in this exercise, investigate the alert file, v$log, and v$log_history tables to determine how best to recover the database.

Look in the alert log file for the log switch that occurred prior to the DROP TABLESPACE command. Other major database events are also recorded in this file. The alert log will note that the tablespace has been dropped. Open the alert log and look for some text like this:

```
Thread 1 advanced to log sequence 223
   Current log# 1 seq# 223 mem# 0: /oradata/PRACTICE/redo01.log
...
Fri Jan 4 09:07:10 2002
drop tablespace indx including contents
Fri Jan 4 09:07:12 2002
Completed: drop tablespace indx including contents
```

This means that on Friday, January 4, somebody issued a drop tablespace command. The command completed in two seconds. Just above that command, the alert log notes that a log switch occurred. The log sequence number 223 was current when the tablespace was dropped. To find what the first change number is in redo log sequence 223, you'll need to look in the v$log_history view with a query like this:

```
SQL> SELECT sequence#, first_change#
   2    FROM v$log_history WHERE sequence# = 223;
```

For illustration, say that the first_change# occurred at SCN 64300.

You must perform your detective work on the PRACTICE database before you restore the datafiles and control files from the consistent backup. Once you copy over the existing control files, you lose the information you need to perform incomplete recovery. You may want to copy this database to another location after shutting it down (as described in Exercise 4.1). You may need this copy if you select the wrong end point to stop recovery. You can then restore and start up the old database and investigate more.

From your investigation, you can conclude that a drop tablespace command occurred at 9:07:10 in the morning on Friday, January 4. The current redo log file was log file sequence 223 and began recording database changes starting at change number 64300. You'll want to recover the database to a point prior to the drop tablespace command. You can perform this incomplete recovery up to a point in time, up to a database change number, or up to a specific log file. When you recover the database incompletely, you will lose database transactions occurring after the end recovery point. However, you gladly make this trade-off because you need the INDX tablespace back.

Task 3: Restore Datafiles and Control Files

When you perform incomplete recovery, you restore all database files except the online redo log files from a backup prior to the time that you want to recover to. No datafile can have a change number greater than the change number of the time you wish to recover up to. Therefore, shut down the database and copy all the datafiles and control files from the closed backup made in Exercise 4.3. Leave the current redo logs in the /oradata/PRACTICE directory because you may require redo in the online redo log files to bring the database to the point before the tablespace was dropped.

Task 4: Recover Database Incompletely

Before you begin incomplete recovery, double-check that the files in the /oradata/ PRACTICE directory contain datafiles and control files from the most recent database consistent backup. The redo log files should be the ones from the database as it existed when you "accidentally" dropped the INDX tablespace.

Recover your database with the alter database command and use the UNTIL clause to specify the duration of the recovery operation. You can recover the database until a specific time, change number, or redo log.

■ **Time-based recovery** By specifying the time of parameter, you instruct the PRACTICE instance to apply redo from the redo files until the moment specified by the date. Redo is found in the archived and online redo files beginning with the lowest change number for any of the datafiles as found in the file headers. The date must be a character literal in the format YYYY-MM-DD:HH24:MI:SS.

Open the alert log and find the date of the drop tablespace command as shown above. Translate that date into the format expected by the ALTER DATABASE command. Perform time-based recovery of the PRACTICE database with a command like this:

```
SQL> ALTER DATABASE RECOVER AUTOMATIC UNTIL TIME '2002-01-04:09:07:10';
```

According to the alert log listing above, the drop tablespace occurred at 12 seconds in the seventh minute. Your recover command will restore the database up to ten seconds in the seventh minute. Redo will be applied up to the moment just before the drop tablespace command occurred. If you don't encounter problems after this recovery operation, you'll get a DATABASE ALTERED response. The datafiles now contain all information as they did two seconds before the accident occurred. To open the database, you'll have to reset the redo logs.

NOTE
Recovery will not always be 100 percent accurate to a specific time. Estimate the time you think the mistake occurred and set your time stop point a little before that time.

■ **Change-based recovery**   You can specify a SCN threshold for recovery. Rather than supplying a time value, you could have provided a SCN like this:

```
SQL> ALTER DATABASE RECOVER AUTOMATIC UNTIL SCN 64300;
```

The CHANGE option on the RECOVER clause indicates change-based recovery. This parameter recovers the database to a transaction-consistent state immediately before the system change number (SCN) specified by integer. The trick is figuring out what SCN value to set on the recover command. The datafiles will be current to change 64300 at the conclusion of this command. When using change based recovery, unless you have the exact SCN value at which the problem occurred, which is rare for non-structural database changes, time-based recovery would be a more accurate method of stopping recovery.

■ **Cancel-based recovery**   You can perform incomplete database recovery using the CANCEL keyword. Cancel-based recovery recovers the database until you type **cancel**. Redo logs are applied one by one until you reach the redo log file that you'd like to stop at.

Start cancel recovery with the ALTER DATABASE command:

```
SQL> ALTER DATABASE RECOVER UNTIL CANCEL USING BACKUP CONTROLFILE;
```

If you use the AUTOMATIC keyword, Oracle automatically derives the archive log file name and location from the init.ora parameters and applies each file found. Recovery will stop when the next suggested log can't be found. This can be useful if an archive log file is missing and prevents complete recovery. For cancel-based recovery in this exercise, you have to manually apply the log file names and then type **CANCEL'** when you reach the log file that was current at the time of the tablespace drop. When you recover to an SCN or time, you don't have to interact with recovery as you do with cancel-based recovery.

You want to apply all redo logs up to the log containing the DROP TABLESPACE command. Keep applying redo logs until the redo log at which you want to stop is displayed. Once you see the file that you don't want to apply, type **cancel**. In Chapter 5, we'll look at cancel-based recovery more closely.

Task 5: Open with Reset Logs

After incomplete recovery, you must reset the online redo logs. When you open the database with the RESETLOGS option, all datafiles get a new RESETLOGS SCN and time stamp. Archived redo logs also have these two values in their header. Oracle software prevents you from corrupting your datafiles with old archived logs by insuring that the datafile RESETLOGS SCN and time stamp match the redo log file.

To open the database and reset the logs, issue this command:

```
SQL> ALTER DATABASE OPEN RESETLOGS;
```

When you type this command, you may notice it takes some time to complete. The online redo log files are rebuilt, every datafile header is updated, and the control files are updated. When all this work is done, the database opens. Note the new sequence number for each online redo log file.

```
SQL> SELECT group#, sequence#, archived, status
  2  FROM v$log;
   GROUP#   SEQUENCE# ARCHIVED STATUS
---------- ---------- -------- ----------------
        1          0 YES      UNUSED
        2          1 NO       CURRENT
        3          0 YES      UNUSED
```

Your redo files have now begun numbering themselves again. You've created a new incarnation of the PRACTICE database. Have a look at the alert log file for some text that looks like this:

```
Mon Aug 27 06:54:49 2001
RESETLOGS after complete recovery through change 64300
```

The resetting of the logs occurred up to a specified SCN. Any redo after SCN 64300 has not been applied to the datafiles.

Task 6: Confirm Database Recovery

After a successful recovery, you can verify that the recovery retained the database objects as desired. Check that the new incarnation of the database contains the INDX tablespace via the v$tablespace or dba_tablespaces views. You should see the INDX tablespace listed. Also select from TINA.DATE_LOG for the latest date/time in the table. Provided that you have not inserted rows into this table since the database has been opened, you will fetch a time that is less than the time that the drop tablespace command occurred. You lost rows that were inserted into TINA.DATE_LOG after the time you dropped the tablespace.

Congratulations. You have successfully performed an incomplete recovery.

NOTE
You MUST take a full database backup after opening it with the RESETLOGS option. It is almost impossible to restore a previous backup and roll it forward through the time when a RESETLOGS was performed.

Troubleshooting

While performing the exercises in this chapter, you may have run across some errors you weren't expecting. If you do encounter an error, check this section for help.

Alter Database Open

During database startup, you may have some problems:

1. **ORA-00313: open failed for members of log group *string* of thread *string*.** The log file is not where the control file thinks it should be. Check that you have a redo log where the control file expects. Also check that you have the correct log files in place. If everything checks out, you will have to carry out incomplete recovery until this wrong log file is reached. Opening the database with RESETLOGS will recreate any missing log files.

2. **ORA-00314: log *string* of thread *string*, expected sequence# *string* doesn't match *string*.** The log file opened is out of sequence. Perhaps you failed to copy online redo log file from backup after a restore.

3. **ORA-01157: cannot identify/lock data file string—see DBWR trace file.** When opening the database, Oracle could not find a datafile. Restore the file and recover the database.

Startup Mount

1. **ORA-00205: error in identifying controlfile, check alert log for more info.**
When the database starts, it finds the control file and mounts it. If the
instance can't find the control files listed in the parameter file, you will
get this message. Make sure the control file exists where the parameter file
says it should.

Alter System Switch Log File

1. **Hangs:** Check that you have not filled the disk containing your
archive log files.

Summary

In this chapter, you learned the fundamentals of user-managed physical database
restore and recovery using a cold backup and archive logs. You learned some of the
key commands to recover a database and can now create a cold backup script via
the dynamic v$ views.

In the next chapter, you'll learn how to make a backup of the database files
while the database is open. Using those files, you'll carry out complete and
incomplete recovery of your PRACTICE database.

Chapter Questions

Here are some questions that review some of the important concepts covered in
this chapter.

1. Why would you want your database to be in ARCHIVELOG mode?

    A. You can recover your database completely or to a specific point in time.

    B. Your server has extra disk space that needs to be filled.

    C. The control files need to be stored away for safekeeping.

    D. Datafiles can be compressed while they are online.

2. Which v$ view will tell you the sequence numbers of your archived redo
log files?

    A. v$datafile

    B. v$log

C. v$log_history

D. v$database

3. How can you know which files need to be recovered when the database won't open?

A. Select from v$recover_file.

B. Look in the alert log file.

C. Check the parameter file.

D. Select from v$broken_datafile.

4. What SQL*Plus command gives you a quick overview of the current archive status of your database?

A. ARCHIVE STATUS

B. SHOW PARAMETER ARCHIVE

C. ALTER SYSTEM SWITCH LOGFILE

D. ARCHIVE LOG LIST

5. Pick the three types of incomplete recovery.

A. Cancel-based recovery

B. Time-based recovery

C. Error-based recovery

D. Change-based recovery

Answers to Chapter Questions

I. A. When the database is in ARCHIVELOG mode, redo log file contents are copied to a destination you specify. By applying these files to a restored portion of the database, you can redo the work performed earlier by the database.

2. C. The v$log_history displays a detailed list of archived redo log files, the history of change numbers, and log sequence numbers for log switches as contained in the current control file.

3. A. Though the alert log does list one file that requires recovery, it does not list all the files that need recovery like v$recover_file does.

4. D. Archive Log List displays the database archiving mode, the archive destination, the oldest and next online redo log groups, and if archiving is automatic or manual.

5. A, B, D. Error-based recovery is not a method of specifying the stop point for recovery.

CHAPTER
5

Recovery from
Open Backup

ou can restore and recover a database from a consistent backup as discussed in Chapter 4. The big drawback to a consistent backup: the database must be shut down. You may not be able to shut down your database because users and applications are constantly using it. If your database must be available almost all the time, a closed database backup won't be an option. How can you back up a database that is constantly in use? You perform a hot backup.

When the database is running, the state of the database files is constantly changing. Datafiles and control files get updated, redo logs get written to and archived. The user-managed method to back up an open database is to place each tablespace in backup mode and back up the datafiles. After you've performed a backup of your datafiles, you return the tablespace back to its normal condition.

After you've created one of these open database backups (also known as a hot backup), you have files that can be restored in the event of a failure. If you have to fix a broken database, you can copy one or more datafiles from the backup location. You won't be able to open the database without recovery when restoring files from an inconsistent backup. The reason: the datafiles are inconsistent. Remember that each data file has a number in its header that defines the latest database state of that datafile. Before a database can open, all online datafiles must have the same system change number (SCN). As you see in Figure 5-1, the SCN is Oracle's own relative timekeeping mechanism. When they all have the same SCN, they are consistent. A backup taken on an open database does not produce consistent datafiles. Therefore, you must perform media recovery before you open a database using restored files from an open database backup. Once any necessary redo information is applied to make the SCNs consistent, you can open your database. Conducting backups on an open database allows users and applications to use the entire database during the backup operation.

SCN Values in Data File Headers

Within a datafile header, there are several SCN values. The creation SCN is allocated when the datafile was created. The checkpoint SCN marks the database or datafile state when the file underwent its last checkpoint. This is the important SCN value that is used to make sure the datafiles are consistent with the control file on startup. Offline SCN marks the datafile state when the file was taken offline; the online SCN will be updated when the file is returned to online status. The backup SCN records when the tablespace is put into hot backup mode and the reset log's SCN is recorded when the database is opened using the RESETLOGS parameter. Similar SCN values recorded in the control file ensure all datafiles are consistent with the control file and each other during database startup and recovery.

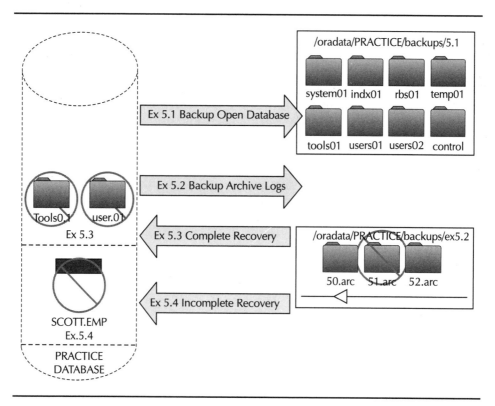

FIGURE 5-1. *Open Backup, Restore & Recovery Operations*

Whole Open Backup

To back up the whole database while it is open, all the datafiles get copied to a different location (typically disk or tape). During the time a datafile is being copied, changes continue to occur to the datafile. When the copy is complete, the database continues to change the datafile that has been copied. How does Oracle allow a datafile to be copied for backup while it undergoes changes? Before you copy the datafile, you place its tablespace in backup mode. Placing a tablespace in backup mode instructs Oracle to update the tablespace's datafile headers. Oracle also modifies its creation of redo entries for those datafiles. When a tablespace is placed in backup mode, several events occur:

- A flag in each file header is set to indicate that a hot backup will be taking place.

- The tablespace datafiles undergo a checkpoint. All dirty blocks in memory are written to the files. The SCN of the checkpoint is written to the datafile headers and the control file. This begins backup SCN marks to the latest change to the files. The SCN structure is now frozen from any changes within the files.

- A begin backup entry is made to the alert log file.

- Before the first change is made to any blocks within the datafiles, a block image of each changed block is copied to the redo. Then the standard redo vector is created for changes to the block. All subsequent changes to the same block create normal redo change vectors.

While the tablespace is in backup mode, you can copy the datafiles to another destination using an operating system copy command. The amount of redo generated during a hot backup can increase significantly if multiple users are updating these tablespaces because the redo must contain a copy of each changed data block (for the first change only). Therefore, conduct open database backups when database activity is light.

When the datafiles have been copied, you take the tablespace out of backup mode. When you mark the end of backup mode for a tablespace, several events occur:

- The hot backup flag is cleared to show the backup has ended.

- The end backup SCN is recorded in the redo stream as a redo vector. Oracle uses this redo entry to know when to take the tablespace out of hot backup mode during recovery of the datafile.

- The file's checkpoint structure is unfrozen and incremented to match the rest of the database.

- The redo generation is returned back to normal, as it was before the tablespace was placed into backup mode.

Since changes made during backup must be stored in the redo stream and can't be lost, your database must be in archive log mode for open database backup.

NOTE
You cannot place a read-only tablespace in backup mode because it cannot be changed by a database. You cannot place a temporary locally managed tablespace in backup mode, either. To restore/ recover a locally managed temporary tablespace, just recreate it.

Exercise 5.1: Backup an Open Database

During this exercise, you will create a whole database backup of the PRACTICE database while the database is open. To do this, you issue the ALTER TABLESPACE...BEGIN BACKUP command and then take an open backup of the datafiles in a tablespace. You take a tablespace out of hot backup mode when you issue the ALTER TABLESPACE...END BACKUP or ALTER DATABASE END BACKUP command. While each tablespace is in backup mode, you copy the datafiles for that tablespace. In addition to making a copy of each online datafile, a whole database open backup includes a backup copy of the current control file.

Task Description	Minutes
1. Generate Database Activity	5
2. Create a Hot Backup Script	15
3. Run a Hot Backup	5
4. Examine Backup Commands	5
Total Time	30

After you confirm that the database has some activity, you will create a script file containing all the commands needed to complete a valid whole open database backup. You will run the backup script and review the work accomplished.

Task 1: Generate Database Activity

Start by inserting rows into Tina's DATE_LOG table. When you are done with your restore, confirm that your recovery was complete. Confirm that the rows are being inserted into the table via the job system. You might set the interval of the job to every minute to increase database activity.

Task 2: Create a Hot Backup Script

Create a hot backup of all the files in your database. In a nutshell, the open database backup script you are about to create will do the following:

■ Switch log files to make sure all changes made before the backup are archived

■ Place one tablespace into hot backup mode

■ Copy this tablespace's files using an OS command

■ Take this tablespace out of hot backup mode

■ Repeat steps 2-4 for each tablespace

■ Switch log files to make sure all changes after the backup have been archived

■ Back up the current control file

When you run this script, you will use SQL, SQL*Plus commands, and PL/SQL to create an executable file of SQL commands and operating system commands. This file (let's call it the backup command file) also creates a file displaying its output. The files you are about to work with are

■ **Backup Script file (open_backup.sql)**   This is the file you create in a text editor (the one listed next).

■ **Backup Command file (open_backup_commands.sql)**   This file gets created and executed within open_backup.sql.

■ **Backup Command file output file (open_backup_output.lst)**   This file captures the output of the file that is executed by open_backup_commands.sql.

Look over the contents of open_backup.sql and refer to the comments on some of the lines. You can either type these commands into the file as listed here or download them from the Web site at Osborne.

```
1.     set feedback off pagesize 0 heading off verify off
linesize 100 trimspool on
2.     define dir = '/oradata/PRACTICE/backup/ch5'
3.     define fil = '/tmp/open_backup_commands.sql'
4.     define spo = '&dir/open_backup_output.lst'
5.     prompt *** Spooling to &fil
6.     set serveroutput on
7.     spool &fil
8.     prompt spool &spo
9.     prompt archive log list;;
10.    prompt alter system switch logfile;;
11.    DECLARE
12.     CURSOR cur_tablespace IS
13.      SELECT tablespace_name FROM dba_tablespaces
         WHERE status <> 'READ ONLY';
```

```
14.    CURSOR cur_datafile (tn VARCHAR) IS
15.      SELECT file_name
16.        FROM dba_data_files
17.        WHERE tablespace_name = tn;
18.    BEGIN
19.      FOR ct IN cur_tablespace LOOP
20.         dbms_output.put_line ('alter tablespace
'||ct.tablespace_name||' begin backup;');
21.         FOR cd IN cur_datafile (ct.tablespace_name) LOOP
22.            dbms_output.put_line ('host cp '||cd.file_name||' &dir');
23.         END LOOP;
24.         dbms_output.put_line ('alter tablespace
'||ct.tablespace_name||' end backup;');
25.      END LOOP;
26.    END;
27.    /
28.    prompt alter system switch logfile;;
29.    prompt 'alter database backup controlfile to ''&dir\backup.ctl''
REUSE;'
30.    prompt archive log list;;
31.    prompt spool off;;
32.    spool off;
33.    @&fil
```

This script will create all the commands necessary to run a whole backup of an open database. The first line sets some SQL*Plus variables, as you have done in previous scripts (feedback=off, pagesize=0, heading=off, verify=off, linesize=100, trimspool=on). Let's look at some lines in this script and explain important points:

- Lines 2-4 set user variables that will be used in the script. The variables include the file containing the backup commands, the directory to make file copies and a file for important script output. The actual backup commands are written to a file in a temporary directory. You don't want to make the mistake of running a backup script using backup commands for a database as it used to exist. Notice that line 4 defines a user variable by referring to the contents of a user variable.

- Line 6 instructs the calls to the dbms_output procedure in the PL/SQL code to display the output on the screen. This screen text gets written to the command file. The dbms_output package is one of many PL/SQL packages supplied by Oracle.

- Line 7 begins the logging of all output from the SQL, SQL*Plus commands, and PL/SQL code to a file defined in the user variable set earlier.

■ Line 8 writes a spool command to the spool file. When you run your backup commands via the script created in /tmp/open_backup_commands.sql, you'll want the output of that script to give you some important archive log sequence numbers.

■ Line 9 instructs your command file to list the current archiving information to the spool file of the command file. When you recover your database from this backup, you will want to know the current log file sequence number.

■ Line 10 switches the log file from the current log file to the next log file. This forces a checkpoint for all online datafiles and creates a new archive log file.

■ Lines 11–27 contain PL/SQL code that places each tablespace in backup mode, copies all the datafiles to a backup destination, and takes that tablespace out of backup mode. The code has two cursors: a list of all database tablespaces and a list of all datafiles for one tablespace. (I am excluding read-only tablespaces because Oracle will not allow you to put them into backup mode.) The tablespace cursor is opened in the first FOR loop. The dbms_output.put_line procedure call displays the command text needed in your backup command script. Each tablespace is placed in backup mode before the datafile cursor is opened using the current tablespace name. Each datafile will be copied using an OS copy command. (For Linux, use the CP command; for Windows, use the copy command.) Once all the datafiles are fetched for this tablespace and the copy command is created, the tablespace is taken out of backup mode. This looping process continues for all the tablespaces in the database. I chose PL/SQL for this part of the backup script so that you can make use of PL/SQL loop mechanisms to copy all the files for each tablespace. You can modify this PL/SQL block to create a backup for only online tablespaces or only certain tablespaces. To do this, you could add a WHERE condition to the tablespaces cursor similar to the READ ONLY predicate.

■ Line 28 switches the log file from the current log file to the next log file. This forces a checkpoint for all online datafiles and creates a new archive log file. This also ensures that the redo entries created during hot backup get archived.

■ Line 29 creates a copy of the control file just after the datafile backups are complete. You may need a copy of this control file when recovering using this backup. The primary method for backing up the control file is to use an SQL statement to generate an exact binary copy of the file. You can use this backup control file for recoveries performed using these backed up datafiles. The REUSE keyword in the script will overwrite a file if it already exists.

■ Lines 30–32 direct the open_backup_commands.sql file to list the archive information to the spool file of the backup script. You'll have a record of the archive sequence numbers if you should have to combine this open database backup with backup archive logs. You can also use the approximate times of when the backup was taken to figure out what archives are needed for recovery. Finally, the command SQL file will stop spooling.

■ Line 33 executes the backup SQL command file you created.

CAUTION
*When using raw devices for your Oracle database,
an alternative to 'cp' must be used. The 'dd'
command is a suitable substitute.*

Once you have typed all these commands to a file named open_backup.sql, you can run this file from the SQL*Plus prompt connected as SYS with the SYSDBA role or a similar privileged user.

Task 3: Run Backup Script
Start the script you just created from the SQL*Plus prompt. While the script runs, tablespaces and datafiles are placed in backup mode. During this backup, you can look at the v$backup view from another SQL*Plus session to see which files are currently in backup mode. After the script completes, you can also place the users tablespace in backup mode and look at the backup status of all online datafiles.

```
SQL> ALTER TABLESPACE users BEGIN BACKUP;
SQL> SELECT d.tablespace_name tablespace, b.file#,
  2          b.status, b.change#, b.time
  3    FROM dba_data_files d, v$backup b
  4   WHERE b.file#=d.file_id
  5   ORDER BY tablespace_name;
TABLESPACE FILE# STATUS      CHANGE# TIME
---------- ----- ----------- ------- ---------------
INDX           6 NOT ACTIVE   84972 05-JAN-02 09:30
RBS            2 NOT ACTIVE   85446 05-JAN-02 09:35
SYSTEM         1 NOT ACTIVE   85458 05-JAN-02 09:42
TEMP           4 NOT ACTIVE   85712 05-JAN-02 09:38
TOOLS          5 NOT ACTIVE   85452 05-JAN-02 09:40
USERS          3 ACTIVE       85722 05-JAN-02 11:59
USERS          7 ACTIVE       85722 05-JAN-02 11:59
SQL> ALTER TABLESPACE users END BACKUP;
```

The users tablespace has two datafiles with file# 3 and 7. The begin backup checkpoint SCN for these files is 85722, and the begin backup command was issued at 11:59 AM on January 5.

During this exercise, you create and run a script file; most backup operations performed by DBAs are accomplished via scripts. To help you become familiar with the script operation, try typing the commands line by line in Task 2 and watch what happens.

TIP

You can compress backed up database files with Linux compress or Windows Zip utilities. This will save space. Be sure not to compress a file until the copy operation is complete, and understand that using a compression utility could introduce corruption into the file.

After the open backup has run, have a look at the alert log file. You'll see backup mode entries like those listed here:

```
Wed Jan 05 09:30:00 2001
alter tablespace SYSTEM begin backup
Wed Jan 05 09:30:05 2001
Completed: alter tablespace SYSTEM begin backup
...
Wed Jan 05 09:31:00 2001
alter tablespace SYSTEM end backup
Wed Jan 05 09:31:05 2001
Completed: alter tablespace SYSTEM end backup
```

This alert log listing shows you some timeline information about the SYSTEM tablespace open backup operation. At 9:30 AM, your script-generaged command file issued the command to place the SYSTEM tablespace in backup mode. Five seconds passed until the SYSTEM tablespace actually made it to backup mode. As previously discussed, Oracle software has to do some work before the tablespace enters backup mode. The time required to copy the one file SYSTEM datafile was a little less than 55 seconds. At 9:31 AM, you issued the command to remove the SYSTEM tablespace from backup mode. After five seconds, the SYSTEM tablespace returned to its normal mode.

CAUTION
Remember to mark the beginning and end of a tablespace backup. If you back up datafiles in an open database without the tablespace being in backup mode, the backup files are not useful for recovery. An attempted recovery may result in file errors and prevent you from opening your database. Why? Oracle cannot guarantee the consistency of these datafiles. Also, you cannot shut down a database cleanly if you leave a tablespace in backup mode. The database will report an error during a clean shutdown attempt.

The commands in this exercise constitute a serial open backup. All the tablespaces are backed up one at a time. You can place more than one tablespace in backup mode simultaneously. Backing up online tablespaces in parallel can reduce the time required to complete the backup. Oracle Corporation recommends the serial backup option because it minimizes the time between ALTER TABLESPACE ... BEGIN/END BACKUP statements. Parallel hot backups of busy tablespaces may generate enormous amounts of redo. Also, if your instance crashes during hot backup, ending backup on a few datafiles in one tablespace is quicker and easier than ending backup in many tablespaces containing many datafiles.

When you back up a database, you will also want to back up related files like the password files, the alert log, NET8 files, and the parameter file. Files outside of the database can be backed up using any of your operating system backup utilities. In Oracle 9*i*, if you are using the new server parameter file feature, you can create a copy of the server parameter file with the CREATE PFILE command:

```
SQL> CREATE PFILE = '/tmp/init.ora' FROM SPILE;
```

The init.ora from this command will contain a text listing of all server parameters.

Task 4: Examine Backup Commands
Take a moment to look at the file your script created that actually performed the backup commands. The script you ran in Task 2 created a file named /tmp/open_backup_commands.sql. Notice the attention given to the redo logs before

the datafile backups begin via the ALTER SYSTEM command. Next, the file contains
the backup commands for each of the tablespaces. In your PRACTICE database,
all tablespaces have only one datafile each except the USERS tablespace. When
the USERS tablespace is placed in backup mode, you back up both datafiles for this
tablespace. By backing up all datafiles in a tablespace, you reduce the overhead
of taking the tablespace in and out of backup mode for each data file. Also, all
the datafiles have the same backup mode SCNs, making recovery simpler and
easier to manage.

```
alter system switch logfile;
alter system archive log all;
alter tablespace SYSTEM begin backup;
host cp /oradata/PRACTICE/system01.dbf /oradata/PRACTICE/backup/ch05
alter tablespace SYSTEM end backup;
…
alter tablespace USERS begin backup;
host cp /oradata/PRACTICE/users01.dbf /oradata/PRACTICE/backup/ch05
host cp /oradata/PRACTICE/users02.dbf /oradata/PRACTICE/backup/ch05
alter tablespace USERS end backup;
…
alter database backup controlfile to '/oradata/PRACTICE/backup/ch05/backup.ctl' REUSE;
```

Once the backup of all the datafiles is complete, the backup command file makes a
copy of the control file. You can use the backup control file if you lose all control files.

Exercise 5.2: Backup Archive Log Files

By now, your PRACTICE database has probably created a number of archive redo
log files. You won't be able to ignore the archive log files. As the database processes
transactions, redo gets generated and archived. Over time, they accumulate and
fill up your archiving destination. Since database activity halts when redo cannot
be archived, usually due to lack of disk space, the archive destination must be
periodically purged. Most database installations move archive files to a tape backup
device or a remote machine. The tapes are then taken to offsite storage. If the machine
is lost because of an environmental disaster (flood, fire, earthquake, and so on), the
offsite archive files can be used to recover the database along with offsite datafile
and control file backups.

In this exercise, you will move the archive files from the current archive destination
to another directory. In a real Oracle database configuration, you move the files from
one or more file systems to another file system, tape, or machine.

Task Description	Minutes
1. Find Archive Files	5
2. Create Archive File Script	10
3. Run Archive File Script	5
4. Confirm Archive File Backup	5
Total Time	25

First, locate the archive log files. Next, create and run a script that will move those files. Finally, verify that the script worked as you wanted and that it placed the file in the backup directory.

This exercise will demonstrate the backing up of a single archive destination. It is possible to have multiple archive destinations, multiple *archive_log_dest_n*, where *n* is a number between 1 and 5. If multiple destinations are being used, each of them must be considered for purging. A script that moves (backs up) archive log files from multiple destinations can be found on the Osborne Web site.

Task 1: Find Archive Files
The archive files will be located in the directory defined by the log_archive_dest parameters configured in the database initialization file. To find the value of this parameter, you can look at the parameter file or select from the v$archive_dest view. Refer back to Exercise 4.3 in Chapter 4 where you turned on archiving for the details on archive log configuration. Once you find out the directory location for redo archiving, open a command prompt and confirm that archive redo files exist. The files in this directory will match up with the contents of the name column in the v$archived_log view.

Task 2: Create Archive File Script
Moving the archived files from the archive destination to another location can be accomplished with an OS move command. In a file named archive_backup.sql, create the commands you need to generate a backup command file, issue the move command for a selected group of archive log files, and run the command file. The

gist of this file: find each archive log in the v$archive_log view that was created yesterday and generate move commands to a backup directory.

```
1.    define dir = '/oradata/PRACTICE/backup/ch5'
2.    define fil = '/tmp/archive_backup_commands.sql'
3.    spool &fil
4.    prompt archive log next;;
5.    SELECT 'host mv '||name||' &dir'
6.      FROM v$archived_log
7.     WHERE completion_time >= trunc(sysdate)-1
8.        AND completion_time < trunc(sysdate);
9.    spool off;
10.   @&fil
```

This script file is similar to those that I've presented earlier. Let me emphasize some highlights:

- Lines 1–2 set SQL*Plus user variables used later in the script. Note the directory to which archive logs get copied is stored in the dir user variable.

- Lines 3 and 9 start and stop the recording of SQL output to a file. Line 10 runs the content of the spool file.

- Line 4 instructs the server to archive any online redo log files that have not been archived. This command is important whether you've configured manual or automatic archiving. Your PRACTICE database has been configured to automatically archive log files. If your archiver needs to catch up due to heavy redo activity, the ARCHIVE LOG NEXT command ensures that all online redo logs in need of archiving get archived before control is returned to the SQL*Plus prompt. Note the two semicolons at the end of this line create one semicolon in the spooled file.

- Lines 5–8 find several archived log file names known to the control file as displayed from the v$archived_log view. Using each file name, a move command gets generated to the new directory. This script moves files that were created yesterday. The TRUNC function removes the time portion of the SYSDATE variable. This script moves all archive logs that were created in the 24-hour-period starting at 00:00:00 through 23:59:59 yesterday. Since most recoveries will only require recent archive files, you keep today's archive log file in place.

In a typical production database environment, the archive files are backed up to tape using OS utilities and then removed from disk. These tapes can be taken to offsite storage. Once the files are safely on tape, they can be removed from disk.

Task 3: Run Archive File Script

After typing in the contents of archive_backup.sql, you can run it from SQL*Plus as SYS on your PRACTICE database. Since this database does not have much redo activity, the script will run quickly. If you run the script more than once, you'll get messages indicating that files are not found by the move command. These messages should not be a surprise because the archive files have already been moved.

CAUTION
You might be tempted to copy all the files in the archive destination to a backup device. During such an operation, you may copy an archive file in the process of being created. This partial archive log file cannot be used for recovery and will prevent full recovery unless you have another valid copy of it. Be careful with your archive log file move scripts to confirm that complete files get copied.

Task 4: Confirm Archive File Backup

From a command prompt, check the archive destination to see which files remain. Locate the archive backup directory and confirm that the files have been moved to the correct place. Check that you have all the sequence values you'd expect. If you miss just one archive log file, you will not be able to completely recover your database.

Now that you have a whole database backup and your archive files are moved, let's see if you can use it to recover in the event of a failure.

Complete and Incomplete Recovery

You can recover your database completely using an open database backup with applied redo in the event of a failure. When you fix a broken database with a user-managed hot backup, you will always have to recover datafiles that have been restored.

Exercise 5.3: Complete Recovery from an Open Backup

In this exercise, you will remove two datafiles and recover them so that your database is completely recovered. This exercise will seem similar to the first recovery that you did in the last chapter. This time, however, when you break and recover the database, you will perform all your operations while the database is open.

Task Description	Minutes
1. Break the database	10
2. Restore the missing datafile	10
3. Recover restored datafile	10
4. Verify database recovery	5
Total Time	35

In this exercise, you will recover while the database is open. The recovery will be complete; no database work will be lost.

Task 1: Break the Database

With the database open, use an operating system prompt and remove the tools01.dbf and users01.dbf files. On Linux, you can remove the files while the datafiles are online. On Windows, you'll need to take the datafile offline to release the OS lock on the file. Take these files offline with the ALTER DATABASE command:

```
SQL> alter database datafile '/oradata/PRACTICE/tools01.dbf' offline;
SQL> alter database datafile '/oradata/PRACTICE/users01.dbf' offline;
```

If you had removed the datafiles while the tablespace was still online, at some point after the files have been removed, the instance will detect that the file(s) are missing. The datafiles may be missing for some time before you experience an error. An "ORA-01157: cannot identify/lock data file" fill will occur when the file must be accessed by the database. On Linux, try selecting from the TINA.DATE_LOG table. If the table blocks requested are in memory, your SQL statement will not produce an error. Even the updates to the table may not produce an error for a while on your Linux database. Why? Oracle caches data blocks in memory. Needed blocks are read from disk if they don't already exist in memory. The same is true for modified blocks. When the blocks are flushed to disk, the instance will realize that the file does not exist. A checkpoint spawned by a log switch will produce this error for one of the missing datafiles on Linux. A log switch on Windows will not produce an error because these two missing datafiles are not online. On Windows, you won't see any error until you bring the files back online.

```
SQL> alter database datafile '/oradata/PRACTICE/tools01.dbf' online;
SQL> alter database datafile '/oradata/PRACTICE/users01.dbf' online;
```

If you try to shut down the database cleanly, the Oracle software will not let you. The shutdown process must successfully complete a checkpoint of all online datafiles before a clean shutdown will succeed. If you decide to shut down a database with missing datafiles, you'll have to take those datafiles offline first or abort the instance. (Aborting the instance is not recommended and should only be used as a last resort.)

Once you have produced an error in your open database, have a look at your alert log file. In this file, you'll see error information that is similar to what you witnessed on your screen.

```
Errors in file /app/oracle/admin/PRACTICE/bdump/practiceDBW0.TRC:
ORA-01157: cannot identify/lock data file 5 - see DBWR trace file
ORA-01110: data file 5: '/oradata/PRACTICE/tools01.dbf'
ORA-27041: unable to open file
OSD-04002: unable to open file
O/S-Error: (OS 2) The system cannot find the file specified.
```

When a datafile is unavailable, you can recover it while the database is open. You can roll the datafile forward to be consistent with the current database only if all required archived redo logs needed are available. Recovering the lost datafile is what you will do in the remainder of this exercise.

Task 2: Restore Missing Datafiles
Use the data dictionary to show which files need recovery. You can look in two views to find out which files that must be recovered:

```
SQL> select * from v$recover_file;
SQL> select name, status from v$datafile;
```

Both of these views alert you of the files you'll need to recover. The v$recover_file also lets you know the specific error you are up against. At this point, the ERROR column should display a "FILE NOT FOUND" value.

When the datafile needs to be recovered, that datafile must be offline. Your two datafiles are probably already taken offline by the instance. When you take a datafile offline, you do not have any offline options. You can also take a datafile offline by taking its tablespace offline. When you take a tablespace offline, you can do so using four different options:

CAUTION
You cannot offline a datafile in a database that's not running in archive log mode. You must offline drop it. Afterward, you should rebuild the tablespace.

- **normal** When you take a tablespace offline normal, its datafiles undergo a checkpoint. All blocks get flushed from the buffer cache to the tablespace, and datafiles and the file headers are updated with a checkpoint SCN. Media recovery is unneeded on this datafile when you bring it back online.

- **temporary** Take a tablespace offline temporary, and Oracle performs a checkpoint for all online datafiles in the tablespace but does not ensure that all files can be written. Any offline files may require media recovery before you bring the tablespace back online.

- **immediate** Take a tablespace offline immediate, Oracle does not ensure that tablespace files are available and does not perform a checkpoint. You must perform media recovery on the tablespace before bringing it back online.

- **for recover** Specify FOR RECOVER to take the production database tablespaces in the recovery set offline for tablespace point-in-time recovery. This option is discussed in Chapter 9.

Copy the users01.dbf and tools01.dbf from the backup destination directory used by the open database backup script. You can copy it from the /oradata/ PRACTICE/backup/ch5 directory. After you copy these two files back to their database location, look at the contents of v$recover_file. Notice that the values in the view have changed and that the change# column now has a value. The selection from the view has read the restored files and found the checkpoint SCN. That value is now displayed in the view. Compare those numbers with the CHECKPOINT_CHANGE# in v$datafile. The online datafiles will have a checkpoint number greater than the restored files. The checkpoint information contained in v$datafile is being read from the control file, as opposed to the datafiles themselves.

Task 3: Recover Restored Datafiles
To recover a tablespace or a datafile, you will perform complete (full) recovery. First, recover the TOOLS tablespace by recovering the datafile. Issue the RECOVER DATAFILE command to apply redo from the archive and online files to the restored datafile. You can instruct Oracle to recover by file number or file name.

```
SQL> recover datafile 5;
```

For my PRACTICE database, the file 5 is the tools01.dbf file. The recover command finds the checkpoint SCN of the restored file, compares that number with SCN ranges in the redo log files, and determines which file is needed to begin recovery. That file is then read from the archive destination and applied to the datafile. You may see feedback like this:

```
ORA-00279: change 83584 generated at 01/05/2002 12:51:17 needed for thread 1
ORA-00289: suggestion : /oradata/PRACTICE/archive/51.arc
ORA-00280: change 83584 for thread 1 is in sequence #51
```

The recover command determined that the redo needed for the recovery begins in archive log sequence from 221 to 51. That file was moved to the backup location in the previous exercise. To get around this situation, the recover command must find the archive file it needs. You can copy the file to the original destination, or you can tell the recover command to look at different locations. Rather than copy the archive files, just tell the recover command where to get the archive log files:

```
SQL> RECOVER FROM '/oradata/PRACTICE/backup/ch5' DATAFILE 5;
```

If you decide to copy the archive files back to the archive file destination, you won't have to include the FROM clause in your RECOVER command. To the entire tablespace containing the restored files, use the RECOVER command like this:

```
SQL> RECOVER FROM '/oradata/PRACTICE/backup/ch5' TABLESPACE TOOLS;
```

You can also recover more than one datafile or tablespace in the same command. Add each datafile or tablespace you want to recover following the RECOVER command separated by commas.

```
SQL> RECOVER FROM '/oradata/PRACTICE/backup/ch5'
  2       DATAFILE '/oradata/PRACTICE/users01.dbf',
  3                '/oradata/PRACTICE/tools01.dbf';
```

When the recovery of your datafiles completes, you'll get a message saying:

```
Log applied.
Media recovery complete.
```

Have a look at the alert log. You can see the time line of the recovery.

```
ALTER DATABASE RECOVER  tablespace tools
Wed Jan 05 16:54:55 2002
Media Recovery Tablespace: TOOLS
Media Recovery Start
Media Recovery Log
ALTER DATABASE RECOVER  FROM '/oradata/PRACTICE/backup/ch5'   CONTINUE DEFAULT
Media Recovery Log /oradata/PRACTICE/backup/ch5/51.arc
...
Recovery of Online Redo Log: Thread 1 Group 1 Seq 14 Reading mem 0
```

```
   Mem# 0 errs 0: /oradata/PRACTICE/redo01.log
Media Recovery Complete
Completed: ALTER DATABASE RECOVER  tablespace tools
Wed Jan 02 16:55:09 2002
alter tablespace tools online
Wed Jan 02 16:55:09 2002
Completed: alter tablespace tools online
```

Before you move to the last task, see if you can follow the trail of redo log files applied for your recovery. When the datafiles are restored, each one contains a checkpoint SCN recorded when they were backed up. That number defines the time up until which all changed blocks have been written to those files. Therefore, any redo information before this SCN is not needed for this file. Each redo log file contains a range of database SCN values and is assigned a unique sequence number. The redo files containing the restored datafile checkpoint SCN changes up to the current online redo log must be applied to that file for it to be current.

Task 4: Verify Database Recovery

Once you have recovered each datafile, you can place it back online as shown earlier with the ALTER DATABASE command. If the datafiles come back online, you can be sure that you have successfully recovered them. A datafile will not come online unless it is synchronized with the control file.

You can also check the latest database time in TINA.DATE_LOG. This time will be at least the time just before you removed the TOOLS tablespace datafile. The latest time entry will probably be more recent because the Oracle job to insert rows will have done some more inserts.

TIP
A temporary tablespace does not need to be recovered. Since it only serves as a sort space, you can just drop it and recreate it instead. Also, you cannot take a temporary tablespace offline. You can take a datafile in a temporary tablespace offline.

Way to go! You just recovered two datafiles from an open backup on an open database.

Exercise 5.4: Incomplete Recovery from an Open Backup

One final exercise will be helpful before I close out this chapter. Using the backup performed in Exercise 5.1, you will perform an incomplete recovery after you "mistakenly" drop a table from your PRACTICE database. This exercise will reinforce the concepts learned so far, give you a little more practice, and allow you to see some other important recovery concepts.

Task Description	Minutes
1. Drop a table	5
2. Rename an Archive Log	5
3. Investigate Recovery	10
4. Restore database	10
5. Recover database to a point	10
6. Verify database recovery	5
Total Time	30

In this exercise, you will drop a table owned by user SCOTT. Then you will restore all the files from the previous open database backup and recover the database using a backup control file.

Task 1: Drop a Table

In this task, you will drop the SCOTT.EMP table. Before you do, take some notes about the current database state to help you with the upcoming incomplete recovery. Either note the latest date/time value in TINA.DATE_LOG, or insert a date that you can check for after recovery. When you recover, the date/time in the TINA.DATE_LOG will be this date/time value (or one close to it). Also, switch the log files and take note of the datafiles' checkpoint SCN by querying the change# from v$datafile. Once you've noted these values, you are ready to drop the table with the DROP command.

```
SQL> DROP TABLE scott.emp;
```

Some SQL commands can be undone via Oracle's rollback feature. The DROP command cannot be undone because data definition language (DDL) is implicitly committed. Once a table is dropped, it's gone.

Before you begin your recovery, note the current date/time in TINA.DATE_LOG. Make sure a few more rows get inserted. You can even insert a time in the future into this table. Insert a row a year in the future.

```
SQL> INSERT INTO tina.date_log VALUES (sysdate+(365*5));  SQL> COMMIT;
```

Once you recover the PRACTICE database incompletely, you will only see rows in this table that are equal to or less than the date/time you recorded before you dropped the table.

Task 2: Rename an Archive Log

You know the time the table got dropped and that the logs were switched just before the drop occurred. In the last chapter, your incomplete recovery was time based. This chapter, try a cancel-based recovery. Cancel-based recovery is common when an archive log file has been damaged or lost.

Determine the current log file with a query from the v$log dynamic view:

```
SQL> SELECT sequence# FROM v$log WHERE status = 'CURRENT';
```

Look in the archive directory and find the archive log file with a sequence number one less than the sequence number returned from this query. For example, if the current log file sequence is 52, you will find a file named 51.arc in the /oradata/PRACTICE/ archive directory. Rename that file to 51.arc.backup. When you recover the database in Task 5, you'll cancel recovery when /oradata/PRACTICE/archive/51.arc is not found.

TIP

You can simulate a corrupted archive file by copying any file to /oradata/PRACTICE/archive/51.arc (for example: a word processing document). When the recover attempts to read this file, you'll get an Oracle error.

Task 3: Investigate Recovery

You will apply each redo log up to the log where the failure occurred. Answer this question: Which redo log file was current when the failure happened? In the previous chapter, you recovered from a drop tablespace command. When a tablespace gets dropped, the alert log specifies the exact time the action occurred. The drop table command does not write an entry to the alert log. You will have to estimate the time of the failure. Using that time, you can approximate the log file sequence when the drop table occurred.

```
SQL> SELECT sequence#, first_change#,
  2         to_char(first_time,'DD-MON-YY HH24:MI:SS') first_time
  3    FROM v$log_history;
```

Find the log sequence with a date and time just before the failure event happened.

NOTE
Determining the time of a database failure (user mistake) is an inexact science. You will not usually have the exact time that a mistaken DDL command was executed. You may need to work from an approximation and try several restore/recoveries before you get it right.

Task 4: Restore Database

Although you can use files created from an open database for recovery, incomplete whole database recovery must be done on a closed database. Why? Once you finish an incomplete recovery, the datafiles will exist in a state that they did earlier. When you have restored an old database that needs to be brought up to date, the only option available to the DBA is to roll it forward using the log files. You cannot restore a newer backup and roll it back as you can an uncommitted transaction. Therefore, to get the SCOTT.EMP table back, you must replace all datafiles as they were from a copy made before the drop statement occurred. Then you will apply redo to all the datafiles to a point just before the table dropped. Note also that you do not want to copy redo files from a backup over the current database online redo log files. The online redo files may have transactions you want to apply during your incomplete recovery.

Before restoring the datafiles, first shut down the database cleanly. In a real recovery scenario, make a whole-database closed backup if time allows (in case the recovery does not go as hoped). Restore all datafiles created in Exercise 5-1 to the current database location. You will be overwriting the datafiles of your PRACTICE database with backup files made while the database was open.

Task 5: Recover Database to a Point

Perform the recover operation on the datafiles and look at the contents of v$recover_file while the database is mounted. You will see that all the datafiles require recovery. Note that all the files have different change numbers and times except the two files in the USER tablespace. Why? These datafiles were copied during an open database backup. The tablespaces were placed in backup mode and copied at different times. They all require recovery from their current SCN up to the ending SCN of the last redo log you will apply.

NOTE
When doing incomplete recovery using a hot backup, you must ensure that the time you are recovering up until includes the last hot backup end marker. Otherwise, you will be trying to open a database with inconsistent datafiles, and you cannot do that. The time of the last end backup command should be recorded in the alert.log.

On my recovery, the last current log file sequence before the drop table occurred is 50. The change numbers in my redo log file range from 83821 to 83850. When I perform recovery, I will continue to apply the logs suggested by the recover command until log sequence number 51 is reached. Then I'll type **cancel**.

```
SQL> SET LOGSOURCE "/oradata/PRACTICE/backup/ch5";
```

Earlier, you pointed the recover command to use a directory other than the default directory. You can also point to the directory location of archive logs with the SET LOGSOURCE command prior to the RECOVER command.

Start Cancel recovery. Keep applying redo logs until the latest one is applied. Open with Reset logs.

```
/oradata/PRACTICE/backup/ch5/51.arc
ORA-00280: change 83851 for thread 1 is in sequence #51
ORA-00278: log file '/oradata/PRACTICE/backup/ch5/50.arc'
no longer needed for this recovery
Specify log: {<RET>=suggested | filename | AUTO | CANCEL}
```

At this prompt, enter the word **CANCEL**. Have a look at the v$recover_file table now from a separate SQL*Plus session. Notice that the change# and time columns have been advanced for each datafile. By applying a redo log file, you have advanced the contents of all the datafiles up to a consistent time and change number. All the change numbers and times may be the same as each other and will equal the last change and time of the last log file you applied.

To open the database, you must specify the RESETLOGS on the ALTER DATABASE OPEN command. The online redo log files will begin numbering at sequence 1. Also, as the database begins archiving, the sequence numbers on the archive will restart at 1 because these archive files are plain file copies of the online redo logs.

NOTE
Because the archive log files are now being numbered using sequence numbers starting from 1, you should clear out the current archive log destinations before you open the database. This will prevent confusion with the files coexisting in the same directory from different database incarnations.

CAUTION
You cannot use a previous backup and roll it forward through a RESETLOGS opening. When the database is opened with RESETLOGS, the outstanding data in the last current online redo log is lost. Therefore, a recovery could also be missing redo. You must take a fresh backup as soon as the database has been opened using the RESETLOGS parameter. This backup will be the oldest starting point of all future recoveries.

Task 6: Verify Recovery

The reason you performed this recovery was to replace the dropped table. Check to see that the SCOTT.EMP table exists. Also, select the latest time and date from the DATE_LOG before the table is dropped. If you inserted a date/time five years in the future after the EMP table was dropped, that date/time should not be in the table.

Troubleshooting

Check out this section for some tips about possible errors or circumstances you don't expect during open backups, archive operations, and recoveries.

Archive Commands

When you configure or use archiving, you might run into these problems.

Archive Log List

When you run this command you might get an error.

```
SQL> archive log list
ORA-01031: insufficient privileges
```

You must be connected as SYSDBA or SYSOPER to use this command.

Archive locations

On Windows, you might notice your archived log files are not in the directory you think they should be. For example, you may have set log_archive_dest_1 = "location=D:\oradata\PRACTICE\archive" and log_archive_format = %s.arc, but your archived log files are named archive%s.arc in the d:\oradata\PRACTICE directory. Confirm that you have created the archive directory under d:\oradata\PRACTICE. If not, you get a file and a directory concatenated together.

Startup or Shutdown Commands

During database startup, you may have some problems.

1. **ORA-01113: file 3 needs media recovery**
   You may have a file that is not current with the database. Also, the database may have crashed when a tablespace was in backup mode. Try to recover the database with the recover database command. The recovery process will remove the tablespace from backup mode.

2. **ORA-01123: cannot start online backup; media recovery not enabled**
   You must be in archive log mode to run open database backup.

3. **ORA-01142: cannot end online backup—none of the files are in backup mode**
   You'll get this error if you try to place a tablespace that is not in backup out of backup mode.

4. **ORA-01078: failure in processing system parameters**
   Check that quoted strings in your parameter file do not have \ at the end. The \ character works on Windows as a directory separator but works in Oracle as a string escape character. During database shutdown, you may get an error.

5. **ORA-01149: cannot shut down—file 3 has online backup set**
   If you try to shut down a database while a tablespace is in backup mode, you will encounter this error. Take the tablespace out of backup mode before shutting down.

Summary

You can perform partial or whole database backups of an Oracle database while the database is open. During this process, you place a tablespace in backup mode prior to making a copy of the datafile(s) in the tablespace. Once the copy is complete, you return the tablespace from backup mode. Be sure to switch your log file before you back up your control file in conjunction with your hot backup. You can recover your database, tablespaces, or datafiles using these backup files.

The best way to test the usability of backups is to restore them to a separate host and attempt to open the database, performing media recovery if necessary. This testing strategy requires that you have a separate computer available for restore and recovery operations.

Later on in this book, you'll see how Recovery Manager can handle a hot database backup much easier and more efficiently. When you make a backup using Recovery Manager while the database is open, you do not need to put the tablespaces in hot backup mode.

For more information on open database backup and recovery, have a look at the Chapters 3 through 6 of the *Oracle 8i Backup and Recovery Guide* and Chapters 3, 6 and 7 in the *Oracle 8i Administrators Guide*.

Chapter Questions

Here are some questions to help you review some of the important concepts covered in this chapter.

1. Datafiles belonging to an online tablespace in backup mode are not changing or being updated with changed data blocks by the database writer.

   A. True

   B. False

2. How does the RECOVER command know which redo log files to apply for recovery? (Pick any that apply.)

   A. Recovery begins with the datafile containing the lowest SCN.

   B. Oracle knows the change ranges of redo log files from the control file.

   C. Oracle knows the location of needed redo log files from the control file.

   D. It's magic.

3. Why would you move archived redo log files out of the archive log destination? (Pick any that apply.)

   A. They may conflict with the database parameter file.

   B. To move them offsite in case of a disaster.

   C. So the archive destination has room for more archive files.

   D. To prevent a new database incarnation from overwriting existing archive files.

4. What v$ view would you use to find out what datafiles require recovery?

   A. v$logfile

   B. v$datafix

   C. v$controlfile

   D. v$recover_file

5. What command places the TOOLS tablespace in backup mode so that you can copy its files from the operating system?

   A. ALTER TABLESPACE TOOLS YOU CAN COPY IT NOW

   B. ALTER TABLESPACE TOOLS SET BACKUP

   C. ALTER TABLESPACE TOOLS BEGIN BACKUP

   D. ALTER TABLESPACE TOOLS BACKUP BEGIN

Answers to Chapter Questions

1. False.   During hot backup mode, datafile blocks continue to be read from and written to. The datafile header and redo entries are handled differently.

2. A, B, C.   The RECOVER DATAFILE command finds the datafile with the earliest checkpoint SCN. Using that SCN, it finds the redo log file names that contain that range of changes and begins to apply them to that data file. The control file keeps track of redo log file change numbers, times, sequences, and file names.

3. B, C, D.   As the database generates redo and archives that information, the archive location will fill up. When the archive destination fills, database operations halt. If you lose the database computer, you can recover your database with an offsite backup, including the redo logs. Finally, a new incarnation will overwrite any existing archive log files if you keep the destination and format of archive files the same.

4. D.   The v$recover_file tells you which datafiles are not synchronized with the other datafiles and control files.

5. C.   When you issue the ALTER TABLESPACE TOOLS BEGIN BACKUP command, the TOOLS tablespace undergoes a checkpoint. All changes for the files in that tablespace get recorded as block images to the redo files.

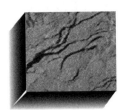

CHAPTER
6

Duplicate Database

ecovering your database does not always have to be performed when a system is down and users are waiting. Some recoveries can actually be planned. I can think of three important reasons to plan a recovery:

- To test that your backups are complete.

- To hone your database administration skills.

- To create a duplicate copy of an existing database.

In this chapter, we'll discuss creating a duplicate database.

A duplicate database can be called a *copy* or a *clone* database. A copy of a database has the same name as the original. A clone of a database has a different database name from the original. When creating both a copy and a clone, a database is physically copied on the same machine or to a different machine. You can easily duplicate a database using the restoration and recovery techniques already presented in previous chapters.

By performing database duplication operations, you provide yourself and your development team several advantages:

- The development team has a simulation database for coding and testing.

- You can verify the quality of your current database backups.

- You can benchmark and validate backup and recovery procedures.

- You can practice your database recovery skills.

You can copy or clone a database in three ways using Oracle utilities. First, you can perform a physical database restore and recovery using operating system file copies and recreating the database control file. Second, you can use Oracle Export and Import utilities to perform a logical restoration from the original database to a new database (see Chapter 8). Finally, you can use Oracle's Recovery Manager to perform a physical file restoration of the datafiles and control file (see Chapter 15). In this chapter, you will clone the PRACTICE database on the same machine using an open database backup (see Figure 6-1). Then we'll look at other duplication scenarios you can perform by modifying the procedures described in the chapter exercise.

Duplicating a database seems like it would be as simple as copying a group of word processing documents. Unfortunately, it isn't. Remember that an Oracle database consists of the triangulation of three file types. These file types—datafiles, redo log files and control file(s)—must be coordinated. When you clone a database, you copy the datafiles to the new database location, create a new control file(s), and reset the redo logs. You've learned how to backup (copy) datafiles and reset redo logs.

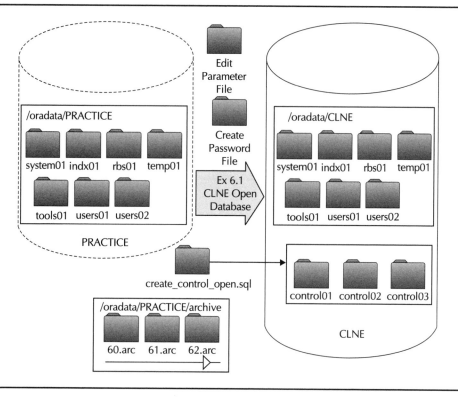

FIGURE 6-1. *Exercises in database cloning*

A duplicate database can be created from a primary database that is either open or closed. In Chapters 4 and 5, you were guided through closed (cold) backups and open (hot) backups. In order to create a duplicate database, the backups files from open and closed backups can be used as the datafile copies. Closed backup datafile backups do not require recovery. Opened backup datafiles require recovery because each file is inconsistent with each other. When you clone a database, you'll have to create a new control file. Let's look at some specifics of the CREATE CONTROLFILE command.

A database control file can be created with the CREATE CONTROLFILE command. This command is useful or necessary in a number of circumstances:

1. You have lost all your control files.

2. You need to change the maximum setting of redo log members or groups.

3. You must change the maximum number of datafiles or instances.

4. You want to change the names and locations of your database files (although this can also be done through different methods when the database is open).

5. You want to change the name of your database.

When you issue a CREATE CONTROLFILE statement, Oracle creates a new control file based on the information you specify in the statement.

The CREATE CONTROLFILE has some similarities to the CREATE DATABASE statement. Refer to Table 6-1 for a brief description of some of the keywords and clauses in the command. I've noted the parameters that pertain to database duplication.

Keyword	Required?	Description
LOGFILE	Yes	Specifies all redo log members and groups that will be used by the database. If you plan to reset the redo logs, these files do not need to exist, they will be created. If you plan to reuse the existing redo logs, each redo log file must be correctly specified.
DATAFILE	Yes	Lists the specific file name of every data file in your database.
REUSE	No	When you create a control file and a file exists of the same name, you will get an error. Use the REUSE parameter to write over the existing control file. The location of the control files is determined by the control_files parameter in your database parameter file.
SET	No	Defines the name of the database you want this database to be. This is required when renaming the database.
RESETLOGS	No*	Indicates that you are disregarding and replacing any log files located after the LOGFILE keyword. If you create your control file(s) with this option, you must open the database with RESETLOGS.
NORESETLOGS	No*	Specifies that the redo log files will be used from the last time that the database was opened. The redo log files must exist as specified by the LOGFILE parameter and will the current ones to the datafiles referred to by the created control file.

*Either the RESETLOGS or the NORESETLOGS must be specified.

TABLE 6-1. *Important Keywords for Creating a New Control File*

Create Control File Considerations

1. The database instance must be started but not mounted. The CREATE CONTROLFILE statement mounts the newly created control file(s) when it succeeds.

2. The user running this command must be granted the OSDBA role.

3. When you create a new control file, you lose stored history like archive log history and RMAN backups.

CAUTION
When a database is opened with the RESETLOGS option, the redo log files are reset, and the database is said to be a new incarnation. Incarnation means to cause to appear in a new form, refurbish, or revitalize. Each time a database is opened resetting the logs, another incarnation of the database is established. Be aware that opening the database and resetting the logs has many critical considerations. You cannot recover your database using a preincarnation backup and post-incarnation redo logs. Consider resetting the logs (creating a new database incarnation) a task to be avoided. If you must reset the logs, back up your database as soon as the database is opened.

Database Duplication

This chapter has one exercise. You will clone the PRACTICE database on the same machine. You'll see how the CREATE CONTROLFILE command can be used in database cloning. The clone of the PRACTICE database will be created while the database is open. After you go through this exercise, we'll look at some other database duplication scenarios you may want to perform. You can build on what you learn here to accomplish real world duplication tasks.

Exercise 6.1: Clone Open Practice Database

To create a clone of the open PRACTICE database, follow these steps. Your task time may be much faster than the time indicated here. I've added extra time for each step assuming this is your first time on each item and you are trying to find your way around.

Task Description	Minutes
1. Prepare Clone Database	10
2. Backup Open Practice Database	10
3. Configure Control File Script	10
4. Run Control File Script	5
5. Recover Clone Database	10
6. Open Clone Database	5
Total Time	50

First, you will prepare the directories, parameter file, and password file (and Windows services) for a new database named CLNE. Next, you'll copy the PRACTICE datafiles to the CLNE database datafile directory. Then you'll generate the commands you need to create a new control file for the CLNE database. Finally, you'll run the script to complete your CLNE database.

Task 1: Prepare CLNE Database

Prepare the CLNE database by creating database directories, parameter file, and password file (and Windows services). If you used the Database Configuration Assistant in Chapter 3 to create your PRACTICE database, you'll see some of the tasks performed by that tool here.

Create all the directories for the CLNE database you are about to build:

```
export ORACLE_SID=CLNE
export ORACLE_BASE=/app/oracle
export ORACLE_HOME=/app/oracle/product/8.1.7
export ORACLE_DATA=/oradata/$ORACLE_SID
export ORACLE_ADMIN=$ORACLE_BASE/admin/$ORACLE_SID
mkdir $ORACLE_ADMIN
mkdir $ORACLE_ADMIN/pfile
mkdir $ORACLE_ADMIN/bdump
```

```
mkdir $ORACLE_ADMIN/cdump
mkdir $ORACLE_ADMIN/udump
mkdir $ORACLE_ADMIN/create
mkdir $ORACLE_DATA/
mkdir $ORACLE_DATA/archive
```

You can use these commands to create database directory structures in subsequent chapters by changing the ORACLE_SID environment variable.

Next, create a parameter file for your CLNE database. Copy the PRACTICE database parameter file to the $ORACLE_BASE/admin/CLNE/pfile directory. Also, add a symbolic link to the default parameter file in the $ORACLE_HOME/dbs directory. You can accomplish these commands on Linux like this:

```
LINUX> cp $ORACLE_BASE/admin/PRACTICE/pfile/initPRACTICE.ora
$ORACLE_BASE/admin/CLNE/pfile/initCLNE.ora
LINUX> ln -s $ORACLE_BASE/admin/CLNE/pfile/initCLNE.ora
$ORACLE_HOME/dbs/initCLNE.ora
```

The symbolic link in the $ORACLE_HOME/dbs points the default parameter file location to the pfile location defined by Oracle Flexible Architecture (OFA). In Windows, you don't have symbolic links like you do in Linux. You can have your default parameter file name include the contents of another parameter file. In Windows, copy the PRACTICE parameter file to the CLNE location and create a new file in the default database containing the IFILE keyword:

```
WINNT> copy %ORACLE_BASE%\admin\PRACTICE\pfile\initPRACTICE.ora
%ORACLE_BASE%\admin\CLNE\pfile\initCLNE.ora
WINNT > notepad $ORACLE_HOME/dbs/initCLNE.ora
 > IFILE=d:\app\oracle\admin\CLNE\pfile\initCLNE.ora
```

With your parameter file set for the CLNE database, open the file in the pfile directory. Change every occurrence of the word 'PRACTICE' to 'CLNE'. When you perform this global search and replace, you'll change the database name, service name, control file location, and many directory paths for parameters

Because you are changing the database name, you will also want to change other parameters in this file from the old database name of PRACTICE to the new name of CLNE. Change these parameters, among others:

```
db_name = CLNE
instance_name = CLNE
service_names = CLNE
```

```
log_archive_dest_1 = "location=/oradata/CLNE/archive"
background_dump_dest = /app/oracle/admin/CLNE/bdump
core_dump_dest = /app/oracle/admin/CLNE/cdump
user_dump_dest = /app/oracle/admin/CLNE/udump
control_files = ("/oradata/CLNE/control01.ctl",
                 "/oradata/CLNE/control02.ctl",
                 "/oradata/CLNE/control03.ctl")
```

Be very careful to change the location of the control file locations. You don't want to write over the current control files. The CREATE CONTROLFILE command creates control files at the file location you specified in the CONTROL_FILE parameter. If you try to create a control file with the name of a file that exists, the CREATE CONTROLFILE will fail. This prevents you from making the mistake of writing over an existing control file. If you choose, you can add the REUSE keyword to avoid this error when you create a control file. But be warned: this could overwrite a control file if you have not changed the init.ora file.

Note that when you create a control file, you will probably be creating several copies of the same control file. In the example, you will be creating three control files in the /oradata/CLNE directory. In a real environment, each of these three locations would be in different physical locations.

Create a password file so that you can connect in SQL*Plus as SYS with the SYSDBA role. The password file is also used for remote administration security.

```
LINUX> orapwd file=$ORACLE_HOME/dbs/orapwCLNE password=CLNE entries=4
```

In Windows, you'll need to create a new database service for the CLNE database. This creates a Windows service named OracleServiceCLNE with the internal password of CLNE.

```
WINNT> oradim -new -sid CLNE -intpwd CLNE
```

Task 2: Backup Open Practice Database
Remember that backup script you built in Exercise 5.1 in Chapter 5? You can use that script again to copy the datafiles to the CLNE data directory while the PRACTICE database is open. Find your file named open_backup.sql and make some minor modifications, as follows:

1. Change the dir user variable from the current value to /oradata/CLNE. When you run the open database backup, you will copy all datafiles to the directory where you are duplicating your database.

2. Remove the line that creates copy commands for the control files. When you duplicate the database, you will create a new control file with a new database name.

Once you have edited the open_backup.sql database, run it as SYS with SYSDBA role on the PRACTICE database. Upon completion, the /oradata/CLNE directory will have an inconsistent copy of all datafiles in the PRACTICE database.

In this simple example, you have only one directory. In a real system containing many large files, you may need to edit your copy script to put files in different locations or on tape.

Task 3: Configure Control File Script

Typing in all the files required by the CREATE CONTROLFILE command can be quite a job. Good thing you have a shortcut available to you. You can let the database generate all the instructions necessary to create a new control file, and you can use the alter database command to do all this work for you. Open a SQL*Plus prompt and log in to the PRACTICE database as user SYS:

```
SQL > ALTER DATABASE BACKUP CONTROLFILE TO TRACE RESETLOGS;
```

When you type this command, the Oracle Server generates a file on the server machine that contains all the commands necessary to create a control file. This will be located in the location defined by the user_dump_dest initialization parameter. In fact, the file will contain a full script that you can modify to duplicate your database. To find the directory where you'll find your trace file, type these commands:

```
SQL > SELECT value FROM v$parameter
  2    WHERE name = 'user_dump_dest';
SQL > SHOW PARAMETER user_dump_dest;
```

The file will be named something like ora123.trc. Look for a file with a date and time stamp about the same time as the moment you issued the command to trace. When you look at that trace file, you will find all the commands you need to create a control file and start up your database. This file includes STARTUP, CREATE CONTROLFILE, RECOVER DATABASE, and ALTER DATABASE OPEN commands.

Locate the file in the user_dump_dest directory as explained above. Once you find the file, rename it to create_control.sql and move it into the $ORACLE_BASE/admin/CLNE/create directory. Name the file create_control.sql.

This trace file has all the commands you need to create a new control for your new CLNE database. Make a few small modifications, and you can run the script to finish the database cloning process.

1. Remove comments from the script. The top of the file contains trace information that you won't need to create the control file and open the database. Also, remove the lines beginning with the # symbol.

> **2.** Change the word REUSE to SET on the CREATE CONTROLFILE command. You will be changing the name of the database rather than retaining the old database name.
>
> **3.** Change the word "PRACTICE" to "CLNE" on the CREATE CONTROLFILE command. The control file created will be for a database named CLNE.
>
> **4.** Change the file location of each datafile and redo log from the /oradata/PRACTICE directory to the /oradata/CLNE directory.

When you have made your changes, the file will look like what you see here:

```
1.    STARTUP NOMOUNT
2.    CREATE CONTROLFILE SET DATABASE "CLNE" RESETLOGS ARCHIVELOG
3.        MAXLOGFILES 16
4.        MAXLOGMEMBERS 2
5.        MAXDATAFILES 30
6.        MAXINSTANCES 1
7.        MAXLOGHISTORY 226
8.    LOGFILE
9.      GROUP 1 '/oradata/CLNE/redo03.log'   SIZE 1M,
10.     GROUP 2 '/oradata/CLNE/redo02.log'   SIZE 1M,
11.     GROUP 3 '/oradata/CLNE/redo01.log'   SIZE 1M
12.   DATAFILE
13.     '/oradata/CLNE/system01.dbf',
14.     '/oradata/CLNE/tools01.dbf',
15.     '/oradata/CLNE/rbs01.dbf',
16.     '/oradata/CLNE/temp01.dbf',
17.     '/oradata/CLNE/users01.dbf',
18.     '/oradata/CLNE/indx01.dbf',
19.     '/oradata/CLNE/users02.dbf'
20.   CHARACTER SET WE8ISO8859P1;
```

Your new control file needs to know where you've copied each database file. The CREATE CONTROLFILE command does not care about the location of each database file. Because the control file needs only to find each file, it does not care about file names or locations.

■ **Line 1** starts the database instance and opens the control file. You can specify the database parameter file with the PFILE option (PFILE stands for parameter file). If you don't specify the parameter file, the Oracle Server opens a file in a default location depending on your ORACLE_SID environment setting and your operating system. On a startup NOMOUNT, you only read the init.ora file and establish the memory structures required by Oracle.

- **Line 2** creates the control file. When you create your control file, you will be renaming the database. The database name in the control file will be initially different from the database name in each of the datafiles. Because you cannot change the database name in the redo logs, they must be recreated. Both the online redo logs and the archived redo logs from the original database can no longer be used once you reset the logs to include your new database name. To change the database name in the control file, use the SET keyword and the RESETLOGS keyword in the CREATE CONTROLFILE command. The SET keyword specifies that the control file will have a different name than the current name. Here you specify the name of the database will be CLNE no matter what database the datafile headers think they belong to. The RESETLOGS option on the control file means that the description of the redo logs will be used to create new redo logs.

- **Lines 8–11** create the control file with a database name; redo log files and groups, datafiles, and a character set. The online redo log files are defined by the text following the LOGFILE keyword. These files will be created when the database is opened with the RESETLOGS.

- **Lines 12–20** define the datafiles that will make up the database.

You have removed the recovery commands and the open database command. You now have to perform cancel-based recovery that must be done interactively, as you'll see in the next step.

Task 4: Run Control File Script
Connect with SQL*Plus and run the create_control_open.sql from the $ORACLE_BASE/admin/CLNE/create directory to actually create a new control file:

```
LINUX> export ORACLE_SID=CLNE
LINUX> cd $ORACLE_BASE/admin/$ORACLE_SID/create
LINUX> sqlplus /nolog
SQL> connect sys/CLNE as sysdba;
SQL> @create_control_open.sql
```

Note that the CREATE CONTROLFILE script can run from any location via a client Net8 SQL*Plus session.

Task 5: Recover Clone Database
Now that you have created a new control file for the CLNE database, you will need to apply redo to each of the datafiles that were copied from the open PRACTICE

Cloning a Database from a Closed Backup

If you clone a database from a closed backup, you will not have to recover the datafiles after you've created a new control file and before you open the database. Why? The files will be consistent when you backed them up with the database when it was closed. Therefore, no recovery will be necessary. If you choose to clone a database from a closed backup, perform every task in this exercise except the recovery task.

database. The datafiles for the CLNE database require recovery because they were copied while the PRACTICE database was open. When the tablespace was placed in backup mode, the datafile checkpoint SCNs were different. Therefore, each datafile must be recovered using archive logs from the PRACTICE database.

When you apply redo, you can perform incomplete recovery or complete recovery. With either recovery, you'll need to make the archive logs from the PRACTICE database available to the CLNE database:

```
SQL> SET LOGSOURCE /oradata/PRACTICE/archive;
```

This command tells the CLNE instance to find archive logs for recovery to look in the archive destination of the PRACTICE database.

You are ready to begin recovery. A good recovery option to choose is cancel-based recovery. If you have many archive log files that you want to recover, you can perform SCN or time-based to avoid the time and effort involved in applying each redo file one at a time. You can supply archive files one by one until you either cancel or until media recovery completes.

```
SQL> RECOVER DATABASE USING BACKUP CONTROLFILE UNTIL CANCEL;
```

At the prompt, apply at least one archive log file. The end backup redo entry for each datafile will probably be contained in this redo file. At the conclusion of the application of this redo file, all the datafiles will be caught up to the same SCN. Once you have applied enough redo to roll the database forward to the desired point in time, type **CANCEL**. In order to open the CLNE database, apply all the archive logs requested up to and including the log containing the end hot backup entry from the open database backup. If you want to completely recover the CLNE database before you open it, you'll have to recover using the current online redo log of the PRACTICE database. Perform recovery until you run out of archived redo logs

Extra Credit Task

You have some freedom with your datafiles in the DATAFILE clause.

1. The file names can be changed along with the file location. For example, the file INDX01.dbf could be copied to INDX01.ora (or to any other name you choose).

2. The datafiles and redo logs do not have to be in the same directory for the CREATE CONTROLFILE command to work.

3. The order of the files following the DATAFILE keyword can change. For example, the tools01.dbf file can be first, and the system01.dbf can be last.

Why is this the case? Each database file has unique database information in the file header that can be used to identify it. The CREATE CONTROLFILE command confirms the file is there and that the database name agrees with the database name for the new control file. Each data file header is read and placed into the new control file. That's why you can change file names, directories, and file name order.

For extra credit, vary the file names, directories, and order. Note that once you get your database open, the file number from the v$datafile dictionary view is the same in the copied database as it is in original database. (I'm not recommending you change the datafile order, but you can try this to help you understand the duplication process better.)

to apply. Once all archived redo logs have been applied from the PRACTICE database, you have two options:

1. Option 1 is to force a log switch on the PRACTICE database and apply that new archive log to the CLNE. Once applied, you'll have all changes applied to the CLNE database that were made to the PRACTICE database up to the log switch. At the CLNE database recover prompt, type **CANCEL**. You are ready to open the CLNE.

2. Option 2 is to shut down the PRACTICE database and apply the current redo log from the PRACTICE database to the CLNE database. With the PRACTICE database shut down, type **/oradata/PRACTICE/redo01.dbf** (if redo01.dbf is the current online file) at the recover prompt of the CLNE. You can also copy the current online redo file to a location for your CLNE

database to read. If you have completely recovered the CLNE database, you'll see the message MEDIA RECOVERY COMPLETE. Because a database is constantly writing to the current online log, don't try to apply the PRACTICE current redo log while the PRACTICE database is open.

Task 6: Open Clone Database

After you see the message media recovery cancelled or completed, you are ready to open the database with RESETLOGS. For this command to work, all datafiles must be consistent with same checkpoint SCN in each file header:

```
SQL> ALTER DATABASE OPEN RESETLOGS;
```

Terrific! You created a clone of your database without ever closing the PRACTICE database.

Duplicate Database Scenarios

After completing this exercise, you will be ready to perform other forms of database duplication. Before I close out this chapter, I'm going to point out some tips and tricks that complement the material you just read.

Clone to a Different Machine

Typically, database duplication does not occur on the same machine. For example, you might create a TEST database as a copy of your PRODUCTION database. You can follow the steps, keeping in mind that files must be transferred from the source database machine to the duplicated database machine. Keep these points in mind:

1. The database versions should be identical when cloning databases between machines. You'll avoid the probability of problems if the Oracle release is the same up to the patch set releases (8.1.7.x.x).

2. Database duplication should only be attempted between machines with the same operating system and release. For example, duplicating a Linux database to a Windows machine won't work.

3. When you clone a database on a different machine, some tasks will be performed on the original database and others will be performed on the clone database machine. On the original database machine, you create a

control file trace script, back up the datafiles to disk or tape and copy the datafiles, parameter file, control file script, and archive logs to the clone database machine. On the clone machine, you prepare your instance (create directories, edit parameter file, establish Windows services, create a password file). Then copy the datafiles to specific directories and edit the control file creation script to point to those file locations. Finally, you create a new control file and recover the database using copied archive logs.

4. When you create a backup and need transfer files, you'll have to transfer the files between machines. The FTP utility is a generic means to copy files from one machine to another. FTP (file transfer protocol) is the file transfer mechanism used primarily by the Internet. Linux and UNIX machines have FTP available as a standard utility. Remember to set the transfer mode to binary. Windows NT/2000 has FTP available also. Alternatively, you could make a network drive between two NT/Windows 2000 servers. Another UNIX command for transferring files is RCP (remote copy).

5. Any database duplication effort will require Net8 configuration of the duplicated machine. You don't want to make the mistake of connecting to the source database when you meant to connect to the duplicated one. You can verify the database and instance you are connecting to by querying the v$database and v$instance views.

6. If you have really big database files and slow network connectivity, you can compress the database files on the source database machine, transfer them, then uncompress them on the duplicated database machine. This may save you significant time. UNIX file compression utilities include compress/uncompress and gzip. Windows file compression utilities include PkZip and WinZip. File compression of any kind is not supported by Oracle. Block corruptions may be introduced when compression techniques get used during file copy operation.

Clone from a Tape Backup

Because you may perform backups to tape, you can restore from the same tape. The backup set you've created from your source database backup can be used to duplicate your database. The big benefit of using your current backup for duplication is that you confirm that your tape backup is a good one. If you duplicate a database using your tape backups and you experience a failure, it points you to an issue you can address in your backups.

Copy a Database to a Different Machine

When you copy a database from one machine to another, you may or may not use the existing control file for the duplicated database. It is possible to copy a database without recreating the control file. You'd be able to accomplish this if:

1. The database copy will have the same name *and* will reside on a different machine

2. You copy all the datafiles, online redo files, and temporary files to identical directories and file system names *or* you rename the datafiles with the copied control file mounted.

To copy a database without recreating the control file, you can create a directory structure on the target machine identical to the original machine. Copy all the database files from the original machine to the target machine. Put them each in the identical directory and file name on the target machine. Open the copied database with copy of the original database parameter file. You're done!

If the duplicated database files cannot reside in identical locations as the source, you can copy a database and mount the control file. Then change the location in the mounted control file with the ALTER DATABASE RENAME FILE command for each file that has been copied to a different directory location.

Say you needed to move the tools01.dbf file from the /u01 file system to the /u02 file system, you can accomplish this with these commands:

```
SQL> STARTUP MOUNT;
SQL> ALTER DATABASE RENAME FILE '/u01/PRACTICE/tools01.dbf'
  2    TO '/u02/PRACTICE/tools01.dbf';
SQL> HOST mv /u01/PRACTICE/tools01.dbf /u02/PRACTICE/tools01.dbf
SQL> Remark Repeat datafile moves for other datafiles
SQL> ALTER DATABASE OPEN;
```

You can modify the file name and location of your files and point the existing control file to the new location.

NOTE
You can also move datafiles while the database is open. Take the tablespace or datafile(s) offline, rename the datafile(s), move the datafile(s) on the OS, and bring the tablespace or datafile(s) back online.

If you choose to create a new control file when copying a database, perform all the cloning tasks described in the chapter exercise with a few exceptions:

1. When you create a control file, use the REUSE keyword and not the SET keyword after the CREATE CONTROLFILE keywords in the create control file script.

2. Because you are retaining the database name, you don't have to reset the logs. If you decide to reuse existing logs from the original database, change the keyword RESETLOGS to NORESETLOGS when you create the control file. You must also copy the online logs from the source database because you won't be resetting the logs for this to work. Then, when you open the database, open it without resetting the logs. You can use the ALTER DATABASE OPEN or ALTER DATABASE OPEN NORESETLOGS commands.

TIP
You can move a database on the same machine by creating a new control file or keeping your current control file. If you create a new control file, follow the procedures listed in this section. If you keep your current control, mount the file, move all the datafiles in your database, and rename each one with the "ALTER DATABASE RENAME FILE" command.

Duplicate Part of a Database

When you duplicate a database (clone or copy), you don't have to copy all the datafiles. If you only want a few of the tablespaces, copy only the datafiles for those tablespaces along with all SYSTEM tablespace files (and perhaps applicable rollback tablespaces as they could be required for opening the database and also prevents you from having to recreate the rollback segments again). You can open the duplicate database with a newly created control file. After the database is open and you look at the datafiles in the database, you might notice some files in the Oracle Home database or dbs directory that start with the letters "missing." If you do not specify a file when you create the control file, the database will open without them. However, the data dictionary contained in the system tablespace expects them to be available. If you need the missing files in your database clone, perform the duplication process again and be sure to include them next time. If the database does not need these missing files, you can drop them from the database. You must drop the whole tablespace, not just an individual file.

Troubleshooting

When you clone a database, you may (and probably will) run into various problems along the way. Usually, those problems show up in an error message during a task in the project. Read further for some common error messages you might encounter. To make the errors easier to find, I've grouped them by the command that you issue. They also are grouped this way because some errors will occur whether you are copying or cloning a database.

Command Connect

When you try to connect to your CLNE database with the SYSDBA, you may see this error:

> **ORA-27101: shared memory realm does not exist**
> If you connect as SYSDBA to a database, you must have a password file. Otherwise, you'll have to connect as internal. Create a password file with the orapwd utility at the OS command prompt.

Command CREATE CONTROLFILE

When you attempt to create a control file, you may get several errors. I've listed some sample error output, the reason for the error, and a possible solution. Each of these errors will be proceeded by the ORA-01503 - CREATE CONTROLFILE failed message. An OS error will accompany the Oracle error and will help pinpoint the cause of the problem.

1. **ORA-00200: controlfile could not be created -**
   ORA-27038: skgfrcre: file exists
   The CREATE CONTROLFILE command expects to create a brand new file. You can remove the existing control file or use the REUSE option on the CREATE CONTROLFILE command. You might also change the control file parameter in the database parameter file. Be careful when using the REUSE clause: do not overwrite the primary database control file.

2. **ORA-01504: database name 'CLNE' does not match parameter**
   db_name 'PRACTICE'-
   Make sure that the database name is the same in the new init.ora file and the created control file script.

3. ORA-01565: error in identifying file '/oradata/CLNE/system01.dbf'
The CREATE CONTROLFILE verifies the existence of each datafile after
the DATAFILE keyword. Confirm that you typed the file name correctly
and that you copied the file correctly.

Command RECOVER DATABASE

When you are recovering the CLNE database, Oracle might ask for an archive log
that has not yet been created from the PRACTICE database. The CLNE database may
need redo in the current PRACTICE database archive log. You switch the logs on
PRACTICE and make the newly archived redo file available to the CLNE database. Try
applying this redo to the CLNE database to complete recovery. You may have
encountered this error because you did not switch the log files after the open database
backup completed:

**1. ORA-01547: warning: RECOVER succeeded but OPEN RESETLOGS would
get error below.**
You must perform incomplete recovery on at least one archive log file to
successfully open a database from an open database backup.

Command ALTER DATABASE OPEN RESETLOGS

The final step and true test of effective database cloning is the moment that you
open the database. You may get some errors like these:

ORA-00283: recovery session canceled due to errors
When you open the database, all the datafiles must have the same current file
checkpoint SCN, which is one of a number of validation checks that Oracle runs
against the file headers before opening the database. This error indicates that the
specified datafile requires recovery. You might get this error for a number of
reasons. If you get this error and are trying to open the database with a new
name, you may have to start over with your original datafiles.

1. The copy of the original database was made when the database was
open or aborted. You can look at the date-time stamps of all the
datafiles and confirm that they all have the exact same date and time.
You'll have to perform recovery using an archive log or perhaps an
online log from the original database.

2. The recover command was issued against redo logs that are not current or are of a database with the wrong name. You may have to copy all the files again.

3. The Oracle software version may be different from the version of the original database. Make sure that the copy database is running the same version as the original database. Check out the environment setting of ORACLE_HOME.

4. When cloning from an open database, you may have not applied enough of the archive log files to cover the time of the last end backup command against one or more of the datafiles.

Summary

You have created a database by copying an existing database. You learned about creating a database with a new name by recreating the control file. The database cloning process lets you test backup and quickly provide alternate database environments for testing and certification. You also got a chance to practice your recoveries. You'll find this procedure useful throughout your Oracle DBA career. Remember, the key to duplicating a database is recreating the control file. For more information on creating a control file, go to Chapter 2 in the *Oracle 8i Backup and Recovery Guide,* Chapter 9 in the *Oracle 8i SQL Reference* and Chapter 5 in *Oracle 8i Administrator's Guide.* Also check Oracle's Metalink Web site (http://metalink.oracle.com) for articles about duplicating a database.

Chapter Questions

The following questions will help you review some of the important concepts and nuances.

1. You can create a copy of a database with a database by recreating a control file. Which one will create the CREATE CONTROLFILE commands?

   A. ALTER SYSTEM BUILD CONTROL FILE

   B. ALTER DATABASE BACKUP CONTROL FILE TO TRACE

   C. ALTER DATABASE RECREATE CONTROL FILE

   D. ALTER SYSTEM BACKUP CONTROL FILE

2. If you want to change the name of an existing database, you'll have to recreate the control file. Which keywords in the CREATE CONTROLFILE command will rename your database?

   A. SET DATABASE

   B. RENAME DATABASE

   C. CHANGE DATABASE

   D. COPY DATABASE

3. Why do you have to open a database that has been renamed with the ALTER DATABASE OPEN RESETLOGS command?

   A. Any existing log files can renamed also.

   B. The database name must be changed in the log files.

   C. Any existing log files from a database backup cannot be used with a new database name.

   D. Log files contain the database data file names and they must be altered.

4. When you clone a database and change the name, you can use a copy of the existing control file and redo logs

   A. True

   B. False

5. By creating a new control file, which of these tasks can you accomplish? (Pick any that apply.)

   A. Change the location of datafiles

   B. Change the location of redo log files

   C. Change the Oracle database version

   D. Rename a database

Answers to Chapter Questions

1. B. To create a control file as a text file containing the CREATE CONTROLFILE command, use ALTER DATABASE BACKUP CONTROL FILE TO TRACE. The file will be located in the user_dump_dest directory.

2. A. By setting the database name in the new control file, you can change the name to a different one.

3. C. When you rename a database, the existing log files are invalid because they contain the old database name.

4. False. The database name (specifically the DBID) cannot be modified within existing control files and redo logs. Therefore, control file and redo logs must be recreated if you change the name of the database.

5. A, B, D. You can change the location of datafiles with a CREATE CONTROLFILE command. You can rename a database with the CREATE CONTROLFILE command using the RESETLOGS options.

CHAPTER
7

Standby Database

epairing a broken database takes time. After you find out that your database has a problem, you must first investigate the problem to find out what's broken and how to fix it. Then, to repair the database, you've got to locate your backup (often on tape), restore the backup, and perform recovery. All these activities can take hours—hours when your users or application cannot use the database. What if your business can't do without a working database for more than several minutes? You have to find a mechanism to provide a working production database quickly. A database solution for this kind of challenge is called a high availability solution.

What if your database center experiences an environmental disaster? A flood, fire, tornado, extended loss of power, or explosion may make the physical facility housing your production database unusable. Recovering from a disaster like this is called disaster recovery. Hours or days may pass while you collect your backup tapes from offsite storage, move them to another machine, and restore and recover your database. If your business cannot afford an extended outage, consider a disaster recovery plan that includes Oracle's standby database feature.

When you think of the word standby, what comes to your mind? The noun standby means:

- One that can always be relied on, as in an emergency.

- One kept in readiness to serve as a substitute.

A standby database can be relied on as a substitute when the production database becomes unavailable. Two important terms apply to a deployment of an Oracle standby database:

- **Primary**   The database source is the *primary* database. This database might also be called the source, production, or active database. In this chapter, the PRACTICE instance serves as the primary.

- **Standby**   The database copy is the *standby* database. This database might also be called the target or recovering database. This database usually has the same name and instance name as the primary. If the standby is on the same server (for testing purposes only, as used in the tasks for this chapter), the instance name will be different. In this chapter, the instance name will be STANDBY.

When you deploy a standby database, you create a copy of the primary database and place it at a standby location. This is typically another host residing at a different physical location. To keep the standby current with the primary database, archive redo logs are transported (shipped) to the standby database and applied. If the primary site fails, the standby database can be activated as the new primary in a matter of minutes. This saves a lot of wasted downtime, which equates to lost time and revenue.

CAUTION
When I say that the standby is current with the primary, it is only as current as the last archive log file that was applied to it. This lag in archived redo represents the difference in "currentness" between the primary and the standby databases.

There are a number of points to consider before implementing a standby database:

- To be truly useful, the primary and standby database should reside on remote systems at different physical locations.

- The servers housing the primary and standby database should have the same machine architecture and operating system.

- The Oracle database versions on both primary and secondary should be the same.

- To maintain performance should the primary site fail, hardware specifications must be duplicated. The standby host should only be used as a standby site and nothing more.

- The shipping of the archive log files relies on Net8, which is completely reliant on the network. If there are network failures, there will be larger time lags between the primary and standby.

- Deploy exhaustive error checking so that you can quickly investigate if the archive propagation and application encounters a problem (for example, archive log files getting corrupted during network transfer or errors during application of archive log files).

- Clients and middle-tier services should be prepared to cope with the moving of the primary database to a different server in the event of a failover. This can be achieved by using different TNS service names, a DNS name change, or the Net8 failover facilities.

- There are a number of database structural changes and object manipulations that will not be propagated to the standby.

- The primary database MUST be running in ARCHIVELOG mode. These log files are used to recover the standby database.

- Be sure to verify procedures that back up the standby database. If a failover occurs and the standby becomes the primary, your backup procedures will protect your new primary.

Oracle's Standby Database

Oracle's standby database (shown in Figure 7-1) was introduced in release 7.3. With the advent of RMAN in 8.0, a whole new approach to backup and recovery was born, including some new methods you could use when creating a standby database (discussed in Chapter 16). Release 8*i* included more new features for the standby database that allowed Oracle to automate some of the maintenance tasks. With 8*i*, it was made possible to open the standby database in a read-only mode and then put it back into recovery. The standby database feature is made even simpler in Oracle 9*i* and renamed as Data Guard.

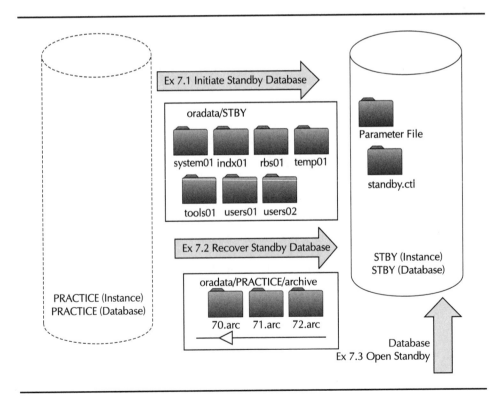

FIGURE 7-1. *Standby Database of the PRACTICE*

In this chapter's four exercises, you will initiate a standby database, propagate redo, open it for queries, and activate it. As I describe the tasks of each exercise, I'll briefly discuss commands, details, and restrictions of a standby deployment.

NOTE
Standby database complexity comes from the maintenance and automatic error checking of a busy production system.

Exercise 7.1: Initiate a Standby Database

In this exercise, you will build a database named STANDBY to function as a standby database to the PRACTICE database.

Task Description	Minutes
1. Prepare for Standby database	5
2. Make Open Database backup	10
3. Create Standby control file	5
4. Configure Standby parameter file	10
5. Mount Standby database	5
Total Time	35

Setting up the STANDBY database starts with creating directories (and services on Windows) for a copy of the PRACTICE database. Next, you'll back up the PRACTICE database datafiles to the STANDBY directory structure. The STANDBY database will mount its own special control file generated from the PRACTICE database. After you configure the standby database parameter file, you'll be able to mount the new database as a standby.

Task 1: Prepare for Standby Database

When you create your STANDBY database, you'll need to create directories for database administration files, database files, and archive logs. You'll also need to prepare the standby instance by copying and configuring a parameter file, creating a password file, and creating Windows services on Windows. Follow the steps outlined in detail in Exercise 6-1, Task 1 in Chapter 6. In this case, create an instance named STANDBY rather than CLONE.

NOTE
If you're using a remote standby, the directory structure is easier to manage if it is identical to the primary site.

Task 2: Make Open Database Backup

With the directories created, you can create a backup of all datafiles in the PRACTICE database. It is possible to take either cold (database shut) or hot (database open) backups for creating the standby. Make a copy of the datafiles while the database is open. Back in Chapter 5, you created a script named open_backup.sql. Edit that file and change the destination directory of the datafile backups. Rather than copying the files to a backup directory named /oradata/PRACTICE/backup/user/ch5, change the value of the dir user parameter to point to the STANDBY database directory:

```
define dir = '/oradata/STANDBY'
```

Also change this line:

```
prompt 'alter database backup controlfile to ''&dir\control.ctl'' REUSE;'
```

To this:

```
prompt ALTER DATABASE CREATE STANDBY CONTROLFILE AS
'/oralog/oradata/STANDBY/standby.ctl' REUSE;;
```

This command creates the special control file that the standby database must use. A standby database cannot be created using a normal backup of the primary database control file.

Running this script now will create a standby copy of the primary database.

NOTE
If you're using a remote standby, the files will need to be backed up and then transferred using a tool such as FTP (Unix) or a mapped networked drive (NT/Windows 2000). If you're using FTP, make sure that the transfer mode is set to binary.

Task 3: Configure Standby Parameter File

A standby database requires a parameter file like any other database. Several parameters in this file require special attention because this database is a standby. After copying the parameter file in Task 1, open the file with an editor and make some modifications. Change the parameters for the STANDBY database and directories:

```
db_name = PRACTICE
instance_name = STANDBY
service_names = STANDBY
control_files = ("/oradata/STANDBY/standby.ctl")
log_archive_dest_1 = 'location=/oradata/STANDBY/archive'
```

```
standby_archive_dest = "/oradata/STANDBY/archive"
background_dump_dest = /app/oracle/admin/STANDBY/bdump
user_dump_dest = /app/oracle/admin/STANDBY/udump
db_file_name_convert = "/oradata/PRACTICE", "/oradata/STANDBY"
log_file_name_convert = "/oradata/PRACTICE", "/oradata/STANDBY"
lock_name_space = STANDBY
```

These parameters require a brief explanation:

- **db_name**   A standby database must have the exact same name as the primary database. In this case, it is PRACTICE.

- **instance_name**   The name linked to the memory structures and background processes is defined by the instance name parameter. The instance name does not have to be the same as the database name.

- **service_names**   An instance connects to one or more database services specified by the service name parameter. The service name STANDBY will be used for archive log transfer between the PRACTICE database and the STANDBY database.

- **control_files**   The control files are opened by the instance defined by the control_files parameter. The STANDBY database control_file parameter is different from the control file on the PRACTICE database.

- **log_archive_dest_1**   This directory is used by Oracle to apply archive logs during manual recovery.

- **standby_archive_dest_1**   This directory is used by Oracle to apply archive logs that have automatically been transferred/shipped from the primary database (PRACTICE). This is called *managed* recovery.

- **background_dump_dest**   The location for the alert.log and debugging trace files for background processes.

- **user_dump_dest**   The location for the user process trace files.

- **db_file_name_convert**   The control file is a special copy from the PRACTICE database but still thinks the datafiles are in the /oradata/PRACTICE directory. This parameter tells the instance to look for those datafiles in the /oradata/ STANDBY directory instead. This parameter serves as path name translation functionality. Because your standby database is on the same computer as the primary database, you must place datafiles in a different path location. If you had separate computers for the primary and standby database, you could place all datafiles in an identical directory structure. In that recommended scenario, you would not have to define this parameter. You can only specify this parameter once, but it is possible to use a subset of the directory names—for example, if your datafiles reside in /u01/oradata/PRACTICE and /u02/oradata/PRACTICE and they need to be in /u01/oradata/STANDBY and /u02/oradata/STANDBY. The db_file_name_convert parameter would look something like this:

```
db_file_name_convert = "/oradata/PRACTICE", "/oradata/STANDBY"
```

- **log_file_name_convert** Once the STANDBY database is activated, its control file expects the online log files to be located in /oradata/PRACTICE. Upon activation, this parameter tells the instance to create online log files in the /oradata/STANDBY directory instead.

- **lock_name_space** This parameter must be used to enable two databases of the same name to exist on the same machine. The namespace value assigned to this parameter is used for naming the memory structures for this instance. It is always used to allow two databases of the same name to coexist on the same machine.

Task 4: Mount Standby Database

Instantiate your STANDBY database by starting the instance and mounting the standby control file. You issue two commands to initiate your new standby database: you set your ORACLE_SID environment variable to STANDBY and connect as SYS in SQL*Plus.

```
LINUX> export ORACLE_SID=STANDBY;
LINUX> sqlplus /nolog
SQL> CONNECT sys/standby AS SYSDBA;
SQL> STARTUP NOMOUNT;
SQL> ALTER DATABASE MOUNT STANDBY DATABASE;
```

If you have configured your initialization file properly for the STANDBY database, the startup command will succeed. If it does not succeed, make sure you have set up the parameters as described. Query v$datafile to check the datafile locations have been properly converted by the DB_FILE_NAME_CONVERT parameter.

That's it. You just initiated a standby database named STANDBY.

Exercise 7.2: Recover Standby Database

Now that you have a standby database, how do you keep this database current with its primary? Changes continue to occur on the PRACTICE database that must be reflected in the STANDBY database. Those changes will be applied to the STANDBY database using the archived redo logs from the PRACTICE database. In this exercise, you will transport archive files from the primary to the standby database and apply them. After the archive files have been applied, the STANDBY will be current with the PRACTICE database up to the last file applied.

Task Description	Minutes
1. Manual recovery – Ship Archive log files	15
2. Manual recovery – Apply Archive log files	5
3. Enable managed recovery	15
4. Confirm managed recovery	10
Total Time	45

There are two methods available for recovering and applying the archive log files from the primary database to the standby. Oracle has called these two methods *manual recovery* and *managed recovery*.

Manual recovery, as the name suggests, is a method of applying the archived logs without Oracle handling it. The DBA must set up an automated script or manually enter the instructions to transfer the files from the primary to the standby locations and then issue a recovery command against the standby database. This was the only way of doing standby recovery before 8*i*. If manual recovery is not the chosen method, it is still required to resolve gaps in the log sequences. This occurs if a log file is missing and once it has been restored, must be applied.

Managed recovery is the opposite of manual recovery. Oracle will take care of the transferring of archived log files from the primary and standby destinations using Net8. The application of these log files to the standby (recovery) is also managed. This is configured through some special init.ora parameter settings and some recovery command options. The standby database spawns a background process named Remote File Server (RFS) to create archive files from Net8 transmission to files in the standby_arch_dest_1 directory.

Task 1: Manual Recovery—Ship Archive Log Files

The key to keeping the standby site current with the primary site is the effective transport and application of archive log files. In our standby training deployment, all you will do is copy archive files from one directory to another to simulate the transport of archive log files.

NOTE

If you're using a remote standby, the log files will need to be transferred over the network. If using FTP, the transfer mode must *be set to Binary.*

To propagate PRACTICE database changes to the STANDBY database, copy the archive logs created since the STANDBY database was created. From an operating system prompt, copy the archive files from PRACTICE archive destination to the STANDBY archive destination:

```
LINUX>cp /oradata/PRACTICE/backup/archive/* /oradata/STANDBY/archive
```

Once the files are copied, you are ready to begin recovery and apply the files.

Task 2: Manual Recovery—Apply Archive Log Files

With the STANDBY database mounted as a standby database, apply the archive files needed with the RECOVER command on the STANDBY database.

```
SQL> RECOVER STANDBY DATABASE;
```

The RECOVER command will prompt you for the archive file.

Accept the recommended file names until you have applied all the archive files copied up to the latest sequence. This recovery is just like the cancel-based recovery you performed in Chapter 5:

```
ORA-00279: change 615858460 generated at 01/07/2002 06:51:49 needed for thread 1
ORA-00289: suggestion : /oralog/oradata/STANDBY/archive/70.arc
ORA-00280: change 615858460 for thread 1 is in sequence #70
Specify log: {<RET>=suggested | filename | AUTO | CANCEL}
```

Apply the suggested log by pressing ENTER. You can keep applying logs until an application of suggested log file yields this message:

```
ORA-00308: cannot open archived log
'/oradata/STANDBY/archive/72.arc'
ORA-27037: unable to obtain file status
SVR4 Error: 2: No such file or directory
```

This indicates you tried to apply an archive log that has not been generated or copied. No harm is done; your recovery is cancelled for you. If you know the last archive log copied, you can type cancel after that last file is applied to avoid this message. Have a look at the alert log of the STANDBY file. You'll see the archive files applied here.

```
ORA-279 signalled during: ALTER DATABASE RECOVER   standby database   ...
Fri Jan 07 06:51:49 2002
ALTER DATABASE RECOVER    CONTINUE DEFAULT
Fri Jan 07 06:51:49 2002
Media Recovery Log /oralog/oradata/STANDBY/archive/70.arc
```

TIP
Use automatic shipping of the log files to reduce the administration involved. If you choose to deploy a standby database using manual recovery, you'll want to pay plenty of attention to the transport and application of redo files. Typically, these processes are scripted to run unattended and detect errors.

Task 3: Enable Managed Recovery

To enable managed recovery, you'll need to configure Net8 so that the archiver process on the primary can communicate with the RFS process on the standby. After you have Net8 configured, you must instruct the primary archiver to write archive log files to a Net8 service in addition to the local directory. Finally, the standby database is configured to recover in managed mode. The archive files get shipped from the PRACTICE database and applied to the STANDBY database automatically until you cancel the recovery.

Configure the Net8 configuration files with the Net8 assistant. Set up an entry for your new STANDBY database for both the listener.ora and the tnsnames.ora. Create a new database service named STANDBY using the IPC protocol for the listener. (The IPC protocol is used because the database is local to the machine.) Configure the tnsnames.ora file for a new service named STANDBY. The goal is to allow the PRACTICE database to connect via the listener to the STANDBY instance. This connection will be created and used each time an archive log is sent from the primary to the standby. Restart the listener so that your changes will take effect.

NOTE
If using a remote standby, the tnsnames.ora for the standby server will be using IPC to communicate with STANDBY. On the primary server, the tnsnames.ora file will use TCP because the archive log files will be transported over the network.

Once connectivity has been configured, instruct the standby database to begin managed recovery. Connect to the mounted STANDBY database as SYS and instruct the managed recovery to begin.

```
SQL> RECOVER MANAGED STANDBY DATABASE;
```

When you issue this command, you might think that the command gets stuck. You don't get any feedback; the SQL prompt does not return. This behavior is expected. The STANDBY database has started the RFS background process to receive any transmitted archive log from the PRACTICE database. When an archive log is sent, it is copied from the Net8 transmission to the /oradata/STANDBY/archive directory. RFS also updates the standby control file with the new archive log information. Once the archive log is reproduced at the STANDBY archive destination directory, the file is applied to the STANDBY database. The recover process checks for new archive logs every 15 seconds. This work of reproducing archive logs and applying them continues until the managed recovery is cancelled.

```
SQL> RECOVER MANAGED STANDBY DATABASE CANCEL;
```

This cancel command must be issued from a different SQL*Plus session on the STANDBY database.

Finally, instruct the primary database to begin writing archive logs to the new service you've configured. Add the second archive log destination to the PRACTICE database parameter file and restart the instance. Because the LOG_ARCHIVE_DEST_N can be set dynamically, connect as SYS to the PRACTICE instance and use the ALTER SYSTEM command to begin writing to a Net8 service also. Whenever a database parameter is set in this way, remember to also add it to the init.ora file to ensure it remains set after the database has been restarted.

```
SQL> ALTER SYSTEM SET LOG_ARCHIVE_DEST_2 = "MANDATORY service=STANDBY reopen=30"
```

The archiver will write archive files to a Net8 service. The mandatory keyword says the transfer must succeed before online redo can be written over. The reopen keyword defines the time in seconds to retry the file transfer operation should an error be returned to the archiver process. Archive files will now be written to the Net8 service named STANDBY.

You can turn archive log transfer off and on by setting the LOG_ARCHIVE_DEST_STATE_N dynamic parameter. If the transfer of archive logs fails for some reason, such as a network problem, you might turn off the transmission of files to the standby:

```
SQL> ALTER SYSTEM SET LOG_ARCHIVE_DEST_STATE_2 = DEFER;
```

Deferring the transmission of archives allows the primary database to continue to write archive files to local disk. You don't want the database to stop because the archiver can't write to a destination. Once the standby archive destination has been reestablished, the archive log files produced during the deferred time will have to be manually copied to the standby site. Then you can re-enable the shipment of archive files via Net8.

```
SQL> ALTER SYSTEM SET LOG_ARCHIVE_DEST_STATE_2 = ENABLE;
```

Task 4: Confirm Managed Recovery

How can you know if the managed archive propagation process is running properly? You can look in three places:.

1. **Archive files** Look at the STANDBY database archive destination for archive logs being transmitted from the primary. New archive log files on the PRACTICE database will be reproduced in the /oradata/STANDBY/archive directory.

2. **Standby alert log** Check the STANDBY alert.log for archive logs application entries. If you haven't seen any activity yet, perform a few log switches on the PRACTICE database. Wait a few minutes and look for evidence that the new archive logs were transported and applied.

```
Media Recovery Log /oradata/STANDBY/archive/71.arc
Media Recovery Waiting for thread 1 seq# 72
```

3. **Log history** The third and final test is to select from v$log_history on both the primary and standby databases. The following query should return the same number, bearing in mind that the standby might be a few seconds behind:.

```
SQL> SELECT MAX(sequence#) FROM v$log_history;
```

Exercise 7.3: Open the Standby Database in Read-Only

You can see that your standby database is mounted and is staying current with the primary database. It is now possible, starting from 8*i*, to open the standby database in read-only mode. Why would you want to do this? It allows the DBA to check the standby database is functioning correctly because it can be opened and data can be queried. The standby can also be used as a reporting database to reduce such an impact on the primary database. No data can be changed when the standby database is opened in read-only mode. The archive log files will continually be transferred from the primary database but not applied. This will only happen when the standby is returned to recovery mode.

NOTE
While the standby database is open in read-only mode, archive log files from the primary database are not *being applied. Therefore, keeping the standby database open for long periods of time will dramatically increase the amount of time required to activate it when the primary fails.*

Task Description	Minutes
1. Generate Database Activity	5
2. Open the Standby Database in Read Only mode	15
3. Return the Standby to recovery mode	10
Total Time	30

This exercise will have you generate some activity in the PRACTICE database, stop the recovery for the standby database, and open it in read-only mode to see that the new activity has been propagated. At the end, you will put the standby database back into recovery mode.

Task 1: Generate Database Activity
Connect to the PRACTICE instance and generate some rows in TINA.DATE_LOG by inserting a row with a timestamp in the future. You can look for this row on the STANDBY database when you open it for queries.

```
SQL> INSERT INTO tina.date_log VALUES (SYSDATE+365*7);
SQL> ALTER SYSTEM SWITCH LOGFILE;
```

Be sure to switch the log files so that a new archive log file is created and propagated on the STANDBY database.

Task 2: Open the Standby Database in Read-Only Mode
Keep the STANDBY database in managed recovery mode until the new archive log(s) are transported and applied. These new archive logs will contain the new row you inserted in the previous task. Cancel the recovery on the STANDBY database.

```
SQL> RECOVER MANAGED STANDBY DATABASE CANCEL;
```

Open the STANDBY database so you can select rows from the TINA.DATE_LOG table.

```
SQL> ALTER DATABASE OPEN READ ONLY;
```

See if the rows you inserted on the PRACTICE database have arrived on the STANDBY database.

To test the continual transfer of log files from the PRACTICE database, insert some more rows into the TINA.DATE_LOG table as described at the beginning of this exercise. After the SWITCH LOGFILE command has been issued, the archive log file should appear in /oradata/STANDBY/archive.

NOTE

If large queries that will require more sort space than defined by SORT_AREA_SIZE are going to run against the standby database, a temporary tablespace must be added to the standby. By using a tablespace of type temporary and a local managed temporary datafile, it will not interfere with the read-only nature of the standby database. This is documented in the Oracle 8i Standby Database Concepts and Administration Guide.

Task 3: Return the Standby Database to Recovery Mode

To place the STANDBY database back in recover mode from being open in read-only, you have to shut down the database first.

```
SQL> SHUTDOWN IMMEDIATE;
SQL> STARTUP NOMOUNT;
SQL> ALTER DATABASE MOUNT STANDBY DATABASE;
SQL> RECOVER MANAGED STANDBY DATABASE;
```

Issuing the recovery command will commence application of the waiting archive log files that were transferred from the primary database during the period of time the standby was open in read-only mode.

Exercise 7.4: Activate the Standby Database

When the primary database fails, the standby database can be activated to become the new primary. When the standby database is activated, it becomes an open database just like the primary was. It is not something that can be practiced, undone, and tried a second time. During activation, the online redo logs are reset (similar to opening with the RESETLOGS option), and the log files from the primary database can no longer be applied to the standby. Don't activate the standby to see if changes are being propagated; instead, open the standby in read-only mode. If the standby is activated by mistake, it must be recreated by following the steps used during its original creation. If the standby is activated unnecessarily, the primary will no longer have a standby until another one is created.

Be sure to take a backup (hot or cold) of the newly activated standby database as soon as it is open. There is no second standby in this example, although this can easily be configured for a more complex environment. If no backups are taken and the standby database failed, you have to resort to a restoration and recovery.

Task Description	Minutes
1. Stop recovery of the standby database	5
2. Activate the standby database	5
Total Time	10

This exercise will guide you through the simple steps necessary to activate the standby database.

Task 1: Stop Recovery of the Standby Database

You can simulate the failure of a primary database by shutting down the PRACTICE instance and activating the STANDBY instance. The standby database will still be in recovery mode at this point, so you need to shut it down and then activate it. Before recovery stops, make sure all the archive log files that were transferred to the standby archive log destination have been applied correctly. This can be achieved by using any of three methods outlined in "Confirm Managed Recovery" (Exercise 7-2, Task 4). Then shut down the standby database cleanly:

```
SQL> RECOVER MANAGED STANDBY DATABASE CANCEL;
```

Task 2: Activate the Standby Database

This is the point of no return. In a production environment, this must be a real emergency. Once the standby database has been activated, it is no different from any other Oracle database. To activate the standby database, first make sure you are connected to the right server (the same host in these exercises), your ORACLE_SID is set correctly, and you are connected to the database as a SYSDBA user. Recovery has just been cancelled, so the standby database is currently in a mounted state.

```
SQL> ALTER DATABASE ACTIVATE STANDBY DATABASE;
SQL> SHUTDOWN;
SQL> STARTUP
```

Online redo log files will be created in the /oradata/STANDBY directory, and the control file now becomes a primary control file. In order to make the database usable after the activation, it must be shut down and restarted.

NOTE

In a production environment, it is important to do two things now: back up your new primary database and create a new standby database. Without doing these two operations, you are in danger of losing your database should another failure occur.

Good going! You built, managed, opened, and activated a standby database.

Recommendations

The exercises in this chapter taught you how to deploy a standby database. This standby is not as complete as one would implement in a production environment. Implementing a true standby site involves use of a different machine at a different site. If you choose the Oracle standby feature, you'll want to follow several best practices:

■   Direct load operations that have occurred on the primary database need special attention. For example, if you use SQL*Loader to load data with the direct option, these operations are logged differently in the redo logs, which will invalidate the affected data blocks on the standby database.

■   Many physical changes to the primary database require a manual response on the standby database. For example, if you add a datafile on the primary, you'll have to add the datafile on the standby.

■   Consider experimenting with switchover and switchback between two database servers. This simulates failing over to a standby database, which becomes the primary. Switchback involves moving the primary database back to the primary server.

■   Look into deploying the Data Guard feature, which is available in Oracle 9*i* and on certain platforms in 8*i*. Data Guard provides many new features that help to prevent or minimize losses due to human errors, propagation problems, disasters, and data corruption.

Troubleshooting

During a standby deployment, you may encounter a number of errors. Here's list of common errors you might run across.

1. **ORA-00283: recovery session canceled due to errors.**
    When you initiate managed standby recovery from a SQL*Plus session, you'll have to cancel managed recovery from a different SQL*Plus session. Once the cancel command completes from the first session, the first session may not respond immediately. Press ENTER in the first SQL*Plus session, and you'll see this error. The error this message refers to is your cancellation of managed recovery. This message is expected, unless a number of other error messages are also reported.

2. **Managed recovery doesn't seem to be working.** If you don't see media recovery messages in the standby alert.log, look at a number of other things:

■ Look at the v$archive_dest on both databases to confirm that the archive logs being produced on the primary database are going to a location that the standby database is reading from.

■ Check that the sequence number of archive logs expected by the standby is correct. You can track archive log sequences by checking the standby alert.log to see which log file it is expecting. This can then be compared against the log files that have been propagated from the primary.

■ Check network connectivity to the STANDBY service with the tnsping utility. If the network link between the primary and secondary becomes unavailable or the standby listener is down, the logs cannot be transferred.

■ Check the primary alert.log for archiver error messages.

Summary

You've now had a taste of standby database deployment. You created a standby database of the PRACTICE database on your Oracle server. You learned the important parameter file settings for a standby database. You also learned the important standby database commands including RECOVER, OPEN READ ONLY, and ACTIVATE. This is a brief study in what can be an advanced solution, but I hope you've gained some confidence and familiarity with the highlights of a standby implementation. You can build on what you've experienced in these exercises when you deploy a true standby solution. Read through the *Oracle 8i Standby Database Concepts and Administration Guide* for all the details on successfully implementing an Oracle standby database. You can also find helpful standby database white papers on the Oracle Metalink Web site.

Chapter Questions

As a refresher, try these questions to reinforce the concepts and exercises in this chapter.

1. What command do you use to mount a standby database?

   A. ALTER DATABASE MOUNT STANDBY;

   B. ALTER SYSTEM MOUNT STANDBY DATABASE;

   C. ALTER DATABASE MOUNT STANDBY DATABASE;

   D. ALTER DATABASE OPEN STANDBY DATABASE;

2. Why do you recover a standby database? (Pick any that apply.)

   A. The standby database is broken.

   B. Changes from the primary archive logs must be applied to the standby.

   C. The online redo logs on the standby have been reset.

   D. Recovery on the standby keeps it current with the primary.

3. You can continue recovering the standby while it is open for queries.

   A. True

   B. False

4. Managed standby recovery will automatically keep the standby database current with the primary database. How does the managed recovery keep the standby current? (Pick any that apply.)

   A. The standby database spawns a background process to reproduce archive logs.

   B. Archive logs are sent from the primary via Net8.

   C. Archive logs are applied to the standby automatically.

   D. Your manager performs recovery while you play golf.

5. When you activate the standby database, you reset the online logs on the standby database.

   A. True

   B. False

Answers to Chapter Questions

1. C   Alter the database and mount it as a standby database. (Funny that you'd have the word database twice in the same command.)

2. B, D   Changes made to the primary must be propagated to the standby. Those changes contained in the primary archive logs. When those logs get shipped and applied on the standby, the changes exist in the standby. The application of archive logs occurs on the standby via the RECOVER command.

3. False   The standby recovery and open states are mutually exclusive. Oracle does not recommend using a standby for queries over extended periods because the archive logs are not being applied to the standby. Therefore, the standby is not being kept up to date with the primary.

4. A, B, C   In manual recovery, you have to send archive files from the primary to the standby and apply them. With managed recovery, the archive files are sent from the primary via Net8 to a background process on the standby. These transferred archive files are periodically applied to the standby database. Your manager has nothing to do with this.

5. True   Your standby database operates without online redo log files until activation. Upon activation, the online logs are reset. This database can no longer serve as a substitute for the primary database.

CHAPTER
8

Export and Import

p to now, each backup and recovery activity discussed in this book has been a physical operation. You've been learning about the physical files that make up the database and how to protect the database by working with those files. What if you just want to copy database data and objects out of and into an Oracle database? You can also copy the logical contents of a database into an Oracle binary-format dump file that is located on disk or tape. The contents of this binary file can be read into an Oracle database to recreate the objects contained within it. This logical transfer of data objects can occur on the same Oracle database or between Oracle databases, even if they reside on platforms with different hardware and software configurations. The two companion Oracle utilities that accomplish this logical database transfer are Export and Import.

When you run Export against an Oracle database, all nondata dictionary objects (such as tables) are extracted to a file. The Import utility reads the object definitions and table data from an Export dump file and creates the objects into an Oracle database. The export files can be used as backups in addition to normal physical backup procedures. Note these points about the Export/Import utilities:

- Export dump files can be read only by the Oracle Import utility.

- The version of the Import utility cannot be earlier than the version of the Export utility used to create the dump file.

- The database must be open when running Export or Import against it.

- Export and Import can run from any Net8 client; the file processed is always local to the client machine. Be aware that a Net8 export or import can cause excessive network traffic.

When you run Export/Import, there are four modes that describe the scope of work to be performed when extracting or inserting database content:

- **Full database mode**   During export, the entire database contents are written to a file with a few exclusions. Certain user's objects are not exported including SYS, ORDSYS, CTXSYS, MDSYS, and ORDPLUGINS. Database structure information like tablespace definitions and rollback segments do get included. The export parameter defining full database mode is FULL. During import, all database objects that are contained in the export file are created in the database. The import parameter defining user mode is FULL=Y.

- **User mode**   During export, all database objects owned by the specified user(s) are written to a file. You specify these users with the OWNER parameter. All tables, indexes, views, triggers, synonyms, database links, objects, stored code, and so on owned by this owner get written to the export file. During import, all database objects owned by named users within the export file are created in the database. The imported users are specified with the FROMUSER parameter.

■   **Table mode**   During export, individual tables and associated objects (for example, indexes, constraints, triggers, grants) are written to a file. Each table must be named using the TABLES parameter. Only privileged users can export tables owned by other owners. During import, tables are read from an export file and created in the database. The import parameter defining table mode is also TABLES.

■   **Tablespace mode**   During export, metadata about the selected tablespaces and all objects contained within these tablespaces gets written to a file. Actual table data (rows) is not written to the export file. The export file produced, along with the tablespace datafiles, is copied from the source database to the target database. During import, the tablespace and object metadata gets added to the target database. The only time this mode of export is used in 8*i* is for transporting a tablespace from one database to another (Transportable Tablespaces). Tablespace export is demonstrated and explained in Chapter 9.

Bear in mind, the mode of a file created by the Export utility execution is exclusive from the mode of import on that file. For example, you can do a table mode import using an export file created in full database mode.

The privileges of the user running the Export utility define which modes that user can invoke. Any user with CREATE SESSION privilege can perform table or owner mode exports on their own schema. Only privileged DBA users, with the DBA, SYSDBA or EXP_FULL_DATABASE roles, can perform table or owner mode exports on schemas other than their own. Also, only privileged users who have been granted the EXP_FULL_DATABASE system privilege can perform full database and tablespace exports.

The privileges of the user running the Import utility work differently from the Export utility. A user with IMP_FULL_DATABASE role can do an import from an export file, even if that user did not create the export file. While an import executes, the connect user must have permission to perform the command specified in the export file. For example, if the import run must execute a CREATE TABLE command from the export file, then the user running the import must have that command privilege for that command to work.

Oracle Export and Import utilities are controlled by a number of parameters. Several parameters are common to both utilities. Table 8-1 contains a list of the common parameters and a brief description of each.

Parameter	Description

Userid	The required userid parameter provides the database user id and password for the user running the Export or Import utility. If you plan to connect locally as SCOTT, you'd type:
	`userid=scott/tiger`
	If you plan to connect over Net8, you'd type:
	`userid=scott/tiger@practice`
	If you must run export or import as SYSDBA, you'd type:
	`userid="scott/tiger as SYSDBA"`

File	The file parameter defines the file name that export will create or the import will read. You can fully qualify the path name. If you supply only the file name, the file will be created or read from the current directory. If you do not supply a file name, both utilities will look for expdat.dmp in the current working directory.
Log	Screen output of an Export/Import can be captured to a file defined by the log parameter. You can fully qualify the path name. If you supply only the file name, the file will be created in the current directory.
Help	At the command prompt, you can type **help=y** to get a brief listing of all parameters for either the Export or Import utility. When you list the contents of export with the HELP parameter, some parameters have a default value shown in parentheses after the description. For example: ROWS Export Data Rows (Y) says that the parameter named ROWS exports the data rows by default.
Parfile	Parameters for an Export/Import can be read from a file called a parameter file. To supply a parameter file, provide a file name to the parfile parameter. This file should contain a list of parameters and their associated values.
Tables	Use the tables parameter for export to extract tables in the tables list or to import tables contained within an export file.
Rows	Use the row parameter to instruct export to extract table rows within each exported table or to instruct the import to insert table rows within each imported table.

TABLE 8-1.   *Important Common Parameters between Export and Import*

Both Export and Import contain many other parameters. Some of them will be explained later in this chapter during the exercises. A few parameters are common between Export and Import but have different meaning or connotation:

- **Full**   A full export means extract all the contents of the entire database. A full import means to read and create all the contents of an export file.

- **Owner versus Fromuser/Touser**   The owner parameter in an export extracts all objects owned by the named owners. If the owners of the objects in the export file need to change during the import, Fromuser will specify the original object owner contained in the export file. Touser specifies the new schema to create and own the imported objects. For example, I can export Stephan's objects and want to import them into Kenny's schema. You would use these import parameters: FROMUSER=STEPHAN TOUSER =KENNY.

The Oracle Export/Import utilities have some valuable uses and features, including:

- **Backup and recovery**   Export and Import are useful for application development, data migration, and transportable tablespaces. They can be handy for various DBA tasks but are not a quality backup and recovery strategy. At best, an export is a snapshot of tables as they existed at a single point in time. If you lose a table or datafile, you'll have a difficult time replacing all data using an export file and the import utility if the tables are dynamic in nature. You cannot apply redo to a table that has been imported. Perhaps, however, exports can be useful to augment a true backup and recovery strategy—for example, exporting key static tables after new data has been loaded into them.

- **Block corruptions**   You can export your entire database or key tables to find block corruptions in tables. An export issues a full table scan against the tables being exported that forces every block to be read and checked for media corruption.

- **Crossing database versions**   You can copy schema and data from a source Oracle database of one version to a target Oracle database of a different version. When you export data from the source database, use the export version of the database with the earliest version of the two databases. When you import data into the target database, use the import version of the target database.

- **Crossing operating systems**   You can use Export/Import to move data from an Oracle database on one OS to another Oracle database on the same or different OS. (Oracle 8*i* transportable tablespaces cannot be transported to a database on a different OS.)

■ **Character support** The National Language Support (NLS) feature in Oracle presents characters, numbers, symbols, calendars, and so on adapted to support native languages. Pay careful attention if you see the words POSSIBLE CHARSET CONVERSION during an export or import. Note the export and import clients' character set values and adjust the NLS_LANG environment variable setting as needed.

In this chapter, you'll have the opportunity to perform a variety of simple Export/Import operations as shown in Figure 8-1. I'll show you how to perform Export/Import on the entire database (database mode), for one or more users (user mode) and for one or more tables (table mode). You'll have the chance to run Export/Import interactively. You'll also see how you can control these utilities via command line parameters and via a parameter file. Most exercises in this chapter will use a parameter file. Next chapter, I'll show you how to use Export/Import with Transportable Tablespaces.

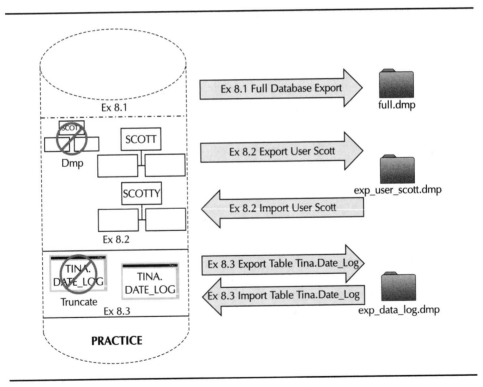

FIGURE 8-1. *Export and Import of the PRACTICE database*

Database Mode Export and Import

The first mode of Export/Import you'll perform involves the full database. Export operations in the first exercise will be performed against the entire database. Import operations will be performed against the entire export file.

Exercise 8.1: Export the Full Database

In this exercise, you will create a full database export of the PRACTICE database.

Task Description	Minutes
1. Export Full Database Interactively	10
2. Export Full Database via Command Line	10
3. Export Full Database via Parameter File	10
4. Export Full Database in Direct Mode	10
5. Import Full Database for Show	10
Total Time	50

You will perform the same full database export several times to illustrate your options in invoking and controlling the Export utility. In the final task, you'll look at the contents of the export file using the Import utility.

Task 1: Export Full Database Interactively

In this task, you can create a full database export file by running the Export utility interactively. As you look at the prompts from the Export utility, you can learn the keywords used to control it. From the OS prompt, start an export run by typing **exp**. Once you press ENTER, you'll be asked a battery of questions:

1. **username** The user name that will perform the export. Any user can export their own schema. (To export objects other than tables you own, connect as a user with the EXP_FULL_DATABASE or a DBA role). For this exercise, connect as SYS. If you want to connect to a database over Net8, enter the username followed by the service name (**sys@practice**).

2. **password** Specifies the password for the username just entered.

3. **buffer size** Specifies the size, in bytes, of the buffer used to fetch rows. Accept the default. When the buffer is filled, its contents are written to the export file.

4. **Export file** The Export utility creates a binary file containing version information, run specifics, object-creation commands and table-insert statements. Accept the default file name of expdat.dmp.

5. **entire database** Defines the scope of your export. You can export the entire database, one or more users, or one or more tables. Choose 1 for a full database export.

6. **grants** Specifies whether or not the Export utility exports object grants. All object grants should get exported on a full database export. Choose yes.

7. **table data** You can export tables with or without table data. Because we want the entire database contents to be included, choose yes.

8. **extents** If you compress extents, the object creation command created in the import consolidates all data into one initial extent upon import. If you do not compress extents, an object will be created with the same extent settings as they existed at export. Choose no.

As the export runs, screen output shows the work performed. When the export completes, a file will have been created named expdat.dmp in the directory where the export command ran. That file contains a copy of all schema objects owned by every user except user SYS, ORDSYS, CTXSYS, MDSYS, and ORDPLUGINS.

Task 2: Export Full Database via Command Line

Typically, you'll want to supply all export parameters at the command line or via a command file. You can put the command-line parameters together on one line to supply all the information needed by the Export utility. If you do not supply a required parameter, Export will prompt you for a parameter value. To export the entire database using command-line parameters to a specific file, supply the USERID, FILE, and FULL parameters:

```
LINUX> exp USERID=sys/practice
FILE=/oradata/PRACTICE/backup/ch08/full.dmp FULL=Y
```

Each keyword is followed by a value or value set. You can omit the userid keyword, and the user and password values are assumed to be the first value.

```
LINUX> exp sys/practice FILE=/oradata/PRACTICE/backup/ch08/full.dmp
FULL=Y
```

The resulting file created from this command is named /oradata/PRACTICE/backup/ch08/full.dmp.

Task 3: Export Full Database via Parameter File

If you don't want to supply keyword values as command-line parameters, you can provide a parameter file that Export can read. You can run the exact same export as you ran in the previous task by placing the parameters into a file. To supply a parameter file name to export, add the parfile keyword with a file name containing commands:

```
LINUX> exp parfile=export_full.par
```

The contents of the export_full.par file look like this:

```
# Export the entire database
USERID   = sys/practice
FILE     = /oradata/PRACTICE/backup/ch08/full.dmp
LOG      = /oradata/PRACTICE/backup/ch08/full.log
FULL     = Y
ROWS     = N
BUFFER   = 10000
COMPRESS = N
```

The USERID, FILE, and FULL keywords are the same as the command-line example above. I also added other useful parameters:

- **Log** All output from the export execution will be logged to a file named /oradata/PRACTICE/backup/ch08/full.log

- **Buffer** The size of the buffer used to fetch rows will be 10,000 bytes. Setting this parameter appropriately will help large exports run faster. I chose an arbitrary value of 10,000 bytes for illustration.

- **Rows** Data rows make up the bulk of the export file contents. You can instruct the export utility to only export the object definitions and not the data rows by setting ROWS = N.

- **Compress** Compress will cause each object to be created on import with one initial extent sized large enough to hold the entire object. This does not mean the export file is compressed using a compression algorithm.

Note the following points about the full export:

1. The export overwrote the previous export file. You will not be warned if the export file already exists.

2. You can specify parameters on the command line and in the parameter file. If the same parameter is specified on both, the command-line parameter takes precedence.

Task 4: Export Full Database in Direct Mode

Conventional path export, which is the default, uses SQL SELECT statements to extract data from tables. In order to do this, the same process is followed as when you manually issue a select against a table. The data blocks are read from the datafiles on disk and passed through the database buffer cache. The data is evaluated and then written out to the export dump file.

Direct path export avoids the buffer cache almost completely. The data is read directly from the datafiles, bypassing the database buffer cache. Certain blocks like the segment header and possibly consistent read data will still pass through the buffer cache. Direct path export will run significantly faster on larger tables because of this.

For your small PRACTICE database, you won't see a big improvement in speed via the direct path. For a large database, you may see a direct path export run several times faster than conventional path exports.

Run a full database export using a parameter file like the one shown here:

```
# Export the entire database with direct option
USERID   = sys/practice
FILE     = /oradata/PRACTICE/backup/ch08/full.dmp
LOG      = /oradata/PRACTICE/backup/ch08/full.log
FULL     = Y
COMPRESS = N
DIRECT   = Y
```

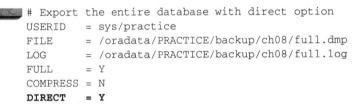

TIP
If you have a very large amount of data for export, you can supply a maximum file size for each export file and name several files to be created. For example: if you have a 2GB operating system file size limit, you could specify FILESIZE=2000m and name your files with the FILE parameter in a list. (FILE=exp1.dmp, exp2.dmp, exp3.dmp). Each file will have a maximum size of 2GB, but the last file could be smaller if not enough data to reach 2GB is exported.

Task 5: Import Full Database for Show

The Import utility uses the export file to copy objects and data into a database. You can also use it to display the contents of an export file. Two parameters that create output and do not change the database are SHOW and INDEX FILE. In this task, you can run an import to see the contents of the export dump file.

Use the show parameter to display the output of the import, as below. Create another parameter file named import_full.par and place these parameter values in that file.

```
USERID = sys/practice
FILE   = /oradata/PRACTICE/backup/ch08/full.dmp
LOG    = /oradata/PRACTICE/backup/ch08/full.dmp
FULL   = Y
SHOW   = Y
```

You can run this file from the Linux prompt using an executable program named *imp*.

```
LINUX> imp parfile=import_full.par
```

The contents of the export file (also known as a dump file) go flying across your screen. They are also recorded to the file specified by the LOG parameter. Using an editor, open up the log file of screen output to see what's inside:

```
. importing TINA's objects into TINA
"ALTER SCHEMA = "TINA""
"CREATE TABLE "DATE_LOG" ("CREATE_DATE" DATE)  PCTFREE 10 PCTUSED 40 INITRAN"
"S 1 MAXTRANS 255 LOGGING STORAGE(INITIAL 196608 NEXT 65536 MINEXTENTS 1 MAX"
"EXTENTS 4096 PCTINCREASE 0 FREELISTS 1 FREELIST GROUPS 1 BUFFER_POOL DEFAUL"
"T) TABLESPACE "TOOLS""
. . skipping table "DATE_LOG"
...
. importing TINA's objects into TINA
"ALTER SCHEMA = "TINA""
"CREATE PROCEDURE INSERT_DATE_LOG_ROW"
"IS"
"-- Purpose: Insert a row with the current time into DATE_LOG."
"BEGIN"
"  INSERT INTO DATE_LOG (create_date) VALUES (SYSDATE);"
"END;"
"ALTER PROCEDURE "INSERT_DATE_LOG_ROW" COMPILE TIMESTAMP '2001-09-12:09:36:29'"
...
"CREATE UNIQUE INDEX "CREATE_DATE_PK" ON "DATE_LOG" ("CREATE_DATE" )  PCTFRE"
"E 10 INITRANS 2 MAXTRANS 255 STORAGE(INITIAL 393216 NEXT 65536 MINEXTENTS 1"
" MAXEXTENTS 4096 PCTINCREASE 0 FREELISTS 1 FREELIST GROUPS 1 BUFFER_POOL DE"
"FAULT) TABLESPACE "INDX" LOGGING"
"ALTER TABLE "DATE_LOG" ADD  CONSTRAINT "CREATE_DATE_PK" PRIMARY KEY ("INSER"
"T_TIME") USING INDEX PCTFREE 10 INITRANS 2 MAXTRANS 255 STORAGE(INITIAL 393"
"216 NEXT 65536 MINEXTENTS 1 MAXEXTENTS 4096 PCTINCREASE 0 FREELISTS 1 FREEL"
"IST GROUPS 1 BUFFER_POOL DEFAULT) TABLESPACE "INDX" ENABLE "
...
. importing TINA's objects into TINA
"ALTER SCHEMA = "TINA""
"BEGIN   sys.dbms_ijob.submit(job=>1,luser=>'TINA',puser=>'TINA',cuser=>'TIN"
"A',next_date=>to_date('2001-10-01:09:48:15','YYYY-MM-DD:HH24:MI:SS'),interv"
"al=>'(SYSDATE + 1/(24*60))',broken=>FALSE,what=>'tina.insert_date_log_row;',nls"
```

```
"env=>'NLS_LANGUAGE=''AMERICAN'' NLS_TERRITORY=''AMERICA'' NLS_CURRENCY=''$'"
"' NLS_ISO_CURRENCY=''AMERICA'' NLS_NUMERIC_CHARACTERS=''.,'' NLS_DATE_FORMA"
"T=''DD-MON-RR'' NLS_DATE_LANGUAGE=''AMERICAN'' NLS_SORT=''BINARY''',env=>'0"
"102000200000000'); END;"
```

I've listed some excerpts from the file that show how parts of the TINA schema look. (Ugly, isn't it? To make this output usable for creating the objects, you'd have to edit this file or clean it up with a script.) First in the file, you see the definition of TINA's tables. Next, you see the source code of her stored PL/SQL code. You can see the code for the INSERT_DATE_LOG_ROW procedure you wrote in Chapter 3. Finally, you see a job entry for the Oracle job, which calls the procedure. By looking through this file, you see a preview of the import process. Notice two things in this output file:

1. You can see the order that database objects were exported and will get imported. Tables are imported before indexes. Stored procedures come before Oracle jobs.

2. The text definitions in the log files have been wrapped within words. Using the show file output to recreate stored code requires significant editing.

If you just want the table and index definitions contained within an export file, use the INDEXFILE parameter. You can create a file containing just the tables and indexes, shown here.

```
USERID = sys/practice
FILE   = /oradata/PRACTICE/backup/ch08/full.dmp
INDEXFILE = /oradata/PRACTICE/backup/ch08/full.idx
FULL   = Y
```

Look at the resulting index file and notice that the table definitions have been remarked. You can remove the comments and recreate the table also by running this file.

Extra Credit
If you want to copy a database, you can follow the steps described in Chapter 6. You can also copy a database using Export/Import. To do this, create a new database with no objects other than default ones (data dictionary objects). Perform a full export of the source database. Using that export file, import the entire file into the newly created database. Export/Import works well if your databases are on different operating systems. Try creating a new database and import a full export from the PRACTICE database. First, you create a new empty database containing the SYSTEM, RBS, TEMP, and other tablespaces identical

in name to those of the PRACTICE database. After you've run all the needed catalog.sql, catproc.sql, and other data dictionary scripts to this new database, you are ready to perform a full import to the new database using the PRACTICE database export file.

User Mode Export and Import

You don't have to export the entire database with each Export run. You might instead choose to copy the logical contents of one or more users into a single export file. The primary reasons for exporting users are to protect application critical users and their data, create test environments, and copy schemas to different databases. Exports don't have to run by a DBA; developers can make schema copies of their own development data, for example.

Exercise 8.2: Replace and Clone User SCOTT

In this exercise, you will export user SCOTT's database objects to a single file. Using that file, you will be able to copy him back into the database and then create another user using this file.

Task Description	Minutes
1. Export User SCOTT	10
2. Drop User SCOTT	10
3. Import User SCOTT	10
4. Import User SCOTTY	10
Total Time	40

In these tasks, you will get some practice with imports. First, you'll create an export file containing all database objects for user SCOTT. After you drop user SCOTT, you will recreate him and import all his objects. Finally, you will copy the database objects owned by SCOTT into a user named SCOTTY.

Task 1: Export User SCOTT

Using a parameter file shown next, you can export the user named SCOTT:

```
# Export user Scott
USERID = sys/practice
```

```
FILE   = /oradata/PRACTICE/backup/ch08/export_user_scott.dmp
LOG    = /oradata/PRACTICE/backup/ch08/export_user_scott.log
OWNER  = SCOTT
```

The OWNER keyword specifies that this file contains data objects owned by SCOTT. If you want to export more than one user, include the owners within parentheses delimited by commas. If you look at the log file of this export defined by the LOG keyword, you will see the screen output created during the export.

Since user SCOTT has connect privileges on the database, he could have created his own export rather than relying on the DBA to do this task for him. If SCOTT were to create run export, he could use a parameter file like you see here:

```
# Export user Scott
USERID = scott/tiger
FILE   = /oradata/PRACTICE/backup/ch08/export_user_scott.dmp
LOG    = /oradata/PRACTICE/backup/ch08/export_user_scott.log
```

Notice that when you run an export connected as SCOTT, you don't have to supply the OWNER parameter. Since SCOTT can only export his own data objects, the Export utility assumes that if he does not specify a table, he wants to export his entire schema.

If you try to export owner TINA connected to SCOTT by specifying OWNER=TINA, you get this error message:

```
EXP-00032: Non-DBAs may not export other users
```

If you want to export one user's schema, you can run export as that user and supply the user password. If you need to export one or more users' schema and don't know the users' passwords, you can run export as a privileged DBA user and use the keyword OWNER. As a privileged user, you can export many user schemas in one pass.

Task 2: Drop User SCOTT
You can drop user SCOTT with the DROP USER command.

```
SQL> SELECT username FROM DBA_USERS;
SQL> DROP USER SCOTT CASCADE;
SQL> SELECT username FROM DBA_USERS;
```

The DROP USER command removes a user and all objects owned by that user. A data dictionary view named DBA_USERS contains a current list of all the database users. If you select from this view prior to the drop command, you will see that SCOTT is a user in the database. After the drop command, you won't see SCOTT in this (or any other) data dictionary view.

Task 3: Import User SCOTT

When you import SCOTT's schema, the SCOTT user account *must* already exist in the database. A user mode import does not create the user to be imported; it only creates the user objects:

```
SQL> GRANT CONNECT, RESOURCE TO SCOTT IDENTIFIED BY TIGER;
SQL> ALTER USER SCOTT DEFAULT TABLESPACE USERS TEMPORARY TABLESPACE TEMP;
```

After creating the user, you can import the objects.

You control the Import utility similar to the way you control the Export utility. You can run Import interactively or with a command-line parameter or a parameter file. To see the parameter keyword available, type the help keyword at the command prompt:

```
LINUX> imp help=y
```

Notice many of the parameters that are the same as export like USERID, FILE, LOG, and PARFILE. One keyword you don't see is OWNER. In Export, you perform user mode using the keyword OWNER. As a DBA, you perform user mode import with the keyword FROMUSER, as shown here:

```
# Import user Scott as a DBA
USERID = sys/practice
FILE = /oradata/PRACTICE/backup/ch08/export_user_scott.dmp
LOG  = /oradata/PRACTICE/backup/ch08/import_user_scott.log
FROMUSER = SCOTT
```

As SCOTT, you can import a file into your own schema without using the keyword FROMUSER, as shown here:

```
# Import user Scott as Scott
USERID = scott/tiger
FILE = /oradata/PRACTICE/backup/ch08/export_user_scott.dmp
LOG  = /oradata/PRACTICE/backup/ch08/import_user_scott.log
```

Task 4: Import User SCOTTY

SCOTT calls you up and says he needs some empty tables to test out his new application. He wants you to replicate all his schema objects into a new schema named SCOTTY. To accomplish this, you can import SCOTT's schema from the Task 1 export into a newly created user:

```
SQL> GRANT CONNECT, RESOURCE TO SCOTTY IDENTIFIED BY KITTY;
SQL> ALTER USER SCOTTY DEFAULT TABLESPACE USERS TEMPORARY TABLESPACE TEMP;
```

After creating the new user, you can import SCOTT's objects into the SCOTTY schema. This time, don't import the data, just the objects, as shown here:

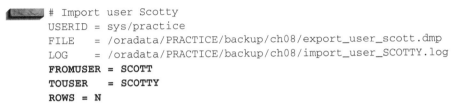

```
# Import user Scotty
USERID = sys/practice
FILE    = /oradata/PRACTICE/backup/ch08/export_user_scott.dmp
LOG     = /oradata/PRACTICE/backup/ch08/import_user_SCOTTY.log
FROMUSER = SCOTT
TOUSER   = SCOTTY
ROWS = N
```

Note some things about this parameter file:

- **Touser**   The contents of user SCOTT are imported from the export file into user SCOTTY.

- **Rows**   SCOTT's objects are created in SCOTTY's schema without any data rows.

In the import log file, you'll see an entry that looks like this, stating the owner translation:

```
. importing SCOTT's objects into SCOTTY
```

Table Mode Export and Import

The last mode we'll discuss in this chapter is table mode. Any user can accomplish this most granular mechanism of data object movement on their own schema. Only

Extra Credit

Sometimes you might need to import into a database that does not have the tablespaces for the database objects in the export file. If you import the contents of the file, objects will be created in the default tablespace of the owner if the requested tablespace does not exist. You are able to create the objects in a different tablespace and then import the rows. Try this: import all SCOTT's objects into SCOTTY's schema, but put all objects in the INDEX tablespace. Here's how to do it: create an index file from an import of the export file. Edit the index file created by removing the remarks and changing the tablespace in the text file for all the objects. Run the index file as a script in SQL*Plus to create all the database objects in SCOTTY's schema in the INDX tablespace. Once the objects are created, import the file with the keyword IGNORE = Y. The data rows will be imported into their new tablespace location using the newly created object structures.

privileged DBA users can Export/Import tables in another user's schema. Each table exported or imported always contains the table definitions and may optionally contain the table's indexes, constraints, triggers, grants, and so on. You can export many tables from multiple users into one export file. When you import in table mode, you can import many tables from multiple users contained within one export file.

Exercise 8.3: Export a Database Table

In this exercise, you will create a file containing one table in the TINA schema in the PRACTICE database.

Task Description	Minutes
1. Export Table	10
2. Truncate Table	10
3. Import Table	10
Total Time	30

You will export the TINA.DATE_LOG table using a where clause as specified by the query parameter. The query parameter allows an export to be taken from a table containing only those rows that meet the predicate in the query's where clause. After you truncate the TINA.DATE_LOG table, you will import the table from the export file. Finally, when you select the data from the TINA.DATE_LOG, it will only include rows created during the export.

Task 1: Export Table

Before you export some tables from the PRACTICE database, insert some rows into TINA.DATE_LOG dated in the future. You can insert 'SYSDATE+ 8' into the table so that the table will contain dates greater than today. Be sure to issue a commit after your inserts.

Create an export with three tables using a parameter file as shown in this example:

```
USERID   = sys/practice
FILE     = /oradata/PRACTICE/backup/ch08/export_date_log.dmp
LOG      = /oradata/PRACTICE/backup/ch08/export_date_log.log
TABLES   = (TINA.DATE_LOG)
QUERY    = "WHERE create_date < SYSDATE"
COMPRESS = N
DIRECT   = N
```

The export file will contain the definition of the TINA.DATE_LOG and the rows for the table meeting the WHERE clause.

Task 2: Truncate Table

You can quickly remove all data from the TINA.DATE_LOG table with the TRUNCATE TABLE command. Removing the data will not break the job and procedure that creates rows in this table.

```
SQL> SELECT count(*) from TINA.DATE_LOG;
SQL> SELECT count(*) from TINA.DATE_LOG
  2  WHERE create_date > SYSDATE;
SQL> TRUNCATE TABLE TINA.DATE_LOG;
SQL> SELECT count(*) from TINA.DATE_LOG;
```

After the truncate, you will not find any rows in the table.

TIP
If you have very large tables to import, use the COMMIT parameter to force a commit each time the buffer contents (specified by BUFFER) is filled and written to the table. By default, Oracle will commit when each table has been completely imported. This can cause the rollback segments to grow extremely large.

Task 3: Import Table

You can replace the rows in TINA.DATE_LOG with the data in the export file. To perform a table import, use the TABLES keyword to specify the rows you'd like to insert, as shown next.

```
USERID  = sys/practice
FILE    = /oradata/PRACTICE/backup/ch08/export_date_log.dmp
LOG     = /oradata/PRACTICE/backup/ch08/import_date_log.log
TABLES  = (TINA.DATE_LOG)
IGNORE  = Y
```

The IGNORE keyword tells import to insert data rows into any tables that already exist. If you don't specify this keyword, any attempt to import tables that already exist will cause an error, and the rows for that table will not be imported. Be aware that using IGNORE=Y could result in duplicate rows being inserted into the table if there are no unique constraints on the table preventing this.

Once the rows have been imported, check that you have rows in the table and none are greater than SYSDATE.

```
SQL> SELECT count(*) from TINA.DATE_LOG;
SQL> SELECT count(*) from TINA.DATE_LOG
  2  WHERE create_date > SYSDATE;
```

You should see plenty of rows now in the DATE_LOG table but none with a date greater than today. Note that when an export file has been created using the query parameter, that query condition is not written into the export file. When you import such a file, you have no way of knowing that the file being imported is not the contents of the entire table. If you keep an export log file with the export file, you'll be able to see parameters used when creating the file.

9*i* New Features

Here is a brief description of features that have been added to the Export/Import utilities in Oracle 9*i*. For a more in-depth technical look at these features, use the *Oracle 9*i *Utilities Guide*.

■ **Tablespace exports**   You can now export all objects that reside in a set of named tablespaces using the TABLESPACE parameter. This feature is different from Transportable Tablespaces. No checking is done to ensure that the objects are self-contained in each tablespace. The export file produced is the same as any other export file. The contents can be imported using a FULL, TABLES or FROMUSER/TOUSER.

■ **Table name pattern matching**   The table level export has been enhanced to allow table names with mixed case to be named for export. Before 9*i*, all tables were assumed to have uppercase names. Import now also allows you to export table names with mixed case characters.

■ **Resumable exports and imports**   You can now suspend an export and import if the Export/Import encounters a storage management related error. Such problems would include running out of disk space for the export file, hitting maximum extents limit on a table being imported, or running out of datafile space for an imported object. When the problem has been resolved, the export or import will continue. If the problem is not resolved within a specified timeout interval, the Export/Import will abort.

■ **Flashback exports**   With Oracle 9*i*, you can run a query and return the results at a previous point in time using an SCN or time value. Export can make use of this server capability. Using the FLASHBACK_SCN or FLASHBACK_TIME parameters, you can export objects the way they were at an earlier point in time. To use this feature, the database must be configured to use Automatic Undo Management with a suitable undo retention period defined.

Troubleshooting

If you run into problems during Export/Import operations, look over this list for possible solutions.

1. **EXP-00026: conflicting modes specified.** The export modes specified conflict with each other. For example, the parameters FULL, TABLES, and OWNER are mutually exclusive.

2. **IMP-00015: following statement failed because the object already exists.** You cannot create an object that already exists during an Import. Specify the IGNORE parameter to Y to disregard this error.

3. **ORA-00001: unique constraint (SCOTT.PK_EMP) violated.** You tried to insert a row that violated the primary key. Perhaps you've already imported the data contained in this export dump file.

4. **Partial Import success and partial failure** An import will perform the work that it can. If it encounters an error when creating a table, no rows will be inserted into that table. If import encounters an error while inserting a row, that row will not be inserted but other rows will. You'll have to look over the log files to figure out which part worked and which part didn't.

Summary

The Export and Import utilities provide you with a logical, file-based mechanism for moving database objects between Oracle databases and tablespaces (using the transportable tablespace feature). You can Export/Import the full database, a user(s) in a database, or a table(s) in a database. Though some use this tool as a logical backup and restore strategy, you will find it even more helpful as a data transfer mechanism. In the next chapter, I'll show you how to transport tablespaces between databases using export and import. If you want to know more about the Export and Import utilities, read Chapters 1 and 2 of the *Oracle 8i Utilities* manual.

Chapter Questions

Try to answer these questions to reinforce the concepts and exercises in this chapter.

1. Which parameters specify that a database export will extract data objects for one or more users? (Pick any that apply.)

    A. SCHEMA

    B. OWNER

    C. USER

    D. TABLES

2. Export dump files can be read only by the Oracle Import utility.

    A. True

    B. False

3. During an import, which of these table data objects are imported first?

    A. Table indexes

    B. Integrity constraints, views, procedures, and triggers

    C. Table definitions

    D. Table data

4. Which keyword(s) would you specify to the Import utility to specify that database objects owned by one user be created in another user? (Pick any that apply.)

    A. TOUSER

    B. OWNER

    C. USER

    D. FROMUSER

5. You can run a full import on an export dump file created with the TABLES mode keyword.

    A. True

    B. False

Answers to Chapter Questions

1. B, D. When you export data objects for a user, you define the users following the OWNER keyword. In an Oracle database, a user that has database objects in its schema is called the owner of those objects. You can use the tables parameter to specify multiple users tables/objects (TABLES=SCOTT.EMP, TINA.DATE_LOG).

2. True. An export dump file is an Oracle binary-format dump file that can only be read by the Oracle Import utility.

3. C. The tables must be created before the indexes, constraints, and data can be added to the table.

4. A, D. The FROMUSER parameter enables you to import a subset of schemas from an export file containing multiple schemas. The TOUSER parameter specifies a list of usernames whose schemas will be targets for import. When these parameters are used together, you can clone user objects from one user to another. If multiple schemas are specified, the schema names are paired.

5. True. The import full keyword specifies whether to import the entire export file. Since the export file contains only table definitions, all the table definitions in that file will be created by the Import utility on the connected database by the connected user.

CHAPTER
9

Tablespace Point In Time Recovery

ou have learned how to perform complete recovery of all or part of the database and incomplete recoveries of your entire Oracle database. You can also recover one or more tablespaces incompletely while keeping the rest of your database current. Under what conditions would an incomplete tablespace recovery option make sense?

- When a table is mistakenly dropped or truncated

- When table data has been logically corrupted

- When a batch job ran incorrectly on a portion of the database

- When a SQL statement mistakenly changed table data

- When full recovery of a very large database might take too long and only a subset of the database is required

You can recover one or more tablespaces of a database with a feature called tablespace point-in-time recovery (TSPITR), as shown in Figure 9-1. TSPITR enables recovery of one or more non-SYSTEM tablespaces to a point in time different from that of the rest of the database. To perform tablespace recovery, a portion of the source database is restored to an *auxiliary* instance. The auxiliary instance is used to recover chosen tablespaces to a point in time. Finally, transport the recovered tablespace(s) to the source database or export only the required objects from the recovered tablespace(s). In this chapter, you'll see how to perform a very simple TSPITR on your PRACTICE database. You can use this example to familiarize yourself with how you might accomplish this task in your real database environment.

In this chapter, you'll be exposed to some new terminology:

- **Auxiliary instance**   The background processes and memory structures that recover specific tablespaces. This instance will open the auxiliary database and will be called AUXY in this chapter.

- **Auxiliary database**   This is a copy or subset of the primary database for the temporary purpose of tablespace recovery. In this chapter, the AUXY instance will open a database named PRACTICE. This PRACTICE database will be a restored backup of the datafiles and control file from your primary PRACTICE database.

- **Primary database**   The database in need of TSPITR. In this chapter, it's the PRACTICE database whose USERS tablespace will be recovered to a different time from all other tablespaces in the primary database.

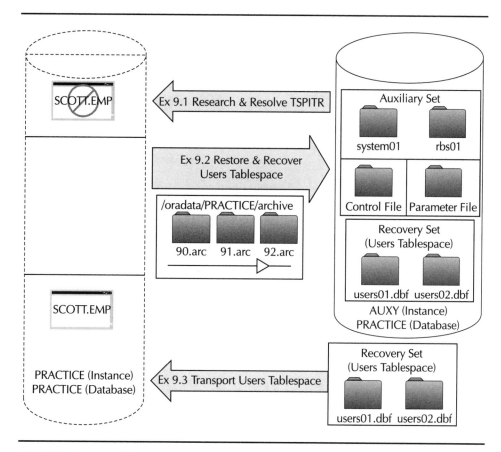

FIGURE 9-1. *Tablespace point-in-time recovery of the PRACTICE database*

- **Recovery set**   Datafiles comprising the tablespace(s) to be recovered to a point in time. The SYSTEM tablespace datafiles cannot be part of the recovery set. In this chapter, the recovery set is the two backup datafiles in USERS tablespace.

- **Auxiliary set**   Any database files required for tablespace recovery. In this chapter, the auxiliary set is the primary PRACTICE database backup control file, backup datafiles of the SYSTEM, RBS and TEMP tablespaces, the auxiliary database parameter file and the primary PRACTICE database archived log files.

When you consider the TSPITR using transportable tablespaces from Oracle, keep in mind several important considerations:

■ After TSPITR is complete, you cannot use existing backups of the recovery set datafiles. You must use new backups instead. This is due to the fact that older archived redo logs cannot be applied to these new files that were transported into the production database.

■ SQL that modifies data on an auxiliary instance used for TSPITR will fail because the auxiliary can only be used for recovery.

■ Some data objects are not allowed in a TSPITR recovery set; for example, tables with varray columns, nested tables, external bfiles, and so on.

■ Be aware of some general restrictions on transportable tablespaces in Oracle 8*i*. Source and target databases run on the same hardware architecture with the same operating system, have the same character set, and have the same block size.

In this chapter, you'll recover one tablespace to a previous point in time from the rest of the database. All this will be done to the PRACTICE database without ever shutting it down.

Tablespace Recovery Investigation

The mechanics of TSPITR are straightforward. In this chapter, when you perform TSPITR on the USERS tablespace, you create a partial copy of the PRACTICE database. This auxiliary database has the auxiliary set tablespace datafiles (system, rollback, and temporary tablespaces) and the recovery set tablespace datafiles of the USERS tablespace. All these tablespaces are recovered to a point in time. When incomplete recovery reaches the defined stop point, you transport the recovered datafiles of the USERS tablespace into the PRACTICE database. Many of these operations are similar to those covered in Chapter 6. The auxiliary database is created using a backup of the primary database (PRACTICE). The auxiliary instance opens the auxiliary database and uses the primary database archived log files to roll it forward in time, as described in Chapters 4 and 5. The restored datafiles can be from a closed or open backup.

When you perform TSPITR, you have to consider some unwanted ramifications. You may lose some objects and data in the recovered tablespace that were created after the time when you choose to stop recovery. You may also compromise relationships between objects in the recovered tablespace and objects not in the recovered tablespace. Unless you restore and recover all tablespaces that contain related objects, you must manually resolve any such relations. Investigating these risks and relationships can be a time-consuming task. Prior to any TSPITR, you should weigh the pros and cons of the operation by comparing the effort of cleaning up after TSPITR to the value gained via TSPITR. In Exercise 9.1, I'll show you a very simple scenario that investigates and resolves any issues that will arise when TSPITR is performed. In a real database, this process will be longer and much more involved.

Exercise 9.1: Research and Resolve Tablespace Recovery

In this exercise, you will break the PRACTICE database by "mistakenly" removing a table. Then you will investigate the trade-offs with a TSPITR.

Task Description	Minutes
1. Perform Open Database Backup	10
2. Drop Table SCOTT.EMP	10
3. Investigate TSPITR	10
Total Time	30

Before you perform TSPITR, you must investigate the possibility of application data inconsistencies between tables in recovered and unrecovered tablespaces. You want to know implicit referential dependencies that may need resolution before proceeding. Task 3 shows how you would find problems and resolve them before you proceed with TSPITR.

Task 1: Perform Open Database Backup

To perform TSPITR, you will need a backup to restore and recover from. You can either perform a closed database backup as shown in Chapter 4 or an open backup as shown in Chapter 5. To perform an open database backup, run the script named open_backup.sql used in Chapter 5 and change the backup directory to /oradata/PRACTICE/backup/ch09 as defined by the SQL*Plus &dir user variable.

When you use this open backup script, note three important things that this script accomplishes for you during the primary database backup:

1. Archives the current online log on the primary database so that any needed redo information will be contained in an archived log.

2. Ensures that all the datafiles that comprise the auxiliary and recovery set tablespace(s) are present in the backup.

3. Creates the control file used in the auxiliary set after the datafile backup.

Task 2: Drop Table SCOTT.EMP

For this chapter, you'll create a typical situation where TSPITR would be a suitable option. Let's pick on poor old SCOTT again and drop his employee table. You will recover this table using TSPITR. Before you drop the table, first create an index on the employee table in the INDX tablespace. You'll need to deal with this index during TSPITR because it is associated to an object in the recovery set tablespace but does not exist in that recovered tablespace. Second, mark the time before the table drop occurs. Later, you'll recover the USERS tablespace up to this time and SCOTT's employee table will be recovered.

```
SQL> CONNECT scott/tiger;
SQL> ALTER INDEX pk_emp REBUILD TABLESPACE indx;
SQL> ALTER SESSION SET NLS_DATE_FORMAT = 'YYYY-MM-DD:HH24:MI:SS';
SQL> SELECT sysdate FROM dual;
SQL> DROP TABLE SCOTT.EMP;
```

A primary key constraint on the SCOTT.EMP table requires that every employee number be present (not null) and unique for each employee row. The ALTER INDEX command moves the index to the INDX tablespace. When you perform tablespace recovery on the USERS tablespace, you'll need to remove and recreate this index. The ALTER SESSION command lets you change the date format used by all date columns within this session. You can see the time in the format expected by time-based recovery. This time will be used again in Task 3 of Exercise 9.2 during incomplete recovery on the AUXY instance.

To better illustrate issues and results with TSPITR, create an object in the USERS tablespace after the drop table command occurs. Also, insert a row into a table contained in the USERS tablespace. Finally, insert a row into a table in a different tablespace than USERS.

```
SQL> CREATE TABLE dept_copy TABLESPACE users AS SELECT * FROM dept;
SQL> INSERT INTO dept (deptno, dname, loc)
  2    VALUES ('50','SUPPORT','DENVER');
SQL> COMMIT;
SQL> CONNECT sys/practice;
SQL> INSERT INTO tina.date_log VALUES (SYSDATE+365*9);
SQL> ALTER SYSTEM SWITCH LOGFILE;
```

After you perform TSPITR, the SCOTT.DEPT_COPY table will not exist in the USERS tablespace on the primary PRACTICE database. Because any data changes made to objects in the USERS tablespace after TSPITR will not be recovered, the support department will not be found in the department table. Finally, the data in TINA.DATE_LOG will remain untouched after TSPITR. You should see a date nine years in the future after TSPITR. The beauty of TSPITR is that all nonrecovered tablespaces lose no data or objects. Objects in non-recovered tablespaces can still be affected if there are direct associations with objects in the recovered tablespace, such as indexes, triggers, and constraints.

Task 3: Investigate TSPITR

You have trade-offs to consider when you perform TSPITR. When you consider whether to perform TSPITR, ask yourself three questions:

1. What objects will be dropped if I perform TSPITR on a tablespace to a specific point in time?
   (Dropped objects)

2. What database-related objects might prevent TSPITR from succeeding?
   (Dependent objects)

3. Are there any objects in the recovery set that cannot be transported?
   (Non-transportable objects)

Here is how you can check the TSPITR option for these potential problems before you proceed.

Dropped objects   If you recover a tablespace to a previous point in time, you will lose objects created in that tablespace after the time of recovery. A data dictionary view that helps you assess the loss of objects is TS_PITR_OBJECTS_TO_BE_DROPPED. By querying this view and providing the tablespace you plan to recover and the time you plan to stop recovery, you'll quickly see any objects that will be lost if you proceed with TSPITR.

```
column owner   format a10
column name    format a10
column tname   format a10
column time    format a20
SELECT owner, name, tablespace_name tname, to_char(creation_time) time
  FROM sys.ts_pitr_objects_to_be_dropped
 WHERE tablespace_name in ('USERS')
   AND creation_time > to_date('2002-01-09:10:30:50',
                                     'YYYY-MM-DD:HH24:MI:SS')
ORDER BY tablespace_name, creation_time;
```

The results of the query performed will be DEPT_COPY. The copy of SCOTT's DEPT table will not be contained in the recovered USERS tablespace if you stop recovery at 10:30:50 AM on January 9, 2002.

```
OWNER      NAME       TNAME      TIME
---------- ---------- ---------- --------------------
SCOTT      DEPT_COPY  USERS      2002-01-09:10:30:48
```

You will also lose data changes made to objects in that tablespace after the time of recovery. If you wanted to find out what data changes would not be applied to data objects in the USERS tablespace, you'd have to be able to see the contents of the log files from 10:30:50 AM on January 9, 2002, to the current log file. To investigate the contents of the log files, you'd make use of Oracle's Log Miner utility as described in Chapter 10.

Dependent objects   The second investigative question asks if any objects will prevent a tablespace recovery to the USERS tables from succeeding. A recovery set must fully contain the following:

- Tables and their indexes

- Primary key/foreign key relationships

- All elements of large object datatypes (LOBs)

- All partitions and subpartitions of a table/index

- All parts of a nested table

To find those objects and dependencies, you make use of a procedure named DBMS_TTS.TRANSPORT_SET_CHECK and a view named TRANSPORT_SET_ VIOLATIONS. This procedure checks if the USERS tablespace is self-contained. The procedure requires two parameters. In the first parameter, provide the names of one or more tablespaces to check. The second parameter is true if you'd like to count in referential integrity constraints when examining if the set of tablespaces is self-contained. After calling this procedure, select from the view to see a list of any violations. If the view does not return any rows, the set of tablespaces is self-contained.

```
SQL> execute dbms_tts.transport_set_check('users', TRUE);
SQL> SELECT * FROM transport_set_violations;
VIOLATIONS
----------------------------------------------------------------------
Index SCOTT.ENAME_UK in tablespace INDX enforces primary constraints of table
SCOTT.EMP in tablespace USERS
```

You can see that the unique constraint and index created earlier on the EMP table will cause a violation when trying to export only the recovered USERS tablespace. If you tried to export the metadata for only the USERS tablespace, you'd get a "The transportable set is not self-contained" error message. Therefore, to export the USERS tablespace, you have to either include the INDX tablespace in the recovery set or drop the index in the INDX tablespace. In Oracle 8*i*, you can also use a view named TS_PITR_CHECK to check for dependencies and restrictions that can prevent TSPITR from proceeding. This view ascertains relationships between objects that straddle the recovery set boundaries. In Oracle 9*i*, this view has been removed, and DBMS_TTS.TRANSPORT_SET_CHECK should be used instead. TS_PITR_CHECK does not provide information about dependencies and restrictions for objects owned by SYS.

```
SELECT *
  FROM sys.ts_pitr_check
 WHERE (ts1_name IN ('USERS') AND ts2_name NOT IN ('USERS'))
    OR (ts1_name NOT IN ('USERS') AND ts2_name IN ('USERS'));
```

You should check for objects residing outside the recovery set on both the primary database and on the auxiliary before you do the export. If there are too many objects outside the recovery set on the primary, you can increase the tablespaces to be included in the recovery set. Including more tablespaces might decrease the amount of time spent on dropping and recreating dependant objects. Typically, you check for dependant objects outside the recovery set before you restore the backup files to the auxiliary set. After recovery on the auxiliary, run DBMS_TTS.TRANSPORT_SET_CHECK on the auxiliary to make sure the export will succeed. Consider also that dependent objects existing in the primary might have been added after the recovery time. Therefore, check that your recovery set is self-contained on both the auxiliary and the primary, and compare any exceptions. In this oversimplified scenario, you will only return one from the query. In a real database scenario, you may find many dependencies that will require attention.

NOTE
These views and procedures check structural dependencies defined within the Oracle database data dictionary, not data dependencies defined and maintained by an application.

Non-transportable objects   Object types that are not allowed in TSPITR recovery sets include:

- Replicated master tables
- Materialized views and materialized view logs
- Function-based indexes
- Scoped REFs
- Domain indexes (user-defined indexes)
- Objects owned by SYS, including rollback segments

Once you've gathered your facts, you can make an informed decision. Is performing TSPITR to get the SCOTT.EMP table back worth the loss of other objects or time spent rebuilding others? Since you have to get the SCOTT.EMP table back and can easily recreate the SCOTT.DEPT_COPY table, proceed with TSPITR of the USERS tablespace.

Tablespace Recovery on an Auxiliary Database

When you recover the USERS tablespace, you'll need an Oracle instance and auxiliary set for recovery. The instance will need a backup control file, the system, and rollback tablespace files. The recovery will use the PRACTICE database archived redo log files.

Exercise 9.2: Restore and Recover USERS Tablespace

In this exercise, you will restore and recover the USERS tablespace using a separate instance on the same machine. This exercise contains similar tasks as ones you performed in Chapter 6. The primary differences are that you'll only recover tablespaces in the recovery and auxiliary sets (USERS, SYSTEM, and RBS) tablespace, and you'll mount the database as a clone database. Other than that, you'll perform many of the same tasks as described in Exercise 6.1.

Task Description	Minutes
1. Create Auxiliary Instance	10
2. Restore SYSTEM, ROLLBACK, and USERS to Auxiliary	10
3. Recover Auxiliary to Specific Time	10
4. Open Auxiliary Instance	10
Total Time	40

The preferred method to perform TSPITR is to create and recover an auxiliary database on a server machine different from the primary database. By doing this, you avoid the risk of corrupting the primary database instance by writing over the control files or online redo logs. You can successfully accomplish TSPITR on the same machine if you are careful and have sufficient machine resources for a second instance. In this exercise, you create an auxiliary instance named AUXY of the primary

PRACTICE database on the same machine. Then, you will recover the recovery set datafiles to prepare them for Export/Import back into the PRACTICE database.

Task 1: Create Auxiliary Instance

Create an instance named AUXY including directories, Windows services, parameter file, and password file, as described in Chapter 6 (Exercise 6.1, Task 1).

In the parameter file, you'll need only one control file set to /oradata/AUXY/auxiliary.ctl. Be sure to set DB_FILE_NAME_CONVERT, LOG_FILE_NAME_CONVERT and LOCK_NAME_SPACE in the parameter file also.

```
DB_FILE_NAME_CONVERT = "PRACTICE","AUXY"
LOG_FILE_NAME_CONVERT = "PRACTICE","AUXY"
LOCK_NAME_SPACE = "AUXY"
```

You can also adjust the parameter file parameter so that the auxiliary instance uses less memory (DB_BLOCK_BUFFERS, SHARED_POOL_SIZE, LARGE_POOL_SIZE, and so on). The DB_NAME parameter remains PRACTICE; you'll be creating the auxiliary instance of the PRACTICE database.

CAUTION
Be sure that the auxiliary instance does not mount the PRACTICE instance control files, use the online log files of the PRACTICE instance or open any datafiles of the PRACTICE instance. You can damage your primary database if you do this.

Task 2: Restore SYSTEM, ROLLBACK, and USERS to Auxiliary

Copy the backup control file created by the open backup in Exercise 9.1 to /oradata/AUXY/auxiliary.ctl. This backup control file will be used to mount the database.

Copy the datafiles in the recovery set from the /oradata/PRACTICE/backup/ch09 directory to the /oradata/AUXY directory where they were saved during the online backup. These datafiles are from the SYSTEM, RBS, and USERS tablespaces. When creating an auxiliary instance for TSPITR, you must not only restore the datafiles from the tablespaces that you are going to recover, but also the SYSTEM and ROLLBACK (undo) datafiles. This is because the SYSTEM tablespace stores the data dictionary. You need this tablespace to open the database, log on to the database, view any objects, export from the database, and so on. The undo tablespace is required because when you perform incomplete recovery against the database, block changes will need to be rolled back for any outstanding transactions that were uncommitted at the time the recovery was cancelled.

NOTE
Sometimes the temporary tablespace datafiles are also required if you wish to do any kind of sort operation against the auxiliary instance. Temporary tablespace is rarely required because as soon as the database is opened, you will be exporting the tablespace. Also, the sort segment on disk will only be needed if the sort will not fit into the sort area defined for the instance.

Issue these commands to mount your backup controlfile with the AUXY instance:

```
LINUX> export ORACLE_SID=AUXY
LINUX> sqlplus /nolog
SQL> CONNECT SYS/AUXY AS SYSDBA;
SQL> STARTUP NOMOUNT;
SQL> ALTER DATABASE MOUNT CLONE DATABASE;
```

When you mount the auxiliary instance of the PRACTICE database as a clone database, that database is taken out of archive log mode and all the datafiles are taken offline. A database mounted as a clone instance cannot assume all the datafiles are located as defined in the control file. This feature gives you the flexibility to restore files to different locations based on disk availability. Also, most datafiles of a clone instance will never be needed in an online status because they are not a part of the recovery set or the auxiliary set. Recovery of a select few datafiles is the sole purpose of this database mounted as a clone.

After the backup control file is mounted, you can see the control file's record of the current datafiles in the database. The DB_FILE_NAME_CONVERT have translated the PRACTICE directory to the AUXY directory for all datafiles.

```
SQL> col name form a30;
SQL> col file# form 99;
SQL> SELECT file#, name, status FROM v$datafile;
FILE# NAME                            STATUS
----- ------------------------------  -------
    1 /oradata/AUXY/system01.dbf  SYSOFF
    2 /oradata/AUXY/rbs01.dbf     OFFLINE
    3 /oradata/AUXY/users01.dbf   OFFLINE
    4 /oradata/AUXY/temp01.dbf    OFFLINE
    5 /oradata/AUXY/tools01.dbf   OFFLINE
    6 /oradata/AUXY/indx01.dbf    OFFLINE
    7 /oradata/AUXY/users02.dbf   OFFLINE
```

Also query v$logfile to make sure that the online log files are in a different location from the primary PRACTICE database location.

Before recovery, place SYSTEM, RBS, and USERS tablespace datafiles online. When you place the datafiles online for recovery, they must exist where the control file thinks they do.

```
SQL> ALTER DATABASE DATAFILE 1,2,3,7 ONLINE;
SQL> SELECT file#, name, status FROM v$datafile;
FILE# NAME                                STATUS
----- ------------------------------      -------
    1 /oradata/AUXY/system01.dbf    SYSTEM
    2 /oradata/AUXY/rbs01.dbf       ONLINE
    3 /oradata/AUXY/users01.dbf     ONLINE
    4 /oradata/AUXY/temp01.dbf      OFFLINE
    5 /oradata/AUXY/tools01.dbf     OFFLINE
    6 /oradata/AUXY/indx01.dbf      OFFLINE
    7 /oradata/AUXY/users02.dbf     ONLINE
```

Look again at v$datafile, and you'll see the datafiles in the recovery and auxiliary sets online; others will be offline. You don't need to recover the TOOLS and INDX tablespaces in this scenario. With the recovery set files online, you can begin recovery to the point in time before the SCOTT.EMP table was dropped from the USERS tablespace.

Task 3: Recover AUXY to Specific Time

Recover the USERS tablespace to the time before the drop command. The archive files will be read from the archive destination of the auxiliary database by default. Since these databases are on the same machine, you can apply the redo contained in files stored in the archive destination of the PRACTICE database. Set the LOGSOURCE SQL*Plus system variable to point the recovery command to the /oradata/PRACTICE/archive directory.

```
SQL> SET LOGSOURCE /oradata/PRACTICE/archive;
SQL> RECOVER DATABASE USING BACKUP CONTROLFILE
  2      UNTIL TIME '2002-01-09:10:30:50';
```

With the recover command, all redo needed to the online tablespaces up to January 9, 2002 at 10:30:50 AM is applied, the time just before the SCOTT.EMP table was dropped. If the recovery completes without errors, you'll get a "media recovery complete" message. Note that you could have performed either cancel-based recovery or SCN-based recovery also.

Task 4: Open Auxiliary Instance

Open the auxiliary instance and reset the logs. Since the auxiliary instance has opened a backup of the primary PRACTICE database as an auxiliary, only the SYSTEM rollback segment is brought online. This prevents any data manipulation language (DML) from being executed against any user objects in the database. Any attempt to bring a non-system rollback segment online will fail.

On the auxiliary instance you can use the DBMS_TTS package as stated previously and compare results and resolve any dependencies as you did on the primary PRACTICE instance earlier. If this view returns no rows, you can be confident that the export phase of TSPITR will succeed. At this point, you can remove the primary key on SCOTT's employee table so that the upcoming tablespace transport will succeed.

The USERS tablespace datafiles are now ready for transport from the auxiliary instance back to the PRACTICE instance.

Transportable Tablespace

Remember the fourth mode of Export/Import that was covered in Chapter 8? You will use this fourth mode to plug a tablespace from one instance into another. The transportable tablespace feature enables you to move or copy a set of tablespaces from one Oracle database to another. To transport one or more tablespaces, you first make the tablespaces read-only on the source database. Extract the database information (metadata) stored in the data dictionary using Oracle Export. Both the datafiles and the metadata export file must be copied to the target database. The transport of these files can be done using any facility for copying binary files, such as the operating system copying facility or binary-mode FTP. Finally, use Oracle Import to include tablespace metadata into the target database data dictionary. You can make the transported tablespace set read write after metadata import.

A transportable tablespace is a combination of two parts:

1. An export of the metadata (instead of the data) of a tablespace and all objects contained within it.

2. A copy of the datafiles belonging to that tablespace.

You transport a tablespace by copying the files of these two parts to a compatible Oracle database and "plug" the tablespace in by doing the following:

1. Restoring the tablespace datafiles to the new location.

2. Importing the metadata of the tablespace.

NOTE
Look at the plugged_in column of
DBA_TABLESPACES and v$datafile to see which
tablespaces and datafiles have been plugged in.

Exercise 9.3: Transport the USERS Tablespace

You currently have the USERS tablespace on the PRACTICE instance of the PRACTICE database without the SCOTT.EMP table. You also have the USERS tablespace in the auxiliary instance with the SCOTT.EMP table. You need to transport this recovered tablespace from the AUXY instance to the PRACTICE instance. You'll use Oracle transportable tablespace feature to accomplish this last leg of the TSPITR operation.

Task Description	Minutes
1. Alter USERS Tablespace on AUXY	5
2. Export USERS Tablespace from AUXY	5
3. Drop USERS Tablespace from PRACTICE	5
4. Copy Datafiles	10
5. Import USERS Tablespace on PRACTICE	5
6. Verify TSPITR on PRACTICE	10
7. Back Up PRACTICE Database	10
Total Time	50

In this exercise, you'll use Export/Import to transport the metadata in the USERS tablespace from the AUXY instance to the PRACTICE instance. You'll use the OS copy command to copy datafiles. Finally, you'll verify the results on the PRACTICE instance and the PRACTICE database. Since you will be working on both instances during these tasks, you might want to open two operating system sessions: one for the AUXY instance and one for the PRACTICE instance.

Task I: Alter USERS Tablespace on AUXY

Changes cannot occur during the tablespace transport process. Therefore, the tablespace must be set to read-only before it can be exported. When making a tablespace read-only, the datafiles that belong to the tablespace are checkpointed, and no more updates to objects within it are allowed.

```
LINUX> sqlplus /nolog
SQL> connect sys/auxiliary as sysdba;
SQL> alter tablespace users read only;
```

Task 2: Export USERS Tablespace from AUXY

Use the Export utility to extract the USERS tablespace metadata to a binary dump file.

```
LINUX> export ORACLE_SID=AUXY
LINUX> exp parfile=exp_transport.par
```

Create the export using a parameter file, as shown here.

```
userid="sys/auxiliary as sysdba"
transport_tablespace=y
tablespaces=users
file=transport.dmp
log=transport.log
```

Several important keywords in this file direct the Export utility to extract the USERS tablespace to a binary dump file.

- **userid** Tablespace export must be done as a user with SYSDBA role. To define the SYSDBA for the userid keyword, you'll have to use quotation marks.

- **transport_tablespace** This parameter enables the export of transportable tablespace metadata. When set to Y, the export runs in tablespace_mode and is used in conjunction with the TABLESPACES parameter.

- **tablespaces** This parameter specifies that all metadata contained in the data dictionary for the segments in the named tablespace be exported.

Using the export dump file from this export along with the datafiles, you'll be able to plug the USERS tablespace datafiles into another database of identical block size, Oracle Version, and operating system.

Task 3: Drop USERS Tablespace from PRACTICE

Before the USERS tablespace can be plugged into the PRACTICE database, no tablespace of the same name can currently exist. When you drop the tables including contents, the objects contained within it are removed from the data dictionary. Also remove the datafiles at the operating system.

```
SQL> ALTER DATABASE DROP TABLESPACE users INCLUDING CONTENTS;
LINUX> rm /oradata/PRACTICE/users01.dbf
LINUX> rm /oradata/PRACTICE/users02.dbf
```

TIP
In Oracle 9i, you can remove the datafiles from the operating system when you drop the tablespace. To remove the USERS tablespace and datafiles, use this command: DROP TABLESPACE USERS INCLUDING CONTENTS AND DATAFILES;

Task 4: Copy Datafiles

The files recovered by the AUXY instance can be moved from their current location to the final location.

```
LINUX> cp /oradata/AUXY/users01.dbf /oradata/PRACTICE
LINUX> cp /oradata/AUXY/users02.dbf /oradata/PRACTICE
```

If you move the datafiles to a different server machine, you can use binary mode FTP to move the files.

Task 5: Import USERS Tablespace on PRACTICE

Now that the USERS tablespace datafiles are in place, you are ready to plug the tablespace into the primary PRACTICE database. Use the Import utility to insert the metadata into the PRACTICE instance:

```
LINUX> export ORACLE_SID=PRACTICE
LINUX> imp parfile=imp_transport.par
```

Use the parameter file shown here.

```
userid="sys/practice as sysdba"
transport_tablespace=y
tablespaces=users
datafiles="/oradata/PRACTICE/users01.dbf","/oradata/PRACTICE/users02.dbf"
file=transport.dmp
log=imp_transport.log
```

Note some of the keyword entries in the parameter file.

- **userid**   Tablespace import must be done as a user with SYSDBA role. To define the SYSDBA for the userid keyword, you must use quotation marks.

- **transport_tablespace**   This parameter enables the import of transportable tablespace metadata. When set to Y, the import runs in tablespace_mode and is used in conjunction with the TABLESPACES parameter.

- **tablespaces**   When TRANSPORT_TABLESPACE is specified as Y, use this parameter to provide a list of tablespaces to be transported into the database.

- **datafiles**   When TRANSPORT_TABLESPACE is specified as Y, use this parameter to list the datafiles to be transported into the database with their correct location.

Task 6: Verify TSPITR on PRACTICE

The tablespace that has been imported is now in read only mode. Place the tablespace in read write mode.

```
LINUX> sqlplus /nolog
SQL> CONNECT sys/practice;
SQL> ALTER TABLESPACE users READ WRITE;
```

Check that the objects and data in the USERS tablespace exist as they existed just before the SCOTT.EMP table was dropped. Check that the SCOTT.EMP table exists and the SCOTT.DEPT_COPY table does not exist. Also see if the SUPPORT department can be found in the SCOTT.DEPT table. You should now have the SCOTT.EMP table back, but you don't have the DEPT_COPY table or the SUPPORT department in the SCOTT.DEPT table. Perform any post-transport cleanup now. In this scenario, be sure to add the primary key back to the SCOTT.EMP table that had to be removed before transport.

Check that data in other tablespaces contains data that was changed after the recovery time of the USERS tablespace. See if the TINA.DATE_LOG table has an insert date nine years in the future.

```
SQL> describe scott.emp;
SQL> describe scott.dept_copy;
SQL> SELECT * FROM scott.dept;
SQL> SELECT max(create_date) FROM tina.date_log;
```

You did it! You performed tablespace point-in-time recovery on the PRACTICE database and never shut it down. Go tell your boss that you have hands-on experience with TSPITR and demand a $10,000 raise. (You may have to explain what TSPITR stands for.)

Extra Credit

You can perform TSPITR a bit differently than is described in Exercise 9.3. Instead of transporting the entire recovered tablespace from the AUXY instance to the PRACTICE instance, you can export specific objects from the USERS tablespace. Once the AUXY instance is recovered and you open it, you can use the Oracle Export utility to create a binary dump file of certain objects. Using that binary dump file, you can import that object into the PRACTICE instance. Try this: rather than transporting the entire USERS tablespace from the AUXY instance, export only the SCOTT.EMP table and import that table into the PRACTICE instance. Using this method, you can retain all other work done on the PRACTICE instance including the creation of the DEPT_COPY table. (Prior to Oracle 8.0, this method of object recovery was the only way to achieve TSPITR.)

Task 7: Back Up PRACTICE Database

Once you've performed TSPITR, you must back up the database again. You won't be able to recover the tablespace(s) using the pre-TSPITR datafiles because the archived logs from that backup do not correspond to the newly recovered tablespace(s). You can perform either a closed database backup as shown in Chapter 4, or an open backup as shown in Chapter 5.

Transportable Tablespace Tips

You can use transportable tablespaces for uses other than TSPITR.

- **Data warehousing systems and large batch operations**   You can move or copy data from one database to another almost a quickly as you can copy the tablespace datafile(s) from one location to another. (When moving tablespaces and the database instances exist on the same machine, you don't even have to move the file.) For running large load operations, they can be done on a second database located on a different server. Once the data is loaded and formatted correctly, the data can be transported to the production environment. This will save on resource consumption of the production server.

- **Resetting data during testing on a development system**   Establish a baseline of data in one or more tablespaces on a development system and use transportable tablespaces to export the metadata and copy the datafiles to back up location. After testing finishes, you can plug in your baseline tablespaces again.

Troubleshooting

If you run into problems during TSPITR operations, look over this list for possible solutions.

1. **ORA-01547: warning: RECOVER succeeded but OPEN RESETLOGS would get error below:**
   ORA-01195: online backup of file 1 needs more recovery to be consistent
   ORA-01110: data file 1: '/oradata/AUXY/system01.dbf'   Check that the time you set for recovery is correct. The datafiles have not been recovered to a time suitable for opening. Perhaps the auxiliary backup originated from a restored open backup, and the end hot backup marker has not been reached yet. You need to apply more recovery before the database can be opened.

2. **Mount database ORA-01103: database name 'PRACTICE' in controlfile is not 'AUXY'**   The auxiliary must have same database name as the source. Check the db_name setting in the AUXY instance parameter file. It should be set to PRACTICE for these exercises.

3. **Mount database ORA-01102: cannot mount database in EXCLUSIVE mode**
This error is seen when you are trying to mount a database that is already mounted by another instance. When you open two databases of the same name on a single machine, they share the same memory space. If you specify a different LOCK_NAME_SPACE, the memory space designator will be different. Check that the ORACLE_SID is set correctly and that the AUXY instance is mounting the controlfile as a clone database.

4. **ORA-01698: a clone database may only have SYSTEM rollback segment online** You will see this error when you are trying to online a non-system rollback segment. To prevent DML on the AUXY database you opened as a clone, Oracle will not allow you to online any non-system rollback segments.

5. **ORA-29303: user does not log in as SYS** To export a tablespace, you must be logged using the SYSDBA role.

6. **ORA-01696: controlfile is not a clone controlfile** If you did not create a backup control file with the ALTER DATABASE BACKUP CONTROL FILE, you will get this error when you mount a database with the clone option. Either find a valid backup control file or create a new one from the primary database.

Summary

You can now perform tablespace recovery on an Oracle database using transportable tablespaces. When you accomplish this work in a real database environment, you'll perform the same procedures, but you'll need to spend more time carefully investigating the ramifications of tablespace recovery on other parts of the database. The primary consideration is the possibility of application-level inconsistency between recovered and unrecovered tablespaces. Understanding these application dependencies helps TSPITR succeed. You should now see that you've got options to protect your database.

For more information on the Export/Import of transportable tablespaces, look at Chapters 1 and 2 or the *Oracle8i Utilities* manual. Read Chapter 9 of the *Oracle8i Administrator's Guide* and Chapter 7 of the *Oracle8i Backup and Recovery* guide for information about transporting tablespaces between databases and using TSPITR.

Chapter Questions

As a refresher, try answering these questions to reinforce the concepts and exercises in this chapter.

1. TSPITR is useful for recovery during which of these scenarios? (Pick any that apply.)

  A. When a table is mistakenly dropped or truncated

  B. When table data has been logically corrupted

  C. When a batch job ran incorrectly on a portion of the database

  D. When full recovery of a very large database might take too long and only key objects are required

2. Which two data dictionary views help you to survey the impact TSPITR might have on your database?

  A. TS_PITR_CONFIRM

  B. TS_PITR_OBJECTS_TO_BE_DROPPED

  C. TRANSPORT_SET_VIOLATIONS

  D. TS_PITR_OBJECTS_LOST

3. Once you've recovered a tablespace set on an auxiliary instance, you can either transport the entire tablespace from the auxiliary instance or export individual objects from the auxiliary instance.

  A. True

  B. False

4. To export a tablespace's metadata using the Oracle Export utility, what keyword parameters are required? (Pick any that apply.)

  A. TABLESPACES

  B. TRANPORTABLE

  C. TRANSPORT_TABLESPACE

  D. DATAFILES

5. To import a tablespace's metadata using the Oracle Import utility, what keyword parameters are required? (Pick any that apply.)

  A. TRANPORTABLE

  B. TABLESPACES

  C. TRANSPORT_TABLESPACE

  D. DATAFILES

Answers to Chapter Questions

1. A,B,C,D. TSPITR can be useful for recovery from a variety of failure scenarios. You have to judge the impact of TSPITR versus any impact that recovery might have on the remainder of the tablespaces in the database.

2. B, C. You can use these views to answer two questions: If I perform TSPITR, will I lose any objects? Are there any object types that will prevent TSPITR from succeeding?

3. True. Once you've recovered a tablespace on an auxiliary instance, you have the option of transporting the entire tablespace or exporting objects within the recovered tablespace.

4. A, C. The TRANSPORT_TABLESPACE parameter specifies that the Export utility should run in tablespace mode. The TABLESPACES parameter defines which tablespaces about which to extract metadata.

5. B, C, D. The TRANSPORT_TABLESPACE parameter specifies that the import utility should run in tablespace mode. The TABLESPACES parameter defines which tablespaces about which to extract metadata. The DATAFILES defines the files that contain the tablespace data.

CHAPTER
10

LogMiner

or the last few chapters, I have been talking about archive redo log files. You backed them up. You used them for recovery. You used them to propagate changes to a standby database and recover a tablespace to a point in time. Have you wondered if there is a way to look inside an Oracle redo log file? It is possible to dump the log file contents to a trace file, but it is very difficult to interpret. Alternatively, starting with Oracle 8*i*, you can look at the contents of one or more log files using a utility named *LogMiner*, which consists of a few data dictionary views and some stored procedures. In this chapter, you'll follow steps to set up and use LogMiner to view and analyze the contents of the database redo log files.

As Oracle makes changes to data blocks, it writes redo information to the current online redo log file. Redo files contain change times, object identifiers, change SCNs, the operations that occurred in the block and other important information. Redo files contain both the changes to the data blocks made by the user and the changes to the undo blocks in the rollback segments. Oracle labels object-related information in the data dictionary using numeric identifiers. For example, a table is assigned an object number, with each column having a column identifier. Each column has a corresponding data type identifier that indicates if it is a varchar2, date, number, and so on. Using LogMiner, you can read the contents of redo file and then recreate or undo the SQL statements that generated the original redo. By using a data dictionary file, LogMiner will translate the Oracle object identifiers into the actual table and column names you recognize. Without a dictionary file, the SQL statements produced by LogMiner are very difficult to understand because the object names and column names are unknown.

I'll quickly define some terms you'll need to know before you begin. Each of these terms will be explained further as you progress through the tasks in this chapter's exercise.

- **Current database** When LogMiner analyzes redo log files using the same server that created the logs, the redo log files come from the current database. The LogMiner procedures and views are accessed using the database that created the mined log files, as shown here and in Figure 10-1.

- **Foreign database** LogMiner can analyze redo log files created from a different database from the one that analyzes them. The database that created the redo log files is a foreign database.

- **Dictionary file** LogMiner uses a dictionary file to correlate Oracle internal object IDs to table names, columns, datatypes, and so on. The dictionary file must be generated by the database that created the redo log files.

You might want to use LogMiner for a variety of reasons. Perhaps data in a table has mysteriously changed; use LogMiner to investigate the circumstances of that

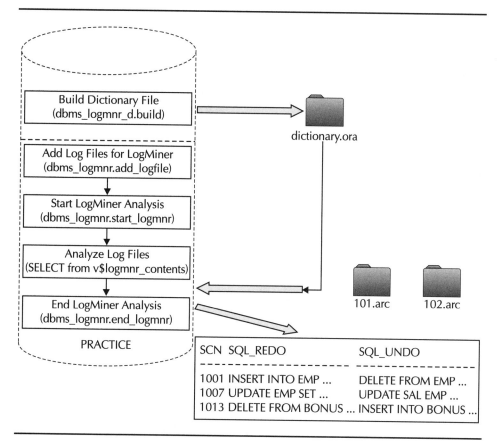

FIGURE 10-1. *LogMiner Activities on the PRACTICE database*

change. You can also use LogMiner to undo those changes. To investigate the workload on tables, you can use LogMiner to investigate the number of SQL changes occurring in one or more tables. With a little extra investigation, LogMiner can point you to the exact time and SCN that a mistaken DROP TABLE or other DDL statement occurred (although it does not record these exact statements).

When you consider using LogMiner, understand these points before proceeding:

- You can run LogMiner on a database that is mounted or unmounted.

- If you analyze redo files from a foreign database, the block size of the current database must be as large or larger than the foreign database. Why? The first change to a block in a tablespace in hot backup mode creates the entire block image in the redo stream as a single redo record. If that redo is being read by LogMiner using a database with a smaller block size, an error will occur because the single redo record cannot fit into one block.

■ Though LogMiner does not interpret DDL in redo logs, DDL statements such as a DROP TABLE create DML in the data dictionary. These dictionary DML statements can be used to investigate DDL commands issued against the database. DDL statements are tracked much better in Oracle 9*i*.

■ LogMiner will not reconstruct the original NOLOGGING SQL operations, but resulting DML performed on the data dictionary will be contained in the log files.

■ Though LogMiner can be used for occasional log file analysis, this is not a feature that should be considered for use on a regular basis, especially when mining redo information in a database that generates a very large amount of redo information. Analyzing enormous amounts of redo information with LogMiner can be quite time consuming.

■ If LogMiner is being used to mine log files from a different database, both the source database and analyzing database must use the same hardware platform and operating system. Also, the source and analyzing database must use the same character sets.

■ LogMiner will not analyze redo generated for some database objects and data types such as index-organized tables, clustered tables/indexes, nonscalar data types, and chained rows.

■ LogMiner will not generate the original SQL from direct path insert operations, although data dictionary DML will be created.

■ LogMiner will show uncommitted transactions because redo logs will contain committed and uncommitted data. It is up to you to query the affected objects to determine if the data was committed or not.

In this chapter, you'll create a dictionary file, generate some database activity, and analyze redo logs using LogMiner.

Analyzing Redo Using LogMiner

Reading redo log transactions via LogMiner involves making use of Oracle-supplied package procedures, data dictionary views, and a data dictionary external file. In brief, here is what you do to analyze redo log files with LogMiner: create an external data dictionary file using a LogMiner stored procedure. Next, create a list of redo log files you'd like to analyze using another stored procedure. Then start

LogMiner by executing another stored procedure. After all these steps, you are ready to select from a data dictionary view, which shows the contents of the log files. When this view is queried, Oracle reads the log files and returns the results in a formatted way. (The contents of the log files are not actually stored in a permanent database object.) Once you are done analyzing the listed log files, you stop LogMiner with a call to another stored procedure. Important LogMiner procedures and views are shown in Table 10-1.

As you proceed through the single exercise in this chapter, you'll see how all these procedures, files, and views work together to let you look at your database redo log files.

Exercise 10.1: Analyze the Redo Files

This chapter has only one exercise. During this exercise, you will find details about a specific change to a row in the SCOTT.EMP table. Next, you'll see how you can investigate the database change activity on a specific table by analyzing the redo log files for changes performed on that table. Finally, you will learn how to determine the exact time and SCN for a specific DROP TABLE command. These three examples

Procedures	Purpose
dbms_logmnr_d.build	Builds a data dictionary file.
dbms_logmnr.add_logfile	Adds log files to a list for analysis.
dbms_logmnr.start_logmnr	Starts LogMiner using an optional dictionary file and log files previously specified for analysis.
dbms_logmnr.end_logmnr	Stops LogMiner analysis.
Views	**Purpose**
v$logmnr_dictionary	Displays information about the dictionary file used for object ID name resolution.
v$logmnr_logs	Displays the list of logs to be analyzed when LogMiner starts.
v$logmnr_contents	After LogMiner is started, you can issue SQL statements at the SQL prompt to query the contents of redo logs using this view.

TABLE 10-1.   *Important LogMiner Procedures and Views*

will demonstrate some of the ways that you might use LogMiner to investigate redo information in a true database environment.

Task Description	Minutes
1. Create Data Dictionary File	5
2. Generate Database Activity	5
3. Specify Log Files for Analysis	5
4. Start LogMiner	5
5. Analyze the Redo Log Contents	15
6. Close LogMiner	5
Total Time	40

The tasks in the exercise serve as a guide to successful LogMiner setup and analysis. I'll cover the files, procedures, and views used by LogMiner to look at redo information in the PRACTICE database. In Task 2, you will execute some DML and DDL that you will then be able to find in Task 5. If you are able to locate these specific database changes using LogMiner views, you can consider this exercise a success.

Task 1: Create Data Dictionary File
A data dictionary file is an optional step when using LogMiner. The dictionary file greatly improves the readability of the contents of the log files. Here is what the log files look like *without* a data dictionary file:

```
SQL> SELECT sql_redo FROM v$logmnr_contents;
SQL_REDO
------------------------------------------------------------------------
set transaction read write;
insert into UNKNOWN.Objn:4273(Col[1]) values (HEXTORAW('c1022'));
commit;
```

Here is what the log files look like *with* a data dictionary file:

```
SQL> select sql_redo from v$logmnr_contents;
SQL_REDO
------------------------------------------------------------------------
set transaction read write;
insert into TINA.DATE_LOG(C1) values (1);
commit;
```

The data dictionary file maps the Oracle internal object ID values to recognizable names for tables, columns, and other data types. The data dictionary file is a text file equivalent of relevant parts of your data dictionary. The file contains SQL statements that look like they could be used to partly recreate your data dictionary. These statements are used by LogMiner and should not be run against any database, as this could corrupt the data dictionary contents. The LogMiner procedures use this file to convert the object identifiers to meaningful names. LogMiner stores information from the dictionary file in the PGA memory area for the current session. Because LogMiner does data manipulation in the PGA also, you should make sure that you have plenty of memory on the system if the dictionary file is very large. If a dictionary file is not being used, less PGA memory will be required. However, be aware that converting these numbers into meaningful names without a dictionary file takes considerable effort. Therefore, you'll create a data dictionary file during this task and direct LogMiner to use it to translate the internal numbers into names you can recognize when you perform log file analysis during Task 4.

- The dictionary file should be current with the date of the log files. If an object analyzed by LogMiner is not found in the data dictionary file, LogMiner will not be able to display the table and column names of database objects.

- The dictionary file must be created on the same database as the log files. For example, you can't use a dictionary file from the CLONE database to analyze the log files of the PRACTICE database.

Before you can create a data dictionary file, the PRACTICE database must be able to write to a directory on the server hard disk. Set a parameter in your database parameter file named UTL_FILE_DIR. This parameter allows you to specify one or more directories that Oracle can use for PL/SQL file I/O. You can declare many directories by repeating the UTL_FILE_DIR contiguously on separate lines in the parameter file. Add this exercise directory to your parameter file.

```
utl_file_dir=/oradata/PRACTICE/backup/ch10
```

Since this parameter is not a dynamic database parameter, you'll have to restart the database for this setting to take effect. Once you restart the database, log on and check that the setting has taken effect.

```
LINUX> sqlplus /nolog
SQL> CONNECT sys/practice;
SQL> SHOW PARAMETER utl_file_dir;
```

To create a data dictionary file, execute the BUILD procedure in the DBMS_LOGMNR_D supplied package. This procedure queries the dictionary tables of the current database and creates a text-based file containing their contents. This file is created in the directory named within the procedure call.

```
SQL> EXECUTE dbms_logmnr_d.build( -
     dictionary_filename => 'dictionary.ora', -
     dictionary_location => '/oradata/PRACTICE/backup/ch10');
```

Notice the hyphen character on the end of each line denotes the continuation of a single command on multiple lines in SQL*Plus. After this procedure completes, open a file named dictionary.ora in /oradata/PRACTICE/backup/ch10 to familiarize yourself with its contents.

Task 2: Generate Database Activity

In this second task, you'll generate SQL activity that can be later found in the log files. You'll change a row in the EMP table, confirm rows are being inserted into TINA.DATE_LOG, and drop the SCOTT.BONUS table.

First, make sure that your Oracle job is generating rows in the TINA.DATE_LOG table. Refer back to Chapter 3 for more information if needed.

Second, change a row in the SCOTT.EMP table. Use this SQL to change the salary and commission of one of the employees:

```
LINUX> sqlplus /nolog
SQL> CONNECT scott/tiger;
SQL> UPDATE emp SET sal = 3000, comm = 5000
  2   WHERE empno = 7844;
SQL> COMMIT;
```

Later you'll be able to mine for this SQL statement to demonstrate how you can make use of LogMiner.

Third, drop the SCOTT.BONUS table. The BONUS table currently doesn't have any rows, and you will not be using it anywhere in the rest of the book.

```
SQL> DROP TABLE bonus;
```

Note the time of these SQL commands either by looking at your watch or using the SQL*Plus command "set time on". This has the effect of adding a timestamp to the SQL prompt, which would look like this:

```
SQL> set time on;
17:21:20 SQL> DROP TABLE bonus;
Table dropped.
17:21:26 SQL>
```

The redo for the UPDATE and DROP (DML against the dictionary) statements will be contained in the current online redo log file. Find the sequence number of that log file by selecting from the v$log view. Finally, force a log switch to cause the current online redo log to be archived. You will run LogMiner to analyze this newly archived log file and see if you can find information in this log about the update and the drop table SQL.

```
17:22:01 SQL> SELECT sequence# FROM v$log WHERE status = 'CURRENT';
17:22:01 SQL> ALTER SYSTEM SWITCH LOGFILE;
```

Note the selection from the v$log view. The sequence number of the current log during your database changes will most likely contain the redo for those changes. In this chapter discussion, the current log sequence number before the log switch will be 102. Thus the archive log file created during the log switch will be named 102.arc.

Task 3: Specify Log Files for Analysis
LogMiner will analyze the log files you tell it to. Therefore, you must create a list of log files to be analyzed. Add log files with the ADD_LOGFILE procedure of the DBMS_LOGMNR Oracle supplied package. As you add them, each log file will show up in the v$logmnr_logs view.

```
LINUX> sqlplus sys/practice
SQL> SELECT db_name, thread_sqn, filename
  2 FROM v$logmnr_logs;
```

You won't see any rows return from selecting this view before you add any log files for analysis to the list. Since you know that the SQL changes you made in the previous task are contained in the log file with sequence 102, include this log file and the two before it for LogMiner analysis.

```
BEGIN
    dbms_logmnr.add_logfile(
        logfilename => '/oradata/PRACTICE/backup/ch10/100.arc',
        options => dbms_logmnr.NEW);

    dbms_logmnr.add_logfile(
        logfilename => '/oradata/PRACTICE/backup/ch10/101.arc',
        options => dbms_logmnr.ADDFILE);

    dbms_logmnr.add_logfile(
        logfilename => '/oradata/PRACTICE/backup/ch10/102.arc',
        options => dbms_logmnr.ADDFILE);
END;
/
```

When you add the first log file to the list, specify that a new list is being created. The first time the add_logfile procedure is called, the option is set to dbms_logmnr.NEW. This creates a new list of log files to be analyzed by LogMiner. Subsequent calls to add_logfile use the ADDFILE option to add to this newly created list. Every time the NEW option is used, the list of log files is reset to the one log file named in the add_logfile call. If you specify the new parameter again, any files previously added will be dropped from the list. Did you notice how quickly the procedure returns when you run these procedures? This procedure call does not analyze the file but adds the file to the list for later analysis.

Select from the v$logmnr_logs view and you'll see the files you've added to the list.

```
SQL> SELECT db_name, thread_sqn, filename FROM v$logmnr_logs;
DB_NAME   THREAD_SQN FILENAME
--------  ---------- ---------------------------------
PRACTICE         100 /oradata/PRACTICE/archive/100.arc
PRACTICE         101 /oradata/PRACTICE/archive/101.arc
PRACTICE         102 /oradata/PRACTICE/archive/102.arc
```

You can remove redo log files by specifying the REMOVEFILE option of the DBMS_LOGMNR.ADD_LOGFILE procedure. In the example, you can be sure that the log file with sequence 100 does not contain the redo information you are hunting for. Therefore, you can remove sequence 100 from the list for analysis.

```
SQL> EXECUTE dbms_logmnr.add_logfile( -
  2     logfilename => 'd:\oradata\PRACTICE\archive\100.arc', -
  3     options => dbms_logmnr.REMOVEFILE);
```

Task 4: Start LogMiner
With a dictionary file in place and your archive files listed, you are ready to start LogMiner.

```
EXECUTE dbms_logmnr.start_logmnr(
    dictfilename => '/oradata/PRACTICE/backup/ch10/dictionary.ora');
```

When you start LogMiner, specify the fully qualified path name of the dictionary file you created earlier.

You have several other parameters that you can optionally specify to this procedure. You can specify the beginning SCN and/or ending SCN for the analysis. You can specify the beginning time and/or ending time for the analysis. These parameters may be helpful if you must analyze many large archive logs and want to view a smaller time period of redo. In your small PRACTICE database, you'll analyze the full range of redo in the log file list. Upon completion of this command, you are ready to analyze the contents of the listed log files.

Task 5: Analyze the Redo Log Contents

You now have the contents of log file numbers 101.arc and 102.arc available to you in the V$LOGMNR_CONTENTS view. Using this view, you can investigate the redo log to answer several sample questions that might arise. When you query the V$LOGMNR_CONTENTS view, the log files contained in V$LOGMNR_LOGS are read sequentially and the data is returned in the row structure defined by the V$LOGMNR_CONTENTS view. This view has 53 columns (see Table 10-2 for a description of the more useful columns). The contents of all log files are not permanently stored in a table or in memory. Consequently, each time you select against V$LOGMNR_CONTENTS contents, the log files are scanned. If you must investigate a large number of log files many times to find what you are looking for, it would be better to create a table segment of the results, using a Create Table As Select (CTAS) command.

Column	Description
OPERATION	The operation recorded in the redo entry (INSERT, UPDATE, DELETE, and so on)
TIMESTAMP	The date and time that the data change occurred
SCN	The system change number of this specific data change
SEG_OWNER	The owner name of the segment (if a change is made to a segment)
SEG_NAME	The segment name where the data change occurred
SEG_TYPE	The segment type of the data change
TABLE_SPACE_NAME	The tablespace name of the segment that changed
ROW_ID	The row ID of the specific row of the data change
USER_NAME	The connect user who performed the data change
SESSION_INFO	The connect user session information when the data change was performed
SQL_REDO	The SQL statement that will reproduce the specific row change for this redo entry
SQL_UNDO	The SQL statement that will roll back or undo the specific row change for this redo entry

TABLE 10-2. *Useful Columns in the V$LOGMNR_CONTENTS View*

In this task, you'll accomplish three things using redo information in the PRACTICE database:

1. Find details of a data change: determine the change details for the salary of an employee.

2. Perform capacity analysis: examine the workload on the TINA.DATE_LOG table.

3. Find details of a DDL command: locate the SCN and time of a table drop.

The v$logmnr_contents data dictionary view displays the contents of your redo log files.

Find Details of a Data Change   Changes in data may occur on your database that are unexpected or made by mistake. The place to look for the details of those changes is the contents of the redo log files. In the example, perhaps a report shows a big change in the salary and commission of an employee. A manager comes to you and says that a salesman named Turner has had his salary and commission changed. She'd like for you to find out what happened and wants to know what the salary and commission values were before the change. She also wants to know any details about who made the change and when the change occurred.

To answer her questions, you need to find any SQL that has run against the SCOTT.EMP table. This table has a column named SAL for current salary and COMM for commission. To find all SQL run against this table, you can run a SELECT statement like this:

```
SQL> SELECT operation, timestamp, scn
  2    FROM v$logmnr_contents
  3   WHERE seg_name = 'EMP'
  4     AND seg_owner = 'SCOTT';
  4     AND seg_type_name = 'TABLE';
OPERATION TIMESTAMP              SCN
--------- -------------------- ----------
UPDATE    10-JAN-2002 10:42:42 340982
```

You can see that at 10:42 AM on January 10, an update statement was run against the SCOTT.EMP table. To find out what the specific change made to the table was, you'd look at the SQL_REDO and SQL_UNDO columns.

```
SQL> SELECT sql_redo, sql_undo
  2    FROM v$logmnr_contents
  3   WHERE seg_name = 'EMP'
  4     AND seg_owner = 'SCOTT'
  5     AND seg_type_name = 'TABLE';
SQL_REDO
------------------------------------------------------------------------
```

```
update "SCOTT"."EMP" set "SAL" = 3000, "COMM" = 5000 where ROWID =
'AAAAyQAADAAAAASAAJ';
SQL_UNDO
----------------------------------------------------------------------
update "SCOTT"."EMP" set "SAL" = 1500, "COMM" = 0 where ROWID =
'AAAAyQAADAAAAASAAJ';
```

The SQL_REDO column defines the specific SQL statement that will produce the same result as the SQL that you ran in Task 2. Notice that the SQL from the redo log is different from the SQL you ran earlier. The redo log contains the actual data change to the specific row applied by the database. It does not contain the actual SQL. The SQL_UNDO column contains SQL that allows you to undo the SQL_REDO change. In effect, it represents the data values before the change occurred. The undo value is collected from the rollback segment undo changes stored in the redo. The undo data changes written to the rollback segment change is also written to the current online redo log. LogMiner can extract all the information stored in the redo log files so that you can see the contents of changed columns before they were changed. It is a good idea to select the same row from the current table to see the values of all the other columns. This is useful when you report to your manager what data has been changed and to make sure that data has not been changed again.

You found the change to the data and the time of the change. Would you like to know who made the change? Look at the USERNAME and SESSION_INFO columns of the V$LOGMNR_CONTENTS. In these columns, you'll find helpful session information that may help you further decipher how the salary and commission of employee Turner was changed.

```
SQL> SELECT username, session_info
  2     FROM logmnr_contents
  3    WHERE seg_name = 'EMP'
  4      AND seg_owner = 'SCOTT'
  5      AND seg_type_name = 'TABLE';
```

```
USERNAME
--------
SCOTT
SESSION_INFO
----------------------------------------------------------------------
LoginUserName = SCOTT, ClientInfo = , OsUserName = SJONES, MachineName = SJCOMP
```

NOTE
Many applications use a single or shared logon to perform database work. These middle-tier connections may make it hard to find valuable session information when investigating data changes via redo analysis.

You can see that someone logged in as user SCOTT and performed this update. You also know the culprit was logged on to a machine named SJCOMP as an operating system named SJONES. It looks like all roads are pointing to Scott! You can provide this information to your manager, and you can return the data to its values before the change by using the contents of the SQL_UNDO column as your command. Don't forget to check the contents of this row as it currently exists in the table to make sure it hasn't changed a subsequent time.

```
SQL> update "SCOTT"."EMP" set "SAL" = 1500, "COMM" = 0
  2   where ROWID = 'AAAAyQAADAAAAASAAJ';
```

CAUTION
The data change scenario here is simple for illustration purposes. In a production database environment, you would not change production data without careful consideration and appropriate approval. You must also consider any foreign key relationships on the tables being changed, or any referential integrity being maintained by an application.

Perform Capacity Analysis   As a DBA, you may need to do some performance tuning or capacity planning. This task might involve the use of many different tools and utilities. As a piece of the puzzle, you can use LogMiner to examine the activity occurring to tables in your databases. For example, LogMiner will help you investigate the amount and frequency of DML on a table. The same function can be achieved using table auditing. Using LogMiner does not degrade runtime performance when the table is being updated, while table auditing can cause some runtime performance overhead.

Let's look at the SQL activity on the TINA.DATE_LOG table. With LogMiner started, you can examine the number of inserts, updates, and deletes on this table. (Select statements do not generate redo; therefore, you won't see them via LogMiner.) This very simple example gives you an idea of some of the ways you might analyze DML activity on your database tables.

```
SELECT operation, to_char(timestamp,'HH') hour, count(*) total
   FROM v$logmnr_contents
  WHERE seg_name = 'DATE_LOG'
    AND seg_owner = 'TINA'
    AND seg_type_name = 'TABLE'
  GROUP BY operation, to_char(timestamp,'HH');
OPERATION HOUR      TOTAL
--------- ----  ----------
INSERT    10           6
```

```
INSERT    11       6
INSERT    12       6
INSERT    13       6
```

The results of this query show you that the DATE_LOG table is adding rows at the rate of six per hour.

When you must analyze a significant amount of redo, understand the tradeoff between comprehensive analysis and speed of analysis. The more log files you add to the LogMiner list for analysis, the more redo information you can analyze. However, more or larger log files in the LogMiner list cause SQL against the V$LOGMNR_CONTENTS view to take longer to complete.

Find Details of a DDL Command   In Chapters 5 and 9, you simulated an accidental drop table as you did in this chapter. In those chapters, I mentioned that you'd find it hard to know the time that the mistaken drop table occurred. Using LogMiner, you can deduce the exact time and SCN of a drop table statement. You can use this time or SCN for incomplete database recovery or tablespace point in time recovery (TSPITR).

As stated earlier, LogMiner only translates redo log information for data manipulation language (insert, update, delete). You will not be able to find a DROP TABLE statement in the V$LOGMNR_CONTENTS view. Since a DROP TABLE statement performs DML on data dictionary tables, you can search the view for occurrences of a deletion from the SYS.OBJ$ or the SYS.TAB$ data dictionary tables.

```
SQL> SELECT seg_name, operation, scn, timestamp, count(*)
  2    FROM v$logmnr_contents
  3    WHERE operation = 'DELETE'
  4    GROUP by seg_name, operation, scn, timestamp
  5    ORDER by scn;
SEG_NAME          OPERATION                SCN TIMESTAMP              COUNT(*)
--------------    ---------------   ----------  -------------------   ----------
FET$              DELETE                362948 2002-01-10:07:59:11           1
COL$              DELETE                362952 2002-01-10:07:59:16           4
OBJ$              DELETE                362952 2002-01-10:07:59:16           1
TAB$              DELETE                362952 2002-01-10:07:59:16           1
SEG$              DELETE                362954 2002-01-10:07:59:16           1
UET$              DELETE                362954 2002-01-10:07:59:16           1
```

From the SQL results above, you can see that at 7:59 AM on January 10, an object, a table, and four columns (the SCOTT.BONUS table had four columns) were removed from the data dictionary. This object deletion from the data dictionary may have been your drop bonus table statement. Next, look at the SQL_REDO of the DROP TABLE command.

```
SQL> SELECT sql_redo FROM v$logmnr_contents
  2    WHERE scn = 362952 and seg_name = 'OBJ$';
SQL_REDO
```

```
-------------------------------------------------------------------------
delete from SYS.OBJ$ where OBJ# = 13079 and DATAOBJ# = 13079 and OWNER# =
38 and NAME = 'BONUS' and NAMESPACE = 1 and SUBNAME IS NULL and TYPE# = 2
and CTIME = TO_DATE('2002-01-10:07:59:16', 'DD-MON-YYYY HH24:MI:SS') and
MTIME = TO_DATE('2002-01-10:07:59:16', 'DD-MON-YYYY HH24:MI:SS') and STIME
= TO_DATE('2002-01-10:07:59:16', 'DD-MON-YYYY HH24:MI:SS') and STATUS = 1
and REMOTEOWNER IS NULL and LINKNAME IS NULL and FLAGS = 0 and ROWID =
'AAAAASAABAAAGXkAAA';
```

Looking at the output of the SQL_REDO column, you see the OBJ#. The value associated to OBJ# corresponds to the Oracle ID for this table as stored in the dictionary table TAB$.OBJ#. (OBJECT_ID can also be seen in the DBA_OBJECTS view.) To tie together the table that was dropped and the actual time and SCN of the SQL statement issued to drop the table, you will need to know approximately when the table was dropped and how many columns the table contained. Using this information, it is possible to find the exact time the table was dropped as well as user information should it be needed . That object ID can be found in the dictionary file (the file that was created in Task 2). Open the dictionary file in an editor and search for the word BONUS. You'll see an insert statement that looks like this:

```
INSERT_INTO OBJ$_TABLE VALUES (13079,13079,38,'BONUS',1,'',2,
to_date('01/10/2001 06:25:28', 'MM/DD/YYYY HH24:MI:SS'),
to_date('01/10/2001 06:25:28', 'MM/DD/YYYY HH24:MI:SS'),
to_date('01/10/2001 06:25:28', 'MM/DD/YYYY H24:MI:SS'),
1,'','',0,,,,,'','', );
```

If you do not see an entry for the BONUS table in the dictionary file, you couldn't have created the dictionary file while this table existed in the database. If this is the case, you will have to use your judgment and piece together the dropped table data. The OBJ# value in the SQL_REDO column will be the exact same number as the first value inserted in the data dictionary file for the dropped table (in the output above, the object ID of the BONUS table is 13079). If you have strung all this together properly, you can be assured that the drop table occurred at SCN 362952 and at time 2002-01-10:07:59:16. Using these values, you can perform TSPITR if you choose to.

To recap, you can find the time and SCN of the drop table command by matching the data dictionary file object number to the object identifier in the SQL_REDO column for a delete against the SYS.OBJ$ data dictionary table.

Task 5: Close LogMiner
When you are done with LogMiner, you should release the resources used by this program. LogMiner has allocated memory and data structures for the analysis of redo

files. When you end your LogMiner work, the contents of V$LOGMNR_CONTENTS will no longer be available to you. If you need to further analyze redo log contents, you might find it helpful to create a permanent database table with the contents of the V$LOGMNR_CONTENTS view. You'll then have the redo file contents available for investigation after you terminate LogMiner.

```
SQL> CREATE TABLE logmnr_contents AS SELECT * FROM v$logmnr_contents;
```

Once your investigation of the redo logs is completed, run the END_LOGMNR of the DBMS_LOGMNR package.

```
EXECUTE dbms_logmnr.end_logmnr;
```

When you end LogMiner, you release session memory allocated for the redo log analysis.

Oracle 9*i* Enhancements

Oracle 9*i* has improved some of LogMiner's capabilities. Most of the enhancements allow you to mine redo information that was not previously available in Oracle 8*i*. LogMiner in Oracle 9*i* can now do the following:

- Analyze redo containing chained rows and clustered tables/indexes

- Provide three access options for data dictionary information:

    - The dictionary object information can be saved as a flat ASCII text file as in Oracle 8*i*

    - The dictionary object information can be stored in the redo stream of database's log files

    - LogMiner can access the database's data dictionary online

- Track DDL statements

- Analyze redo information generated during direct load operations if the database is running in archivelog mode

- Show only committed transactions and not the transactions that have not yet been committed.

Finally, Oracle Enterprise Manager provides the ability to access LogMiner functionality via a graphical user interface called the LogMiner Viewer.

Troubleshooting

If you run into problems using LogMiner, you might encounter one of these errors. These notes may point you in the right direction to solve log analysis problems.

1. **ORA-06532: Subscript outside of limit**
   ORA-06512: at "SYS.DBMS_LOGMNR_D", line 793 When you create a data dictionary file, you may encounter this error as I did. To fix this, you'll need to change the Oracle supplied script in the $ORACLE_HOME/rdbms/ admin directory. Open the file named dbmslmd.sql and change this line:

   ```
   TYPE col_desc_array IS VARRAY(513) OF col_description;
   ```

   to

   ```
   TYPE col_desc_array IS VARRAY(700) OF col_description;
   ```

   After you've changed the script, rerun dbmslmd.sql as user SYS. (I found this solution by going to Metalink and entering "ORA-06532: Subscript outside of limit" in the search screen. Other people had encountered the same error as I did, so I was able to quickly resolve my problem. Be very careful, though, whenever you modify a script supplied by Oracle.)

2. **ORA-01306: dbms_logmnr.start_logmnr() must be invoked before selecting from v$logmnr_contents** The order that you run the steps for LogMiner is important. You must specify log files for LogMiner and start LogMiner before you can select for the LogMiner contents view.

3. **ORA-01292: no log file has been specified for the current LogMiner session** Before you can select from the LogMiner view, you must add a log file(s) to the list for analysis and start logmnr. Then you can select from V$LOGMNR_CONTENTS.

Summary

Occasional analysis of the online redo log file can help you find out when table data is changed or perform capacity analysis on your Oracle database. LogMiner serves as a handy means to look at the contents of Oracle 8 or 8*i* database redo logs. In this chapter you have been introduced to LogMiner and its components. You have been shown how to mine your archive log files to find out when and who changed some table data, when a table was dropped so you can more accurately perform some form of recovery and also how to show the amount of DML activity over a time period. Advantages of using the data dictionary file have been clearly demonstrated and LogMiner restrictions have also been highlighted. Finally, a list of new features in Oracle 9*i* are listed, which make LogMiner more versatile and easier to use.

For more information on LogMiner, see Chapter 7 ("Managing Archived Redo Logs") of the Oracle 8*i* Administrators Guide. Also look at *Oracle8i Supplied PL/SQL Packages Reference* for specifics on LogMiner procedures and the *Oracle8*i *Reference* for specifics on the LogMiner views.

Chapter Questions

As a refresher, try answering these questions to reinforce the concepts in this chapter.

1. What purpose does a dictionary file serve for Oracle's LogMiner?

   A. Translates object ID numbers into readable object names during LogMiner analysis

   B. Looks up words for correct spelling

   C. Backs up the SYSTEM tablespace

   D. Stores errors during LogMiner analysis

2. Which view contains the contents of the currently analyzed redo log files?

   A. V$LOGMNR_DICTIONARY

   B. V$LOGMNR_LOGS

   C. V$LOGMNR_CONTENTS

   D. V$LOG

3. LogMiner can find DML and DDL in the redo log files during analysis?

   A. True

   B. False

4. What procedure adds log files to the list for LogMiner analysis?

   A. DBMS_LOGMNR_D.BUILD

   B. DBMS_LOGMNR.ADD_LOGFILE

   C. DBMS_LOGMNR.START_LOGMNR

   D. DBMS_LOGMNR.END_LOGMNR

5. The contents of LogMiner V$LOGMNR_CONTENTS view are available only to the session running LogMiner and will not be available after that session ends LogMiner.

   A. True

   B. False

Answers to Chapter Questions

1. A. LogMiner uses a dictionary file to translate Oracle internal object IDs for the object name and column names in SQL statements.

2. C. When you select from V$LOGMNR_CONTENTS, you are sequentially reading through files in the LogMiner analysis list and optionally translating Oracle object ID into readable n11ames.

3. False. LogMiner will not find the DDL commands to change object definitions. It will find SQL that changes table values. Using the SQL changes made to data dictionary tables, you can deduce some DDL statements.

4. B. The DBMS_LOGMNR.ADD_LOGFILE procedure specifies the log file or files that you want to read. You can view information about specified log files using a view named V$LOGMNR_LOGS.

5. True. Though you can have multiple sessions on a database running LogMiner, the contents of the V$LOGMNR_CONTENTS are only available to that session while LogMiner is started. Each session could see different data values if they analyze a different set of log files.

PART
III

Server Managed
Recovery

CHAPTER
11

RMAN Configuration

ecovery Manager (RMAN) is an Oracle tool you can use to back up, restore, and recover your Oracle databases. RMAN was introduced with Oracle 8.0 and has changed the way DBAs handle database backup and recovery strategies. RMAN is a command-line interpreter that translates user commands into PL/SQL. These PL/SQL commands are then run on the desired database to back up, restore, and recover it. Each backup created using RMAN is stored on either disk or tape media, and the information about the backup is recorded in the control file of the backed up database and in an optional storage area called a *Recovery Catalog*. Using various database views or RMAN commands, you can query the control file or the recovery catalog to show the status of backups taken. RMAN is called server-managed recovery because it manages most aspects of backup, restoration, and recovery.

In this chapter, you will learn the architecture and terminology used by RMAN. You'll also learn how to configure RMAN. The remaining chapters of the book will describe how to accomplish backup and recovery tasks using RMAN based on the configuration you've set up in this chapter.

RMAN Architecture

Before we start looking at RMAN, let's take a moment to understand the architecture and how each component interacts with each other, as shown in Figure 11-1. The following list describes the different RMAN components:

- **RMAN executable**   The actual command-line tool used to back up, restore, and recover your databases. This executable will translate commands that you provide into a sequence of steps required to carry out the desired result. These steps execute PL/SQL on the target database. The RMAN executable is also responsible for updating the recovery catalog with new information. The program is automatically installed when you install the Oracle server and can be called from the server where the database is being backed up or from another, different host.

- **recover.bsq**   A separate file that forms part of the RMAN executable. This file resides in the $ORACLE_HOME/rdbms/admin directory and must be present for RMAN to function. This file contains structural information and other data (such as functions and SQL cursors) for RMAN's use.

- **Target database**   The database that is being backed up, restored, or recovered.

- **Target database control file**   The control file of the database being backed up, restored, or recovered. Whenever an RMAN backup is taken of a database, the backup information is *always* stored in the target database control file. To prevent the control files from getting too large, older backup records are overwritten after a certain number of days.

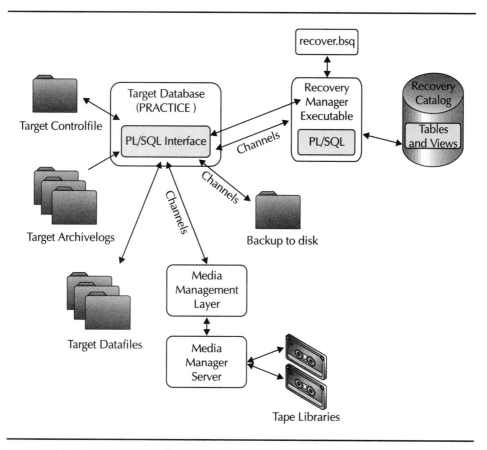

FIGURE 11-1. *RMAN architecture*

■ **Channels**   Communication pathways that allow the RMAN executable to pass data from the target database to the backup media. When a channel is opened, a server session process to the database is created (just as a session process is created when you connect to the database using SQL*Plus). This channel is then used to handle the data moving in and out of the database during some RMAN commands.

■ **Recovery catalog**   An optional user schema containing RMAN information stored on a different database than the target database. The catalog is a set of tables, views, and PL/SQL packages that are contained within a user's schema located on a separate database and server from the database being backed up. The catalog stores the same backup information found in the control file (with the addition of stored scripts). This backup information is stored indefinitely in the catalog (though it can be manually purged), while the control file stores backup information for a finite period. The recovery catalog can keep a historical repository of all backups taken using RMAN, store RMAN scripts, and improve the use of the automated restoration and recovery options of RMAN.

■ **Media Management Layer (MML)**   A software layer allowing RMAN to write to and read from a vendor tape device. To back up to tape, RMAN uses the Media Management Layer (MML) that communicates with the physical tape drives. The MML passes the data being backed up from the target database to the media manager server (Legato Networker, Veritas Netbackup, and so on), which then puts the data onto tape. If you are backing up to disk, the MML is not necessary. Similarly, RMAN restore files from tape via the MML.

Key Features of RMAN

Now that you are familiar with the main components, how does RMAN make backing up and recovering your many Oracle databases easier? Many RMAN features make it a more desirable tool for handling backup and recovery than employing the user manager recovery techniques already discussed in previous chapters.

■ **Automated backup, restoration, and recovery**   If the physical database structure changes when datafiles are added, tablespaces are dropped, more archive log files are created, etc., RMAN will automatically back up the newly created structures. As you have seen before, the control file of a database contains its physical structure. RMAN reads the control file each time the database is backed up to make sure the correct structural contents (datafiles, control files, and archive log files) are backed up.

■ **Automatic backup recording**   RMAN automatically records each backup being taken in the target database control file (the number of records is restricted) and in the optional recovery catalog. This means that RMAN will also know which backup should be restored and which log files are needed for recovery. This takes the burden off of the DBA to keep accurate backup records.

■ **Incremental levels of backup**   To back up a datafile with user-managed backups, the whole file must be copied to another location (disk or tape). This means that if your database occupies 200GB of disk space, your database backup will also occupy 200GB of space. The incremental levels of backup offered by RMAN enable you to back up used blocks that have been used (as opposed to empty, unused blocks) or back up only the data blocks that have only changed since the last incremental backup. This reduces the amount of data being backed up *and* improves recovery performance.

■ **Recovery through NOLOGGING operations**   Oracle recommends that you take a fresh backup of the datafiles when a NOLOGGING operation occurs on an object within that datafile. If you must apply redo to a restored file from log files generated during a NOLOGGING operation, the data in those changed blocks will be inaccessible. The reason? Applied redo records from the NOLOGGING operations mark those blocks as corrupt. Using RMAN to perform incremental backups, the blocks that were changed during the NOLOGGING operation are backed up. When recovering using an incremental backup, the entire block changed by the NOLOGGING operation is restored. Therefore, the redo during the previous NOLOGGING operation is not required, and the data blocks changed remain accessible.

■ **Corruption detection**   RMAN can check each data block read during backup for a number of different corruptions (media corruption, checksum invalidation, and logical structure corruptions). These corruption checks can also be performed during a restoration. Any corrupt blocks found during a backup will be reported in the target database alert.log and can also be viewed in the V$BACKUP_CORRUPTION and V$COPY_CORRUPTION views of the target database.

■ **Smarter open database backup**   During open database backup, RMAN does not require each tablespace to be placed into hot backup mode (this means no more tablespace BEGIN/END backup statements). Therefore, open database backups do not require the increased amount of redo generated as user-managed open backups do and, thus, RMAN open backups run faster and don't create extra redo activity.

■ **Performance tuning enhancements**   RMAN allows you to adjust the performance for backup, restoration, and recovery operations. You can operate on your database in parallel, multiplex the reading and writing to tape devices or disks, and limit read rates of the files being backed up to reduce overhead on the I/O system.

■ **Easy archive log backups**   Just like datafiles, archived redo log files can easily be backed up using RMAN. There is no need to manually create a list of archive log files that need to be backed up and then removed—RMAN can do all of this for you. During a recovery, RMAN detects which log files are needed, restores them, and applies them.

These features, among others, make RMAN a better option for backup and recovery than typical user-managed techniques. In this chapter and the next three, I'll display these features and explain them in greater detail.

Recovery Manager Catalog

Protecting the Oracle database is a primary job role for the database administrator. Performing backups regularly becomes routine. With user-managed recovery, you must know where backups are stored and what the backup contains. When the time comes to recover a database, the DBA has to *quickly* find and restore the correct backup(s) and find the archive log files needed for recovery. One of the big advantages of using server-managed recovery is that records of the backups are stored in control file and optionally, the recovery catalog. Therefore, during restoration and recovery, you simply issue the correct RMAN commands, and RMAN will translate them into a list of required datafiles and archive log files that are needed to bring the database back.

Because all RMAN information is stored in the target database control file, why would you go to the extra effort to maintain an RMAN catalog? See Table 11-1 for a list of advantages in using an RMAN catalog.

The target database control file will store a maximum number of days worth of backup and archive log information, which is determined using the CONTROL_FILE_RECORD_KEEP_TIME init.ora parameter. By default, this parameter is set to seven days. This means on the eighth day, the oldest information (from day 1) may be overwritten.

The recovery catalog retains more RMAN activity history than the target database control file. If a recovery catalog is not being used and you are just relying on the control file for recording your backups, what happens if you lose all of your current control files? Unless you have the backup history recorded elsewhere, you lose the information for the most recent RMAN backups. Even if you do have the information recorded elsewhere (not using a catalog), restoration and recovery will require more manual activity from you and the assistance from Oracle Support. Using a catalog, a complete database loss (including all control files) can be recovered from, assuming that you keep the catalog up to date.

The Recovery Manager catalog contains information about your target database(s) (tablespaces, datafiles, log files, and so on), which is copied from the target control file. RMAN uses catalog information to perform backup, restore, recovery, and maintenance operations. For example, the catalog stores a history of the names and locations of all the target datafiles and archive log files. RMAN provides reporting facilities, which allow you to query the catalog to see information about RMAN backups performed on the target database(s). The catalog can optionally contain groups of RMAN commands known as stored scripts (explained in Chapter 13). Table 1 shows the differences between using a target control file only and a recovery catalog.

Target Control File Only	**Target Control File and Catalog**
If all target database control files are lost, recovery is possible but very difficult.	If all target database control files are lost, recover is as easy as a few simple commands. The up-to-date catalog contains the location of the control file backups.
The control file contains a time-restricted amount of backup information.	The catalog contains an unlimited history of all RMAN backup operations.
The control file keeps only the current database structure schema information. For example, the control file only knows the datafile names and tablespaces as they currently exist.	The catalog stores any schema information as it changes over time each time the catalog is updated with target control file information. Therefore, you can report on the structural schema as it existed in the past.
RMAN commands can be run from the RMAN prompt and via script files.	RMAN commands can be run from the RMAN prompt, via script files *and* stored scripts.
Without the catalog, target control file backups must occur *after* each RMAN backup (the control file now contains the new backup information). Also, the DBA must keep careful records about the location and details of control file backups.	The catalog contains all necessary information about backups as contained in the target control file. Therefore, the catalog provides a backup record keeping function *and* can be used to restore a control file from RMAN backups.

TABLE 11-1. *Advantages to Using an RMAN Catalog*

When you deploy a recovery catalog with RMAN, keep in mind these considerations:

- Locate the catalog on a separate database and machine from any of the target databases registered in it. You can also use a production database as a catalog database for another production database, and vice versa. For example, you can create a catalog on database PRD1 to manage RMAN activities on PRD2 and create a catalog on PRD2 to manage RMAN activities for PRD1.

■ To avoid upgrade and compatibility issues when using different RMAN versions with various target database versions, use a separate catalog owner for each Oracle database version you plan to manage with RMAN. Create a different user schema for each different version of the database you will be backing up. For an 8.0.6 database, create a schema called rman806 and use the 8.0.6 instructions for creating a catalog (using the catrman.sql script). When backing up an 8.0.6 database, you should use the 8.0.6 RMAN executable. For an 8.1.7 database, create a new schema called rman817 and use the create catalog command to create an 8.1.7 recovery catalog. For these backups, the 8.1.7 RMAN executable would be used. One RMAN catalog can manage multiple target databases. Note that Oracle does support using one version of the catalog to store multiple versions of the target databases. For example, you can create an 8.1.7 catalog and store backups from 8.0.6, 8.1.6, and 8.1.7 databases. By setting up a catalog user for each version, you avoid the series of configuration steps that must be followed (as detailed in the *Oracle 8i Recovery Manager Users Guide and Reference*) to get RMAN to work on an older database version.

■ Be sure to back up the catalog database (with or without RMAN) or at least any catalog users on the catalog database (using Export). The information contained in the recovery catalog becomes crucial in managing a large number of database backups.

Exercise 11.1: Create a Recovery Manager Catalog

The exercise in this chapter shows you how to create a Recovery Manager catalog. You'll also register the PRACTICE database within the newly created catalog. Once you've accomplished these tasks, you can explore the catalog with RMAN commands and SQL*Plus queries.

Task Description	Minutes
1. Prepare the Catalog Database	10
2. Create the Recovery Manager Catalog	5
3. Register the PRACTICE Database	5
4. Resync Control File to Catalog	5
5. Back Up Catalog User	5
Total Time	30

The tasks in this exercise are very simple to perform. As you accomplish each step in each task, I'll talk a little about why you are doing it.

Task 1: Prepare the Catalog Database

Since the catalog is a schema that resides in a database, you must choose a database to house the catalog. Though the catalog owner (a database user) can be created on any Oracle database, you can create a database just for the purpose of holding RMAN repositories. Back in Chapter 3, you created a database to be used for the RMAN catalog called *RCAT*. In a real-world environment, the database holding the recovery catalogs will be located on a different server from any databases being registered in it.

When creating a catalog user, you'll need space for the repository tables, indexes, views, and PL/SQL objects. Though the catalog schema can be in any tablespace, create a separate tablespace on the RCAT database for this purpose:

```
SQL> CREATE TABLESPACE cattbs DATAFILE '/oradata/RCAT/cattbs01.dbf'
  2     SIZE 20M EXTENT MANAGEMENT LOCAL AUTOALLOCATE;
```

With the catalog in a separate tablespace, you can transport the catalog tablespace, Export it (with Oracle 9*i* tablespace Export), and back it up separately from other tablespaces. Next, create a user that will contain the catalog schema using SQL like this:

```
LINUX> sqlplus sys/rcat@rcat
SQL> CREATE USER rman817 IDENTIFIED BY rman
  2     TEMPORARY TABLESPACE temp
  3     DEFAULT TABLESPACE cattbs
  4     QUOTA UNLIMITED ON cattbs;
SQL> GRANT connect, recovery_catalog_owner TO rman817;
```

The RECOVERY_CATALOG_OWNER is a special role that should only be granted to the recovery catalog owner. It indirectly grants many system privileges to the selected user. The user must exist before Recovery Manager can create the catalog. In the next task, you'll use RMAN to create the catalog in the RMAN817 schema.

Task 2: Create the Recovery Manager Catalog

Before you create the catalog, I'll describe some command line options when invoking RMAN from the operating system prompt. Start RMAN by typing **rman**. You can add command-line arguments when you invoke RMAN. Table 11-2 shows useful command-line parameters you can use.

Command Line Parameter	Description
target	String that defines a connect-string for target database. When you connect to a target database, your connection is an SYSDBA connection. This user will have privileges to start up and shut down the database. This user must either belong to the OS DBA group, or you must have set up a password file allowing SYSDBA connections.
catalog or rcvcat	String that defines a connect-string for a recovery catalog user. When you connect to a catalog database, your connection is not an SYSDBA connection. This is the same as using rcvcat, which was introduced with 8.0.
nocatalog	Specifies that RMAN will not use a recovery catalog. This parameter is mutually exclusive to the catalog parameter.
cmdfile	String that defines a name of input command file. When you run RMAN, you can run either a command file or you can run interactively.
log or msglog	String that defines a file containing RMAN output messages. The log parameter can only be specified on the command line. You cannot start spooling in RMAN like you can with the SQL*Plus spool command. When using a logfile, the output messages are not displayed to the screen.
trace	Similar to log/msglog which will produce a file showing the RMAN output messages. Using trace will also display the messages to the screen.
append	Specifies that messages will be appended to the message log file if it already exists. This parameter is used in conjunction with the log parameter.

TABLE 11-2. *RMAN Command-Line Parameters*

When passing parameters to RMAN on the command line, the values can be either a quoted string or an unquoted string. For example, each of the following is equivalent when defining the catalog database on the command line:

```
LINUX> rman target sys/practice@practice    # no equal sign
LINUX> rman target 'sys/practice@practice'  # enclosed in '
LINUX> rman target "sys/practice@practice"  # enclosed in quotes
LINUX> rman target /                         # OS authentication
LINUX> rman
RMAN> connect target sys/practice@practice
```

In this book, you'll start RMAN and connect using the connect command from the RMAN prompt. This way, the connection information won't be easily seen from the operating system.

These same connection options can be used for catalog connections by swapping the keyword target with the keyword catalog. Create a catalog from the RMAN command prompt:

```
LINUX> rman
RMAN> connect catalog rman817/rman@rcat
RMAN> CREATE CATALOG TABLESPACE cattbs;
```

During the creation process, tables, indexes, views, and PL/SQL packages get created that will store target database metadata. You can see a list of the objects by connecting via SQL*Plus as the catalog owner:

```
LINUX> sqlplus /nolog
SQL> CONNECT rman817/rman@rcat
SQL> SELECT object_name, object_type FROM user_objects;
```

Task 3: Register the PRACTICE Database

Before RMAN can operate on a database with a catalog, you must register that target database in the catalog. During registration, RMAN populates the catalog tables with the target database structure information from its control file. Information such as the database ID, database name, tablespaces, datafiles, redo log files, and archive log history get stored into the catalog.

When you register the PRACTICE database, you'll connect to both the catalog database and the target database in the same RMAN session. Establish these connections by using the connect command at the RMAN prompt. After that, register the connected target database in the catalog:

```
LINUX> rman
RMAN> connect catalog rman817/rman@rcat
RMAN> connect target sys/practice@practice
RMAN> register database;
```

When complete, the rman817 catalog user will contain all PRACTICE database information it needs to begin backups of the PRACTICE database.

From the RMAN prompt, you have two commands that will provide information about the current target database status. You can see the database you have registered with the LIST INCARNATION command. If there are multiple databases registered in this catalog, the following command will show all of them:

```
RMAN> list incarnation;
RMAN-03022: compiling command: list
List of Database Incarnations
DB Key  Inc Key DB Name  DB ID              CUR Reset SCN  Reset Time
-------  ------- --------  ----------------  --- ----------  ----------
1       2       PRACTICE 2629144163         YES 64301       10-JAN-02
```

You can use the report command to find out registered information about the PRACTICE database now stored in the catalog.

```
RMAN> report schema;
RMAN-03022: compiling command: report
Report of database schema
File K-bytes     Tablespace            RB segs Name
----  ----------   -------------------   ------- ------------------
1     102400 SYSTEM                YES     /oradata/PRACTICE/system01.dbf
2      20480 RBS                   YES     /oradata/PRACTICE/rbs01.dbf
3      10240 USERS                 NO      /oradata/PRACTICE/users02.dbf
4      20480 TEMP                  NO      /oradata/PRACTICE/temp01.dbf
5      20480 TOOLS                 NO      /oradata/PRACTICE/tools01.dbf
6      20480 INDX                  NO      /oradata/PRACTICE/indx01.dbf
7      10240 USERS                 NO      /oradata/PRACTICE/users01.dbf
```

If you see output like this for your PRACTICE database, you know that you've successfully registered your PRACTICE database in the catalog on the RCAT database.

Task 4: Resync Control File to Catalog

When using RMAN with a recovery catalog, you must keep the catalog information synchronized with the target database control file. RMAN uses two types of synchronization, *full* and *partial*. A full resync will update the catalog with any changed nonreusable records in the control file. Nonreusable records include datafiles, tablespaces and online redo log files. A partial resync will update the catalog with reusable records from the control file. Reusable records include the log history, the archive log information, and any RMAN backup records. You resynchronize the control file with the RESYNC CATALOG command. In order for a full resync to occur, RMAN makes a snapshot copy of the current target control file. The snapshot control file ensures that the control file information is not changing while the catalog is being updated. On Linux, the default snapshot control file is named snapcf_$ORACLE_

SID.f (snapcf_PRACTICE.f for the PRACTICE database) and can be found in the $ORACLE_HOME/dbs directory. On Windows NT, the snapshot control file is named SNCF%ORACLE_HOME%.ORA (SNCFPRACTICE.ORA for the PRACTICE database) in the %ORACLE_HOME%\database directory. You can move this file to a different location during the next resync using the following commands:

```
LINUX> rman
RMAN> connect catalog rman817/rman@rcat
RMAN> connect target sys/practice@practice
RMAN> set snapshot controlfile name to
2>      '/oradata/PRACTICE/snap_PRACTICE.ctl';
RMAN> resync catalog;
```

This resync command is an example of an explicit resynchronization. Some RMAN operations automatically synchronize the database control file to the catalog. RMAN will detect if a partial or full resync is necessary. If only a partial resync is necessary, a snapshot control file is not used. You can also issue the RESYNC CATALOG command. During this command, your catalog tables are updated with the latest control file information using the full resync mechanism. The commands that trigger a partial or full resync of the catalog include Backup, Copy, Crosscheck, List, Report, Delete Expired Backup Set, Duplicate, Restore, Recover, and Switch.

To illustrate control file and catalog synchronization, open a second command prompt and execute these commands to rename a datafile (when you are done with this test, you can rename the datafile back to its original name):

```
LINUX> sqlplus sys/practice@practice
SQL> ALTER DATABASE DATAFILE 6 OFFLINE;
SQL> host mv /oradata/PRACTICE/indx01.dbf
  2    /oradata/PRACTICE/indx1.dbf
SQL> ALTER DATABASE RENAME FILE
  2    '/oradata/PRACTICE/indx01.dbf' TO
  3    '/oradata/PRACTICE/indx1.dbf';
SQL> ALTER DATABASE DATAFILE 6 ONLINE;
```

The control file of the PRACTICE database now knows the true location of the INDX tablespace datafile. But the catalog does not know the current location. When you run the report schema from the RMAN prompt, you'll see a full resync performed. Before the report command runs, RMAN automatically carries out a catalog resync:

```
RMAN> report schema;
RMAN-03022: compiling command: report
RMAN-03024: performing implicit full resync of recovery catalog
RMAN-03023: executing command: full resync
RMAN-08002: starting full resync of recovery catalog
RMAN-08004: full resync complete
Report of database schema
```

```
File K-bytes    Tablespace             RB segs Name
---- ---------- ---------------------- ------- --------------------
1       102400 SYSTEM                  YES     /oradata/PRACTICE/system01.dbf
2        20480 RBS                     YES     /oradata/PRACTICE/rbs01.dbf
3        10240 USERS                   NO      /oradata/PRACTICE/users02.dbf
4        20480 TEMP                    NO      /oradata/PRACTICE/temp01.dbf
5        20480 TOOLS                   NO      /oradata/PRACTICE/tools01.dbf
6        20480 INDX                    NO      /oradata/PRACTICE/indx1.dbf
7        10240 USERS                   NO      /oradata/PRACTICE/users01.dbf
```

Notice the messages after the REPORT SCHEMA command. During the REPORT SCHEMA command, RMAN automatically checks that the catalog is current with the target control file. Thus, a full resync is performed. Also note that the latest information is contained in the target control file. The synchronization passes information from the target control file to the catalog.

TIP

Schedule a resync *against the catalog several times a day to make sure that the catalog is up to date with the target control file. If the target database is producing many archive log files during each day, the catalog needs to be updated to include these log files. This will ensure that the catalog can successfully carry out automatic restoration and recovery of the database in the event of a failure.*

Task 5: Back Up Catalog User

As you protect your Oracle databases, you should also protect your catalog database contents. You can back up the entire catalog database via user-managed or server-managed methods. You can also regularly Export the catalog user. When you Export the catalog user, use an Export parameter file as shown here:

```
USERID = rman817/rcat@rcat
FILE   = /oradata/PRACTICE/backup/ch12/export_user_rman817
LOG    = /oradata/PRACTICE/backup/ch12/export_user_rman817
OWNER  = rman817
```

When you execute export using this parameter file, you create a binary Export file that can be later used to restore the recovery catalog.

NOTE

I'll use a catalog during all RMAN exercises in this book. If you plan to use only a target control file instead, use the nocatalog option at the RMAN catalog for the exercises and do not connect to the catalog. However, some exercises in the rest of this chapter may require a catalog.

Create a Redundant Catalog

You can further protect a target database RMAN deployment by registering that database with a second recovery catalog. In the event of a target database failure and first recovery catalog failure, you'll have a second catalog available for fast and easy recovery. Try this trick to set up and manage a redundant catalog: create a user with required privileges on a different database from the target and first catalog databases, as in Task 1. Using the Export created in Task 5, Import the user into a different database. Each time the original catalog is resynchronized with the target database, using an explicit resync command, connect to the other catalog and issue the same resync command. After each backup, the second catalog also needs to be resynced to ensure that it contains the newly created backup. Managing two recovery catalog schemas like this is easy and provides added protection in the event of a target database and primary recovery catalog failure.

Media Management Layer

Oracle's Recovery Manager is automatically configured to back up your database files to disk. RMAN can also perform backup and recovery operations to one or more tape devices. To do this, you need to configure your Oracle server software to communicate with the tape vendor software. The communication layer between the Oracle RMAN components and the tape vendor software is called the Media Management Layer (MML). Oracle maintains a list of tape management software vendors that work with Recovery Manager at Oracle's Web site (http://www.oracle.com/database/recovery).

Oracle established the Oracle Backup Solutions Program, which provides certification for a range of tape management software products that are compliant with Oracle's Media Management Layer (MML) API specification. Oracle published this specification, and software vendors write software that is compliant with the MML interface. Therefore, an Oracle server session can issue commands to the media manager to back up or restore a file without knowing (or caring) what vendor has supplied the tape access.

A media manager is a utility that loads, labels, and unloads sequential media such as tape drives for the purpose of backing up and recovering data. When you configure the MML for Oracle backup, you obtain a library file from the tape backup vendor and link it in with the Oracle executables (relinking is unnecessary on some versions of Oracle). That shared library is analogous to a driver for an installed hardware device on a computer. When RMAN interacts with the SBT (System Backup to Tape) interface, this shared library communicates with the tape management software. Once the MML is configured with the Oracle server software, RMAN can write and read to the tapes via the tape management software. Thus, the media manager layer translates the RMAN commands into instructions that the media manager can understand. For example, RMAN says copy this file to the SBT interface and the MML translates that command into the native instructions that can be understood by the tape management software. A simple copy command may mean that a tape has to be mounted and then positioned before the copy can begin. This way, RMAN issues simple instructions and the tape software handles all the tape device details.

Configure the Media Management Layer

When Oracle ships, it supplies a dummy shared library on UNIX named libobk.so. You typically configure the MML on UNIX by renaming that file to something like libobk.so.backup for safekeeping. Then create a symbolic link named libobk.so to point to the tape software vendor's RMAN compatible library. Therefore, when Oracle calls the libobk.so from RMAN, it is actually sending commands to the tape management software's library instead.

As a generic example, say your UNIX server is connected to a tape device that is managed by a software company named XYZ Software. If you want to configure RMAN to write to the XYZ Software media manager, first find out if XYZ Software has a library that is compatible with the Oracle specification in the Backup Solutions Program. You can check the Oracle website to see if XYZ Software participates or contact XYZ directly. Once XYZ Software is loaded and successfully writing to and from tape, locate the library that you must link in with the Oracle server software. The tape software company can provide support in locating the library file name and special configuration instructions. When you find the name of that library, you will link it in with the Oracle software by following these steps (the library file is named libxyz.so in this example):

1. Shut down all Oracle databases sharing the current ORACLE_HOME directory.

2. Rename the old symbolic link for libobk.so:

   ```
   mv $ORACLE_HOME/lib/libobk.so $ORACLE_HOME/lib/libobk.so.backup
   ```

3. Create a symbolic link between libobk.so and the shared library that you want to use:

   ```
   % ln -s $ORACLE_HOME/lib/libobk.so $TAPE_SOFTWARE/lib/libxyz.so
   ```

4. Verify that the link is successful by using the sbttest test utility to back up a file. For example, enter:

   ```
   % sbttest testfile.txt -trace sbtio.log
   ```

On Unix platforms (not Windows), you can use a utility named SBTTEST to aid in troubleshooting media management. With this utility, you can test the media management software without running RMAN. This utility writes a sample file (like testfile.txt) to tape and then removes it. Consult Chapter 9 of the *Oracle8i Recovery Manager User's Guide and Reference* for details on troubleshooting the media management layer.

If you are using Oracle 8.0.x, you will need to manually link your RDBMS with your MML software after you set up the symbolic link as just shown. Be sure to relink your Oracle software while all Oracle software in your 8.0.x Oracle Home is shut down. The way each MML is linked into Oracle is normally dependent on the MML chosen. Refer to the MML documentation pertaining to its use with Oracle for exact instructions.

Here is a brief example of how to integrate Oracle8*i* with Legato Storage Manager on Windows NT/2000:

1. Ensure that you installed Legato Storage Manager from the Oracle Server CDROM. On the Oracle Installation CDROM, you'll find a zipped file in the \disk1\lsm directory named lsm57_nt.zip. Unzip this file and install Legato Storage Manager by executing setup.exe. The tape drive must be visible in Settings | Control Panel | Tape Devices.

2. Add the bin directory where you've installed Legato to your path environment setting in your Control Panel. For example, if you've installed Legato in the c:\Program Files\nsr directory, add c:\Program Files\nsr\bin to your path.

Many of the details of setting up the MML is operating system and tape software vendor–specific, so I have not included much detail in configuring the MML in this section, although I hope this section will point you in the right direction toward successful configuration of the MML in your environment. You can also get help on Metalink and from your tape software vendor.

Consult Your Tape Management Vendor

With your shared library linked and tested, you are ready to perform RMAN operations to tape. Your tape management vendor will probably have some specific parameters for their software when writing to and reading from tape at the RMAN prompt. Consult with your tape vendor for specifics about your tape vendor's requirements.

Not only can you perform RMAN operations to tape from an RMAN prompt, many tape management vendors have scheduling software that can call RMAN scripts to perform the backups. The tape software jobs perform similar operations that you perform from the RMAN prompt. Therefore, RMAN processes can be run or they can be executed from the tape management vendor's software. You can purchase backup software described here from third-party software to back up their OS file systems and to manage and automate the RMAN backup processes. Products such as Legato Networker, Veritas Netbackup, HP OmniBack, Solstice Backup, and ARCserve interface well with Oracle's Recovery Manager.

NOTE
All RMAN operations in this book will write to disk. Throughout the examples in the book, you can substitute disk for tape (SBT_TAPE) in an environment where you have set up your MML.

Oracle 9*i* New Features

Oracle 9*i* has introduced a whole set of enhancements to RMAN to make it even more usable than before. A few of them are outlined here:

- **Automatic channel configuration**   Before backing up, copying, or restoring database files with RMAN version 8.x, a channel has to be allocated for the communication in and out of the target database. The CONFIGURE command can now be used to create a set of persistent reusable channels using a number of different parameters. These channels are automatically allocated by Oracle whenever you issue commands like backup, copy, restore, or recover.

- **Retention policies**   Just like those retention policies that are available with media manager software, RMAN can be configured to manage backups as they age out. You can mark backups as obsolete or delete them when they get to be a specified age or have been backed up more than a specified number of times.

- **Block media recovery**   Pre-Oracle9*i*, if one or more data blocks were found to be corrupt within a datafile, the file would have to be taken offline, restored from a backup, and then rolled forward using archive logs. Using block recovery, you can leave the affected file online, allowing access to unaffected blocks, and apply the archived redo to only those blocks that need recovery.

- **Resumable backups**   If the backup of the database fails part way through, it is now possible to restart the backup, only backing up the files that were not backed up the first time.

- **Backup optimization**   RMAN can detect if an identical file has been backed up a specified number of times. If this number has been reached and the file is identical, it will not be backed up again. This is ideal for archive log files because it reduces the number of times an archive log will be backed up to tape.

- **Restore optimization**   This new feature forces RMAN to check if the datafile being restored is already on disk. If the current datafile is found and would be more suitable for recovery than an older backup, the datafile will not be restored by RMAN and the current datafile will be used for recovery.

Troubleshooting

I hope the simple setup exercise in this chapter didn't give you any problems, but if it did, you probably encountered one of the following errors. These notes should help you solve the problem.

1. **RMAN-20002: target database already registered in recovery catalog**
   If you've already registered a database with the catalog, you'll get this error after the register database statement. If you want to unregister a database from the catalog, connect to the catalog database as the catalog owner. Before unregistering the catalog, remove all backup sets for this database as described in Chapter 13. Execute a stored procedure using the db_key and db_id for the database you want to unregister. Find the db_key and db_id by querying the db table owned by the catalog user. For example, if you find that the PRACTICE database has a db_key of 2 and a db_id of 13231834, unregister this database like so:

   ```
   EXECUTE dbms_rcvcat.unregisterdatabase(2, 13231834);
   ```

2. **RMAN-06008: connected to recovery catalog database**
   RMAN-06428: recovery catalog is not installed This error is received if you connect to the catalog database as a user that does not own the catalog schema or the catalog has not yet been created. Check that you've provided the correct user and password for the catalog database. If you have provided the correct user and password, use the create catalog command to create the catalog.

3. **RMAN-06004: ORACLE error from recovery catalog database:**
   ORA-01658: unable to create INITIAL extent for segment in tablespace
   CATTBS This error indicates that the catalog creation process ran out of space when creating catalog schema objects. When creating the catalog, tables and indexes must be created in the catalog tablespace or the default tablespace for the catalog owner. If you run out of space, you will not be able to successfully complete catalog creation. Drop and recreate the catalog user and allocate more space to the tablespace used for the catalog objects. Then recreate the catalog. If the catalog owner owns objects other than the catalog objects, you'll have to remove the catalog objects one by one before creating the catalog. For this and other reasons, the catalog owner should only own catalog objects.

In addition to these troubleshooting tips, I think it will be helpful to give you a brief explanation on interpreting RMAN messages and troubleshooting tips for the MML.

RMAN Messages

When you run RMAN commands, many of them will produce a load of output. Most of the time, the output is only informational. Sometimes the output contains errors. Usually, an RMAN error message will contain text like this:

```
RMAN-00571: ============================================================
RMAN-00569: =============== ERROR MESSAGE STACK FOLLOWS ===============
RMAN-00571: ============================================================
```

Once you see this text, the messages that follow will let you know the problem that caused the error. Read through the trailing messages. Sometimes you'll see an ORA- error message. Generic Oracle and RMAN error messages can be found in the *Oracle8i Error Messages* manual. Other RMAN messages that really are errors will often contain all the information you'll need to figure out what went wrong. When reading these error messages, start from the bottom up. Read the last message on the stack and proceed up, as the bottom message is often the cause of the problem.

Media Management Layer

When you configure RMAN with a tape vendor media management layer (MML), you may encounter some problems. You can examine the output messages as just described, and you can also proceed through these tasks to diagnose the RMAN/MML problem.

- Your platform may contain an MML test utility named sbttest utility. You can simulate access to tape using this utility to test your MML. Type **sbttest** at the command prompt to see the command-line options.

- The Media Management Layer may write important information to a log file named sbtio.log in either $ORACLE_HOME/rdbms/log/ or in the user dump destination.

- The alert log file, the target, and the catalog database may contain helpful information for troubleshooting the MML.

- Check with your tape management vendor about their tracing and logging utilities and files. You can correlate these files to your RMAN output to pinpoint which RMAN actions generate tape management problems.

- Check Metalink for issues with your tape vendor and RMAN. Search using your tape vendor and MML and see if someone else might have already solved the problem you are now facing.

Although I don't cover the many intricacies of the MML in this book, I think this brief troubleshooting guide can point you in the right direction as you deploy RMAN in your Oracle database environment.

Summary

In this chapter, you learned the architecture of RMAN, which is classed as server managed recovery. I described the basic components and detailed benefits of using a recovery catalog. You created an RMAN catalog with the create catalog command and learned that it is possible to create multiple catalogs containing information about different versioned databases. You learned about the register database command and how the recovery catalog stays synchronized with the target database control file. The Media Manager Layer (MML) was discussed and you were shown (generically) how to configure Oracle to use your chosen media manager software. For more information on RMAN concepts and configuration, look at Chapters 1, 2, and 3 in *Oracle8i Recovery Manager User's Guide and Reference*. For further help with setting up the MML with RMAN, contact your tape management software vendor.

In the next chapter, you'll perform closed and open database backups. You'll also learn how RMAN can back up your control file and archived redo log files.

Chapter Questions

As a refresher, try these questions to reinforce the concepts and exercises in this chapter.

   1. What command do you use from the RMAN prompt to create a recovery catalog?

      A. register database

      B. create catalog

      C. resync database

      D. list database

   2. What advantages do you have when you use a RMAN catalog instead of just the target control file? (Pick any that apply.)

      A. Recovery is easy using RMAN backups if the target control files are lost.

      B. The catalog information can be used to update the target control file.

      C. The catalog keeps historical backup information that the target control file can't.

      D. A catalog has lower prices and free shipping.

   3. RMAN is called Server Managed Recovery because it manages all aspects of backup, restoration, and recovery.

      A. True

      B. False

4. You can connect to the catalog from the RMAN prompt or using RMAN command line parameters. To connect from the RMAN prompt to a catalog user named rman817 on the RCAT database, type this:

   A. connect target <u>rman817/rman@rcat;</u>

   B. connect target <u>rman817/rman@rcat</u> as SYSDBA

   C. connect <u>rman817/rman@rcat</u> as catalog

   D. connect catalog <u>rman817/rman@rcat</u>

5. The Media Management Layer allows RMAN to write backup to disk and tape.

   A. True

   B. False

Answers to Chapter Questions

1. B.   When you create the catalog, database schema objects are created in the catalog user schema.

2. A, C.   The biggest advantage in using a catalog is that you can easily recover using RMAN backups if the target control files are lost. The recovery catalog will contain historical information beyond what the target control file contains.

3. True.   RMAN and all the related components keep up with backup files, times, locations, media: everything. All you have to do is set things up, connect, and issue a backup command. Then sit back and let RMAN manage the work.

4. D.   The connect command allows you to connect to the catalog or the target database. After the keyword connect, specify what you are connecting to and what user credentials you are connecting with.

5. False.   The MML is necessary to write backups to and read backups from tape. The MML is not necessary when backing up to disk.

CHAPTER
12

RMAN Backup

n the user-managed backups performed in earlier chapters, you learned how to copy entire files using operating system commands. You copied datafiles, control files, and archive log files. You used these coordinated file backups to restore and recover the PRACTICE database. During those operations, you (as the user) had to manage the backup and recovery operations. You had to create lists of database files to copy and restore. In this chapter, you'll see how RMAN uses server components to handle the backup details for you. When you instruct RMAN to back up the database, it knows which files to work on. In addition, RMAN will only back up the blocks of the database files that currently contain data or have had data in them. Therefore, your backup file sizes will be smaller than the size of your datafiles.

The fundamental difference between user-managed and server-managed backup and recovery is this: the DBA must know what to back up and what to restore and recover for user-managed operations. For server-managed operations, RMAN will determine what to back up and what to restore and recover through a very simple interface. The majority of administration tasks have been removed or simplified. For example, remember the open database backup described in Chapter 5? During user-managed backup, you had to create a list of datafiles for each tablespace and place the tablespace in backup mode before you could copy its datafiles. While in backup mode, the server generated additional redo. With RMAN open database backup, additional redo is not automatically generated.

How does RMAN handle open datafile backup differently from user-managed backup? RMAN is clever enough to keep track of the increasing SCNs of any changing data blocks contained within the datafiles being backed up. Changes to the file being backed up can continue to be made through database activity. During the recovery phase, RMAN will automatically apply the redo needed to bring the file to a consistent state. During the backup, it is possible that a data block being copied by RMAN has not been fully written to disk by the DBW (database writer) process, making the header of the block inconsistent with the tail section. This phenomenon is known as a *split*, or *fractured*, block. When such a block is detected, RMAN will reread the block until a consistent copy can be made. Therefore, RMAN is able to perform open database backup with minimal performance degradation.

Recovery Manager Backup Options

Recovery Manager provides three different ways of backing up your database: backups, image copies, and proxy copies. Although each of these methods supplies the same end result of a database backup that can be used for recovery in the event of a database failure, they each have different advantages and disadvantages.

Backups

RMAN backups create one or more physical files on the selected backup media (disk or tape) using its own format. These physical files are called *backup pieces*. The backup can be made of the database, selected tablespaces, datafiles, control files, or archived redo logs or combinations of each.

- Datafiles and control files can be combined in the same backup.

- Archive log files must be backed up separately from datafiles and control files.

The backup files that RMAN creates (backup pieces) are not readable by any other tool and can therefore only be recreated using RMAN. To understand how these backups are created, it is important to understand a few basic terms that will be used throughout the remainder of this book:

- **Channel**   Already introduced to you in Chapter 11, the channel is the communication pathway from the target database to the backup media. The channel type can be defined as either *disk* or *'SBT_TAPE'* (the SBT stands for System Backup to Tape). There are a number of parameters that can be associated with a channel to limit the size of the backup pieces, the number of files that can be opened at one time, and the rate at which those files are read (bytes per second). At least one channel must be allocated before a backup is run. Multiple channels can also be used.

- **Backup set**   A backup set is a logical grouping of physical files (backup pieces) created when the backup command is run. At least one backup set is created for a backup, but there are often more. It is possible to control the number of files being backed up within a backup set using the *filesperset* parameter or to define a maximum size of each backup set using the *setsize* parameter. If multiple channels have been allocated, RMAN will create at least one backup set per channel. RMAN also tries to divide up the files being backed up among the backup sets so that each set is an equal size and each channel works an equal amount. A datafile/control file/archived log file will only belong to one backup set, but a backup set can contain many such files.

- **Backup piece**   A backup piece is the physical file that RMAN creates during a backup. This file will contain the actual data blocks copied from the target datafiles, control files, or archived redo logs. Each backup set will contain at least one backup piece but may contain several. A datafile can also span multiple backup pieces.

■ **Format**   The format is the file name given to the backup pieces created during the backup. When backing up to disk, the full path name for the backup pieces must also be provided. For tape backups, only the file name is required.

■ **Tag**   The tag is a meaningful name that can be used to label a backup. For example, the Sunday level 0 backups might have a tag called Sun-Lev0. This tag can be used to direct RMAN to restore files from a particular backup. The maximum tag length is 30 characters, and a single tag name can be used for more than one backup.

■ **Backup key**   Each backup set created by RMAN is given a unique sequence number that is used to identify it.

When you execute a backup command, ask yourself the following questions:

1. What will be the state of the database when it is backed up? (database state)

2. Where do I want my RMAN backup to be stored? (set destination)

3. What part of the database do I want to back up? (database files)

4. Which data blocks in the database files do I want copied? (incremental level)

The answers to these four questions will dictate how you'll instruct RMAN to take a backup using the BACKUP command. Let's look at the four parts to consider when taking an RMAN backup.

Define the Backup Set Database State

First, RMAN backups can be performed during two different database states. Like user-managed backups, a backup can be taken when the database is closed or open.

■ **Closed database backup**   As with the user-managed closed (cold, consistent) backup, the target database will not be open. Unlike a user-managed backup, RMAN expects to see the database in a mounted state. RMAN must access the target control file to gather structural information during a closed backup.

■ **Open database backup**   As with the user-managed open (hot, inconsistent) backup, the target database will be open. The main difference is that RMAN will not place tablespaces in backup mode during backup or cause extra redo to be generated.

Define the Backup Set Destination

Second, let's talk about items that involve the destination *set* of the backup. When you execute an RMAN backup command, RMAN creates one or more files (backup pieces) that store RMAN control information plus the data blocks being backed up. It is important to give meaningful names to the backup pieces that RMAN creates to prevent having files on tape or disk of which no one knows the origin or contents. This can be achieved within the backup command using the *format* parameter. A number of substitution variables are available for use in creating a file name, which has to be unique for backups to disk and should ideally be unique for tape backups, too. The following are the possible format variables:

- **%d** The database name.

- **%n** The database name padded up to 8 characters by appending one or more *x* letters.

- **%s** The backup set number. These numbers originate from the target control file, beginning with 1 and incremented by 1. If the control file is recreated, the number will start back at 1.

- **%p** The backup piece number within the backup set. The first backup piece is numbered 1 and will be incremented by 1 for each new backup piece within the same backup set.

- **%t** The backup timestamp. This value derives from the seconds elapsed from a reference time in the past.

- **%u** An 8-character value derived from the backup set number and the time the backup was made.

- **%c** The copy number of the backup piece with the backup set. This number will be 1 unless you specify backup duplexing.

- **%U** A guaranteed unique file name made up of %u_%p_%c. If you don't specify a backup file format, %U is used by default.

Some examples of using these format variables are listed in Table 12-1. Remember that only the file name needs to be specified for backups to the SBT_TAPE channels. Backups to disk must also specify the path name and the file name. If no path name is specified, the backup is normally stored in $ORACLE_HOME/dbs.

Format Specified	Example Result
dbinc0_%d_%s_%p_%t	dbinc0_PROD_21_1_447001901
tbsUSERS_%U	tbsUSERS_08dae506_1_1
al_%n_%t_%s_%p	al_PRODxxxx_447157468_41_3

TABLE 12-1. *Example Backup Format results on a Database Named PROD*

CAUTION
*Before choosing a file name, check the maximum
file name size is of the media that you are backing
up to. If you choose a file name format that extends
beyond this limit, you will end up with duplicate file
names that could overwrite each other.*

Define the Backup Set Database Files

Next, let's define terms pertaining to the *scope* of an RMAN backup. During the
execution of a single backup command, you specify the database files to include in the
backup set. RMAN BACKUP commands will only copy data blocks from the datafiles,
control files, and archive logs. These are the backup options available to you:

- **Whole database backup**   The data blocks in all datafiles and control file
  of the target database are included in the backup set. To specify a whole
  database backup, use the keyword DATABASE after the backup command.
  For example: BACKUP (DATABASE).

- **Tablespace backup**   The data blocks in all the datafiles for the specified
  tablespace(s) get copied to the backup set. To specify a tablespace backup,
  use the keyword TABLESPACE after the backup command, followed by a
  comma separated list of tablespaces. For example: BACKUP (TABLESPACE
  SYSTEM, USERS).

- **Datafile backup**   The data blocks in each named datafile get copied to the
  backup set. To specify a datafile backup, use the keyword DATAFILE after
  the backup command. For example: BACKUP (DATAFILE 1,2,3,4).

- **Control file backup**   All data blocks in the database control file get
  copied to the backup set. To specify a control file backup, use the

keyword CONTROLFILE after the backup command. For example: BACKUP CURRENT CONTROLFILE. When a backup is taken of the system tablespace, the control file is automatically included in the backup. A full database backup will therefore include the current control file.

■ **Archive log backup**   All data blocks in each included archive log file get copied to the backup set. To specify an archive log backup, use the keyword ARCHIVELOG after the backup command. Though you can back up datafiles, control files, and archive logs with the same backup command, RMAN will create a separate backup set for the archive logs. For example: BACKUP (ARCHIVELOG ALL).

Define the Backup Set Level

Finally, let's talk about the options available for the *level* of an RMAN backup. When RMAN copies data blocks during a backup, you can specify which data blocks to copy during the backup. As you recall, datafiles are comprised of blocks, and each block is stamped with a system change number (SCN) the last time it is updated. As a backup is taken, every block is read from a datafile and copied to the backup set only if that block meets the level criteria for backup. The level of backup only pertains to datafile backup because all data blocks are copied in each archive log and control file that gets backed up. RMAN will not copy empty blocks from a datafile to the backup set. Empty blocks are only copied when using the Image Copy functionality.

RMAN Backup Compression

When a datafile is added to the database, all blocks within the file are formatted as unused empty blocks. Oracle does this by adding some structure values to the block header and the tail section. The block is classed as used the moment it contains data. If you insert rows into a table and then delete all of the rows, or even if you truncate the table, those blocks that contained the deleted data are still considered used blocks. RMAN will therefore back them up even though they contain no current data. RMAN will not back up the unused empty blocks that have never contained data. RMAN calls this *backup compression*, as the backup being created will be smaller than the original file. Note that whole data blocks are copied during backup, the data blocks are *not* compressed within the backup piece files.

When taking RMAN backups of datafiles, there are two modes of operation: *incremental* or *full.*

Incremental Backups   Using an incremental backup strategy makes it possible to back up only the data blocks that have changed since the last incremental backup. This can greatly reduce the amount of data being backed up and therefore decrease the time and space required to make and store database backups.

Incremental backups contain the notion of a backup *level.* The incremental backup level is an integer between 0 and 4. When an incremental backup is performed, the datafile checkpoint SCN is stored in the target control file with the incremental level. Subsequent incremental backups determine which data blocks to copy in relation to the previous incremental backup level and the SCN of the time it was taken. Backup level 0 is the all-inclusive backup level. During a level 0 backup, all used data blocks get backed up for the chosen datafiles.

An incremental backup can be one of two types: differential or cumulative. A differential backup copies all data blocks that have changed since the most recent same or lower-level incremental backup. For example, during a level 1 differential incremental backup, all data blocks get copied since the last level 1 backup. If a previous level 1 backup has not been taken, all blocks changed since the last level 0 backup are copied. The differential backup is the default incremental backup type used by RMAN when the incremental keyword is used within the backup command.

A cumulative backup copies all data blocks that have changed since the most recent lower-level incremental backup. For example, during a level 2 cumulative incremental backup, all data blocks get copied since the last level 1 incremental backup. If a level 1 backup has not been taken, all blocks since the last level 0 backup are copied.

NOTE
RMAN will always take a copy of the file header, which is block 1 of each datafile.

To help conceptualize a differential incremental backup, look at Figure 12-1, which shows a timeline of differential incremental-level backups. The backup sets are created on each day of the week for a single datafile. The backups taken have the following descriptions (this simplistic example does not take into account any changes made to data dictionary objects that can occur during data changes made by users):

- **Sunday**   A level 0 incremental backup is made. Data block numbers #2, #3, #4, #5, and #6 get copied to backup set 120. These blocks comprise all the used data blocks in the datafile selected for backup (although you'll have

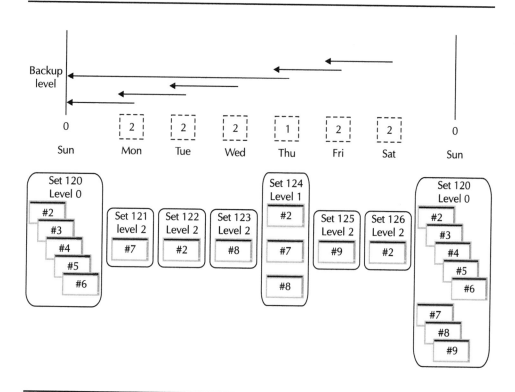

FIGURE 12-1. *Differential Incremental Backup Timeline Example*

a hard time finding a datafile with only five used data blocks in a real world database). A level 0 incremental backup is neither cumulative nor differential. It is a backup used as a baseline for an incremental backup strategy.

- **Monday**   A level 2 differential incremental backup is made. Since Sunday's backup, the data block change to the datafile is block #7, which gets filled with data. Therefore, only this data block is the only one that gets copied to backup set 121 (plus the file header and maybe some blocks from the data dictionary or space management blocks).

- **Tuesday**   A level 2 differential incremental backup is made. Since Monday's backup, a row in data block #2 was updated. Since this data block is the only one that changes, only this data block gets copied to backup set 122.

■ **Wednesday**   A level 2 differential incremental backup is made. Since Tuesday's backup, data block #8 has had data inserted into it. Since this data block is the only one that changed, only this data block gets copied to backup set 123.

■ **Thursday**   A level 1 differential incremental backup is made. All data blocks changed since the most recent level 1 or lower backup are copied to backup set 123. There has not been a level 1 backup since the level 0 backup. Therefore, all changed data blocks since the level 0 backup on Sunday are included in the backup set (#2, #7, and #8).

■ **Friday**   A level 2 differential incremental backup copies data block #9 to backup set 125 because data was added to this data block since Thursday's level 1 backup.

■ **Saturday**   A level 2 differential incremental backup copies data block #2 to backup set 126 because data in that block was changed since Friday's level 2 backup.

■ **Sunday**   A level 0 incremental backup copies all used data blocks to backup set 127. And you're back to the beginning of the cycle.

Cumulative incremental backups are similar to differential, with a small difference, as you can see in Figure 12-2. This diagram shows a timeline of cumulative incremental-level backups. The backup sets are created on each day of the week for a single datafile. The backups taken have these descriptions:

■ **Sunday**   A level 0 incremental backup is made. Data block numbers #2, #3, #4, #5, and #6 get copied to backup set 120. These blocks comprise all the used data blocks in the datafile selected for backup. A level 0 incremental backup is neither cumulative nor differential. It is a full backup used as a baseline for an incremental backup strategy.

■ **Monday**   A level 2 cumulative incremental backup is made. Since Sunday's backup, the data block change to the datafile is that block #7 gets filled with data. Therefore, only this data block is the only one that gets copied to backup set 121.

■ **Tuesday**   A level 2 cumulative incremental backup is made. Since Monday's backup, a row in data block #2 was updated. The two changed data blocks since Sunday's backup get copied to backup set 122.

■ **Wednesday**   A level 2 cumulative incremental backup is made. Since Tuesday's backup, data block #8 has data inserted into it. The three changed data blocks since Sunday's backup get copied to backup set 123.

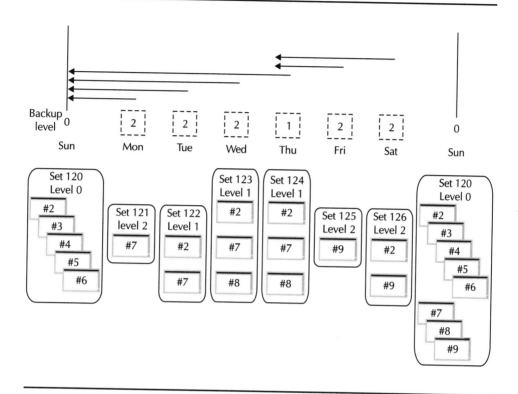

FIGURE 12-2. *Cumulative incremental backup timeline example*

- **Thursday** A level 1 cumulative incremental backup is made. All data blocks changed since the most recent level 1 backup are copied to backup set 123. All changed data blocks since the level 0 backup on Sunday are included in the backup set (#2, #7, and #8).

- **Friday** A level 2 cumulative incremental backup copies data block #9 to backup set 125 because data was added to this data block since Thursday's backup.

- **Saturday** A level 2 cumulative incremental backup copies data blocks #2 and #9 to backup set 126 because these data blocks changed since Thursday's backup.

- **Sunday** A level 0 incremental backup copies all used data blocks to backup set 127. Back to the beginning of the cycle again.

These two figures and their related explanations demonstrate how RMAN performs both differential and cumulative incremental backups.

You now know about incremental backups, but how does RMAN restore a datafile? Chapter 14 covers this in detail, but briefly, incremental backups are restored on top of each other to roll datafiles forward in time. If the differential incremental strategy is employed (as shown in Figure 12-1), if the datafile was lost on Saturday afternoon after the Saturday level 2 incremental backup was taken, the following backups would be restored by RMAN:

1. **Sunday's incremental level 0**   Contains all used blocks in the datafile. A level 0 backup *must* be restored as the base level for subsequent restores.

2. **Thursday's incremental level 1**   Restores all changed blocks since the Sunday backup that has been restored.

3. **Friday's incremental level 2**   Restores all changed blocks since the Thursday backup.

4. **Saturday's incremental level 2**   Restores all changed blocks since the Friday backup.

5. **Finally**   All the redo generated since the time of the Thursday backup will be applied.

Thus, four backups will be used to restore and recover the database to Saturday afternoon using the differential incremental strategy described earlier.

If the cumulative incremental strategy is employed (as shown in Figure 12-2), if the datafile was lost on Saturday afternoon after the Saturday level 2 incremental backup was taken, the following backups would be restored by RMAN:

1. **Sunday's incremental level 0**   Contains all used blocks in the datafile. A level 0 backup *must* be restored as the base level for subsequent restores.

2. **Thursday's incremental level 1**   Restores all changed blocks since the Sunday backup that has been restored.

3. **Saturday's incremental level 2**   Restores all changed blocks since the Thursday backup.

4. **Finally**   All the redo generated since the time of the Thursday backup will be applied.

Thus, three backups will be used to restore and recover the database to Saturday afternoon using the cumulative incremental strategy described earlier.

The decision to use differential or cumulative backups depends on the priority of backup speed/size versus the speed of a restoration and recovery:

- Differential incremental backups copy fewer blocks than cumulative backups and therefore create smaller backup pieces in less time. The drawback to differentials: restoration takes more time because more backup sets must be used.

- Cumulative incremental restore faster because less backup sets are needed to rebuild the database files. The drawback to cumulative: the same data blocks are copied with the same level backups. Copying the same data blocks again creates larger backup piece files and the backups usually take longer.

Since backup sets contain only used and/or changed database blocks, backup sets will be much smaller than image copies. The primary reason to use backup sets is that the backup files saves space over image copies or user-managed operations. When you use the RMAN backup command to protect a database consider these restrictions and guidelines:

- You can run a backup from an RMAN client, but backup sets are always created on tape or a disk connected to the server.

- RMAN does not back up the SQL*Net configuration files, parameter file, alert log, or password file.

- You must use the same version of RMAN executable as the target database you are backing up.

Full Backups   During a full backup, all used data blocks within each datafile are copied to the backup set. A full backup can then be restored using RMAN and archive redo logs can be applied to roll the database forward in time. A full backup copies the exact same blocks as an incremental level 0 but does not take part in an incremental backup strategy. Incremental backups choose to copy data blocks based on prior incremental (not full) backups. For example, consider a datafile that is backed via an incremental level 0 backup on Sunday. On Monday, a full backup is taken. On Tuesday, an incremental level 1 is taken. The blocks being backed up on Tuesday do not consider the backup that was taken on Monday but instead will back up all the blocks that have changed since the last incremental (taken on Sunday).

Image Copies

The copy command creates an *image copy* of an entire database file, which can either be a datafile, control file, or an archive log file. The file copy created by RMAN is identical to the original, without any special formatting applied to it. It can therefore be used just like a file copied from the operating system when the database is opened or closed (as in Chapter 4). The only difference is that the copy is automatically registered in the target database control file and the optional recovery catalog. The tablespace containing the datafile being copied does not have to be put into *hot backup* mode because RMAN keeps track of the changing block SCNs, which are used to detect which redo log files need applying in the event of a recovery. The datafile copies created using RMAN can be used as an incremental level 0 backup, which serves as a base for subsequent incremental backups to be applied.

A level 0 incremental or a full backup creates a backup of all used data blocks within a datafile; an image copy does the same, but it also copies all empty blocks. RMAN can use either the image copy, a full or the level 0 backup as the base incremental to restore before applying further incrementals or redo. Image copies cannot be created using any other of the incremental levels (1–4). RMAN can only create image copies to disk. They cannot be created using the SBT_TAPE channels.

Image copies have one major advantage over differential and incremental backups: they can be put to use during a restore quickly. For example, if you lose a datafile, instruct RMAN to switch to the image copy, apply redo, and the datafile should be accessible again. This is a much quicker process than recovering a datafile from a backup set stored on tape or even on disk, assuming that they both need the same amount of redo to be consistent with the rest of the database.

The big disadvantage to using image copies is that they will occupy the same amount of disk space as the original. If you decide to copy them to tape to save disk space, they must be copied back to disk before RMAN can use them. It's far more efficient on space to use backups instead of image copies.

Proxy Copies

Oracle has enhanced the published Media Management Layer (MML) API by adding a feature called *proxy copy*. The proxy copy allows the MML to take control of how the datafiles are read and backed up. RMAN passes a list of datafiles to the MML layer that needs to be backed up, which in turn decides how best to back them up. The advantage to using proxy copy is that it allows the media manager to use its advanced features, such as direct data transfer from disk to tape. One drawback to using proxy copy is that each datafile being backed up is internally put into a pseudo hot backup mode when the database is open. This means that more redo could be generated during backup times, similar to when the tablespace is manually put into hot backup mode. Oracle automatically handles the status change of each datafile, so less administration is required compared to hot backups. RMAN still catalogs the backups that are taken during a proxy copy, so all of the RMAN automation still applies.

Proxy copy is a relatively new feature to RMAN and is only supported by a few MMLs. You should contact your media manager vendor for more information.

Backup Types Compared

Now that you've read about image copies, backup sets, and proxy copies with RMAN, you might wonder which one makes best sense in your Oracle environment. Each of the backup types has advantages and disadvantages. You can deploy all three types if you choose. Table 12-2 provides a quick list of the advantages and disadvantages of each backup type.

Throughout this chapter, you'll be able to protect your PRACTICE database using the RMAN COPY and BACKUP commands as shown in Figure 12-3. You'll create image copies of all the datafiles and the control file of your database. You'll also create backup sets containing only the used data blocks in your datafiles and all the blocks in your archive log files and control files.

Backup Type	Advantages	Disadvantages
Backup	Contain only used or changed data blocks, making backups smaller. Create backup sets if backup space must be conserved. Backup sets dynamically determine database files for backup. Scripts can be simple. Can be written to tape or disk.	Restoration from backup sets requires reconstructing database files from one or more backup pieces so recovery time takes longer.
Image Copy	File copies can be restored very quickly. Use these if a short recovery time is critical.	File copies are the same size as database files, so they take more space than backup sets. Each image copy must be explicitly named in backup commands. Dynamic scripts are difficult to generate. Image copies can only be written to disk.
Proxy Copy	Can take advantage of MML features. Less consideration for backup pieces and backup set sizes.	Supported mostly by a third-party vendor, adding to support complexity. The feature is not very well documented.

TABLE 12-2.   *Advantages and Disadvantages of RMAN Backup Types*

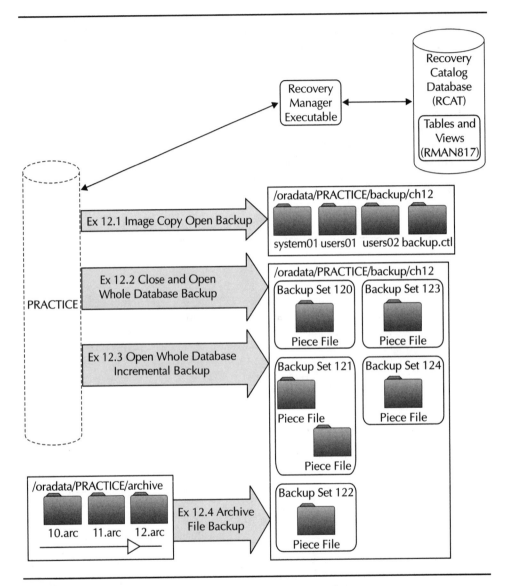

FIGURE 12-3. *RMAN backups of the PRACTICE database*

For the exercises in this chapter, you'll connect to the target database as a user with SYSDBA privilege. You'll also connect to the catalog that you set up in Chapter 11. The connection steps look like this:

```
LINUX> export ORACLE_SID=PRACTICE
LINUX> rman
RMAN> connect target sys/practice;
RMAN> connect catalog rman817/rman@rcat;
```

(You can set the ORACLE_SID to RCAT and use a connect string to connect to the PRACTICE database, or you can use Net8 to connect to both databases.) Since every script in the exercises of this chapter will be run connected to the PRACTICE database as the target and the RCAT database as the catalog, I will omit these steps from the script listings.

Exercise 12.1: Create Recovery Manager Image Copies

In this exercise, you will create image copies off all datafiles and the control file of the PRACTICE database. You must explicitly name each file you plan to copy in the COPY command.

Task Description	Minutes
1. Create an RMAN Copy Script	10
2. Run the RMAN Copy Script	10
3. Verify the RMAN Copy Script	5
Total Time	25

This exercise is very similar to the user-managed backup exercises in Chapters 4 and 5. You are simply going to use RMAN to create a copy of all datafiles and the control file in the PRACTICE database.

Task 1: Create an RMAN Copy Script

During the datafile copy command, you must explicitly specify each file you are going to copy and the file name you plan to create with the copy. A handy way to quickly generate a list of database files is to run the REPORT SCHEMA command. Using that list, create an RMAN copy script. You can copy the datafile names from the output and paste them into a file named b_copy.rcv. Edit the b_copy.rcv file until it looks like the listing shown next. This script copies the datafiles and the control file. (Though RMAN scripts can have any name and extension, you'll typically see an rcv (ReCoVery) extension on these files).

```
run {
allocate channel d1 type disk;
copy
datafile 1 to '/oradata/PRACTICE/backup/ch12/system01.dbf.bak',
datafile 2 to '/oradata/PRACTICE/backup/ch12/rbs01.dbf.bak',
datafile 3 to '/oradata/PRACTICE/backup/ch12/users01.dbf.bak',
datafile 4 to '/oradata/PRACTICE/backup/ch12/temp01.dbf.bak',
datafile 5 to '/oradata/PRACTICE/backup/ch12/tools01.dbf.bak',
datafile 6 to '/oradata/PRACTICE/backup/ch12/indx01.dbf.bak',
datafile 7 to '/oradata/PRACTICE/backup/ch12/users02.dbf.bak',
current controlfile to '/oradata/PRACTICE/backup/ch12/backup.ctl';
}
```

After allocating the channel, the copy command directs RMAN to make image copies of the datafile numbers to the file name provided. The current control file also gets copied. The channel is automatically released at the end of the run block.

Task 2: Run the **RMAN Copy Script**

Run the script you just created by connecting to the target and catalog and then use the @ symbol to run an RMAN command file:

  RMAN> @b_copy.rcv

During the execution of the script, you'll see many messages such as the following:

  RMAN-03022: compiling command: allocate
RMAN-03023: executing command: allocate
RMAN-08030: allocated channel: d1
RMAN-08500: channel d1: sid=16 devtype=DISK

These messages are expected from the allocate channel command in the run block, and RMAN creates them as informative messages. In 9*i*, these messages have been changed so they don't show what appears to be an error message number. These show that RMAN successfully compiled and executed the allocate command. The channel name is d1 and the session ID number on the target PRACTICE database is 16, which created this channel of type DISK.

RMAN-08501: output filename=/oradata/PRACTICE/backup/ch12/system01.dbf.bak
recid=1 stamp=446229077

You can see the copy command making an image copy of datafile 1 to the system01.dbf.bak file.

At the conclusion of the script, you see a partial resync of the recovery catalog:

```
RMAN-03023: executing command: partial resync
RMAN-08003: starting partial resync of recovery catalog
RMAN-08005: partial resync complete
RMAN-08031: released channel: d1
```

During this resync, the RMAN copy records are synchronized with the recovery catalog. At the end of the run block, d1 channel is automatically released from the database.

Task 3: Verify the RMAN Copy Script

You can verify that the image copies worked by looking at the output of the RMAN script. Let's look at several other ways you can confirm that you created a successful image copy of your datafiles and control file. First, look in your /oradata/PRACTICE/backup/ch12/ directory. You will see a copy of all the files you created. Second, you can issue a list copy command from the RMAN command prompt:

```
RMAN> list copy;
RMAN-03022: compiling command: list
List of Datafile Copies
Key File S Completion time Ckp SCN Ckp time  Name
--- ---- - --------------- ------- --------- ------
224  1    A 12-JAN-01      78045   12-JAN-01 /oradata/PRACTICE/backup/ch12/system01.dbf.bak
225  3    A 12-JAN-01      78047   12-JAN-01 /oradata/PRACTICE/backup/ch12/users01.dbf.bak
226  7    A 12-JAN-01      78051   12-JAN-01 /oradata/PRACTICE/backup/ch12/users02.dbf.bak
```

This output shows each datafile that has been copied by RMAN from the previous script, plus any other copies that might have been made before. Each datafile has its own backup key (unique identifier). The backup key can be used for maintenance on each image file copy. The column labeled S provides the status of the backup piece (AVAILABLE, UNAVAILABLE, or EXPIRED). Notice the checkpoint SCN and time of each file. As the copy command proceeds, each datafile undergoes a checkpoint. If these image copies are restored while the database is open, redo must be applied to get these files current with the rest of the database. The control files do not show up in the LIST COPY command because the default file type displayed is datafile. To show copies of the control file, append the OF CONTROLFILE clause to the LIST COPY command:

```
RMAN> list copy of controlfile;
```

There you have it. You just performed an open database backup using RMAN.

How can you create an RMAN script that will create image copies of all datafiles and the control file of your database? From SQL*Plus, you can select from the control file dynamic view v$datafile to get a list of all datafiles in your database. Spool that output to a file along with other needed RMAN commands. See the listing shown next for an example of the commands you can use in SQL*Plus to create an RMAN script file. The only tricky part is striping just the datafile name from the path for each datafile using the INSTR and SUBSTR built in SQL functions.

```
set feedback off pagesize 0 heading off verify off
 set linesize 100 trimspool on
 define dir = '/oradata/PRACTICE/backup/user/ch12/'
define fil = '/tmp/b_copy_whole.rcv'
define div = '/'
spool &fil
prompt run {
prompt   allocate channel d1 type disk;
prompt   copy
select 'datafile ' || file# ||' to ' ||
    '&dir.'||substr(name,(instr(name,'&div',-1)+1))||'.bak ,'
from v$datafile;
prompt current controlfile to '&dir.backup.ctl; }';
spool off;
```

Exercise 12.2: Create Recovery Manager Whole Backup

During this exercise, you will create a full block-level backup of the whole PRACTICE database, including the control file. You will run this whole database backup while the database is open and then again while it is closed. If you are not running the target database in ARCHIVELOG mode, you must perform backups on the database while it is mounted but not open.

Task Description	Minutes
1. Create an RMAN Open Backup Script	5
2. Run the RMAN Open Backup Script	5
3. Verify the RMAN Open Backup Script	5
4. Run an RMAN Closed Backup Script	5
Total Time	20

During this exercise, I'll show you the basic commands to perform a whole database backup. As you run the scripts, the output on the screen will correlate to the output of the list command. I'll point out the correlations so you can connect the backup run output to the list command output.

Task 1: Create an RMAN Open Backup Script

In this task, you'll back up the database while it is open. The script shown next is
the same as the script is in Task 1 with one exception: the database is open instead
of closed.

```
1.   run {
2.      allocate channel d1 type disk;
3.       backup database incremental 0
4.       format '/oradata/PRACTICE/backup/ch12/db_%d_%s_%p_%t'
5.        tag = 'WHOLE_INC0';
6.   }
```

- ■ **Line 1**   A backup command must be enclosed within the run command.
  The run command must be followed by the open curly brace either on the
  same line or on the next nonspace, noncommented line. The run command
  marks a block of code that must be run as a unit. All commands contained
  within curly brackets make up the unit of commands.

- ■ **Line 2**   A backup uses channels to copy data blocks from database files
  to the backup media. Assign this one backup channel a name that is used
  during the duration of the run block.

- ■ **Line 3**   The backup command defines what database files you plan to
  protect. On this line, you will back up data blocks for the entire PRACTICE
  database. When backing up the system tablespace, RMAN includes a backup
  of the current control file. The backup database command concludes with
  the semicolon at the end of line 5.

- ■ **Line 4**   The format keyword tells the backup command where to put
  the backup piece file and what to call it. This line instructs RMAN to
  create a file in the /oradata/PRACTICE/backup/ch12 directory. If you don't
  specify a format, RMAN will name the backup piece %U and put it in the
  $ORACLE_HOME/dbs directory on Linux and $ORACLE_HOME/database
  on Windows.

- ■ **Line 5**   Tags let you provide easily recognizable names to identify backups
  in an RMAN deployment. You can always find a specific backup set by its
  numeric key, but tags help you more easily administrate backups. Tags are
  reusable; if you run this backup script again, both backup sets will have the
  WHOLE_INC0 tag.

- ■ **Line 6**   This closed curly brace matches the opening curly brace after the
  run command on line 1. This brace marks the end of the run command. All
  commands within the run command get compiled and run as a unit.

The most impressive part of this script is that it's so simple! All you have to do is tell RMAN to back up the database. RMAN queries the target database control files to generate a list for datafiles to back up and creates the file to store the data blocks in the backup set. RMAN knows which blocks to copy and skips blocks that don't need to be copied. RMAN records the backup activity in the control file *and* in the catalog. All you have to do is create and run a few simple commands and let the server manage the whole thing.

Task 2: Run the RMAN Open Backup Script

Connected to the target PRACTICE database and the catalog RCAT database, execute the backup database script in the previous task:

```
RMAN> @b_whole_inc0.rcv
```

As the script runs, you'll see numerous RMAN messages. The following is some of my backup output; I have bolded some of the more important output messages and described them to tie them to the actual commands and operations we've just discussed.

```
RMAN-08500: channel d1: sid=14 devtype=DISK
RMAN-08008: channel d1: starting incremental level 0 datafile backupset
RMAN-08502: set_count=120 set_stamp=446988820 creation_time=12-JAN-02
RMAN-08522: input datafile fno=00001 name=/oradata/PRACTICE/system01.dbf
RMAN-08011: including current controlfile in backupset
RMAN-08522: input datafile fno=00002 name=/oradata/PRACTICE/rbs01.dbf
RMAN-08522: input datafile fno=00004 name=/oradata/PRACTICE/temp01.dbf
RMAN-08522: input datafile fno=00005 name=/oradata/PRACTICE/tools01.dbf
RMAN-08522: input datafile fno=00006 name=/oradata/PRACTICE/indx01.dbf
RMAN-08522: input datafile fno=00003 name=/oradata/PRACTICE/users01.dbf
RMAN-08522: input datafile fno=00007 name=/oradata/PRACTICE/users02.dbf
RMAN-08013: channel d1: piece 1 created
RMAN-08503: piece handle=/oradata/PRACTICE/backup/ch12/db_PRACTICE_120_1_44698882E
RMAN-08525: backup set complete, elapsed time: 00:00:57
RMAN-08005: partial resync complete
RMAN-08031: released channel: d1
RMAN-06400: database opened
```

The output shows several important things:

- **sid=14**   When the channel is allocated on the PRACTICE database to perform the backup, that connection has a session id of 14.

- **starting incremental level 0 datafile backupset**   This backup is an incremental level 0 backup. All used data blocks in all datafiles will be copied to the single backup piece.

- **set_count=120**   The backup set number is 120. This is the 120th RMAN backup set for this database. Note: this number is *not* the same as the backup key.

- **including current controlfile in backupset** The current control file is copied with the system tablespace datafile. This message line comes right after the system datafile copy.

- **piece handle=/oradata/PRACTICE/backup/ch12/db_PRACTICE_120_1_ 44698882E** The actual file containing the block-level backup for the entire PRACTICE database is this file. The substitution variables used in the format statement have been incorporated in the file name (%d - database name = PRACTICE, %s - backup set count = 3, %p - backup piece number = 1, %t - backup time = 44698882E). The backup time is not a time you can recognize.

- **elapsed time: 00:00:57** The backup took 57 seconds to complete.

Task 3: Verify the RMAN Open Backup Script

Now that you've run a backup, how can you check the execution results? You can use the LIST command to check the backup has run:

```
RMAN> list backup;
RMAN-03022: compiling command: list
List of Backup Sets
Key      Recid      Stamp      LV Set Stamp  Set Count  Completion Time
-------  ---------- ----------  -- ----------  ----------  ---------------------
256      120           446988874  0  446988820   120          12-JAN-02
    List of Backup Pieces
    Key      Pc# Cp# Status    Completion Time        Piece Name
    -------  --- --- ---------- ---------------------  ---------------------
    257      1    1   AVAILABLE  12-JAN-02              ./db_PRACTICE_120_1_44698882E
    List of Datafiles Included
    File Name                                     LV Type Ckp SCN  Ckp Time
    ---- ------------------------------------      -- ----  ---------- -------------
    1      /oradata/PRACTICE/system01.dbf          0  Inc  78342      12-JAN-02
    2      /oradata/PRACTICE/rbs01.dbf             0  Inc  78342      12-JAN-02
    3      /oradata/PRACTICE/users01.dbf           0  Inc  78342      12-JAN-02
    4      /oradata/PRACTICE/temp01.dbf            0  Inc  78342      12-JAN-02
    5      /oradata/PRACTICE/tools01.dbf           0  Inc  78342      12-JAN-02
    6      /oradata/PRACTICE/indx01.dbf            0  Inc  78342      12-JAN-02
    7      /oradata/PRACTICE/users02.dbf           0  Inc  78342      12-JAN-02
```

This output gives you plenty of information about the backup set created:

- **List of backup sets** The backup set key is 120. This key uniquely identifies this occurrence of an RMAN backup run. Notice that this number agrees with the output you saw when you actually ran the backup. The backup was run and completed on January 12. LV is the level of the backup. A backup level 0 includes all used blocks in each datafile.

- **List of backup pieces** This backup set only has one piece. The actual operating system file containing the blocks is named db_PRACTICE_120_

1_44698882E in the /oradata/PRACTICE/backup/ch12 directory. The RMAN format statement in your script generates this file name.

- **List of datafiles included**   Each datafile included in the backup is listed. The LV column defines the level of block copy and the type shows that the backup was an incremental file backup. You can see the checkpoint SCN value for each datafile backed up.

There's one last thing you can do to verify your backup worked: at the operating system, navigate to the /oradata/PRACTICE/backup/ch12 directory. You'll see your backup piece file named db_PRACTICE_120_1_44698882E. All the used datafile blocks and the entire control file are contained in one file!

The size of the file will probably be around 60MB. Think about this: your sum of all your datafile sizes is 200MB. The control file is about 3MB. How does 203MB fit into a file of only 60MB? Because only the used data blocks have been copied to the backup piece! Take the 20MB index tablespace. Because you've only got a few indexes contained there, you are only using 20 to 50 data blocks. The rest of the data blocks in that tablespace are not (and have never been) used. Therefore, when RMAN only copies the used blocks in that datafile, not much data gets copied. This is how RMAN saves on space in its backup files.

That's all there is to it! RMAN has backed up every data block in the whole database to one files.

CAUTION
When you name your backup file pieces, be sure to use a unique file name or you run the risk of copying over a backup piece file from a previous backup. Many RMAN users specify the format specification of %d_%s_%p_%t, which produces a name that is unique and contains the database name, backup set number, backup piece number, and the encoded timestamp of when the backup is taken.

Task 4: Run an RMAN Closed Backup Script

A closed database backup allows RMAN to back up a database while the control file is mounted but the database is not open. If the database was shut down cleanly, all the datafiles will have a consistent SCN value in their headers. During datafile backup, that consistent SCN for the datafiles is stored in the control file for this RMAN backup, as shown here:

```
1.   shutdown immediate;
2.   startup mount;
3.   run {
4.      allocate channel d1 type disk;
5.      allocate channel d2 type disk;
6.      backup database incremental 0
7.        format '/oradata/PRACTICE/backup/ch12/db_%d_%s_%p_%t'
8.        tag = 'WHOLE_INC0_CLOSED';
9.   }
10.  alter database backup controlfile to ''/temp/backup.ctl'' reuse;
11.  alter database open;
```

The eleven lines in this file contain everything you need to perform an incremental baseline block-level backup of all datafiles and the control file for your PRACTICE database while the database is closed. Let's look at each line in the script and describe what each command accomplishes.

When you allocate several channels, RMAN attempts to create backup sets files that are of similar size. The goal is to evenly divide I/O throughput between allocated channels. RMAN assumes that every block in each datafile being backed up will be included in the backup set. If there are fewer blocks that actually get backed up, the backup sets will be different sizes.

The RMAN commands to back up a closed database are the same commands used to back up an open database. In fact, you can run the script file as shown above to back up the database by simply adding the SHUTDOWN, STARTUP, and ALTER DATABASE commands. For illustration, I've changed the file script to make some points about RMAN backups:

- **Line 1** Before you can back up a closed database, the database must be closed. From the RMAN prompt, you can execute database control commands like shutdown and startup.

- **Line 2** The database control files must be mounted to run any RMAN backup commands. Why? All database schema information is stored in the target control files. Also, RMAN backup operations get stored in this control file so the target control file must be opened by the target instance.

- **Lines 4-5** During this backup, RMAN will open two channels for backup. Each channel creates a session on the target database and opens a backup piece on disk. Multiple channels allow RMAN to perform the data block copies in parallel. Using more than one channel allows RMAN to increase throughput to disk or tape. On the PRACTICE database, one channel is enough. (I am using two for demonstration purposes.)

- **Lines 7-8** Notice that the order of the FORMAT and TAG keywords are in a different order. Within the backup command, you can interchange the order of the keyword phrases.

- **Line 10**   From the RMAN prompt, you can issue other database control commands. In this line, a backup copy of the control file is placed in the backup directory. This alter database command is different from the RMAN backup command because this copy of the control file will not be logged in the target database control file or the catalog tables.

- **Line 11**   After completing the backup, you can open the database for users.

To run the backup script you just created, start RMAN and connect to the PRACTICE database as the target and the RCAT database as the catalog. Use the @ symbol to run the command file you just created:

```
RMAN> @b_whole_inc0_closed.rcv
```

After you run the closed backup script, use the list command to see the backup set number, backup pieces, and files backed up. Particularly notice that the one backup command created two backup sets and two backup pieces. Why? Because two channels were allocated to do the backup.

Note the output is similar to that of Task 2 with one exception: two backup sets are created and written to their own backup piece.

```
RMAN-08502: set_count=121 set_stamp=446987639 creation_time=12-JAN-02
RMAN-08522: input datafile fno=00002 name=/oradata/PRACTICE/rbs01.dbf
RMAN-08522: input datafile fno=00004 name=/oradata/PRACTICE/temp01.dbf
RMAN-08522: input datafile fno=00005 name=/oradata/PRACTICE/tools01.dbf
RMAN-08522: input datafile fno=00006 name=/oradata/PRACTICE/indx01.dbf
RMAN-08502: set_count=122 set_stamp=446987639 creation_time=12-JAN-02
RMAN-08522: input datafile fno=00001 name=/oradata/PRACTICE/system01.dbf
RMAN-08011: including current controlfile in backupset
RMAN-08522: input datafile fno=00003 name=/oradata/PRACTICE/users01.dbf
RMAN-08522: input datafile fno=00007 name=/oradata/PRACTICE/users02.dbf
RMAN-08503: piece handle=/oradata/PRACTICE/backup/ch12/db_PRACTICE_121_1_44698763E
RMAN-08013: channel d2: piece 1 created
RMAN-08503: piece handle=/oradata/PRACTICE/backup/ch12/db_PRACTICE_122_1_44698763E
```

The output shows that two backup sets and pieces were created. The SYSTEM and USERS tablespace datafiles are contained in backup set 122 in backup piece db_PRACTICE_122_1_44698763E. The other tablespace datafiles were placed in backup set 121 in backup piece db_PRACTICE_121_1_44698763E. One backup set took 50 seconds to complete, and the other took 47 seconds.

During backup, RMAN begins copying used blocks from several datafiles. At the conclusion of the backup, the PRACTICE database control file gets updated. Finally, the catalog is synchronized with the PRACTICE control file so these newly created backup records are included.

Check the backup directory to see the actual backup piece file names for this backup. Notice the backup set 122 is larger than backup set 121. Why? Because the datafiles passed to each channel/backup set had a different number of used data blocks.

To recap, you've created an RMAN backup script that will back up all datafiles in the PRACTICE database, including the current control file. You ran that script and took note of the output. Then you verified the backup occurred using the RMAN LIST command, SQL against the catalog, and by checking the file on the operating system. Congratulations! You just completed your first RMAN backup.

NOTE

If you perform a closed database backup with RMAN, you can restore that backup and open the database without performing recovery. The reason: the datafiles were consistent during the backup. Therefore, they are consistent when they are restored. If you perform an open database backup with RMAN, recovery is required to make the file consistent after that open backup is restored.

Exercise 12.3: Create Recovery Manager Incremental Backups

Each of the datafile backup options I've covered up to this point require that you copy the entire datafile or all the used data blocks of that datafile. For a small database like the PRACTICE database, copying the entire file or all the data block contents does not take much time to finish or space to store. However, very few production databases are as small as the PRACTICE database. Very large databases with large datafiles take a lot of time *and* a lot of space to back up. Often, much of the database data remains unchanged from backup to backup. Oracle now offers an option to copy only the data blocks that have recently changed called block-level incremental backups. At any time, you can restore and recover your database by combining the baseline incremental level 0 backup with any needed subsequent incremental level-backups. The backup pieces created with an incremental level backup save an enormous amount of space because you are not backing up the same unchanged data blocks over and over again.

Task Description	Minutes
1. Create an RMAN Incremental Backup Script	5
2. Run the RMAN Incremental Backup Script	5
3. Verify the RMAN Incremental Backup Script	5
4. Run Another RMAN Incremental Backup Script	5
Total Time	20

In the last exercise, you created a baseline incremental level 0 backup of the whole PRACTICE database, including the control file, while the database is open. In this exercise, you will create a cumulative incremental level 1 backup. Next, you will create an incremental level 2 backup. The level 1 backup will copy any data blocks that have changed since the level 0 backup. The level 2 backup will copy any changed data blocks that have changed since the level 1 backup.

Task 1: Create RMAN Incremental Backup Script

The code below contains commands to execute a differential incremental backup of the whole PRACTICE database:

```
run {
    allocate channel d1 type disk;
    backup
      incremental cumulative level = 1
      database
      format '/oracle/PRACTICE/backup/ch12/db_%d_%s_%p_%t'
      tag = 'WHOLE_INC1';
}
```

The commands shown above should look very similar to the previous backup script files in this chapter. Other than the tag name and the format name of the backup piece file, there is only one difference: this listing includes a directive to RMAN that the backup of the datafiles will be a cumulative incremental level 1. Since the script calls for a backup of the entire database, every changed data block in all datafiles will be copied to backup pieces in the backup set.

Task 2: Run the RMAN Incremental Backup Script

As before, run the backup connected to the target PRACTICE database and the catalog:

```
RMAN> @b_whole_inc1.rcv
```

When you run b_whole_inc1.rcv, you'll notice that the backup takes about the same amount of time but the backup piece files are much smaller. This is because very few (if any) of the data blocks containing data dictionary items have changed. Neither have SCOTT's tables. Only a few rows have been inserted into TINA.DATE_LOG.

Task 3: Verify the RMAN Incremental Backup Script

Once again use the list command to examine the results of your backup and check the operating system to make sure that the backup piece files exist. Are you beginning to see a simple pattern here? The output of this command will be similar to previous backup command output with these exceptions:

- The key and piece names are different

- The incremental column value is different

Task 4: Run Another RMAN Incremental Backup Script

Before I talk about an RMAN archive log backup, I want you to run one more backup like the one you just ran in this exercise. Run an incremental level 2 backup. To do this, create a file named b_whole_inc2.rcv as a copy of b_whole_inc1.rcv. Open the script file you just created and change the 1's to 2's. For example: in the b_whole_inc2.rcv change:

- incremental = 1 to incremental = 2

- `tag = 'WHOLE_INC1'` to `tag = 'WHOLE_INC2'`

Therefore, none of the data blocks unchanged other data blocks that were copied again in the level 1 or level 2 backup.

Exercise 12.4: Create Recovery Manager Archive Log Backup

As the PRACTICE database continues operation, archive log files will be generated to the archive dump destination. These files *must* be protected to be absolutely sure that you can recover your database to a point in time in the past or to the current time. In Chapter 5, you learned how you could manage the backup of these archive files with user-managed methods. How do you let RMAN manage the backup of these critical files? Use the BACKUP ARCHIVELOG command to copy the contents of the archive log files to a backup piece in a backup set. When you instruct RMAN to back up the files, you can tell RMAN which files you want to back up using such qualifiers as log sequence ranges or log creation date ranges. Or you can copy them all to a backup set.

RMAN also allows you to perform mandatory housekeeping on these files. Remember, as a database operates, redo gets generated and stored in archive log files. Eventually, these files will fill up the disk destination where they are stored. RMAN has a handy DELETE INPUT option that will remove copied archive log files from disk. Using this option within a careful archive backup strategy, RMAN can be trusted to protect these files for you.

Task Description	Minutes
1. Create an RMAN Archive Log Backup Script	5
2. Run the RMAN Archive Log Backup Script	5
3. Verify the RMAN Backup Script	5
Total Time	15

During this exercise, you'll see the basic commands to back up and remove the PRACTICE database archive log files. I'll talk about the basic commands and how you can employ them cautiously to protect and clear out these files as they get generated for your PRACTICE database.

Task 1: Create an RMAN Archive Log Backup Script

It's easy to use RMAN to back up the archive files: simply create a file with RMAN commands to back up the archive logs. RMAN can do all that work for you with a few commands, as shown here:

```
run {
    allocate channel d1 type disk;
    sql "ALTER SYSTEM ARCHIVE LOG CURRENT";
    backup archivelog all
      format '/oradata/PRACTICE/backup/ch12/ar_%d_%s_%p_%t';
}
```

Within the confines of a run command, define the location you want to back up your archives to, disk or tape. Next, you can optionally be sure that the current online redo log file is archived. Finally, instruct RMAN to copy all the archive logs to a backup piece in a backup set. The location of the backup piece will be in the /oradata/PRACTICE/backup/ch12 directory.

Task 2: Run the RMAN Archive Log Backup Script

Run this script connected to the target database and the catalog database:

```
RMAN> @b_archive.rcv
```

During the execution of the script commands, you'll see output messages generated from RMAN. These messages show you the backup piece name and the archive sequences being backed up:

```
RMAN-08502: set_count=124 set_stamp=446989243 creation_time=12-JAN-02
RMAN-08014: channel d1: specifying archivelog(s) in backup set
RMAN-08504: input archivelog thread=1 sequence=126 recid=1 stamp=446985969
RMAN-08504: input archivelog thread=1 sequence=127 recid=2 stamp=446986041
RMAN-08504: input archivelog thread=1 sequence=128 recid=3 stamp=446989240
RMAN-08013: channel d1: piece 1 created
RMAN-08503: piece handle=/oradata/PRACTICE/backup/ch12/ar_PRACTICE_7_1_44698924E
```

Task 3: Verify the RMAN Backup Script

Run the LIST command and look at v$ tables. Check the output directory for the file.

```
RMAN> list backupset of archivelog all;
```

This command will list all backups you've created of your archive log files. If you've made many backups, the output will scroll across your screen. It shows the sequence numbers of the archive log sequences copied, along with the SCN range for each log file. After listing the archive backups, have a look at the operating system. You should be able to see the backup piece file you created in the output of your backup in the /oradata/PRACTICE/backup/ch12 directory. In the deployment section to follow, I'll show you how you might incorporate archive backups in a sample backup strategy.

RMAN Backup of Multiple Archive Destinations

If you have two or more archive destinations for your target database, the backup archive command will only back up one (usually the first) destination. To back up the archive log files in each of your destinations, create a separate channel for each archive destination. Then, add the LIKE keyword when backing up each destination to its allocated channel. The string following the LIKE keyword should contain the archive destination directory and the % wildcard character to back up any archive log files in that directory.

RMAN Deployment

Now that you know how easy incremental and archive log backups can be, let's talk about how you might put incremental backups together into a sample schedule. This sample schedule includes a strategy for daily backup of datafiles, control files and archive logs. When you deploy an incremental backup strategy, you want to balance the time window available to you in case you need to recover your database after a failure with the backup resources (disk space, tape drives, machine capacity) you have for backups. A fairly standard backup scenario involves a level 0 incremental backup on the weekend. Then, throughout the week, various incremental level 1 and 2 backups are taken. This weekly rotation gives you a baseline incremental database backup once a week with smaller incremental backups during the week. For example, take your backups when database activity is light (for example, 2 A.M.):

- **Sunday early morning**   Level 0 backup (run b_whole_inc0.rcv)

- **Monday early morning**   Level 2 backup (run b_whole_inc2.rcv)

- **Tuesday early morning**   Level 2 backup (run b_whole_inc2.rcv)

- **Wednesday early morning**   Level 2 backup (run b_whole_inc2.rcv)

- **Thursday early morning**   Level 1 backup (run b_whole_inc1.rcv)

- **Friday early morning**   Level 2 backup (run b_whole_inc2.rcv)

- **Saturday early morning**   Level 2 backup (run b_whole_inc2.rcv)

With this cumulative incremental backup deployment, you'd be able to restore and recover using, at most, three backup sets. For example, if you had a failure on Saturday afternoon, the RMAN restore command would require the Sunday, Thursday, and Saturday backup sets. To run cumulative incremental backups, simply add the CUMULATIVE keyword after incremental to scripts described in this exercise.

When you deploy a backup strategy for your archive log files, you must be absolutely sure that you've got at least one (preferably two or more) copies of each archive log file backed up. You also must clear the archive log destination so that it does not fill up the file system and halt database operation. With a careful deployment of the DELETE INPUT option available with RMAN, you can accomplish both goals. The archive log backup strategy is to make three copies of each archive log file before you delete your input.

Here is how you might accomplish a triple copy backup of each archive log file for the PRACTICE database:

1. Make a baseline backup of all existing archive log files for your PRACTICE database using the ARCHIVELOG ALL option for the first two days of your new backup schedule (run b_archive.rcv).

2. Each day, make a backup of all existing archive log files containing redo from the last two days (run b_archive_2days.rcv).

3. Each day, make a backup of the log files containing redo from three days ago until two days ago (run b_archive_delete3.rcv).

This strategy ensures that you have at least three copies of every archive log file created by your database. Two scripts, as shown next, will be needed to enact this archive log backup strategy: b_archive_2days.rcv and b_archive_delete3.rcv.

```
run {
    allocate channel d1 type disk;
    sql 'ALTER SYSTEM ARCHIVE LOG CURRENT';
    backup archivelog
      from time 'SYSDATE-2'
      format '/oradata/PRACTICE/backup/ch12/ar_%d_%s_%p_%t';
}
```

After allocating a channel to disk and archiving the current online redo log, back up all the archive logs created since two days ago. Running this script, each day will back up an archive log file from the previous two days. This script does not delete the archive logs backed up.

```
run {
    allocate channel d1 type disk;
    sql 'ALTER SYSTEM ARCHIVE LOG CURRENT';
    backup archivelog
      from time 'SYSDATE-3' until time 'SYSDATE-2'
      format '/oradata/PRACTICE/backup/ch12/ar_%d_%s_%p_%t'
      delete input;
}
```

When you run archive_delete, the DELETE INPUT qualifier instructs RMAN to delete the archive log files that have been backed up after they have been successfully backed up. While running the b_archive_delete3.rcv script file, you'll see output like this:

```
RMAN-08071: channel d1: deleting archivelog(s)
RMAN-08514: archivelog filename=/oradata/PRACTICE/archive/126.arc recid=125 stamp =443360938
```

The file(s) deleted is shown in the output. After this run completes, look at the operating system in the archive dump destination. The deleted file, 126.arc, won't be on disk anymore. To make this clearer, look at Figure 12-4. Follow the backup

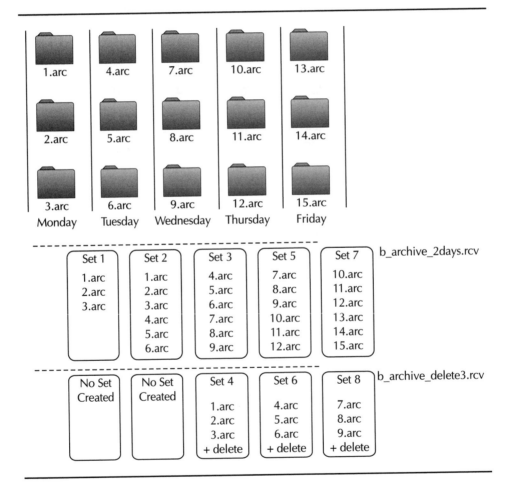

FIGURE 12-4. *Archive Log Backup Time Line*

sets and archive files. The database creates three redo logs a day. Two backup scripts run daily at 1 A.M.: b_archive_2days.rcv and b_archive_delete3.rcv.

- **Tuesday backups**   Backup set 1 contains archive logs 1, 2, and 3. No archive logs get deleted.

- **Wednesday backups**   Backup set 2 contains archive logs 1–6. No archive logs get deleted.

- **Thursday backups**   Backup set 3 contains archive logs 4–9. Backup set 4 copies archive logs 1–3 and removes them from disk.

- **Friday backups**   Backup set 5 contains archive logs 7–12. Backup set 6 copies archive logs 4–6 and removes them from disk.

- **Saturday backups**   Backup set 7 contains archive logs 10–15. Backup set 8 copies archive logs 7–9 and removes them from disk.

This process of backing up and removing files continues indefinitely.

TIP
When including backups within a time range, any archive logs containing redo within the date/time range are included in the backup.

If you want to see how many times a specific archive log file has been backed up, use an RMAN list command like this:

```
RMAN> list backupset of archivelog like '%archive/126.arc'
```

With these scripts created, schedule them to run on your Linux OS using cron (or another scheduling utility). The crontab entries on Linux can look like this:

```
#min   hour   date   month   day   command
0      1      *      *       0     <path>/b_whole_inc0.sh #Sunday
0      1      *      *       1     <path>/b_whole_inc2.sh #Monday
0      1      *      *       2     <path>/b_whole_inc2.sh #Tuesday
0      1      *      *       3     <path>/b_whole_inc2.sh #Wednesday
0      1      *      *       4     <path>/b_whole_inc1.sh #Thursday
0      1      *      *       5     <path>/b_whole_inc2.sh #Friday
0      1      *      *       6     <path>/b_whole_inc2.sh #Saturday
0      2      *      *       *     <path>/b_archive_2days.sh #Every Day
30     2      *      *       *     <path>/b_archive_delete3.sh #Every Day
```

Cron will schedule scripts to run during the week to implement the RMAN backup strategy. Each script will call RMAN with two arguments: cmdfile and log. Also, each script can call another RMAN script containing connection information for the target database and the catalog. For example, a scheduled job to run a whole database incremental level 0 backup would look like b_whole_inc0.sh:

```
$ORACLE_HOME/bin/rman cmdfile=<path>/b_whole_inc0.rcv log=/tmp/b_archive_2days.log
```

Add a line to the beginning of b_whole_inc0.rcv to call a connection script named connect.rcv:

```
@@connect.rcv
```

where connect.rcv contains two connection commands:

```
connect target sys/practice@practice
connect catalog rman817/rman@rcat
```

The double @ before the call to connect.rcv means that this script file will be run from the same directory in which the current script is running. Also, add an exit statement to the b_whole_inc0.rcv so that the backup will exit upon completion when run as a scheduled job. This is an example of how you can deploy an RMAN incremental backup strategy on Linux.

Windows can schedule these RMAN jobs using AT with entries like this:

```
at 1:00 /every:Sunday    cmd /c <path>\b_whole_inc0.bat
at 1:00 /every:Monday    cmd /c <path>\b_whole_inc2.bat
at 1:00 /every:Tuesday   cmd /c <path>\b_whole_inc2.bat
at 1:00 /every:Wednesday cmd /c <path>\b_whole_inc2.bat
at 1:00 /every:Thursday  cmd /c <path>\b_whole_inc1.bat
at 1:00 /every:Friday    cmd /c <path>\b_whole_inc2.bat
at 1:00 /every:Saturday  cmd /c <path>\b_whole_inc2.bat
at 2:00 cmd /c <path>\b_archive_2days.bat
at 2:30 cmd /c <path>\b_archive_delete3.bat
```

The RMAN backup commands can be run from Windows batch files similarly to the script shown for Linux.

RMAN Backup Performance

RMAN backup jobs can be monitored and tuned to make the best use of machine resources. Before tuning RMAN backups, first monitor the backups to see if they are performing as expected and within acceptable time frames. If your backups move quickly, then there's no need to tune. To increase backup performance, balance the options RMAN provides with your disk and/or tape devices.

Monitor Backup and Copy Jobs

When you run large backup jobs, you may wonder if RMAN is making any progress on the backup. To monitor the progress of the backup and copy commands, you can open another SQL*Plus session on the target database and look at the progress. First, you can check that RMAN is actually connected to the target by looking at the V$PROCESS and V$SESSION data dictionary views:

```
LINUX> sqlplus  sys/practice@practice
SQL> SELECT sid, spid, client_info
   2    FROM v$process p, v$session s
   3   WHERE p.addr = s.saddr
   4     AND client_info LIKE '%id=rman%';
```

You should see the RMAN connections from this query: one connection for querying the target database and one connection for each channel allocated for the currently running backup. Then you can select from V$SESSION_LONGOPS to see the progress being made on the backup. As RMAN runs, it populates this data dictionary view with its progress. You should see the % Complete column increasing as the backup runs.

```
SQL> SELECT sid, serial#, context, sofar, totalwork,
   2          round(sofar/totalwork*100,2) "% Complete"
   3    FROM v$session_longops
   4   WHERE opname LIKE 'RMAN:%'
   5     AND opname NOT LIKE 'RMAN: aggregate%';
```

These two queries can be very handy when tracking long running RMAN backups.

Performance Tips

The PRACTICE database is so small that you don't need to enhance the performance. In a real production system, however, you may need to consider carefully how you might take backups on a very large or busy database. Take advantage of RMAN's parallelization and configuration of channels to get the right throughput and output on your backups:

- ■ If you want the backup to run faster, allocate multiple channels during backup. The copy or backup command will run in parallel. When using multiple channels, you must consider how many tape drives or disks can be used in parallel. You do not want to use more channels than tape drives or too many disk channels to cause flooding in the I/O subsystem.

■ If you want to limit the workload on a busy Oracle system, limit the read rate for the channel by using set limit channel <name> read rate = <integer>. This will reduce the amount of reads RMAN puts through the I/O subsystem.

■ If you want to fit your backup of very large files into a file size limitation, limit the size of the file that a channel can create with set limit channel <name> Kbytes = <integer>. For example, if you have a 2GB file size limit on your disk operating system, set Kbytes = 2097152 (that is 2*1024*1024).

■ During backup, too many files concurrently backed up can cause a throughput bottleneck on hardware devices. This can be monitored using regular file monitoring tools such as sar -d or the NT performance monitor. To limit the number of files backed up simultaneously, limit each channel's number of concurrently open files from the default of 32 using the set limit attribute within the backup run block.

As noted throughout this chapter, remember that incremental backups can run much more quickly than full backups. However, you should be aware that during backup, each block has to be read to determine if it should be backed up, no matter what level of incremental backup you are performing. The time savings results from reduced block copy time because less blocks are being copied.

Troubleshooting

If you run into problems taking backups with RMAN, you might encounter one of these errors. These notes may point you in the right direction to solve the issue.

1. **RMAN-04014: startup failed: ORA-01078: failure in processing system parameters** When starting up a remote database, RMAN uses a local database initialization file to open the database. Copy the parameter file to the local hard disk from where RMAN is running. Then use the pfile option on the startup command:
RMAN> startup pfile=initPRACTICE.ora
RMAN looks in the %ORACLE_HOME%\dbs directory on Windows NT instead of the %ORACLE_HOME%\database. You may want to add a parameter file that points to the pfile directory using the IFILE parameter.

2. **ORA-27040: skgfrcre: create error, unable to create file**
OSD-04002: unable to open file
O/S-Error: (OS 3) The system cannot find the path specified. If you set

the format for the backup to a path that is not found, the backup command will fail with this error. Make sure your format command points to a directory that you've created.

3. **RMAN-06004: ORACLE error from recovery catalog database: RMAN-20242: specification does not match any archive log in the recovery catalog**   If there are no archive log files that match the specification during a backup, you get an error. Disregard this error. This pesky error has been removed in Oracle 9*i*.

Corruption Detection

RMAN provides three different ways of detecting block corruptions during the backups. During normal database operations when a data block is read from disk into the buffer cache, Oracle will always check that certain structures in the header portion of the block match the structures in the tail of the block. If they do not match, after several attempts at reading the block, the block will be reported as corrupt. RMAN also performs this data block checking.

By default, RMAN also verifies the checksum is correct in each data block that currently contains a checksum (created by using the init.ora parameter DB_BLOCK_CHECKSUM). The checksum value is then stored with the block being backed up. If the checksum does not match after it is recomputed, the block is reported to be corrupt. If the block does not contain a checksum, RMAN will calculate one and store it in the block in the backup piece. When the blocks are restored, this checksum will be validated to ensure the restored blocks are not corrupt. This feature can be turned off by specifying NOCHECKSUM within the backup command. However, this is *not* recommended because you need to be alerted if corruption problems are found.

It is also possible to add a further block checking routine called *logical* block checking. This feature is enabled by specifying CHECK LOGICAL within the backup command. The logical checks make sure all the structures with the data block, such as the row offsets, space available, number of rows, and so on, appear to be correct. If a structure is found to be invalid, the block will be reported as corrupt. This is turned off by default and may increase the time taken to make a backup when used. This increase should be tested before applying to production database backups.

By default, RMAN will terminate execution as soon as a single corrupt data block is detected. This can be adjusted using the SET MAXCORRUPT option within an RMAN run block (defaults to 0 for all files). This can be set to a different threshold for each datafile but must be used carefully so as not to create backup files with many corrupt blocks. When the threshold has been reached, the next corrupt block found will cause the backup to terminate. When the blocks are restored from a backup that contains corrupt blocks, the same blocks will be corrupt and an error (usually an ORA-1578) will be reported when they are accessed by a query.

If corrupt blocks are found by RMAN within the MAXCORRUPT thresholds, they are recorded in the target control file and recovery catalog. They can be seen in the V$BACKUP_CORRUPTION or V$COPY_CORRUPTION views within the target database. The same data is also kept in the RC_BACKUP_CORRUPTION and RC_COPY_CORRUPTION views in the recovery catalog. Each row in these views represents a backup set and a contiguous range of corrupt blocks found. For example, if RMAN finds blocks 90, 92, and 93 to be corrupt, the following results can be found in V$BACKUP_CORRUPTION:

```
RECID      STAMP  SET_STAMP  SET_COUNT  PIECE#  FILE#  BLOCK#  BLOCKS  MAR
-----  ---------  ---------  ---------- ------  -----  ------  ------  ---
    3  449013231  449013230          22      1      2      90       1  YES
    4  449013231  449013230          22      1      2      92       2  YES
```

This shows that for your one backup set (#22), you have one corrupt block starting at block #90 and two corrupt blocks starting from block #92. If you were to look in the alert.log of this target database, you would also see corruption errors for these three blocks.

The corruption entries in the control file (seen in the two views) will remain viewable until the backup set has been aged out. The entries in the recovery catalog will remain until the backup set information is removed. If the corruption is fixed and a new backup is taken, no new rows will show up in the V$BACKUP_CORRUPTION view. The existing corruptions are kept so that you can see if datafiles being restored with RMAN will contain any corrupt blocks.

Summary

In this chapter, you learned about the RMAN COPY and BACKUP commands. You learned the details of each type of backup RMAN provides (backups, image copies, and proxy copies), and why you might use each method. You used the COPY command to produce image copies of datafiles. With the BACKUP command, you created files on disk or tape containing datafiles, control files, or archive logs. You also learned how you can deploy a simple incremental backup strategy into your production environment. Throughout this chapter, the LIST command was used to show how you can make sure RMAN's backups are recorded correctly in the control file or recovery catalog. Backups with RMAN are simple. With a clear understanding of RMAN components (Chapter 11) and RMAN commands, you are well on your way to a successful database protection strategy and to letting the server manage the work for you. If you want more details on RMAN backup, look at Chapters 1, 2, and 5 of the *Oracle 8i Recovery Manager User's Guide and Reference*. Also, look at some sample scripts provided with your Oracle Server installation. You'll find them in $ORACLE_HOME/rdbms/demo*.rcv.

Chapter Questions

Now that you've made it through this enormous but critical chapter, see if you can answer a few little questions:

1. What RMAN command creates a copy of database file blocks?

    A. Copy

    B. Backup

    C. Allocate

    D. Run

2. The database must be shut down but mounted to make image copies of datafiles using RMAN.

    A. True

    B. False

3. If you plan to copy all the datafiles in your database, use the BACKUP DATABASE command. This is called a _____ backup.

    A. Full

    B. Complete

    C. Whole

    D. Incremental

4. How can you back up archive log files that have been created in the last two days?

    A. backup archivelog two days

    B. backup archivelog from time sysdate –2;

    C. backup archivelog sysdate –2

    D. You can't do this with RMAN

5. Why does an incremental backup strategy save space in backup file pieces?

    A. Only used and changed blocks are copied.

    B. Backups occur during daily increments.

    C. Only parts of data blocks get copied.

    D. Data blocks are compressed when they are copied.

Answers to Chapter Questions

1. B. The BACKUP command reads data blocks in datafiles, control files, or archive logs and copies them to disk or tape. The files created are called backup pieces. The set of backup pieces that contain the entire backup is called a backup set.

2. False. You can make image copies of database files while the database is open or shut down.

3. C. A whole database backup will include every datafile in the backup set. A full database backup will include all used data blocks in the backup set.

4. B. Using the from time qualifier, you specify the beginning range of archive log files you want to include in your backup set.

5. A. RMAN only copies blocks that have changed during backup. On a level 0 or full backup, all blocks ever used by the datafiles are copied. During level 1 or above incremental backups, only blocks changed relative to the most recent backup are copied. RMAN copies the entire block and does not compress them.

CHAPTER
13

RMAN Catalog
Maintenance

hy is a chapter on RMAN catalog maintenance important? Because as a database administrator, you must be able to manage the backups taken to make sure your database is always protected against any kind of failure. Once your backups are automated, you should ask yourself several questions:

- What backups do I currently have?

- Can I recover my database completely?

- Do I have a good copy of my archive log files?

- Have unrecoverable database operations occurred that might prevent recovery?

- Which backups have become obsolete and can be removed?

- What backups do I need to meet my recovery requirements?

- Will I be able to recover quickly enough?

Once the RMAN backups are configured and are running successfully, they still need attention. As a DBA, you must verify that backups are working properly and that older, unneeded backups are removed. In Chapter 12, I recommended a typical incremental backup strategy. As daily automated backups occur, those backups begin to accumulate. Look at Figure 13-1 to see how, over several weeks, daily backups build up. This diagram shows daily incremental backups of the database with a baseline incremental backup executed on Sunday. Each day, archive logs get backed up also. If every backup runs as planned without a hitch, you can rest easy knowing your database is protected.

To show proper diligence, regularly check that your backups function properly and that the database is protected as planned. Sometimes an automated backup might fail because of a lack of disk space, hardware problems, and so on. Perhaps your RMAN backups work successfully but the tape media manager experiences problems. Finding out your backups are incomplete or unavailable during an emergency is no fun, and it's not good for your career.

This chapter will describe some key commands and concepts and show you how to check your backups via the RMAN catalog as well as get rid of older unneeded backups.

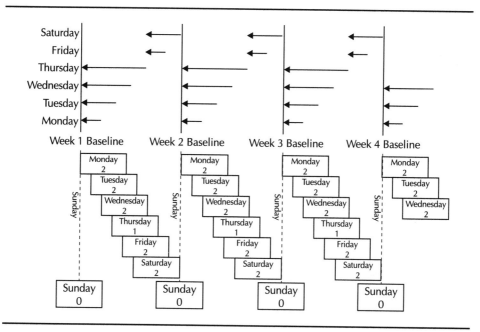

FIGURE 13-1. *RMAN backup timeline for the PRACTICE database*

Throughout this chapter, you'll see many RMAN commands applied toward checking and maintaining catalog backups of the PRACTICE database, so I have included an introduction to these commands. In the exercises in this chapter, you will explore three areas to a successful RMAN deployment:

1. How can I use stored scripts to run common RMAN tasks? (See the section "Recovery Manager Scripts.")

2. How can I be *sure* that my database is protected with my RMAN backups? (See the section "Recovery Manager Backup Confirmation.")

3. How can I clean up older, unwanted backups to free up backup storage space and keep the catalog to a manageable size? (See the section "Recovery Catalog Cleanup.")

RMAN Commands

RMAN provides several commands to help you maintain your backups. Some of these commands have already been used in Chapters 11 and 12 but will be covered in more detail here. The following sections cover the LIST, REPORT, CHANGE, CROSSCHECK, and VALIDATE commands.

LIST

The LIST command causes RMAN to read the catalog or the control file to display details about backups. If you list a single backup set, you'll see the backup pieces created, their times, SCN values, file names, and so on that pertain to that backup. The output of a listing is displayed on the screen unless you've specified a message log file on the command line or at the RMAN prompt. If you list the contents of a backup, you either display database incarnations, RMAN backups, or RMAN copies. If you want to display details about specific backups, you can ask for a list by backup key, backup tag, time range, or device type, or you can specify a pattern to match. You can also request details about specific objects within backups and specify the tablespaces, datafiles, control files, or archive logs.

REPORT

The REPORT command highlights areas in your database backup that require you to take action. Like the LIST command, issuing a REPORT command, causes RMAN to read the catalog or target control file and gather the backup information. Results of the report are then displayed on the screen. Reports help you ensure that you will be able to recover your database quickly and help you find old backups you don't need anymore. You can also run reports to find out things like:

- which files need to be backed up
- which files don't have recent backups
- which files can't be recovered because of unrecoverable operations.

Reports will find an *obsolete* backup, a backup that has been taken several times and been made obsolete by newer backups. The Redundancy option defines the number of backups that need to be in place before it can be considered as obsolete. The default value of redundancy when reporting on obsolete backups is one backup.

CHANGE

The CHANGE command lets you manage the status of known RMAN backups. For each file, RMAN uses an allocated maintenance channel to access files on disk or tape. The CHANGE command has several options to modify the catalog and the backup files:

- **Delete** Removes the backup piece file from the operating system (disk or tape) and marks the backup records as deleted. If using a tape Media Manager Layer (MML), RMAN requests that the backup pieces be removed from tape but does not do it directly.

- **Available** Changes the status of an image copy or backup piece to Available for restores. By default, all backups are set to Available.

- **Unavailable** Changes the status of an image copy or backup piece to Unavailable for restores.

- **Uncatalog** Removes backups from the catalog.

CROSSCHECK

The CROSSCHECK command verifies that a backup file piece known to an RMAN backup exists on disk or tape. A crosscheck can be performed as an option of the CHANGE command. When running the CROSSCHECK command for backups to disk, RMAN reads the catalog to find the location of the backups taken. A maintenance channel must be created for use during the crosscheck operation. For each file, RMAN uses the maintenance channel to confirm the file exists. If the backup file is found, RMAN confirms that the backup piece header is valid. If you are running a crosscheck of backups made to tape, RMAN only queries the media manager. If the media manager says the file does not exist, RMAN marks the file as Expired or Deleted.

VALIDATE

The VALIDATE command determines whether one or more backup sets can be restored and if they have been damaged. A validation is a more exhaustive confirmation than a crosscheck. When executed, RMAN finds all the backup pieces on the media and scans through each file. When it reads each block from within the backup piece, the checksum that was stored when the backup was taken is recomputed and validated. If each file's checksum values are correct, RMAN confirms all the pieces of the backup set are in place and valid. Any errors in backup piece validation are written to the alert log file, a server trace file, or the V$BACKUP_CORRUPTION or V$COPY_CORRUPTION dynamic views. The backup set can contain datafiles, control files, or archive log files. Not only can you perform a validation of a specific backup set, but you can also simulate a restore of the database or portions of a database using the Validate option on the RESTORE command. Finally, RMAN can validate that a recovery can be made to a previous point in time using an UNTIL parameter to set the desired stop point of recovery.

In addition to these commands to manage your backups and catalog, you can use the CREATE, REPLACE and DELETE commands to store RMAN backup and restore scripts in the repository. In Chapter 12, you recorded your RMAN commands in files and then executed those commands by running the file. Alternatively, you can store your RMAN commands into the recovery catalog. Then you can call the scripts you've stored to execute a series of RMAN commands.

Recovery Manager Scripts

Recovery Manager commands can be run from the RMAN prompt or executed from a script. You can also save scripts to the repository and execute these stored scripts for the RMAN prompt. Each registered database must have its own stored script; scripts cannot be shared across databases. For example, if two databases are registered in the catalog and they both run a stored script named b_whole_inc0, this script must be created for each database in the catalog. Stored scripts can be created, replaced, executed, deleted, and listed.

Exercise 13.1: Stored Scripts

In this exercise, you'll learn how to store a few of the script files used in the last chapter as stored scripts.

Task Description	Minutes
1. Create and Replace Stored Scripts	5
2. List and Display Stored Scripts	5
3. Execute and Delete Stored Scripts	5
Total Time	15

In this exercise, you'll take the command files created in Chapter 12 and store them as scripts in the RMAN catalog. You'll then list and print the scripts, and then execute them.

Task 1: Create and Replace Stored Scripts

Create several backup stored scripts using the files in the last chapter, b_whole_inc0.rcv, b_whole_inc1.rcv, b_archive_2days.rcv, and b_archive_delete3.rcv, as shown here.

```
create script b_whole_inc0 {
    allocate channel d1 type disk;
    backup
```

```
      incremental level = 0 cumulative
      database
      format '/oradata/PRACTICE/backup/ch13/db0_%d_%s_%p_%t'
      tag = 'WHOLE_INC0';
   release channel d1;
}
create script b_whole_inc1 {
   allocate channel d1 type disk;
   backup
    incremental level = 1 cumulative
    database
    format '/oradata/PRACTICE/backup/ch13/db1_%d_%s_%p_%t'
    tag = 'WHOLE_INC1';
   release channel d1;
}
create script archive_log_current {
   sql "ALTER SYSTEM ARCHIVE LOG CURRENT";
}
create script b_archive_2days {
   allocate channel d1 type disk;
   execute script archive_log_current;
   backup archivelog
    from time 'SYSDATE-2'
    format '/oradata/PRACTICE/backup/ch13/ar_%d_%s_%p_%t';
   release channel d1;
}
create script archive_delete3 {
   allocate channel d1 type disk;
   execute script archive_log_current;
   backup archivelog
    from time 'SYSDATE-3' until time 'SYSDATE-2'
    format '/oradata/PRACTICE/backup/ch13/ar_%d_%s_%p_%t'
    delete input;
   release channel d1;
}
```

The script definitions shown above accomplish the same tasks as script files used for backups performed in Chapter 12. Some things to note about the contents of scripts.rcv:

■ Within a stored script, run blocks are not required. The commands within a script are compiled when loaded and get executed as a group.

■ Syntax of stored scripts is checked when saved to the catalog. This verifies that any stored script will not have a syntax error. Storing scripts does *not* check for the existence of subdirectories in format statements.

- A stored script can call another stored script. Notice the stored script named archive_log_current. This script is called by two other scripts with the EXECUTE SCRIPT command.

- Allocated channels are not automatically released when an RMAN-stored script completes, so be sure to explicitly release them.

- When this stored script file is run, the create script command creates the scripts for the first time. It is also possible to use the REPLACE SCRIPT command to replace already existing scripts with new ones.

- Stored scripts can be generated from many files or at the RMAN prompt; they all don't have to be loaded at the same time in one script file.

- Using the REPLACE SCRIPT command instead of CREATE SCRIPT will create the stored script if that script does not yet exist or will replace that script if it does.

To create the stored scripts, you must be connected to the recovery catalog and the target database. Though you can create stored scripts by typing in each line of the script at the RMAN command prompt, instead just run the scripts.rcv file.

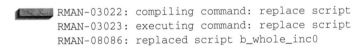

```
LINUX> export ORACLE_SID=PRACTICE
LINUX> rman
RMAN> connect target sys/practice;
RMAN> connect catalog rman817/rman@rcat;
RMAN> @scripts.rcv
```

Why do you have to be connected to the target database if you are just adding data into the recovery catalog? The scripts created in the catalog will be used only for this target. (If you had another database registered in this catalog, you'd need to run scripts.rcv while connected to that target database.) As the replace script file runs, the individual scripts undergo syntax checking and are stored on the catalog database. Messages like this should appear for each stored script in the script file:

```
RMAN-03022: compiling command: replace script
RMAN-03023: executing command: replace script
RMAN-08086: replaced script b_whole_inc0
```

If you mistyped something and RMAN cannot compile the commands, RMAN displays an error and some message describing the line of the file in violation. Correct these errors by changing the incorrect lines in scripts.rcv and run the file again. If no errors are found, the scripts are now created in the catalog.

Task 2: List and Display Stored Scripts

How can you know if the scripts created are in the catalog? RMAN does not have a convenient means to show all stored scripts from the RMAN prompt. A catalog view named RC_STORED_SCRIPT stores one row for each stored script for each registered database. You can use **host** to execute a command outside of RMAN like this:

```
RMAN> host;
LINUX> sqlplus \nolog
SQL> connectrman817/rman@rcat
  2    FROM rc_stored_script
  3    WHERE db_name = 'PRACTICE';
DB_NAME    SCRIPT_NAME
--------   -------------------
PRACTICE   archive_log_current
PRACTICE   b_whole_inc0
PRACTICE   b_whole_inc1
PRACTICE   b_archive_2days
PRACTICE   b_archive_delete
SQL> exit;
LINUX> exit;
```

Return to the RMAN prompt by exiting from SQL*Plus. At the command prompt, type **exit** again, and you will be back at the RMAN prompt.

To print the contents of stored scripts, use the PRINT command at the RMAN prompt. Display the command contents of each stored script:

```
RMAN> print script archive_log_current;
RMAN> print script b_whole_inc0;
RMAN> print script b_whole_inc1;
RMAN> print script b_archive_2days;
RMAN> print script b_archive_delete3;
```

The scripts created for the PRACTICE database are displayed on the screen. Since you just created these scripts, it doesn't make much sense to print them to the screen this way right now. You can also display script contents by selecting from the RC_STORED_SCRIPT_LINE catalog view.

Task 3: Execute and Delete Stored Scripts

The RMAN EXECUTE SCRIPT command runs a stored script from the RMAN prompt. Try one of the scripts you just created by running a full database backup. Back up the PRACTICE database by running the b_whole_inc0 script you just stored in the catalog database:

```
RMAN> run { execute script b_whole_inc0; }
```

Script execution commands must be placed in a run block. Run several stored scripts by placing them in individual run blocks. To demonstrate, take a whole database incremental backup level 1 and back up the archive log files created in the last two days.

```
RMAN> run {
2>   execute script b_whole_inc1;
3>   execute script b_archive_2days;
4>   }
```

To remove a stored script, use the REMOVE SCRIPT command and specify the name of the script:

```
RMAN>  delete script b_whole_inc1;
```

In this exercise, you only create a few small scripts. In a larger deployment, you can create more complex scripts to accomplish backup, maintenance, and recovery tasks. A good example of those scripts can be found in the $ORACLE_ HOME/rdbms/demo directory of your Oracle installation. Several files beginning with demo and ending with .rcv contain Oracle-supplied examples of stored scripts you can use. Open the files and modify portions like the format clause to cater these scripts to your environment. The big advantage of running backups from stored scripts is that they are stored in a centrally accessible location. Separate script files do not have to be maintained elsewhere on the server, and RMAN can be run from a server separate from the server that houses the target database. Using stored scripts means that you don't have to have copies of the scripts on different machines.

Recovery Manager Backup Confirmation

Is the database protected against failure? Can you recover the database using your server-managed backups as dictated by the business requirements? These questions are the acid test for a successful RMAN deployment. As you've heard before, you must be sure to test and verify that your backups can be used for restoration and recovery of an Oracle database. These tests can take a lot of time and disk space on a very large database. Is there a way in RMAN to find out if the target database is protected with the current backup? Yes, there is. Is there a way to simulate a restoration with current RMAN backups? Yes, there is. Can you find out if any part of your database is unprotected because of unrecoverable operations? Yes, you can. Can you confirm that the backups known to the catalog still exist on disk or tape? You'd better believe it!

Exercise 13.2: Confirm Backups

Backups can be confirmed in many ways with RMAN and SQL*Plus. To do this, you'll make use of the LIST, CHANGE, REPORT, and VALIDATE commands. You'll also query the target control file and the catalog to examine the current backup inventory. By using these methods, you'll confirm that you have adequately backed up your PRACTICE database.

Task Description	Minutes
1. Confirm Backups with LIST	10
2. Confirm Backups with REPORT	10
3. Confirm Backups with SQL*Plus	10
4. Crosscheck Backups	10
5. Validate Backups	10
Total Time	50

The focus of this exercise is to provide you with the methods you need to verify that your database can be recovered using existing RMAN backups.

Task 1: Confirm Backups with LIST

In this task, you'll learn what category of information and the database files you can list and how you can filter that list so you don't see every backup taken. Before I show you how the LIST command can confirm your backups, let me walk you through LIST command options with some examples.

Category   The LIST command will display RMAN-related backup information in one of three categories. Ask RMAN for a list of database incarnation information, backups, or image copies:

- **Incarnation**   Shows the known incarnations of the database, including the reset log's SCN and date/time. The database key and incarnation key uniquely identify each database incarnation.

- **Backup**   Shows the backups of the database files, including the backup set count, backup level (incremental number or full), and completion time. This key uniquely identifies each backup set. By default, the backup list shows backup sets and pieces for datafiles instead of archive logs or control files.

■ **Copy**   Shows the image copies of the database files, including the checkpoint SCN and time, file name, and completion date/time of the copy. This key uniquely identifies each image copy. By default, the copy list shows image copies of datafiles instead of archive logs or control files.

Database Files and Filters   When listing backups and copies, tell RMAN what database file type you want to see: datafiles, control files, or archive log files. If you don't specify the file type to display, backup and copy listings show datafiles by default. For the backup and copy information, you can set boundaries (filters) on what backup occurrences you want to display. To see a list of various database object qualifiers (datafile, tablespace, control file, archive log file, or database), append these keywords to your LIST BACKUP or COPY command:

■ **Database**   Shows backups or image copies of all datafiles of the target database.

■ **Tablespace**   Shows backups or image copies of all datafiles for the list of tablespaces contained within the single quoted string. You can list more than one tablespace.

■ **Datafile**   Shows backups or image copies of a datafile for the list by file number or file name within the single quoted string. You can list more than one datafile.

■ **Controlfile**   Shows backups or image copies of the control file in the target database.

■ **Archivelog**   Shows backups or image copies of archive log files.

Datafiles   To illustrate the different ways to see an inventory of the backups and image copies of the SYSTEM and USERS tablespace datafile, enter the commands shown here at the RMAN prompt:

```
# List backup sets & pieces for the SYSTEM and USERS tablespaces
RMAN> list backup;
RMAN> list backup of database;
RMAN> list backup of tablespace 'SYSTEM', 'USERS';
RMAN> list backup of datafile 1, 3, 7;
RMAN> list backup of datafile
2>       '/oradata/PRACTICE/system01.dbf',
3>       '/oradata/PRACTICE/users01.dbf',
4>       '/oradata/PRACTICE/users02.dbf';
# List image copies for the SYSTEM and USERS tablespaces
RMAN> list copy;
RMAN> list copy of database;
```

```
RMAN> list copy of tablespace 'SYSTEM', 'USERS';
RMAN> list copy of datafile 1, 3, 7;
RMAN> list copy of datafile
2>        '/oradata/PRACTICE/system01.dbf',
3>        '/oradata/PRACTICE/users01.dbf',
4>        '/oradata/PRACTICE/users02.dbf';
```

When you list the backup and copies of the database, you get all backups and image copies made of all parts of the database.

Control Files   To see backups and image copies of the control file, tell the list command that you want to see only the control files:

```
RMAN> list backup of controlfile;
RMAN> list copy of controlfile;
```

Notice that the output of the backup listing contains the words "Controlfile Included," indicating that the control file was included in a backup of the SYSTEM tablespace. The list displayed is different from the list displayed for datafile output.

Archive Logs   Listing archive logs has different filtering options from listing datafiles and control files. You must tell the list command which archive log files you want to take inventory of. Use the keyword Archivelog to specify a list of archive log file backups or image copies. You can see all the archive log files (ALL), match a pattern of archive log files (LIKE), or specify a range of files to list. The range must be bounded by one of the following:

- **Time**   The time span that the redo file log was populated with redo information. Specify the range with keywords FROM TIME, UNTIL TIME, or both, along with a single quoted date string. Date strings can be string literals, string literals combined with the TO_DATE function, date arithmetic with SYSDATE, other date functions like LAST_DAY, ADD_MONTHS, and so on. The FROM TIME will include the archived redo log files containing redo changes starting from this time. The UNTIL_TIME will include the archived redo log file that contains this last time of a redo change.

- **SCN**   The SCN span for the redo log file. Specify the range with keywords FROM SCN, UNTIL SCN, or both, along with an integer value. The FROM SCN will include the archived redo log files containing that SCN value and above. The UNTIL_SCN will include the archived redo log file containing that SCN value and below.

- **Log Sequence**   The redo log sequence value for the redo log file. Specify the range with keywords FROM LOGSEQ, UNTIL LOGSEQ, or both, along with an integer value. The FROM LOGSEQ includes the archived log file with this log sequence number and above. The UNTIL LOGSEQ includes the archived log file with this log sequence number and below.

To illustrate how you might list archive log backups and copies, look at this example:

```
#  List archive log backup sets & pieces
RMAN> list backup of archivelog all;
RMAN> list backup of archivelog like '%oradata%';
RMAN> list backup of archivelog from time 'SYSDATE - 14';
RMAN> list backup of archivelog until time 'SYSDATE - 7';
RMAN> list backup of archivelog
2>    from time 'SYSDATE - 14'
3>    until time 'SYSDATE - 7';
RMAN> list backup of archivelog from SCN 100000;
RMAN> list backup of archivelog until SCN 110000;
RMAN> list backup of archivelog from SCN 100000 until SCN 110000;
RMAN> list backup of archivelog from logseq 130;
RMAN> list backup of archivelog until logseq 139;
RMAN> list backup of archivelog from logseq 130 until logseq 139;
```

The examples shown above are how you might see backups taken by RMAN and copies known to RMAN of archive log files. I've listed several examples to help you see the pattern of how the ranges can be defined. Run these commands while connected to your PRACTICE target database and catalog database. Adjust your SCN values and log sequence numbers so that you'll see different output. To see image copies archive log files, replace the keyword BACKUP with COPY.

NOTE
The specification of the database objects for the LIST command is mutually exclusive. For example, you can't see datafiles and control files in the same listing. Display either datafile, control file, or archive log file backups.

Date Format Options   You've got a variety of options when specifying dates with RMAN. Look at the date samples in Table 13-1 for some illustrations of how you can establish date values with RMAN in lists (or other RMAN commands that can use date parameters).

Date String	Value
SYSDATE	The current date and time
TRUNC (SYSDATE)	Midnight of the current day
SYSDATE	The current date and time less seven days
'13-JAN-2002'	Midnight on January 13, 2002, if the session value for NLS_DATE_FORMAT = 'DD-MON-YYYY'
TO_DATE ('13-JAN-2002 13:00', 'DD-MON-YYYY HH24:MI'	1 PM on January 13, 2002, no matter what the session value for NLS_DATE_FORMAT
ADD_MONTHS(SYSDATE, 1)	One month after the current date and time
ADD_MONTHS(SYSDATE, -1)	One month before the current date and time
LAST_DAY(SYSDATE, 1)	The last day of the current date and time
NEXT_DAY(' SYSDATE', 'SUNDAY')	The date of the next Sunday from the current date and time

TABLE 13-1. *RMAN Date String Options*

More Filter Options   Now that you've established the database objects you want to show in the listing, you can filter the output based on several criteria. If you've been using RMAN a while and haven't removed obsolete backups, you'll be overrun with output. The lists can be filtered using criteria. The filter criteria include:

- **Completion time**   Limit the list output to only those backups and image copies complete within a time range. Specify a lower time bound with the AFTER keyword. Specify an upper time bound with the BEFORE keyword. Specify a time range with the BETWEEN keyword. Provide a time range as shown in Table 13-1.

- **Tag**   Limit the list output to only those backups or image copies with this specific tag name. If no tag name is provided, all tagged backups and image copies are included.

- **Recoverable**   Limit the list output to only those backups that can be used to recover the database. Optionally specify a stop point for recoverability. This option will display all those backups that have suitable base-level backups and correct incarnation numbers to be suitable for recovery. For example, if you take a level 3 incremental backup without having a base level (incremental 0, full, or image copy), this backup cannot be used for recovery.

- **Device type**   Limit the list output to only those backups or image copies of type disk or 'SBT_TAPE'.

- **Like**   Limit the list output to only those image copies containing datafiles that match a file name pattern. The '%' wildcard matches any characters and the '_' matches a single character.

These list filters can be used with other filter criteria, as shown here.

```
#  List backup sets of the system datafile with filter criteria
RMAN> list backup completed after 'SYSDATE - 14';
RMAN> list backup completed before 'SYSDATE - 7';
RMAN> list backup completed between 'SYSDATE - 14' and 'SYSDATE - 7';
RMAN> list backup tag = WHOLE_INC0;
RMAN> list backup recoverable;
RMAN> list backup device type disk;
RMAN> list copy like = '%system%'; #image copies only for like filter
RMAN> # Combine filters
RMAN> list backup completed after 'SYSDATE - 14'
2>                tag = WHOLE_INC0
3>                device type disk
4>                recoverable;
```

These examples show how you might use the filter criteria to limit the output of the list. To see the inventory of image copies, replace the keyword BACKUP with COPY. You can combine the filters with the many of database object options shown next. Say, for example, you wanted to see the backups to disk of the RBS tablespace completed this month having a tag named 'WHOLE_INC0. Try this:

```
RMAN> list backup of tablespace 'RBS'
2>      completed after 'LAST_DAY(ADD_MONTHS(SYSDATE,-1))+1'
3>      TAG = WHOLE_INC0
4>      device type disk;
```

This list command will get what you are looking for, if that backup exists. Note that the order of the filter criteria doesn't matter, and each filter phrase does not have to be on its own line.

Putting Lists to Work   With all these options when listing backups and image copies, how can you confirm that the PRACTICE database is protected? You create lists that confirm that your backups agree with the intended strategy. Consider a backup scenario that concurs with the simple strategy described in Chapter 12. The business requires that you be able to recover the database to any point in the last 21 days. You perform an incremental strategy as described here:

- **Sunday**   Cumulative incremental level 0 backup with tag SUN_LEVEL0.
- **Monday**   Cumulative incremental level 2 backup with tag MON_LEVEL2.
- **Tuesday**   Cumulative incremental level 2 backup with tag TUE_LEVEL2.
- **Wednesday**   Cumulative incremental level 2 backup with tag WED_LEVEL2.
- **Thursday**   Cumulative incremental level 1 backup with tag THU_LEVEL2.
- **Friday**   Cumulative incremental level 2 backup with tag FRI_LEVEL2.
- **Saturday**   Cumulative incremental level 2 backup with tag SAT_LEVEL2.
- **Every day**   All archive logs from the past two days get backed up.
- **Every day**   All archive logs that are three days old get backed up and removed from disk.
- **Every day**   The current control is copied in each of the whole database incremental backups.

With this backup strategy, what backup output would you expect to find for each database file? For each archive log? For each control file? Assuming that backups older than 21 days are removed, this listing shows what you'd like to see from the list output.

```
RMAN> # One backup set each day, total of 21
RMAN> list backup completed after 'SYSDATE - 21';
RMAN> # 21 backup sets completed in the last 21 days
RMAN> list backup of controlfile completed after 'SYSDATE - 21';
RMAN> # 3 backup sets completed on Sunday
RMAN> list backup completed after 'SYSDATE - 21' tag = SUN_LEVEL0;
RMAN> # Repeat above for other tag values
```

```
RMAN> # 42 backup sets - two backups daily for 21 days
RMAN> list backup of archivelog all completed after 'SYSDATE - 21';
RMAN> # For a specific archive log, should have 3 backups
RMAN> list backup of archivelog from logseq 130 until logseq 130
 2>    completed after 'SYSDATE - 21';
RMAN> # Make sure we can recover to 21 days previous
RMAN> list backup recoverable until time 'SYSDATE - 21';
```

The list output from these commands will be quite large. Therefore, use the RMAN log command to run these. Then inspect the log file output. Examine the list output file to see if you received an inventory of backups you'd expect.

```
LINUX> rman log=/tmp/list.out
RMAN> connect target sys/practice@practice
RMAN> connect catalog rman817/rman@rcat
RMAN> @list.rcv
RMAN> exit
LINUX> vi /tmp/list.out
```

Task 2: Confirm Backups with REPORT

The LIST command tells you what you've got. REPORT tells you what you need. There are four report options, and two of them (Need backup and Unrecoverable) come in very handy for confirming that your current backups will allow you to recover.

- **Need backup**   Identifies datafiles that require a new backup for a specified threshold (days, incremental count, or redundancy number) to achieve a complete recovery. Recovery will require archived redo logs and perhaps incremental backups. With this report you can ascertain if datafiles in your database require more than the threshold value of incremental backups applied or days of redo applied. Also, you can report datafiles that don't have enough redundant backups.

- **Unrecoverable**   Identifies any datafiles that require backup because an unrecoverable operation (that is a NOLOGGING operation) has occurred to data blocks in that datafile.

- **Obsolete**   Identifies backups that are not needed and can be deleted. You can specify the number of extra backups (redundancy) to this report. For example, if you are comfortable with two redundant backups to the most current one, you can report on any backups that were made earlier than those two redundant backups.

- **Schema**   Shows you the database physical schema for the target database. When using a catalog, you view the physical schema at a specific point in time, log sequence, or SCN.

Since reports fill an analysis function, the parameters used for a specific report pertain to the type of report generated. In this exercise, you'll look at each of the reports and discuss how they can be used to find any holes in your backup strategy.

Need Backup Report   The need backup option shows parts of your database that have not been backed up in a specified number of days.

```
RMAN> report need backup days 2 database;
RMAN-03022: compiling command: report
Report of files whose recovery needs more than 2 days of archived logs
File Days  Name
---- ----- -------------------------------------------------------
1    2     /oradata/PRACTICE/system01.dbf
2    2     /oradata/PRACTICE/rbs01.dbf
3    2     /oradata/PRACTICE/users01.dbf
4    2     /oradata/PRACTICE/temp01.dbf
5    2     /oradata/PRACTICE/tools01.dbf
6    2     /oradata/PRACTICE/indx01.dbf
7    2     /oradata/PRACTICE/users02.dbf
```

This report displays datafiles that have not been backed up in two days and tells you that complete recovery will require the application of all the redo logs from the last two days. This report shows the oldest datafile that has not been backed up. Even if all your datafiles but one have been backed up today and that one file has not been backed up in the last two days, that datafile will show up in this report.

Another reason a recovery would take a long time for complete recovery is that too many incremental backups must be applied. The restoration of, say, 20 incremental backups, especially from tape, may take a long time. The incremental option on the need backup report tells you how many incremental backups must be applied for a complete recovery. This report alerts you if the target database requires more than three incremental backups for recovery:

```
RMAN> report need backup incremental 3 database;
```

CAUTION
The need backup options will not display datafiles that have never been backed up. Don't be deceived if the need backup returns no rows; you may not have any backups at all! In order to implement a complete backup and recovery strategy, you must make sure all datafiles within the database are backed up at least once before incremental backups are taken. It is your responsibility to make sure all parts of the database are backed up.

Unrecoverable Report   Unrecoverable operations on the target database will invalidate data blocks changed by the operation should the invalidation redo records be applied. RMAN can report when you need to take another incremental backup to prevent issues when applying redo from a NOLOGGING operation:

```
RMAN> report unrecoverable;
```

If this report displays any output, take an incremental (or full) backup to copy the database blocks that cannot be recovered with redo application.

Schema Report   The schema report does not alert you of a slow recovery or of unrecoverable blocks. You can look at the current datafiles comprising the target database or see the schema as it existed in the past:

```
RMAN> report schema;
RMAN> report schema at time 'SYSDATE-7';
RMAN> report schema at time "TO_DATE('01/13/2002','MM/DD/YYYY')";
RMAN> report schema at scn 1000;
RMAN> report schema at logseq 131;
```

Task 3: Confirm Backups with SQL*Plus

Add SQL commands against the catalog user that produce similar results to the LIST command. Using SQL to query the catalog, look at the catalog contents that describe the backup set, backup pieces, and datafiles that make up current backups. You can use either the backup set tag or the backup set key to find the information you are looking for. Queries can be run against the target control file or against the catalog user tables. The primary advantage of queries to these views: control over the presentation of the output. Lists have fixed output format, while SQL can be formatted a number of ways. The key views containing backup and image copy information are shown in Table 13-2.

Target Database View	Catalog View	Description
V$BACKUP_SET	RC_BACKUP_SET	RMAN backup set information
V$BACKUP_PIECE	RC_BACKUP_PIECE	RMAN backup piece file information
V$BACKUP_DATAFILE	RC_BACKUP_DATAFILE	RMAN backup datafile information
V$DATAFILE_COPY	RC_DATAFILE_COPY	RMAN image copies of datafiles
V$BACKUP_CONTROLFILE	RC_BACKUP_CONTROLFILE	RMAN backup control file information
V$CONTROLFILE_COPY	RC_CONTROLFILE_COPY	RMAN image copies of the control file
V$BACKUP_REDOLOG	RC_BACKUP_REDOLOG	RMAN backup archive log information

TABLE 13-2. *Important Dictionary and Catalog Views for RMAN Backups and Copies*

The columns and data in the control file view compare closely with those in the catalog view. Though similar, there are some important differences:

- The catalog view will have a column to identify the database and database incarnation, while the target dictionary view will not. A control file will only contain the current incarnation number.

- Catalog views contain a backup key used as an internal RMAN catalog reference number for backups and copies. The control file views do not have this key.

- The target control file or the catalog may have rows that the other does not. Over time, backup records age out of the target control file and won't show up in the v$ view. If you remove backups from the catalog, they will not exist in the catalog view but may still exist in the target control file.

Backup Sets and Pieces   The backup sets taken by RMAN can be seen on the target database and in the catalog database. Queries on these views will show backup set and piece information, as shown here.

```
SQL> connect sys/practice@practice
SQL> SELECT recid, set_count,
  2          decode(backup_type, 'D', 'FULL',
  3                              'I','INCREMENTAL',
  4                              'L','LOGS') Type,
  5          incremental_level ILevel, completion_time Completed
  6     FROM v$backup_set;
SQL> connect rman817/rman@rcat
SQL> SELECT recid, set_count,
  2          decode(backup_type, 'D','FULL',
  3                              'I','INCREMENTAL',
  4                              'L','LOGS') Type,
  5          incremental_level ILevel, completion_time Completed
  6     FROM rc_backup_set
  7    WHERE db_key =
  8      (SELECT max(db_key) FROM rc_database
  9        WHERE name = 'PRACTICE');
```

To compare backup pieces known to the target control file with the catalog user, perform similar queries against V$BACKUP_PIECE and RC_BACKUP_PIECE, respectively. These views contain important columns like handle (the backup piece file name for disk and tape backup) and *tag* (for backup piece tag names).

Datafiles   In addition to the RMAN LIST command, you can select from the views on the catalog to see the details of the datafile copies and backups. Run the queries below to get information similar to what you just saw with the RMAN LIST COPY and LIST BACKUP commands.

```
SQL> connect system/practice@practice
SQL> SELECT file#, completion_time time,
  2          checkpoint_change# change#, name
  3     FROM v$datafile_copy;
SQL> SELECT file#, completion_time time,
  2          checkpoint_change# change#, set_count
  3     FROM v$backup_datafile;
SQL> connect rman817/rman@rcat
SQL> SELECT file#, completion_time time, checkpoint_change# change#, name,
  2          cdf_key key,
  3          decode (Status, 'A','AVAIL','U','UNAVAIL','D','DELETED') Status
  4     FROM rc_datafile_copy
  5    WHERE db_name = 'PRACTICE';
SQL> SELECT file#, completion_time time, checkpoint_change# change#,
  2          bdf_key key, set_count,
```

```
3          decode(status,'A','AVAIL','O','UNUSABLE','D','DELETED') Status
4     FROM rc_backup_datafile
5     WHERE db_name = 'PRACTICE';
```

Backup Control Files   Control file image copies and backups can be found in
the V$CONTROLFILE_COPY, V$BACKUP_CONTROLFILE,
RC_CONTROLFILE_COPY and RC_BACKUP_CONTROLFILE views. These two
catalog views provide more information about control file backups than the LIST
command. Using SQL in SQL*Plus, you can see these additional columns and
format your output.

Backup Archive Logs   In addition to the LIST BACKUP ARCHIVELOG
command, you can query the catalog user to show information about a specific
backup. Open an SQL*Plus session as the catalog owner and run queries like
you've done in previous tasks (select from V$BACKUP_REDOLOG and
V$BACKUP_REDOLOG instead).

For handy SQL statement to check all the archive log files backed up and the number
of occurrence for each file, query the recovery catalog with SQL, as shown here.

```
SQL> connect system/practice@practice
SQL> SELECT sequence#, count(*)
2      FROM v$backup_redolog
3      GROUP BY sequence#;
SQL> connect rman817/rman@rcat
SQL> SELECT sequence#, count(*)
2      FROM rc_backup_redolog
3      WHERE db_name = 'PRACTICE'
3        AND status = 'A'
4      GROUP BY sequence#;
```

With a backup strategy for archive logs as described in Chapter 12, you'd expect
to see three backups of each archive log file. If you have a gap in the sequence, you
do not have an RMAN backup of that archive log file!

NOTE
*The queries shown here are simple. Once you get
familiar with these views, tailor them as you see fit
in your RMAN deployment. Also, if you have
several databases and incarnations of those
databases registered in your catalog, make sure the
where clauses on your queries include the correct
database and incarnation using the db_key and
dbinc_key columns.*

Task 4: Crosscheck Backups

Finding backup information requires the most effort when determining if your current backup situation is in order. When using lists and reports, you are told what RMAN knows of your current backups. If a backup piece has been deleted from the operating system, the control file and catalog will not know about this. Therefore, run a crosscheck occasionally to confirm that the catalog contains the correct information about backup pieces. Keep in mind that a crosscheck can be a very resource-intensive operation, especially if your backups have been made to tape. When a crosscheck occurs, RMAN determines whether the backup set exists. If you crosscheck a larger number of backups on tape, you may keep the tape subsystem busy, loading, unloading, and positioning tapes. Some MMLs query their catalog and report back to RMAN, which is not as intensive as checking the physical tapes for the existence of files. Since the PRACTICE database backups are on disk and you don't have that many backups, a crosscheck operation runs quickly.

NOTE
*Channels for maintenance don't need a name like
backup, restore and recovery channels do.*

The following command will check *all* backups known to either the target control file or catalog:

```
RMAN> allocate channel for maintenance type disk;
RMAN> crosscheck backup;
RMAN> release channel;
```

The output looks like this:

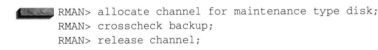

```
RMAN-08074: crosschecked backup piece: found to be 'AVAILABLE'
RMAN-08517: backup piece
handle=/oradata/PRACTICE/backup/ch13/db_PRACTICE_130_1_446974818 recid=19
stamp=446974822
```

The word *available* means that the backup piece was found as expected. You can limit the crosscheck to backups that contain tags or specific tag names with the tag option. You can also limit crosschecks to all backups bounded by a time range. Finally, you can define the database object that the backup pertains to.

CAUTION
*The crosscheck command must be used judiciously on
a production system with many RMAN tape backups.
You don't want to tie up your tape subsystem or MML
library and prevent backups from running.*

```
RMAN> crosscheck backup of datafile 1;
RMAN> crosscheck backup completed between 'SYSDATE-7' and 'SYSDATE';
RMAN> crosscheck backup completed between '01-JAN-2002' and '30-JAN-2002';
RMAN> crosscheck backup tag WHOLE_INC0;
RMAN> crosscheck backup of archivelog like '%/100.%';
RMAN> crosscheck backup of archivelog from logseq 100 until logseq 110;
RMAN> crosscheck backup of archivelog from 'SYSDATE-7' and 'SYSDATE';
```

To crosscheck specific backup sets or image copies, use the change command with the crosscheck option rather than just the crosscheck command:

```
RMAN> change backupset 311 crosscheck;
RMAN> change datafilecopy 545 crosscheck;
```

Backup sets look like this when they are found:

```
RMAN-08074: crosschecked backup piece: found to be 'AVAILABLE'
RMAN-03022: compiling command: change
RMAN-06154: validation succeeded for datafile copy
RMAN-08513: datafile copy
filename=/oradata/PRACTICE/backup/ch12/system01.dbf.bak recid=1
stamp=446972315
```

The words you'd like to see are VALIDATION SUCCEEDED.

Task 5: Validate Backups

RMAN provides the ability to simulate a restore with the validate option on the restore command. This method of validation allows RMAN to choose the backup sets or copies to use for restore. RMAN can also validate the restoration of a specific backup set using the VALIDATE BACKUPSET command. Either method of restoration validation can be performed on the entire database, tablespaces, datafiles, control files, or archive log files.

CAUTION
RMAN validation does not test recovery (the application of incrementals and redo). Therefore, validation is not a comprehensive test. You can validate a restore and then validate incremental backup restores only.

Restore Validate   First, validate the restore of the entire database and let RMAN pick the backup sets and copies to use. This method of validation uses the restore command within a run block. Validate the restore of the backup sets and copies.

The following example validates the restore of the backup control file, all tablespaces, and all archived redo logs from disk:

```
RMAN> run {
    allocate channel d1 type disk;
    restore database validate;
    restore archivelog all validate;
}
RMAN-08096: channel d1: starting validation of datafile backupset
RMAN-08502: set_count=40 set_stamp=447343243 creation_time=01-DEC-01
RMAN-08023: channel d1: restored backup piece 1
RMAN-08511: piece handle=/oradata/backup/ch13/DB_PRACTICE_40_1_447343 243
tag=WHOLE_INC0 params=NULL
RMAN-08098: channel d1: validation complete
RMAN-08096: channel d1: starting validation of datafile backupset
RMAN-08502: set_count=41 set_stamp=447343280 creation_time=01-DEC-01
RMAN-08023: channel d1: restored backup piece 1
RMAN-08511: piece handle=/oradata/backup/ch13/DB_PRACTICE_41_1_447343 280
tag=WHOLE_INC1 params=NULL
RMAN-08098: channel d1: validation complete
```

If the output displays a message that the validation is complete, the validation succeeded. Otherwise, an error message will be displayed.

Validate Backupset The second method of validation requires details of specific backup sets. Take two backup sets created as incremental backups against the PRACTICE database. For example, backup set 130 is a level 0 incremental backup, and backup set 131 is a level 1 backup. Each of them contain a copy of the control file:

```
RMAN> run {
    allocate channel d1 type disk;
    validate backupset 130, 131;
}
```

During validation, the backup pieces are read and the restore is simulated. If the restore worked:

```
RMAN-08024: channel ch1: restore complete
```

Otherwise, you'll get an error message.

To simulate a failed validation, rename a backup piece in a backup piece to a new file name. Validate the backup set. You'll get an error. Next, copy any word processing document to the original file name of the backup piece. Validate the backup set again and you'll get a different error. Remove the word processing file you just copied to simulate a corrupted backup piece and rename the original backup piece to the original file name. A final validation will yield a successful message.

Recovery Catalog Cleanup

Say you take an RMAN database backup each day. After one year, you'd have 365 database backups and 365 archive log backups. Unless you plan to recover to a point in time 364 days ago, you really don't need the backup you made one year ago. How do you get rid of all these old backups? Use the change command.

Exercise 13.3: Remove Redundant Backups

In this exercise, you'll see three ways to remove old backups that are no longer needed.

Task Description	Minutes
1. Find Obsolete Backups	5
2. Remove Obsolete Backups	5
3. Remove Old Backups	5
4. Find Expired Backups	5
5. Remove Expired Backups	5
Total Time	25

To purge the old backups, RMAN provides the change command with the delete option. Obsolete backups not needed for current recoveries are first identified using reports, crosschecks, and SQL. Once identified, they can be removed.

Task 1: Find Obsolete Backups

During a complete recovery, RMAN will use the most recent backup or image copy to restore a database file. When point-in-time recovery is required, RMAN restores the backups that are most recent to that time in the past. Any backup that RMAN will not use for recovery because there are more recent backups is an obsolete backup. Obsolete backups may be needed if you choose to recover to a time that is earlier than the most recent backup. Therefore having a few extra backups around is a good thing. However, when too many of them accumulate, you can choose to remove some of them.

RMAN has a handy report that displays obsolete backup sets that exceed a redundancy threshold. Perhaps your business is comfortable with a three-week backup retention window. They will never call on you, the DBA, to recover the database as it existed more than three weeks ago.

Find backups that have become obsolete and have been created over 21 days (three weeks) ago:

```
RMAN> report obsolete redundancy 1
2>        until time 'SYSDATE-21' device type disk;
```

Any backups or copies returned in this report can be deleted; they are not needed anymore. Because the redundancy default value is "1", you can omit the redundancy clause:

```
RMAN> report obsolete until time 'SYSDATE-21';
```

These commands will still leave one copy of a backup taken later than 21 days ago. This is to give you a safety margin in case you run into a situation where the 21–day-old backup is an incremental level 1. In order to use this for a recovery, you would need the incremental level 0 backup taken 22 days ago, which you might have already removed. This would compromise the 21-day backup retention policy because you are unable to recover the database as it was 21 days ago.

If this problem does not bother you and you can only keep 21 days worth of backups stored on disk or tape—no matter what they are—you can use the list command to show a list of backups taken more than 21 days ago:

```
RMAN> list backupset complete before 'SYSDATE-21';
```

CAUTION
You'll only be able to recover to a point after you have a full or incremental level 0 backup and all incrementals or archive log files created since that time. Therefore, consider keeping one copy of old backups around for safekeeping and all archive logs if you suspect you'll ever have to recover to a point in the distant past. The number of backups that you keep is dependent on what your business dictates. If you can only store tape backups for three months before the tapes are recycled, then you will only be able to recover backups from three months ago.

Task 2: Remove Obsolete Backups

Once the backup sets have been identified for deletion, how do you remove them with RMAN? Allocate a channel for deletion and remove the backup sets or image copies using the change command. For instance, if the REPORT command identified three backup sets (131, 132, and 133) that can be deleted, use these commands to remove those backup pieces from the operating system and change their status to deleted in the catalog:

```
RMAN> # Report obsolete backups on disk.
RMAN> report obsolete redundancy 4 device type disk;
RMAN> # Allocate a channel of type delete.
RMAN> allocate channel for delete type disk;
RMAN> # Delete the backup set(s).
RMAN> change backupset 131, 132, 133 delete;
RMAN> # Release the allocated delete channel.
RMAN> release channel;
```

The trouble with this operation is that you have to run the report and create the deletion commands based on the output of the report. The next task shows a different method for removing older backups.

To find and remove obsolete backups, run several incremental level 0 backups:

```
RMAN> run {execute script b_whole_inc0; };
RMAN> run {execute script b_whole_inc0; };
RMAN> run {execute script b_whole_inc0; };
RMAN> run {execute script b_whole_inc0; };
RMAN> report obsolete redundancy 4 device type disk;
```

The obsolete report will now display obsolete backups. Get rid of the obsolete backups as just shown. The backup files created will be removed from disk and removed from the catalog.

Task 3: Remove Old Backups

Finding backup set numbers and deleting them one by one can be done manually. To automate the removal of old backup sets, however, select the backup sets from the recovery catalog views and spool the change commands to a file. This spooled file can be run from RMAN to remove old backups. The following code contains SQL*Plus commands needed to create such an RMAN script file.

```
define fil = '/tmp/delete_copies.rcv'
spool &fil
prompt allocate channel for delete type disk;;
SELECT 'change backupset '||bs_key||' delete;'
  FROM rc_backup_set
 WHERE completion_time > SYSDATE - 21;
prompt release channel;;
spool off;
```

Calling file /tmp/delete_copies.rcv from an RMAN prompt while connected to the target will cause the catalog to remove the backups set created more than 21 days ago.

NOTE

Oracle has provided a script that will retrieve the obsolete backups from the recovery catalog using the report command and then delete them for you automatically. The script can be found in $ORACLE_HOME/rdbms/demo/rman1.sh on Linux and on NT. It is written as a Unix shell script, so for it to work on NT you must edit it dramatically as a DOS script or use a Unix shell environment. To change the number of redundant days, simply edit the script accordingly.

Task 4: Find Expired Backups

Most media managers have a retention period for files. For example, if a file is older than three months and the media manager retention period is set to three months, that file will be marked as expired. It can no longer be accessed by the media manager and will be removed by newer backups. You can combine the notion of a retention period and the RMAN crosscheck option to remove old backups. For users that require backups to be retained for three weeks and that write RMAN backup piece files to disk, you can remove those backup pieces from the Linux operating system older than three weeks:

```
LINUX> find /oradata/PRACTICE/backup/ -mtime -21 -print | xargs rm
```

Once the files are removed, you can perform a crosscheck on the backup sets.

```
RMAN> allocate channel for maintenance type disk;
RMAN> crosscheck backupsets;
RMAN> release channel;
```

All the files that were deleted at the operating system will be marked as expired by the crosscheck command.

CAUTION
Be careful that you do not remove backups from disk that may be required in the near future. It might be better to make sure that you have several older backups stored somewhere safe or to move the backups to a different directory before issuing the crosscheck command. Then, when you have queried the catalog and are 100 percent sure these backups are no longer needed, remove them.

For users that are using RMAN to back up to tape, issuing a CROSSCHECK command will check to see if the backups are still accessible when the MML has expired old backups. If the MML has expired them, RMAN will also mark them as expired in the catalog.

Task 5: Remove Expired Backups
In this task, you'll delete obsolete backup sets and image copies marked as expired in the previous task. To remove thephysical backups and update their repository records to status DELETED, use the following:

```
RMAN> delete expired backup;
```

After removing the backup pieces, run reports and list to make sure you can recover to a point three weeks in the past:

```
RMAN> # Make sure we can recover to 21 days previous
RMAN> list backup recoverable until time 'SYSDATE - 21';
```

> ### Oracle 9*i* Retention Policy
> In Oracle 9*i*, RMAN has a new feature called a *retention policy*. Just like media managers can define a retention policy for their tapes, RMAN allows you to define a retention policy for the backups, image copies, or proxy copies according to a *recovery window* or *backup redundancy*. With a recovery window, RMAN will mark all backups as obsolete when they are no longer needed to recover a database within the defined number of days for the current time. With backup redundancy, RMAN will mark backups as obsolete when the number of backups has been repeated more than the defined number of times. Nothing is deleted from the catalog; backups are only marked as obsolete. Later, you can use the DELETE OBSOLETE command to remove these old backups.

Troubleshooting

If you run into problems maintaining catalog and backups RMAN, you might encounter one of these errors. These notes may point you in the right direction to solve the issue.

1. **RMAN-01005: syntax error: found "identifier": expecting one of: "double-quoted-string, disk, equal, single-quoted-string" RMAN-01008: the bad identifier was: diskx RMAN-01007: at line 4 column 29 file: scripts.rcv** When creating a stored script in the catalog, you will encounter errors if the syntax of the commands is incorrect. Go to the line and column of the file, correct the line, and run the creation script file again.

2. **RMAN-06091: no channel allocated for maintenance (of an appropriate type)** The change, crosscheck, and validate commands require a maintenance channel of the appropriate type (disk or sbt_tape). Allocate the channel first before attempting to manage the backups.

3. **RMAN-10035: exception raised in RPC: <file> is not a backup piece** This message means a file exists with the name of a backup piece but is not a valid backup piece. Find the correct backup piece file or remove this backup piece.

Summary

In this chapter, you learned how to list backups and image copies that have information stored in the catalog or target control file. You also learned about the four reports you can create with RMAN (need backup, unrecoverable, obsolete, and schema). The crosscheck and validate options allow you to confirm that backups exist and can be successfully restored. The change command allows you to delete and manage existing database backups and image copies. For details about the various list and report options and output, look at Chapter 10 of the *Oracle8i Recovery Manager User's Guide and Reference*. In the same manual, look at Chapters 3 and 4 for explanations about managing the RMAN repository and creating lists and reports.

Chapter Questions

Test your knowledge of this chapter by answering these five questions.

1. Which two commands would you use to look at the contents of the target control file and the catalog from within RMAN?

   A. Select

   B. Report

   C. List

   D. Display

2. Which catalog view shows backup sets made by RMAN?

   A. V$BACKUP_SETS

   B. RC_COLA_SETS

   C. V$BACKUP_PIECES

   D. RC_BACKUP_SETS

3. With RMAN, the command to remove backups from the catalog and from the media is the DELETE command.

   A. True

   B. False

4. RMAN-stored scripts can call other stored scripts registered for the same target database in the same catalog schema.

   A. True

   B. False

5. How is the RMAN validate operation different from the crosscheck options?

   A. The crosscheck operation compares backups with each other; validate compares backups against the catalog schema.

   B. The crosscheck operation checks that a file exists on the backup media and reads the backup piece header; validate reads the entire backup piece file from the backup media performing checksum validation.

   C. The crosscheck operation and validate do the exact same thing.

   D. The crosscheck operation transfers money between bank accounts; validate pays for parking.

Answers to Chapter Questions

1. B, C. The REPORT and LIST commands display formatted output from the catalog.

2. D. The RC_BACKUP_SETS view displays catalog information on backup sets for all registered databases. The V$BACKUP_SETS view on a target database displays backup set information for only that database as contained in the control file.

3. False. The CHANGE command with the DELETE option removes backups and image copies from the catalog and the backup media. A maintenance channel of the correct media type (disk or SBT_TAPE) must be allocated prior to the CHANGE or DELETE.

4. True. Stored scripts can execute other stored scripts within the catalog for the same target database.

5. B. Crosscheck and validate perform the same functions, but validate simulates a restore by reading entire backup piece files for completeness. Therefore, validate is a more thorough and resource-intensive test.

CHAPTER
14

RMAN Recovery

ou configured RMAN in Chapter 11 to use a recovery catalog. In Chapter 12, you made backups of your PRACTICE database. In Chapter 13, you learned how to maintain your RMAN catalog. Now, let's see if all this works together by recovering your PRACTICE database using RMAN. You'll notice that the failure scenarios in this chapter are the same as some of the scenarios in Chapters 4 and 5. This is so you can compare and contrast server-managed recovery to user-managed recovery. Bringing a failed database back to working order with RMAN revolves around two important commands: restore and recover.

RMAN Restore

The restore command, as the name suggests, will restore files from the backups that RMAN has created. The restored files are ready to be used or can be recovered via incremental and redo application. Back in Chapter 12, I explained that RMAN will back up all blocks contained within a control file or an archive redo log. For datafiles, only those blocks that have been used, or that have changed since the last backup according to the incremental level you have defined, will be backed up. When any file is restored using RMAN, the file will then exist exactly as it did when it was originally backed up. For control files and archive redo logs, this means that all the blocks are restored. For datafiles, the used blocks are stored, and the empty blocks that were not backed up are created.

If an incremental backup strategy similar to the ones demonstrated in Chapter 12 is being used, a restore command will only restore the correct base-level files. For example, if you are taking an incremental level 0 backup every Sunday and incremental levels 1 and 2 during the week, RMAN will restore the last incremental level 0 backup. The subsequent incremental backups will be applied during the recover command.

An RMAN baseline backup used by the restore command can be any of these datafile backup types: an image copy, a full backup, and an incremental level 0 backup. Which datafile baseline backup RMAN chooses is mostly dependent on when they were created and what time you are recovering up until. RMAN will try to choose the backup that is newer and will require less recovery.

When restoring datafiles, RMAN can restore a single datafile, several named files, all the datafiles belonging to a tablespace or several tablespaces, or all the datafiles in the database. Tell RMAN to restore a datafile and it will find the most suitable backups or copies to recreate the datafile.

What state must the database be in when you restore database files? Table 14-1 provides a quick list that answers this question. Here is the rule: a database file cannot be in use by the instance when that file is being restored. Why? Because the instance cannot be writing to a database file while it is being restored. During any database file restore, the target database instance must always be started. When restoring any non-system datafile from a backup set, that datafile (or its tablespace) must be offline for the restore to succeed. If you restore any system tablespace datafiles, the database

Database File	Database State
Any non-system datafile	Mounted or open, but the file or tablespace must be offline
System datafile	Mounted
Database (all datafiles)	Mounted
Archive logs	Not mounted, mounted, or open
Control file	Not mounted

TABLE 14-1.   *Database States for Restore Operations*

must be started in mount mode. When restoring a control file, the instance must be started in nomount mode (when the database is mounted, the control file is in use). Archive logs can be restored while the target database is mounted or open.

Why does RMAN expect the database to be mounted during the restoration of datafiles and archive logs? Because RMAN backup and database structural information is in the control file and RMAN needs to access it. Be aware that a restore operation will, by default, replace the existing database file unless you prescribe otherwise.

RMAN Recovery

Once the datafiles have been restored, the recover command can be issued to roll them forward in time. RMAN will use information retrieved from the recovery catalog or the target control file to find out what further incremental backups or which redo logs need to be applied.

RMAN applies recovery in four distinct phases, which can be seen in numbered items here. These phases are:

1. The target control file is sometimes updated to reflect information that is stored in the recovery catalog that is more recent. Log file records and datafile records are most often updated in the control file at this point. This can happen if a backup control file has been restored.

2. Any incremental backups that can be applied are applied at this point.

3. All the restored datafiles are checked that they are present and can be used for recovery. Datafiles that should not be present (any datafiles created after the recovery stop time) are dropped from the database. Any redo logs that are required to roll the database forward are looked for on disk. If they are found they are applied.

4. Redo log files that were not found on disk and are required for recovery are restored to disk and applied to the datafiles.

Each incremental backup gets laid on the top of the previous one, so only changed blocks that were backed up are being replaced. When it can, RMAN chooses to restore incremental backups rather than apply redo from archived log files (applying incremental backups is quicker than application of redo). Once no more incremental backups can be applied, redo is applied to bring datafiles needing recovery forward. Recovery continues until all redo information is applied to specific datafiles or until a specific stop point. By default, RMAN performs complete recovery (all datafiles are rolled forward in time to the latest change in the current online redo log file). If the control file is also restored, RMAN cannot apply the online redo log files, and incomplete recovery must be carried out. Recovery can also continue until a specific point in time by specifying an UNTIL keyword.

TIP

When recovering from backed up archive logs, the archive logs are restored to disk first, then applied. Check that you've got disk space for the restoration of many archive log files prior to recovery.

To help pull this discussion of restore, recovery and incrementals together, look at Figure 14-1. This figure depicts an incremental backup strategy as discussed in Chapter 12. Suppose a datafile is lost on Saturday morning before the level 2 incremental backup. When RMAN restores and recovers this lost datafile, it performs the following steps to accomplish complete recovery:

1. **Restore the datafile.** Using backup set 120, RMAN recreates the entire lost datafile from the whole database incremental level 0 backup taken on Sunday. This base level backup contains all used blocks in the datafile. This level 0 backup *must* be restored as the base level for subsequent restores.

2. **Recover the datafile.** Once the datafile has been restored using the baseline backup, RMAN will recover the datafile using appropriate incremental backups. The first incremental backup applied will be backup set 124 (Thursday's incremental level 1). Backup sets 121, 122, and 123 are not required because all the changed data blocks from those backups are contained in set 124. Next, RMAN finds that backup set 125 has data blocks that can be applied to the restored datafile to make it current. Had there not been any changed blocks for this datafile in backup set 125, that backup set would not have been applied. Next, RMAN finds that no more incremental backups are needed. RMAN then locates needed redo log files for media recovery. If those files exist on disk, they are read from disk. If any archive files cannot be found, RMAN locates an image copy or backup sets containing the required redo files and restores them to disk. Once restored, they are used for complete recovery, along with the current online redo log file.

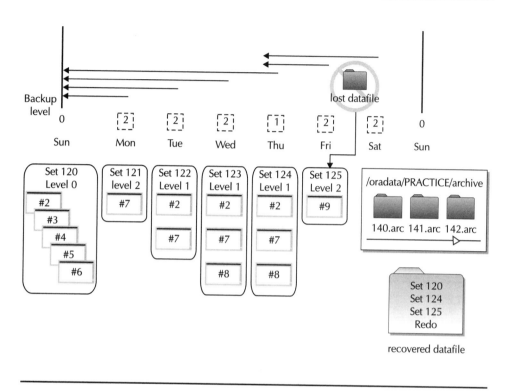

FIGURE 14-1. *Incremental Block Level Recovery using RMAN*

By default, RMAN will restore all datafiles to the original locations when the file was backed up. For example, RMAN restores the /oradata/PRACTICE/users01.dbf back into a file named users01.dbf in the /oradata/PRACTICE directory. Archive logs are restored by default to the archive dump destination directory. The control file is restored to the control file location stipulated by the CONTROL_FILES parameter in the database initialization (init.ora) file. You can change the location of file restores with the *set* attribute within a run block. The set attribute defines values for the commands within a run block. (The run block is a set of commands beginning with the word *run* and enclosed in brackets.) The set attribute can also specify the point in time of recovery and the location where archive log files are restored and read from during recovery. Table 14-2 provides a quick list of useful options that the run block set attribute provides for restore and recovery. Note that the set command is different from the set attribute within a run block. The set command issued at the RMAN prompt allows you to define file names during tablespace point in time recovery and duplicate database commands, among other things.

Set Keyword	Description
set newname for datafile	Defines a new file name and directory for a specific datafile. If not defined, RMAN restores files to their current directory and file name.
set archivelog destination to	Defines a different directory location for archive log files for the restore and recover commands. If not defined, RMAN uses the first archive dump destination as defined in the target init.ora file.
set until	Defines the stop point for recovery. Incomplete recovery can occur up to a specific time, log sequence, or SCN. If not defined, RMAN will restore the most recent baseline backup and recover datafiles using incremental backups and redo until all datafiles are made current.

TABLE 14-2. *Use Set Options for Recovery in an RMAN Run Block*

Environment variables play an important role when restoring and recovering with RMAN. You may need to set environment variables so that the character set of your session matches the character set of your database. Set the NLS_LANG environment variable to match the character set of your target database. If you'll be using a specific time during RMAN commands like LIST, REPORT, or SET UNTIL, set the NLS_DATE environment variable to match the date string in your commands. You can also use the TO_DATE function when specifying dates in your scripts.

```
LINUX> export NLS_LANG=AMERICAN_AMERICA.WE8ISO8859P1
LINUX> export NLS_DATE_FORMAT=YYYY-MM-DD:HH24:DD:SS
WINNT> set NLS_DATE_FORMAT=YYYY-MM-DD:HH24:MI:SS
WINNT> set NLS_LANG=AMERICAN_AMERICA.WE8ISO8859P1
```

Throughout this chapter, you are going to create two new backups using backup script files as created in Chapter 12. (You can also use the backups created during exercises in Chapter 12.) Figure 14-2 shows the operations you'll be performing. Using those backups, you'll recover the PRACTICE database using the RMAN. You will restore and recover the entire database and the datafiles of the USERS tablespace and perform an incomplete recovery after a mistaken drop table command.

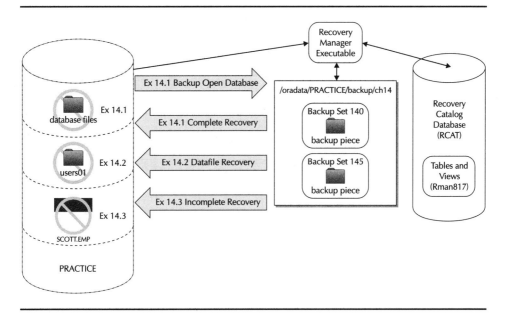

FIGURE 14-2.   *Recovery exercises using RMAN on the PRACTICE database*

RMAN Restore and Recover

Now that you've had a brief overview of the restore and recover commands, try the following exercises to get some hands-on experience using the PRACTICE database as the target and the RCAT database as the catalog database.

You'll see in these exercises that you can restore and recover a part of the database using a backup of the whole database. For example, you can restore the TOOLS datafile using whole database backups. The reverse is not true, however: you cannot restore the whole database from only a backup of the TOOLS tablespace.

Exercise 14.1: Restore the Whole Database

Imagine that you have a catastrophic failure and lose all the datafiles in your database, but the control files and the online redo logs remain intact. How can you recover from such a failure using RMAN backups? This exercise gives you a chance to put RMAN restore and recovery to work.

Task Description	Minutes
1. Perform Whole Database Backups	5
2. Simulate PRACTICE Failure	5
3. Restore and Recover Database	10
4. Verify Restore and Recover Database	5
Total Time	25

In this exercise, you'll perform two whole database backups. Then you'll remove all the datafiles in the PRACTICE database. Using the whole database backups, you'll then restore and recover all the datafiles of the PRACTICE database.

Task 1: Perform Whole Database Backups

Create two backups of your PRACTICE database using the stored scripts you created back in Chapter 12. The first backup you'll take is a whole database incremental level 0 backup that includes the current control file. Before you take the second backup, open a SQL*Plus session to make a data change to a table in the database. After committing that change, return to the RMAN prompt and run a second backup. The second backup is a whole database backup incremental level 1 and will only copy the data blocks that have changed since the first level 0 backup you just made. Enter the commands you see here:

```
LINUX> export ORACLE_SID=PRACTICE
LINUX> rman
RMAN> connect target sys/practice
RMAN> connect catalog rman817/rman@rcat
RMAN> @b_whole_inc0.rcv
RMAN> host;
LINUX> sqlplus /nolog
SQL> connect sys/practice
SQL> DELETE FROM tina.date_log WHERE create_date > SYSDATE;
SQL> INSERT INTO tina.date_log VALUES (SYSDATE+(365+14));
SQL> COMMIT;
SQL> exit
LINUX> exit
RMAN> @b_whole_inc1.rcv
```

CAUTION
Using the host command in RMAN and SQL*Plus can provide a convenient way to run OS commands. Be careful to return to RMAN or SQL*Plus. Otherwise, you may get confused about which programs you have running and make a mistake.

At the conclusion of these commands, you'll have the following backups and data. The backup pieces will be in the /oradata/PRACTICE/backup/ch12 directory, unless you changed the backup script files.

- **Backup: Incremental level 0**   The first backup ran the backup script file created in Chapter 12 named b_whole_inc0. This backup creates a single backup set and piece containing all used data blocks in all datafiles and the current control file for the PRACTICE database. This backup set has a backup set number of 140 (yours will be a different number) and a backup piece key value of 141.

- **Table data**   After the first backup, the TINA.DATE_LOG table was changed: a row was inserted with a create_date column value of 14 years in the future. The table change produced a data block change somewhere in the TOOLS tablespace datafile (assuming this table is still in the TOOLS tablespace). The data block that changed will be included in the next incremental backup.

- **Backup: Incremental level 1**   The second backup ran a backup script created in Chapter 12 named b_whole_inc1. This backup creates a single backup set and piece containing all used data blocks in all datafiles as well as the current control files that have changed since the previous backup. The changed data block for the TINA.DATE_LOG table (and others) was written to this backup. This backup set has a set number of 145 and a backup piece key value of 146.

NOTE
Why are you creating two backups with a change in between? It's because when you restore the database in Task 3, RMAN will extract data blocks saved in the first backup set. Then, during recovery, the second backup set gets applied to the restored datafiles.

Task 2: Simulate PRACTICE Failure

Remove all the datafiles from the /oradata/PRACTICE directory from the operating system. Keep the online redo logs and control files intact. On Linux, you'll be able to remove the files while the database is open. On Windows, you'll have to shut down the database to remove the database files. To perform the same operations no matter which OS you are using, shut down the database from RMAN and remove all database files on either operating system.

```
LINUX> rman
RMAN> connect target sys/practice@practice
RMAN> connect catalog rman817/rman@rcat
RMAN> shutdown abort
RMAN> host;
LINUX> rm /oradata/PRACTICE/*.dbf
LINUX> exit
```

Now that the database files are gone, you'll encounter an error when you attempt to start up the database. After the instance starts and mounts the control file, the instance attempts to find datafile number 1 (system01.dbf). Because the file does not exist, RMAN displays an error. This is the same error you'd receive if you attempted to start the database with SQL*Plus.

```
RMAN> startup
RMAN-06193: connected to target database (not started)
RMAN-06196: Oracle instance started
RMAN-06199: database mounted
RMAN-00571: ===========================================================
RMAN-00569: =============== ERROR MESSAGE STACK FOLLOWS ===============
RMAN-00571: ===========================================================
RMAN-06003: ORACLE error from target database:
ORA-01157: cannot identify/lock data file 1 - see DBWR trace file
ORA-01110: data file 1: '/oradata/PRACTICE/system01.dbf'
RMAN-06097: text of failing SQL statement: alter database open
RMAN-06099: error occurred in source file: krmk.pc, line: 4228
```

At this point, the instance is started and the database control file is mounted, but the database cannot be opened.

Task 3: Restore and Recover Database

At the RMAN prompt, list the two backups just taken in Task 1. Using the tag and the time (the last seven days), issue these list commands to see the two incremental backups:

```
RMAN> list backup completed after 'sysdate-7' tag = WHOLE_INC0;
RMAN> list backup completed after 'sysdate-7' tag = WHOLE_INC1;
```

Notice the backup levels, set counts, and backup piece names in the list output.

Using RMAN, use this script shown here to restore and recover the PRACTICE database:

```
# Restore and Recover Database using RMAN
shutdown abort;
startup mount;
run {
    allocate channel d1 type disk;
    restore database;
    recover database;
}
alter database open;
```

The recovery script doesn't have many lines, but each one accomplishes plenty of work, as explained in the following list. The database must not be open when restoring the entire database. A shutdown abort makes sense because the datafiles are not on disk any more.

- **Run**   The restore and recover commands must be contained within a run block. All the commands within the block function as a group.

- **Allocate**   This allocated channel will read the backup piece files and recreate datafiles in the restore command. This channel is also used when recovering the datafiles by applying incremental backups and redo.

- **Restore**   The catalog knows which files exist in the entire database. Using this information, the restore database command finds the most recent baseline backup (full backup, image copy, or incremental level 0).

- **Recover**   After the datafiles have been restored, the recover command will find and apply any subsequent incremental backups. The data blocks in the backup pieces are written to the datafiles restored from the base level backup. Because this scenario includes both an incremental level 0 backup and an incremental level 1 backup, the incremental level 1 backup will be used to roll forward the changed blocks contained within its backup piece. After incremental backups are applied, redo must be applied to bring the datafiles current with the control file. RMAN will find and apply archive log files needed for recovery (if necessary) and then use the current online redo log file. Most likely, only the current online redo log file will be needed in this first recovery because there is not much activity occurring on the PRACTICE database.

After the RMAN completes the restore and recovery, it releases the d1 disk channel. Finally, you can open the database for users.

Run the commands in the script shown previously and watch RMAN go to work. The lengthy output of the RMAN commands are shown here.

```
RMAN> @r_whole.rcv
RMAN> # Restore and Recover Database using RMAN
RMAN> run {
2>      allocate channel d1 type disk;
3>      restore database;
4>      recover database;
5> }
RMAN-03022: compiling command: allocate
RMAN-03023: executing command: allocate
RMAN-08030: allocated channel: d1
RMAN-08500: channel d1: sid=14 devtype=DISK
RMAN-03022: compiling command: restore
RMAN-03022: compiling command: IRESTORE
RMAN-03023: executing command: IRESTORE
RMAN-08016: channel d1: starting datafile backupset restore
RMAN-08502: set_count=140 set_stamp=447707604 creation_time=14-JAN-02
RMAN-08089: channel d1: specifying datafile(s) to restore from backup set
RMAN-08523: restoring datafile 00001 to /oradata/PRACTICE/system01.dbf
RMAN-08523: restoring datafile 00002 to /oradata/PRACTICE/rbs01.dbf
RMAN-08523: restoring datafile 00003 to /oradata/PRACTICE/users01.dbf
RMAN-08523: restoring datafile 00004 to /oradata/PRACTICE/temp01.dbf
RMAN-08523: restoring datafile 00005 to /oradata/PRACTICE/tools01.dbf
RMAN-08523: restoring datafile 00006 to /oradata/PRACTICE/indx01.dbf
RMAN-08523: restoring datafile 00007 to /oradata/PRACTICE/users02.dbf
RMAN-08023: channel d1: restored backup piece 1
RMAN-08511: piece handle=/oradata/PRACTICE/backup/ch14/db_PRACTICE_140_1_44770760L
RMAN-08024: channel d1: restore complete
RMAN-03023: executing command: partial resync
RMAN-08003: starting partial resync of recovery catalog
RMAN-08005: partial resync complete
RMAN-03022: compiling command: recover
RMAN-03022: compiling command: recover(1)
RMAN-03022: compiling command: recover(2)
RMAN-03023: executing command: recover(2)
RMAN-08039: channel d1: starting incremental datafile backupset restore
RMAN-08502: set_count=145 set_stamp=447707833 creation_time=14-JAN-02
RMAN-08089: channel d1: specifying datafile(s) to restore from backup set
RMAN-08509: destination for restore of datafile 00001: /oradata/PRACTICE/system01.dbf
RMAN-08509: destination for restore of datafile 00002: /oradata/PRACTICE/rbs01.dbf
RMAN-08509: destination for restore of datafile 00003: /oradata/PRACTICE/users01.dbf
RMAN-08509: destination for restore of datafile 00004: /oradata/PRACTICE/temp01.dbf
RMAN-08509: destination for restore of datafile 00005: /oradata/PRACTICE/tools01.dbf
RMAN-08509: destination for restore of datafile 00006: /oradata/PRACTICE/indx01.dbf
RMAN-08509: destination for restore of datafile 00007: /oradata/PRACTICE/users02.dbf
RMAN-08023: channel d1: restored backup piece 1
RMAN-08511: piece handle=/oradata/PRACTICE/backup/ch14/db_PRACTICE_145_1_4477078L
RMAN-08024: channel d1: restore complete
RMAN-03022: compiling command: recover(3)
RMAN-03023: executing command: recover(3)
RMAN-08054: starting media recovery
RMAN-08055: media recovery complete
RMAN-03022: compiling command: recover(4)
RMAN-08031: released channel: d1
RMAN> alter database open;
```

```
RMAN-03022: compiling command: alter db
RMAN-06400: database opened
RMAN> **end-of-file**
```

Take a moment to look through your output and notice several important messages:

- **channel d1: sid=14 devtype=DISK**   When you allocate a channel of type disk, that channel makes a connection to the target database instance. That connection gets a system identifier (SID) on the target instance that can be found by selecting from the v$session while connected via SQL*Plus.

- **set_count=140**   The restore command finds that the most recent incremental level 0 database backup is backup set 140. RMAN reconstructs all the datafiles of the PRACTICE database using the backup piece from this backup set.

- **db_PRACTICE_140_1_44770760L**   The single backup piece for backup set 140 contains all the data blocks needed for restoration. This operating system file is found, read, and used to reconstruct each of the datafiles.

- **restore complete**   Once the restoration of the datafiles completes, RMAN notifies you. Upon restoration completion, the datafiles exist as they did when the backup was taken. Once the datafiles are restored from a baseline backup, the restore command completes.

- **set_count=145**   The application of the set 145 in the recovery output takes place as part of the recovery process (even though the output says that the backup is restored). The second set found for recovery is the incremental level 1 backup. The incremental level 1 application is a result of the recover command. The changes made to the TINA.DATE_LOG table made in Task 1 changed a data block. That data block and others are contained in this backup set. Now, RMAN will lay the changed blocks of this on top of the datafiles just restored from backup set 140.

- **db_PRACTICE_145_1_4477078L**   Backup set 145 is completely contained in this one backup piece file. Data blocks are read from this file through the d1 channel and applied to the recently restored datafiles.

- **restore complete**   When the second backup set is applied, RMAN lets you know that this incremental data block restore is done. Once this restore is complete, the datafiles have the same data they did when the b_whole_inc1 backup script was run.

- **starting media recovery**   After all recent incremental backups have been applied, redo is required to make the database current with the specified recovery stop time (defaults to current/complete recovery). The redo logs are read and applied to the restored datafiles. That redo application includes rolling forward database changes and rolling back changes that were not committed.

- **recover(1) through recover(4)** RMAN recovery is done in four phases; hence, you see recover (1) through (4). Phase 1 changes the control file if new data in the catalog must be reflected in the control file. Phase 2 restores and applies the incremental backups. Phase 3 applies the redo information if the log files are on disk. Phase 4 restores log files that are not on disk and applies redo information to datafiles.

- **media recovery complete** When media recovery brings the database current to the control file, RMAN lets you know that the database is ready to open.

After complete recovery, you can open the database without resetting the redo log files because complete recovery was possible.

Task 5: Verify Restore and Recover Database

Check that the restored datafiles now exist on the operating system. From an operating system prompt, look at the contents of /oradata/PRACTICE directory. You should see the datafiles as they existed before you removed them in Task 2. Open a SQL*Plus session and check the TINA.TIME_LOG table. Find the maximum create_date in the table to make sure the most recent change made exists in the table.

```
SQL> SELECT max(create_date) FROM tina.date_log;
```

If you see a date of 14 years in the future, you have verified that the latest data change to the this table occurred.

See? Recovery with RMAN is easy!

Exercise 14.2: Restore and Recover a Datafile

If an individual datafile comes up missing or corrupted, it can easily be recovered using RMAN while the database remains open (as long as that datafile does not belong to the system tablespace or contain active rollback segments). RMAN can restore and recover the datafiles in one or more tablespaces.

Task Description	Minutes
1. Simulate PRACTICE Failure	5
2. Restore and Recover a Datafile	5
3. Verify Tablespace Recovery	5
4. Restore and Recover Using Backed Up Archive Logs	5
Total Time	20

In this exercise, you'll perform complete recovery on a subset of the database as you did in the previous exercise. This time, however, you'll only restore and recover a datafile of a single tablespace while the database remains open.

Task 1: Simulate PRACTICE Failure

Before you break the database, you need to add a row to one of Scott's tables: add a new department to the department table with an insert statement. Then add a second department but roll back the change. Once restore and recovery completes, you will see the Support department but not the MIS department.

```
SQL> connect sys/practice@practice;
SQL> INSERT INTO dept (deptno, dname, loc) VALUES (50, 'SUPPORT', 'ATLANTA');
SQL> COMMIT;
SQL> INSERT INTO dept (deptno, dname, loc) VALUES (60, 'MIS', 'DENVER');
SQL> ROLLBACK;
SQL> ALTER SYSTEM SWITCH LOGFILE;
SQL> ALTER SYSTEM SWITCH LOGFILE;
SQL> ALTER SYSTEM SWITCH LOGFILE;
```

Next, remove the first datafile from the USERS tablespace. At the operating system, remove the file. Because Windows places a lock on an online datafile, take the tablespace offline normal before removing the datafile

```
SQL> ALTER TABLESPACE USERS OFFLINE NORMAL;
SQL> host;
LINUX> rm /oradata/PRACTICE/users01.dbf
LINUX> exit
SQL> ALTER TABLESPACE USERS ONLINE;
ERROR at line 1:
ORA-01157: cannot identify/lock data file 3 - see DBWR trace file
ORA-01110: data file 3: '/oradata/PRACTICE/users01.dbf'
```

In the next task, you'll see how you can recover the tablespace.

Task 2: Restore and Recover a Datafile

When a datafile requires recovery, you can recover that single datafile using commands shown here. The tablespace containing the datafile is taken offline, the datafile is restored and recovered, then the tablespace is placed online again.

```
sql 'alter tablespace users offline immediate';
run {
    allocate channel d1 type disk;
    restore datafile 3;   # Specify the datafile number or name
    recover tablespace users;
    sql 'alter tablespace users online ';
}
```

Consider this brief explanation of commands for the recovery scenario just given:

- **restore** Using the catalog or the target control file, RMAN finds the most recent image copy, full or incremental level 0 backup of the restored datafile. Using a suitable backup piece, the datafile is restored.

- **recover** Once the missing datafile has been restored via the incremental level 0 backup piece files, this file must be brought current with the rest of the database. The recover command first determines if any data blocks from incremental backups can be applied to this datafile. After restoring data blocks to the restored datafile, RMAN reads the redo logs (both archive and online) and applies that redo to the datafiles of the USERS tablespace. Because all other datafiles are current except the recently restored one, the only redo that gets applied is to the restored /oradata/PRACTICE/users01.dbf file and /oradata/PRACTICE/users02.dbf. The additions of the Support and MIS departments are not contained in the RMAN backups; they are contained in the redo log files. Therefore, the insert of the Support department will be applied using the redo. The insert of the MIS department and subsequent rollback of that insert gets applied from the redo stream as well.

Before you offline a tablespace or datafile for recovery, it is a good idea to check what objects will be affected and consequently unavailable for a short period. To do this, use either of these two SQL statements:

```
SQL> rem For offlining a tablespace:
SQL> SELECT owner, segment_name, segment_type
  2    FROM dba_extents
  3    WHERE tablespace_name = '<tablespace being recovered>'
  4    ORDER BY owner, segment_type, segment_name;
SQL> rem For offlining a datafile:
SQL> SELECT owner, segment_name, segment_type, count(*) extents
  2    FROM dba_extents
  3    WHERE file_id = <file number being offlined>
  4    GROUP BY owner, segment_name, segment_type;
```

As in the previous exercise, run the script file just listed from the RMAN command prompt:

```
LINUX> rman
RMAN> connect target sys/practice@practice
RMAN> connect catalog rman817/rman@rcat
RMAN> @r_datafile.rcv
```

When the restore and recover script runs, output similar to that of shown previously is displayed on the screen. I've included a few output snippets to point out what RMAN is doing while the script is run: RMAN allocates a channel for restoring and recovering the datafiles; RMAN chooses the backup set with count 140 to restore the users01.dbf datafile; that file has a datafile number of 00003, which is the file# found in the v$datafile control file view.

```
RMAN-08016: channel d1: starting datafile backupset restore
RMAN-08502: set_count=140 set_stamp=447680630 creation_time=14-JAN-02
RMAN-08089: channel d1: specifying datafile(s) to restore from backup set
RMAN-08523: restoring datafile 00003 to /oradata/PRACTICE/users01.dbf
```

Once the datafile is restored, the recover command goes to work. RMAN chooses any more recent incremental backups that can be applied to this datafile. Determining that backup set count 145 contains a backup of this datafile, RMAN reads the backup piece file and applies any changed blocks to the newly restored file.

```
RMAN-08039: channel d1: starting incremental datafile backupset restore
RMAN-08502: set_count=145 set_stamp=447680803 creation_time=14-JAN-02
RMAN-08089: channel d1: specifying datafile(s) to restore from backup set
RMAN-08509: destination for restore of datafile 00003:
/oradata/PRACTICE/users01.dbf
```

Once RMAN has applied any necessary incremental backups to the restored datafile, media recovery can commence. Next, the restored datafile must be brought current to the rest of the database via media recovery. During recovery, redo log files are read and applied as needed to catch up the restored datafile. I added the three log switch commands to make sure that archive log files would be required during the recovery. Redo is needed beginning with the redo log file sequence number that was current when the final backup applied was completed. In this output listing, log sequence number 141 was the current online redo log file when the latest incremental backup began. All redo log files must be applied to the restored datafile up to and including the current online redo log file.

```
RMAN-06050: archivelog thread 1 sequence 1 is already on disk as file
/oradata/PRACTICE/archive/141.arc
RMAN-06050: archivelog thread 1 sequence 2 is already on disk as file
/oradata/PRACTICE/archive/142.arc
RMAN-06050: archivelog thread 1 sequence 3 is already on disk as file
/oradata/PRACTICE/archive/143.arc
...
RMAN-08055: media recovery complete
```

These archive log files were found on disk by RMAN. Once all these log files are applied, you'll get the welcome message that media recovery is complete. After this, the tablespace can be successfully brought online and made available for use.

You can also have restored the entire tablespace of the one missing datafile. Restoring the entire tablespace will cause RMAN to write over all existing datafiles in the tablespace. Each of the lines in the next listing and on page 15 would accomplish the same thing.

```
sql 'alter tablespace users offline immediate';
run {
   allocate channel d1 type disk;
   restore tablespace users;
   recover tablespace users;
   sql 'alter tablespace users online';
}
```

Task 3: Verify Tablespace Recovery

After the successful restore and recovery of the missing USERS tablespace datafile, look on the operating system to see the file that RMAN restored. Also, select from the department table owned by SCOTT. You ought to see a Support department but not an MIS department.

```
SQL> connect scott/tiger;
SQL> select * from dept;
    DEPTNO DNAME          LOC
---------- -------------- -------------
        10 ACCOUNTING     NEW YORK
        20 RESEARCH       DALLAS
        30 SALES          CHICAGO
        40 OPERATIONS     BOSTON
        50 SUPPORT        ATLANTA
```

Task 4: Restore and Recover Using Backed Up Archive Logs

In the previous three tasks, you saw how a single datafile can be restored and recovered using incremental backups and existing archive log files on disk. What if, during recovery, some archive log files needed for recovery are *not* found on disk? If the archive log files are contained in an available backup or image copy, RMAN will restore and apply the needed archive files for recovery.

To experiment with how RMAN recovery will restore archive log files to disk and use the restored files during recovery, repeat Tasks 1–3 in this exercise and recover a missing datafile. This time, though, add a small twist: back up the archive log files on disk after several log switch commands. After the backup, rename the files to these recent archive log files on disk. When RMAN performs recovery, it will look for the renamed archive log files on disk. When it can't find them, RMAN will restore the archive files from your backup to disk. Using these restored archive files, RMAN will complete the recovery of the restored users01.dbf datafile. (Rename the files rather than remove them during this task just in case a mistake is made.)

```
RMAN> connect target sys/practice
RMAN> connect catalog rman817/rman@rcat
RMAN> @b_archive_2days.rcv
RMAN> host;
LINUX> cd /oradata/PRACTICE/archive
```

```
LINUX> mv 141.arc 141.arc.bak
LINUX> mv 142.arc 142.arc.bak
LINUX> mv 143.arc 143.arc.bak
LINUX> exit
```

In Chapter 12, I showed you a script named b_archive_2days.rcv that backs up the archive log files that have been created in the last two days. During execution of that script, you saw a message like this:

```
RMAN-08502: set_count=148 set_stamp=447945049 creation_time=08-DEC-01
RMAN-08014: channel d1: specifying archivelog(s) in backup set
RMAN-08504: input archivelog thread=1 sequence=141 recid=105 stamp=447941127
RMAN-08504: input archivelog thread=1 sequence=142 recid=106 stamp=447941449
RMAN-08504: input archivelog thread=1 sequence=143 recid=107 stamp=447945030
```

This means the archive logs in the archive dump destination were copied to a backup set. As the files are backed up, the redo log file sequence numbers are displayed.

When the archive files are moved after the backup has completed, RMAN will not be able to find them on disk. In response to the recover command in r_datafile.rcv, RMAN must use the backup of the archive files made during execution of script file b_archive_2days.rcv. Next, remove the first datafile from the USERS tablespace. At the operating system, remove the file. Because Windows places a lock on an online datafile, take the tablespace offline normal before removing the datafile:

```
SQL> ALTER TABLESPACE USERS OFFLINE NORMAL;
SQL> host;
LINUX> rm /oradata/PRACTICE/users01.dbf
LINUX> exit
SQL> ALTER TABLESPACE USERS ONLINE;
ERROR at line 1:
ORA-01157: cannot identify/lock data file 3 - see DBWR trace file
ORA-01110: data file 3: '/oradata/PRACTICE/users01.dbf'
```

The archive files have been backed up and the archive files on disk have been moved so they cannot be used by the RMAN recovery. Run the recovery as you did in Task 2 of this exercise.

```
LINUX> rman
RMAN> connect target sys/practice@practice
RMAN> connect catalog rman817/rman@rcat
RMAN> @r_datafile.rcv
```

As the restore proceeds, this recovery will use the same datafile incremental backups it used before because you have not taken any new backups between the last task. The difference between this recovery and the previous one is the archive log files needed for recovery restored from backups. You'll see a message stating that the archive log files are being restored to the default destination. The backup piece named ar_PRACTICE_148_1_447946582 is read and used to create the archive log files 141.arc, 142.arc, and 143.arc in the /oradata/PRACTICE/archive destination. Once this restore portion of the recovery command is complete, the restored archive log files can be used to recover the restored datafile.

```
RMAN-08017: channel d1: starting archivelog restore to default destination
RMAN-08022: channel d1: restoring archivelog
RMAN-08510: archivelog thread=1 sequence=141
RMAN-08022: channel d1: restoring archivelog
RMAN-08510: archivelog thread=1 sequence=142
RMAN-08022: channel d1: restoring archivelog
RMAN-08510: archivelog thread=1 sequence=143
RMAN-08023: channel d1: restored backup piece 1
RMAN-08511: piece
handle=/oradata/PRACTICE/backup/ch12/ar_PRACTICE_148_1_447946582
tag=null params=NULL
RMAN-08024: channel d1: restore complete
RMAN-06050: archivelog thread 1 sequence 2 is already on disk as file
/oradata/PRACTICE/archive/142.arc
RMAN-06050: archivelog thread 1 sequence 3 is already on disk as file
/oradata/PRACTICE/archive/143.arc
RMAN-08515: archivelog filename=/oradata/PRACTICE/archive/141.arc thread=1
sequence=141
RMAN-08515: archivelog filename=/oradata/PRACTICE/archive/142.arc thread=1
sequence=142
RMAN-08515: archivelog filename=/oradata/PRACTICE/archive/143.arc thread=1
sequence=143
RMAN-08055: media recovery complete
RMAN-08031: released channel: d1
```

In this example, the archive log files had just been backed up into a backup set with count 148. RMAN knew about this backup and its backup piece file named ar_PRACTICE_148_1_447946582. The archive files were restored to the default archive dump destination as part of the recovery step. Once the needed archive logs were restored, the archive log file could be applied to the restored datafile to roll it forward, so RMAN was able to perform recovery even when the archive file could not be found on disk. This illustrates one of the most powerful features of RMAN. Server-managed recovery keeps track of backups and can quickly call upon those backups to restore and recover the Oracle database. You don't have to remember where the backups are: RMAN handles all those details for you.

Because RMAN restored the archive log files you renamed in the archive dump destination, you can remove the original archive log files you renamed earlier to clean things up:

```
LINUX> rm 141.arc.bak
LINUX> rm 142.arc.bak
LINUX> rm 143.arc.bak
```

Exercise 14.3: Incomplete Database Recovery

To recover if a user/developer accidentally drops a table, you can perform incomplete database recovery as you did in Chapters 4 and 5. Using RMAN, you recover all the datafiles by issuing restore and recover database commands while the database is closed. Tell RMAN the stop point for recover by specifying a time, a log sequence, or an SCN. Based on the stop point, RMAN picks the most suitable backups and image copies that will restore the database to a point most recent to the stop point prescribed. Redo is applied until the stop point is defined. After RMAN does all this work, all that remains is to open the database while resetting the logs. The logs have to be reset because recovery is incomplete.

Task Description	Minutes
1. Simulate PRACTICE Failure	5
2. Incomplete Restore and Recover Database	10
3. Verify Tablespace Recovery	5
Total Time	20

In this exercise, you'll see how RMAN can recover a database to a point in time in the past. I'll show you how to create a scenario that might prompt you to perform incomplete recovery. You'll drop a table and use backups taken earlier in this chapter to recover the PRACTICE database to a time just before the table was dropped.

Task 1: Simulate PRACTICE Failure

During this task, you will remove a table named SCOTT.EMP from the PRACTICE database. To confirm that incomplete recovery works as expected, do a little cleanup and setup on the TINA.DATE_LOG table. Dates have been inserted into Tina's table to mark time in the PRACTICE database. In previous chapters, you inserted future dates in this table for demonstration purposes. Before dropping the employee table, remove all of those future dates so that only past dates can be found. After dropping the employee table, insert one row into TINA.DATE_LOG for 14 years in the future. Finally, switch the logs three times. These log switches ensure that the recovery performed later must use archived redo logs.

```
SQL> CONNECT sys/practice
SQL> SET TIME ON
12:01:02 SQL> DELETE FROM tina.date_log WHERE create_date > SYSDATE;
12:02:12 SQL> DROP TABLE SCOTT.EMP;
12:03:23 SQL> INSERT INTO tina.date_log VALUES (SYSDATE+(365*14));
12:03:27 SQL> COMMIT;
12:03:27 SQL> SELECT MAX(create_date) FROM tina.date_log;
```

At 12:01:02, any future dates existing in the DATE_LOG table are removed. At 12:02:12, the employee table is dropped. After the table drop, a future date is inserted into the DATE_LOG table. When you recover the PRACTICE database up to the point in time prior to the drop table statement, you will not see a CREATE_DATE of 14 years in the future (the last date record inserted). The recovery will stop applying redo records just before the drop table command.

Task 2: Incomplete Restore and Recover Database

An incomplete recovery is accomplished by first restoring a backup set that was taken prior to the point in time you wish to recover to. Assuming that backups before this time are available, RMAN will choose the best one.

```
run {
    # set time to just before data was lost
    set until time "TO_DATE('01/14/2002 12:02:10','MM/DD/YYYY
HH24:MI:SS')";
    shutdown immediate;
    startup mount;
    allocate channel d1 type disk;
    restore database;
    recover database;
    alter database open resetlogs;
}
```

Incomplete recovery means that the entire database must be restored to a previous point in time, including the control file. The trick to effectively performing point-in-time recovery is using the set command. The set until command instructs RMAN to restore the database to the most recent backup prior to the time of recovery. Then recovery will bring the datafiles forward to the specified time. In this example, you know the exact time the employee table got dropped and can set the recovery end time to just before that time. Alternatively, you could set the point of recovery by specifying a log sequence number or an SCN number.

In this table drop scenario, time-based recovery makes sense. Incomplete recovery can be performed by different methods than shown earlier. If you must recover but have a missing or corrupt archive log file, you can recover until a specific log file (that is, the log file before the corrupt or missing one). To specify a log sequence stop point, change the set run option attribute to something like this:

```
set until logseq 1400 thread 1;
```

This set command will apply archive log files up until log sequence 1399 has been applied.

The least commonly used option for incomplete recovery is SCN-based recovery. Specify an SCN stop point of 100000 by changing the set run option attribute to like this:

```
set until SCN 100000;
```

This recovery might be used if some corruption occurred in the database and the alert log provides you with an SCN value related to when the corruption occurred (or you can use LogMiner, as you did in Chapter 10, to find the SCN of a particular command/error). Once the stop point for recovery has been set, you can turn all the work over to RMAN.

While looking at the previous r_whole_incomplete.rcv script, note these points about incomplete database recovery with RMAN:

- The database is shut down before the restore and recovery begins.

- The allocate channel statement must occur after the database instance is restarted. The allocate channel command opens a connection on the database that will be lost during the shutdown.

- The alter database open command can occur outside of the run block.

RMAN accomplishes incomplete recovery just as it does complete recovery with a couple differences:

- RMAN restores all datafiles from a baseline backup prior to the recovery stop point. Those restored files may or may not be the most recent baseline backup, depending on the stop point.

- Recovery continues until the stop point. RMAN is smart enough to know which incremental backups to restore and apply. RMAN will find and apply archive redo log files (and possibly current redo files) until the stop point is reached.

The output of the incomplete recovery will look much like the complete recovery performed in Exercise 14.1. There will be nothing in the output that indicates point-in-time recovery. When you open the database with reset logs, RMAN updates the new incarnation in the catalog, effectively performing the RESET DATABASE command. (The RESET DATABASE command updates the RMAN catalog with new database incarnation information from the target database control file.)

```
RMAN> alter database open resetlogs;
RMAN-03022: compiling command: alter db
RMAN-06400: database opened
RMAN-03023: executing command: alter db
RMAN-08006: database registered in recovery catalog
RMAN-03023: executing command: full resync
RMAN-08002: starting full resync of recovery catalog
RMAN-08004: full resync complete
```

Before you validate recovery, I want to add a footnote. You could have set the stop point for restore and recovery with an until clause after each of these commands:

```
restore database until time "TO_DATE('01/14/2002 12:02:10','MM/DD/YYYY HH24:MI:SS')";
recover database until time "TO_DATE('01/14/2002 12:02:10','MM/DD/YYYY HH24:MI:SS')";
```

The stop point can be defined for the restore and recover command by log sequence or SCN as well as time. Also, the stop point of the restore and the recover don't have to be the same time. By using the set run option on page 22, the stop point on the restore and recover commands is implied.

Task 3: Verify Tablespace Recovery

After a reset logs operation, you'll have a new incarnation of the database. You can see the incarnations of the database with the LIST INCARNATION command.

```
RMAN> list incarnation;
List of Database Incarnations
DB Key  Inc Key  DB Name  DB ID             CUR  Reset SCN   Reset Time
-------  -------  -------  ----------------  ---  ----------  ----------
232      233      PRACTICE  2630335893       NO   83852       03-JAN-02
232      1190     PRACTICE  2630335893       YES  476863      14-JAN-02
```

Notice that the date of the incarnation will be the date that you performed the reset logs operations. You'll also see the SCN value for the database when the redo log files were reset. Though the redo logs have been reset and log sequence numbers restart numbering from one, the SCN values for the datafile headers and the control file are not reset and continue on in sequence after the reset logs operation.

With incomplete recovery now finished, let's see if you got Scott's employee table back. Open a SQL*Plus session and select from the table. You should see that you've accomplished the primary goal of your incomplete recovery:

```
SQL> SELECT * FROM scott.emp;
```

Next, check the maximum create date value of the DATE_LOG table. See if the row you inserted 14 years in the future is in the table. It shouldn't be there because recovery stopped prior to the table drop statement, which should also be prior to the insert of a date 14 years in the future. Therefore, the redo containing that table insert into the DATE_LOG table will not be applied (along with any other redo past the recovery stop point).

```
SQL> SELECT MAX(create_date) FROM tina.date_log;
```

With your PRACTICE database recovered, you have some important things to do now. Because the logs have been reset make sure that you do the following:

- Perform a new baseline backup. The database can not easily be recovered through a reset logs operation (using current redo logs with a prereset logs backup).

- Protect or remove any prereset logs backups. You can recover the database using preresetlogs backups but will find it very difficult to roll forward through a reset logs operation. Therefore, protect at least one baseline backup made prior to reset logs. After a period of time, if there is no potential that you'll want to recover your database again prior to the reset logs, you can remove any backups for the previous database incarnation. Use the REPORT OBSOLETE ORPHAN command to show backups that apply to previous database incarnations.

- Clean up your archive log files in the archive dump destination. New archived redo log files will overwrite any existing archive log files as the sequences grow. Either move those existing archive logs to a new location or remove them.

TIP

In Exercise 14.3, you recovered the entire database to bring back a dropped table with RMAN. In Chapter 17, you'll see how RMAN can perform tablespace point-in-time recovery to accomplish the same table recovery feat without full database incomplete recovery.

Recovery Tips

In this brief introduction to RMAN restore and recovery, you only saw the basics of what RMAN can accomplish. The exercises in the chapter provide a few simple scenarios and explanations of how RMAN can restore and recover your database. These recovery tips touch on other points to consider or to take advantage of in more complex recovery situations:

- When restoring multiple backup sets and pieces, add several channels when restoring a database. Additional channels allow datafile restores to run in parallel.

```
run
{
    allocate channel d1 type disk;
```

```
    allocate channel d2 type disk;
    allocate channel d3 type disk;
    restore database;
    recover database;
}
```

■ If you lose a datafile and need to recover quickly from an image copy, instruct RMAN to switch to the new datafile copy like this (recovery of the datafile may be required):

```
run
{
    allocate channel d1 type disk;
    sql 'alter database datafile 5 offline';
    switch datafile 5 to datafilecopy
'/oradata/PRACTICE/tools01.dbf';
    recover datafile 5;
    sql 'alter database datafile 5 online';
}
```

■ If you lose file systems on your database server, you'll need to recover your database by restoring datafiles to a different location from the original location. Use the SET NEWNAME attribute during a run job to restore and recover lost datafiles. Also use the SWITCH attribute to instruct the target control file to use the restored datafiles in the new locations. Restore and recover a datafile to a new directory location like this:

```
run
{
    allocate channel d1 type disk;
    set newname for datafile 5 to '/u01/PRACTICE/tools01.dbf';
    sql 'alter database datafile 5 offline';
    restore datafile 5;
    switch datafile 5 to datafilecopy
'/u01/PRACTICE/tools01.dbf';
    recover datafile 5;
    sql 'alter database datafile 5 online';
}
```

■ If you lose all copies of your current control file and you have an up to date catalog for this database, use the RESTORE CONTROLFILE command to recreate the control file as it existed in a previous backup. RMAN will automatically place the control file to the locations specified in the init.ora file. After the restore and any recovery, you'll have to open the database by resetting the logs. Restore a control file like this:

```
run
{
   allocate channel d1 type disk;
   restore controlfile;
}
```

■ You can restore your archive log files from an RMAN backup and then manually recover from SQL*Plus.

■ By default, RMAN restores archive log files to the archive dump destination directory. You can instruct RMAN to restore files to a different directory by using the SET ARCHIVELOG DESTINATION command like this:

```
run {
   set archivelog destination to '/tmp';
   allocate channel d1 type disk;
   restore archivelog from logseq 2 until logseq 4;
}
```

■ By default, RMAN recovers datafiles using archive log files in the archive dump destination. If you have instructed RMAN to restore archive files to different locations during a run job, RMAN will automatically find the restored archive log files and apply them during recovery.

■ You can track the speed of restores and recovery as you tracked backup performance in Chapter 12 (V$SESSION_LONGOPS, V$PROCESS and V$SESSION).

Troubleshooting

If you run into problems performing restores and recoveries with RMAN, you might encounter one of these errors:

1. **RMAN-06004: ORACLE error from recovery catalog database:**
   RMAN-20003: target database incarnation not found in recovery catalog
   After opening a target database with the reset logs option from SQL*Plus, the catalog will not contain the new incarnation information of the database. Issue the RESET DATABASE command in RMAN while connected to the target and the catalog. Check that the incarnation update worked with a LIST INCARNATION command.

2. **ORA-00376: file 3 cannot be read at this time**
   ORA-01110: data file 3: '/oradata/PRACTICE/users01.dbf'   After a datafile
   has been restored and recovered, it must be placed online before it can be
   read from. You would get this error when trying to access data from a table
   stored in the users01.dbf file.

3. **PLS-00553: character set name is not recognized**
   RMAN-06031: could not translate database keyword   When recovering
   a database, the session character set must match the character set of
   the target database. To find out the character set of the target database,
   select the character set from V$NLS_PARAMETERS, (SELECT * FROM
   V$NLS_PARAMETERS WHERE PARAMETER = 'NLS_CHARACTERSET';).
   Exit RMAN and set the NLS_LANG environment variable to match the
   character set to this value. For example, set the NLS_LANG parameter on
   Linux to character set we8iso8859p1 for America, like this:
   ```
   LINUX> export NLS_LANG=american_america.we8iso8859p1
   ```

4. **RMAN-04005: error from target database:**
   ORA-00604: error occurred at recursive SQL level 1
   ORA-02248: invalid option for ALTER SESSION   When connecting at
   the RMAN prompt, environment variables like NLS_DATE_FORMAT
   and NLS_LANG that have been set incorrectly may spark this error. For
   example, if you used single quotation marks on Windows to set variables
   rather than a double quotation mark, you'll get this error. Check your
   environment variable settings used prior to starting RMAN for accuracy.

5. **RMAN-10035: exception raised in RPC:**
   ORA-19573: cannot obtain exclusive enqueue for datafile 3   If you
   attempt to restore a datafile that is currently online, you get this error. Take the
   datafile offline before restoring it. If you are restoring a system tablespace
   datafile, shut down and then mount the database.

6. **RMAN-11001: Oracle Error: ORA-01113: file 3 needs media recovery**
   When opening the database or placing a datafile online, the file may have
   not been recovered fully. Make sure that you recover any restored datafiles
   before bringing them online.

Summary

I hope that what stands out about this chapter is that server managed restore and
recovery, under typical circumstances, is very easy. You let the server do the work. You
say "restore," and RMAN figures out what to do. You issue a "recover" command, and
RMAN takes care of the rest. For more information on RMAN recovery, look at Chapter 6
in *Oracle 8i Recovery Manager User's Guide and Reference*. If you want the syntax
specifics of the restore, recover, and set option look in Chapter 10 of this book.

Chapter Questions

As a refresher, try these questions to reinforce the concepts and exercises in this chapter.

1. What command recreates a file from an RMAN backup?

    A. Replace

    B. Recover

    C. Channel

    D. Restore

2. Which types of datafile backups create a baseline for datafile restores? (Pick any that apply.)

    A. Image copy

    B. Incremental level 0

    C. Incremental level 1

    D. Full

3. When you recover a datafile, RMAN may restore archive log files to disk before they can be used for recovery.

    A. True

    B. False

4. During which restore command must the database be closed (assuming the TOOLS tablespace has one datafile named tools01.dbf and does not contain rollback segments)?

    A. restore database

    B. restore tablespace tools

    C. restore datafile 'tools01.dbf'

    D. restore archivelog

5. Incremental level 1–4 backup sets get applied to datafiles when the datafile is restored.

    A. True

    B. False

Answers to Chapter Questions

1. D.   Restore. Comparable to performing an OS copy from backup to destination during user managed recovery.

2. A, B, D.   An image copy, an incremental level 0 datafile, and a full datafile backup all make a copy of all the used data blocks in a datafile. These backups and copies can be used by RMAN to restore a datafile. Incremental level 1–4 backups can be applied to a baseline (image copy, full, or incremental level 0) backup to roll changed blocks forward.

3. True.   During recovery, RMAN first looks on disk for required archive log files in either the archive dump destination or in the directory defined by the SET ARCHIVELOG DESTINATION TO command. If they are not found, they get restored to disk from backup so that recovery can proceed.

4. A.   The database must be closed (but mounted) to restore the system tablespace. A restore and recovery can occur on any nonsystem offline datafile. Archive log files can be restored with the database open and all tablespaces online.

5. False.   During a restore, only baseline backups are used to restore the datafile. During recovery, incremental level 1–4 backups are applied to a datafile followed by redo application.

CHAPTER
15

RMAN
Duplicate Database

y using the database backups, a DBA can make a duplicate database on the same server or on a different server. That duplicate database can have the same name as the primary (a *database copy*) or a different name from the primary (a *database clone*). The only difference that Oracle draws between a database copy and a database clone is that the copy does not have its name changed. Using the RMAN duplicate database feature, you can create a new database from an RMAN backup and keep the existing database name for the duplicate or to give it a new one. Back in Chapter 6, you were introduced to this concept of duplicating a database. In Chapters 12 and 14, you learned how to take backups and carry out restorations and recoveries using Recovery Manager (RMAN). Using the knowledge you gained in these three chapters, I'll show you how to put these things together here to create a duplicate database using RMAN. This database duplication feature using RMAN was introduced with Oracle 8*i*.

How does RMAN create a duplicate database from its backups? During duplication, RMAN connects to the primary database and to the duplicate instance. The duplication process includes restoration and recovery of primary database backup files on the duplicate server. A base level primary database backup taken with RMAN is first restored to the duplicate database server. During recovery, the required primary incremental backups and archive redo logs are then applied to the duplicate database. The recovery of the duplicate database cannot be complete because the online redo logs will not be restored (they are not backed up using RMAN). Therefore, incomplete recovery is carried out to a specified point in time or until the last archive log file known to RMAN is applied. RMAN will not apply any redo from the online logs.

The duplicate database matches the primary database as it was in the past. During duplication, a new control file and online redo log files are created. RMAN will also give the database a new database identifier (DBID).

As in each RMAN chapter, I've defined new RMAN terms or commands that pertain to the content of this chapter. During this chapter, you'll be introduced to these new RMAN terms and commands:

- **Auxiliary database** RMAN duplicates the target (primary) database to this database instance. You create this database parameter file, directories, and password file. You must start the auxiliary instance in NOMOUNT mode prior to RMAN database duplication. Think of this as the duplicate database instance.

- **Duplicate** Creates a new database from the RMAN backups of another database. The auxiliary database is a configured and started Oracle instance where RMAN will perform its duplication activities. From RMAN's perspective, *the target database is duplicated to the auxiliary database.*

- **Set newname** Sets a new name for a datafile within an RMAN run block. The filename supplied to this parameter will override any auxiliary name for this datafile (using SET AUXNAME) or auxiliary database parameters (using DB_FILE_NAME_CONVERT). This newname value persists only for the duration of the run block.

■ **Set auxname** Sets an auxiliary name for a datafile. This auxiliary name persists between RMAN sessions. You must reset the name to null if you don't want subsequent RMAN sessions to use this set name.

■ **Log file** The online redo log files created by the duplicate database can be designated using this keyword with the duplicate command. If you don't specify this keyword, RMAN creates the log files in the location determined from the LOG_FILE_NAME_CONVERT parameter in the auxiliary parameter file. If neither of the RMAN keyword or the auxiliary parameter is set, RMAN will create the log files in the same location as they are in the target database (provided you've specified the NOCHECKFILENAME option).

■ **Nocheckfilename** By default, RMAN will check for datafiles being restored in the original target datafile location on the duplicate host to make sure it is not overwriting datafiles by mistake. You can override this default behavior using this option. It is then up to you to make sure RMAN will not be overwriting any existing datafiles. Be careful when using this command so you don't overwrite a datafile.

During the duplication command, RMAN performs a lot of work. While connected to the target, auxiliary, and the optional catalog database, RMAN will do the following:

1. Determine which baseline backups will be used for duplication based on the most recent taken or the recovery stop point you provide.

2. Determine where to place the datafiles on the auxiliary instance based on auxiliary database parameters or RMAN set commands and options.

3. Read the backup pieces or image copies and restore datafiles for the auxiliary database. This is exactly the same function RMAN uses when you normally carry out a database restoration.

4. Apply any incremental backups to the restored datafiles based on the recovery stop point. This incremental application works as it does when you issue a recover database command within RMAN.

5. Apply any archived log files from disk or backups to the restored datafiles based on the recovery stop point. Just like a normal recovery using RMAN, the archives are the last things to be applied to the restored database.

6. Create a new control file for the auxiliary database.

7. Open the duplicated database while resetting the online redo log files. The new online redo log files are created as specified in the RMAN duplicate database command or as translated in the auxiliary parameter file.

Why would you use RMAN to create a duplicate database? You must use RMAN if your only backups are RMAN backups. If you have RMAN backups and user-managed backups, RMAN makes duplication easier. RMAN creates a new control file for you and handles the restoration and recovery of datafiles.

When you undertake the duplication of a database using RMAN, keep in mind these important considerations:

- You don't have to use a catalog. RMAN information is stored in the target database control file. You must make sure that the backups you wish to create the duplicate database from still reside in the target control file. For example, if you have the init.ora parameter CONTROLFILE_RECORD_KEEP_FOR_TIME set to 21 days, you may not be able to restore from two months ago.

- If the backup is taken while the database is open, you should include a log switch afterward to make sure any redo changes made while the backup was being taken have been archived.

- Be sure to take a backup containing the archive logs needed. RMAN must know about the archive logs to apply them.

- You cannot perform a complete recovery during duplication: recovery must have a stop point. That stop point will either be a stop point that you have specified or the point of the last known archive redo log. You can specify a stop point based on time, log sequence, or SCN.

- To create a copy of a database during duplication, use the same database name as the target database in the auxiliary database parameter file.

- If the duplicate database is residing on a different server and that server has the same directory structure as the primary server, you do not have to rename any of the files during duplication. By default, the DUPLICATE command will notify RMAN that the restored auxiliary file locations are the same as the original files when the target database files were backed up.

- The database name of the new duplicate database can be the same or different from the primary. The database name must be different from any currently existing database sharing the same ORACLE_HOME directory. Therefore, if the primary and duplicate databases reside on the same server and share the same ORACLE_HOME, the duplicate must be given a new name. If they are on the same server and have separate ORACLE_HOME directories or will reside on different servers, they can have the same database name.

In the exercise in this chapter, you'll create a duplicate database with RMAN. You'll have the opportunity to alter the names and locations of the datafiles via the auxiliary initialization parameter file and via RMAN commands. Look at Figure 15-1 as representation of the RMAN duplication you'll perform in this chapter's exercise.

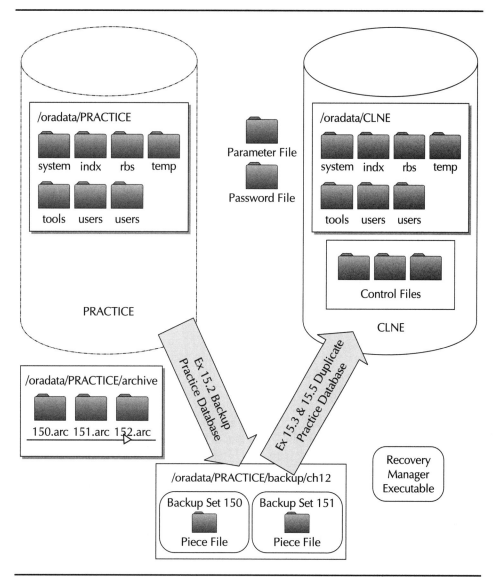

FIGURE 15-1.   *Duplicate the PRACTICE database with RMAN*

Recovery Manager Duplication

Creating a duplicate database involves a series of coordinated steps. In my description of these steps, the primary database is called the target and the duplicate database is the auxiliary.

1. Make the RMAN backups accessible to the server that will house the duplicate database.

   If backups are created on disk, they can be transferred using binary mode ftp or by using a disk-sharing scheme like NFS.

2. Prepare the duplicate database parameter file.

   Before the duplicate database can be created, RMAN needs to connect to an auxiliary instance. This is a similar to the auxiliary instance in Chapter 9 when you carried out tablespace point-in-time recovery. RMAN connects to the auxiliary instance and then restores the datafiles from a backup to make the duplicate database. To start up the auxiliary instance, an initialization parameter file must be created with some special parameters. When creating a duplicate database on the same server as the primary database, you must make sure that the control files, data files, and online redo logs do not overwrite existing files. To do this, you can instruct RMAN to rename files to new locations during the DUPLICATE command, or you can specify some initialization parameters that will do this automatically. You will see how both these methods work in the chapter exercise.

3. Create the duplicate database password file.

   For DBA authentication, a password file is needed for the duplicate database. This can be created following the steps in Exercise 6.1, Task 1, Chapter 6.

4. Create Net8 connectivity files.

   RMAN needs to connect to the primary database (target instance) and the duplicate database (auxiliary instance) at the same time. If both databases are located on different servers, the listener needs to be configured on the duplicate server and the tnsnames file needs to be configured on the server that you are running RMAN from. This is usually the primary database server.

5. Start the auxiliary instance.

   Before RMAN can create the duplicate database, the auxiliary instance needs to be started in nomount mode. The parameter file that was created in step 2 reads the file at startup.

6. Mount or open the primary database.

RMAN requires that the primary database is either mounted or open in order to create a duplicate database.

7. Create the duplicate database.

When you instruct RMAN to create the duplicate database, it automatically restores the required base-level backup and then applies incremental level backups and archive redo log files. When recovery has been applied, the duplicate database is opened with the RESETLOGS option.

The exercise of this chapter combines some of these steps into a single task. Now comes the time for you to practice RMAN database duplication for yourself.

Exercise 15.1: Duplicate PRACTICE Database with RMAN

This chapter has only one exercise, which is to duplicate the PRACTICE database. The database clone you will create is named CLNE (short for Clone). Therefore, the PRACTICE database will be the primary/target database in this exercise. The duplicate database will be a clone because you will assign a new name to the database. If you perform this exercise with an additional server, you can create a database with the same name (PRACTICE) by using the word PRACTICE instead of CLNE throughout this exercise.

Task Description	Minutes
1. Prepare Clone Database	10
2. Back Up Practice Database	10
3. Duplicate Practice Database	10
4. Verify Clone Database	5
5. Duplicate Practice Database Again	10
Total Time	45

Though RMAN will do the bulk of the database duplication work, you still have to prepare the directories and supporting database files.

Task 1: Prepare Clone Database

Start by creating database directories, a parameter file, and a password file (and Windows services) for the CLNE database. Each of these steps will have already been accomplished if you performed the exercise in Chapter 6.

Directories   Create all the directories for the CLNE database you are about to build:

```
export ORACLE_SID=CLNE
export ORACLE_BASE=/app/oracle
export ORACLE_HOME=/app/oracle/product/8.1.7
export ORACLE_DATA=/oradata/$ORACLE_SID
export ORACLE_ADMIN=$ORACLE_BASE/admin/$ORACLE_SID
mkdir $ORACLE_ADMIN
mkdir $ORACLE_ADMIN/pfile
mkdir $ORACLE_ADMIN/bdump
mkdir $ORACLE_ADMIN/cdump
mkdir $ORACLE_ADMIN/udump
mkdir $ORACLE_ADMIN/create
mkdir $ORACLE_DATA/
mkdir $ORACLE_DATA/archive
```

Parameter File   Next, create a parameter file for the CLNE database by copying the PRACTICE database parameter file to the $ORACLE_BASE/admin/CLNE/pfile directory. Also add a LINUX symbolic link to the default parameter file in the $ORACLE_HOME/dbs directory or to a Windows parameter file in the %ORACLE_HOME%\database directory.

Open the new parameter file in the pfile directory and change every occurrence of the word 'PRACTICE' to 'CLNE'. When you perform this global search and replace, you'll change the database name, service name, control file location and many directory paths for parameters. Be sure that you've changed parameters, including: DB_NAME, INSTANCE_NAME, SERVICE_NAMES, CONTROL_FILES, and destination directories. Add two parameters to the CLNE database parameter file:

```
db_file_name_convert     = ("PRACTICE", "CLNE")
log_file_name_convert    = ("PRACTICE", "CLNE")
```

During duplication, these two parameters translate file names and locations from the old value to a new value. In this example, any occurrence of PRACTICE in the full name of any datafile is changed to CLNE. Therefore, the PRACTICE database datafile named /oradata/PRACTICE/system01.dbf will be created in the CLNE as /oradata/CLNE/system01.dbf. The log file name /oradata/PRACTICE/redo01.log will be created as /oradata/CLNE/redo01.log on the CLNE database.

Password File   During RMAN duplication, you'll have to connect to the CLNE database with the SYSDBA role. Create a password file. The password file is also used for remote administration security.

```
LINUX> orapwd file=$ORACLE_HOME/dbs/orapwCLNE password=CLNE entries=4
WINNT> orapwd file=%ORACLE_HOME%\database\PWDCLNE.ora password=CLNE
entries=10
```

Windows Service   On Windows, create a new database service for the CLNE database named OracleServiceCLNE using the oradim utility.

```
WINNT> oradim -new -sid CLNE -intpwd CLNE
```

Net8 Connectivity   Finally, configure Net8 connectivity for the CLNE database. This was not necessary when you duplicated a database in Chapter 6 because you did not have to connect to the CLNE instance while also being connected to the PRACTICE database. Use Net8 Assistant (netasst on Linux or a start menu shortcut on Windows) to update your Net8 configuration.

If you created a clone database as described in Chapter 6, all of these steps may not be necessary (with the exception of adding the two convert parameters to the CLNE parameter file). The database files may already be in the /oradata/CLNE directory. You can leave those previous database files (datafiles, log files, and control files) created earlier, or you can remove them now if you'd like. To remove them, just delete all the files from the /oradata/CLNE directory.

Task 2: Back Up Practice Database

By now, you probably have sufficient backups of the PRACTICE database to duplicate it to the CLNE database. To make sure, go ahead and create two more backups of the PRACTICE database that can be used for the duplication.

The first backup will be a baseline backup (incremental level 0) using the command script created in Chapter 12 named b_whole_0.rcv. The datafile and control file baseline backup could also be a full whole database backup or image copies of all the datafiles and the control file in the database. An incremental level 1-4 without a baseline backup will not suffice as a source backup for database duplication.

The second backup taken after the baseline datafile and control file backup is an archive log file backup. Run the b_archive_2days.rcv RMAN command file created in Chapter 12. The commands contained in this file force a log switch and back up any archive log files containing redo information from the last two days:

```
LINUX> rman
RMAN> connect target sys/practice@practice
RMAN> connect catalog rman817/rman@rcat
RMAN> @b_whole_inc0.rcv
RMAN> @b_archive_2days.rcv
```

Mark the current log file on the PRACTICE database. During duplication, I'll use this log file as my stop point.

```
SQL> connect sys/practice@practice
SQL> SELECT sequence#, thread# FROM v$log WHERE status = 'CURRENT';
```

Task 3: Duplicate Practice Database
In this task, RMAN will perform a lot of work in response to just a few commands. All the commands you need are shown here.

```
connect target sys/practice@practice
connect catalog rman817/rman@rcat
connect auxiliary sys/clone@clne
# Duplicate the PRACTICE database to the CLNE database
run {
    set until logseq 151 thread 1;
    allocate auxiliary channel d1 type disk;
    duplicate target database to CLNE;
}
```

The commands shown in this listing are explained in the bullets below. This RMAN script file contains connection commands to the target, catalog, and auxiliary. During duplication, a target database connection and an auxiliary connection are required. The catalog connection is optional.

- **connect target**   The database to be duplicated is the target database connection. This database can be mounted or open.

- **connect catalog**   The catalog, if one is being used, should contain all the backup history for the target database. RMAN can then use the appropriate backup to restore the duplicate database. This database must be open.

- **connect auxiliary**   The duplicate database is the auxiliary database connection. This database must be started in nomount mode.

- **set until**   Because database duplication must be incomplete if the target database is open, a stop point of the log sequence one greater than the sequence of the last archived redo log file can be used. If the current log file on the target database is 151, recovery on the auxiliary database will include log sequence 150 but not 151. The thread value must be included and will have a value of one for a database that is not a part of an Oracle Parallel Server configuration. The stop point that you choose must be a point in time greater than the time of the oldest backup that RMAN can restore from.

- **allocate auxiliary channel**   Operations on the auxiliary database are performed via an auxiliary channel. Backup pieces of the target database are read by this channel and are restored to the CLNE database. Recovery of the CLNE database is performed via this channel, too.

- **duplicate target**   The target database will be duplicated to the auxiliary database named CLNE. The duplicate command restores datafiles from the target database backup to the new location(s) on the auxiliary. After restoration, RMAN creates a new control file then recovers the database. Finally, the auxiliary database is opened while resetting the log files.

The output of the DUPLICATE command is lengthy, so I won't display it all here. I do want to point out some of the highlights that illustrate all the work RMAN is doing, however:

```
RMAN-08500: channel d1: sid=13 devtype=DISK
```

During the duplication, the auxiliary channel connects to the CLNE instance. While the duplication operations proceed, you can connect in SQL*Plus to the CLNE instance and see the RMAN connection using this session identifier (sid) (not to be confused with the system identifier (SID):

```
RMAN-03027: printing stored script: Memory Script
{
   set until scn 598838;
   set newname for datafile  1 to "/oradata/CLNE/system01.dbf";
...
   restore
   check readonly
   clone database;
}
```

The duplicate command spawns the execution of RMAN scripts. RMAN has chosen to use scripts that it creates dynamically in memory. Because they are not stored statically anywhere, it means the duplicate command will work the same with or without a catalog. In this first memory script, RMAN determines that log sequence 151 on the PRACTICE database begins with SCN 598838, setting this as the stop point for the duplication process. Then RMAN restores the most suitable baseline backup taken prior to this SCN value. RMAN will then recover using incremental backups and archived redo up to this SCN value. Just like normal RMAN recovery, RMAN will first look in the auxiliary database archive_log_dest directory to see if the archive log files needed for recovery are there. If they are not, they must be restored and applied from a backup. Next, RMAN determines the new file names for datafiles based on the DB_FILE_NAME_CONVERT init.ora parameter for the CLNE database. All occurrences of PRACTICE are translated to CLNE, effectively changing the directory for every datafile when the datafiles are restored. Finally, the restore command is issued to the clone database. The keyword clone in the RMAN-generated script (you see it in the RMAN output during duplication) will write to the CLNE auxiliary database. If I had connected to an auxiliary database named TST1, the command would still say RESTORE CLONE DATABASE.

```
RMAN-08502: set_count=153 set_stamp=449676306 creation_time=15-JAN-02
RMAN-08089: channel d1: specifying datafile(s) to restore from backup set
RMAN-08523: restoring datafile 00001 to /oradata/CLNE/system01.dbf
RMAN-08523: restoring datafile 00002 to /oradata/CLNE/rbs01.dbf
...
RMAN-08511: piece handle=
/oradata/PRACTICE/backup/ch12/db_PRACTICE_102_1_44966306 tag=WHOLE_INC0
```

The restore command found the backup taken in Task 2 and uses it to restore the datafiles from the target database (PRACTICE) to the auxiliary database (CLNE). The datafiles are restored from backup, not copied from the target database. Therefore, the performance impact on the target database is minimal.

```
RMAN-08024: channel d1: restore complete
RMAN-06162: sql statement: CREATE CONTROLFILE REUSE SET DATABASE CLNE ...
LOGFILE
   GROUP  1 ( '/oradata/CLNE/redo01.log' ) SIZE    1048576  REUSE,
   GROUP  2 ( '/oradata/CLNE/redo02.log' ) SIZE    1048576  REUSE,
   GROUP  3 ( '/oradata/CLNE/redo03.log' ) SIZE    1048576  REUSE
DATAFILE ...
```

After the restore completes, RMAN creates a new control file. In the control file creation command, the database name is set to CLNE rather than PRACTICE. The location of the log files has been changed from /oradata/PRACTICE to /oradata/CLNE because of the CLNE database init.ora parameter LOG_FILE_NAME_CONVERT set in Task 1.

```
switch clone datafile all;
```

All the non-system datafiles in the clone database (named CLNE) must be switched from the target database location to the new database location.

```
RMAN-03027: printing stored script: Memory Script
{
    set until scn  598838;
```

```
    recover
    clone database
    check readonly
    ;
}
RMAN-03021: executing script: Memory Script
```

The datafiles have been restored to the CLNE database location and the new CLNE control file has been created. Next, RMAN recovers the restored database files on the clone database using first incremental backups and then archived redo log files. Because no incremental backups have been taken in this exercise, you won't see any incremental backups being restored and applied. You should see media recovery using archive log files from the PRACTICE database during RMAN recovery phase 4:

```
RMAN-08054: starting media recovery
RMAN-03022: compiling command: recover(4)
...
RMAN-03023: executing command: recover(4)
RMAN-08515: archivelog filename=/oradata/PRACTICE/archive/149.arc
thread=1 sequence=149
RMAN-08515: archivelog filename=/oradata/PRACTICE/archive/150.arc
thread=1 sequence=150
RMAN-08055: media recovery complete
```

After media recovery, the CLNE database is opened using the resetlogs option:

```
Alter clone database open resetlogs;
...
RMAN-06400: database opened
```

If, during all the output from the duplicate command script, you do not encounter an error script and you see the RMAN-06400: database opened message, the RMAN database duplication operation was a success!

Task 4: Verify Clone Database

To check that the CLNE database has been successfully created, connect via SQL*Plus and run some queries. The SYS password (without SYSDBA role) will be the same as the SYS password on the PRACTICE database. Why? Because the CLNE database is a duplicate of the PRACTICE database!

```
SQL> CONNECT sys/practice@clone
SQL> SELECT sequence#, first_change#, status FROM v$log ORDER BY
status;
 SEQUENCE# FIRST_CHANGE# STATUS
---------- ------------- ----------------
```

```
1        598839 CURRENT
0             0 UNUSED
0             0 UNUSED
```

The sequence number of the current online redo log file is—drum roll, please—1! When the CLNE database is opened with resetlogs, the log sequence resets to 1. The first change of that log sequence is 598839. When the database is opened and the redo logs are reset, the SCN first change of the current redo log is one greater than the SCN change where recovery ended. During recovery, all the datafiles were rolled forward to SCN 598838. The reset logs operation at database open occurred at SCN 598839.

```
SQL> SELECT instance_name FROM v$instance;
SQL> SELECT name FROM v$database;
SQL> SELECT name FROM v$datafile;
SQL> SELECT member FROM v$logfile;
SQL> SELECT name FROM v$controlfile;
SQL> SELECT max(create_date) FROM tina.date_log;
```

By running these queries, you can see the location of the database files and examine data in one of the database tables. Feel free to look at the /oradata/CLNE directory to see the database files created by the RMAN duplication operation. Because RMAN automatically assigns a duplicated database a new DBID, you can register your new database in the recovery catalog and start taking backups of it. Even if the duplicate database has the same name as the primary database, the DBID is different, so it can also be registered in the recovery catalog.

Task 5: Duplicate Practice Database Again

This final task gives you the opportunity to duplicate a database but control the names and locations of datafiles and log files using RMAN keywords and commands. (The control file location is determined by the control_file setting in the auxiliary database parameter file). Control the datafile locations with set newname or set auxname, as shown here.

```
set auxname for datafile 2 TO '/oradata/CLNE/auxname02.dbf';
set auxname for datafile 4 TO '/oradata/CLNE/auxname04.dbf';
set auxname for datafile 6 TO '/oradata/CLNE/auxname06.dbf';
run {
   allocate auxiliary channel d1 type disk;
   set until logseq 152 thread 1;
   set newname for datafile 1 TO '/oradata/CLNE/newname01.dbf';
   set newname for datafile 3 TO '/oradata/CLNE/newname03.dbf';
   set newname for datafile 5 TO '/oradata/CLNE/newname05.dbf';
   set newname for datafile 7 TO '/oradata/CLNE/newname07.dbf';
   duplicate target database to CLNE logfile
     group 1 ('/oradata/CLNE/redo01_1.log',
```

```
                '/oradata/CLNE/redo01_2.log') size 500K reuse,
     group 2 ('/oradata/CLNE/redo02_1.log',
                '/oradata/CLNE/redo02_2.log') size 500K reuse,
     group 3 ('/oradata/CLNE/redo03_1.log',
                '/oradata/CLNE/redo03_2.log') size 500K reuse;
}
set auxname for datafile 2 TO null;
set auxname for datafile 4 TO null;
set auxname for datafile 6 TO null;
```

This shows how you can specify a new file name (or location) for each datafile in the CLNE database during duplication. Thus, each file can be specifically renamed when restoring the PRACTICE backup to the CLNE location. Log files can be specified as an addition to the DUPLICATE TARGET DATABASE command. In the example above, each datafile has been renamed, and the log files have been resized, renamed, and mirrored. For illustration, I use newname for odd-numbered datafiles and auxname for even-numbered datafiles. Also, I added a set until clause for incomplete recovery. The duplication will use a baseline backup and apply redo up to but not including log sequence 152.

Create your backup with the script shown above. Be sure to shut down the CLNE database and open the instance without mounting it prior to running this duplication script. (On Windows, shut down the Windows service prior to starting the CLNE instance. If you don't, the control files remain in a mounted state). Though the datafile and log file conversion parameters from the initCLNE.ora file added back in Task 1 remain in place, the datafile and log file names prescribed via RMAN set commands overrides the init.ora parameters.

NOTE
If you specify auxname and newname in the same script, newname takes precedence over auxname.

Once the database duplication works by running either (or both) of these scripts, look at the datafile and log file locations as described in Task 4. You'll see different file names in the /oradata/CLNE directory. This confirms that you can control the file name locations of a duplicate database using RMAN commands and keywords.

TIP
Reset each auxname to null so that subsequent RMAN commands don't mistakenly use the same name. For example, in this chapter you will create datafile 1 as /oradata/CLNE/auxname1.dbf. Next chapter, your datafile 1 will again be /oradata/CLNE/auxname1.dbf unless you reset the auxiliary name for this file or override it with set newname.

Duplicating a Database on a Different Server

Much of the time, duplication will take place on a different server from the primary database server. How do you handle this?

- If RMAN backup of the target has been made to disk, the backup piece must be copied to the duplicate server. For example, if on hostA an RMAN backup has a backup piece file named /oradata/df_100_12345_1, that file must be copied to the same location on hostB. RMAN will then be able to use this backup piece for the restoration.

- If RMAN backup of the target has been made to tape, the tape vendor software and tape library must be available to the server hosting the auxiliary database.

- If the clone database will have the same directory structure as the primary, add the NOCHECKFILENAME option. This stops RMAN from checking restored datafile existence, and will write over anything already there with the same filenames.

Troubleshooting

RMAN expects several things to be in place prior to database duplication.
The target database must be opened or mounted.

- The environment variable for the RMAN session must be set to the same NLS Language as the target database.

- A whole database backup must be taken of the PRACTICE database followed by an archive log backup that includes a log switch. The archive log backup will only be required if the archive logs needed for recovery cannot be found in the duplicate database archive log destination directory. If the primary archive logs have been copied to the duplicate server, the archive backup will not be required.

- The auxiliary instance (CLNE) must be started in nomount mode.

If you run into problems creating a duplicate database with RMAN, you might encounter one of these errors.

    I. RMAN-05001: auxiliary filename /oradata/PRACTICE/tools01.dbf conflicts with a file used by the target database The RMAN duplication feature by default, prevents you from writing over the datafiles and log files as they existed during the backup being restored. If you get this error, be sure you've renamed your datafile with auxiliary parameter settings or RMAN commands. If you intend to re-create this datafile on the auxiliary in the same location as the target on a different server, use the NOCHECKFILENAME option of the duplicate command. RMAN will not error out when overwriting existing files if you do this.

2. **PLS-00553: character set name is not recognized** If the RMAN client character setting is different than the target database setting during duplication, RMAN will display this error. Change your client character set value like this for your operating system:
```
LINUX > export NLS_LANG=AMERICAN.WE8ISO8859P1
WINNT>  set NLS_LANG=AMERICAN.WE8ISO8859P1
```

3. **RMAN-08060: unable to find archivelog**
   RMAN-06054: media recovery requesting unknown log: thread 1 scn 598778
   RMAN duplication cannot perform complete recovery. Specify a stop point up to the last archived log file using the set until run option, or make the archive log available by switching the online log files on the target database and copying them to the duplicate or backing it up with RMAN.

4. **ORA-12571: TNS:packet writer failure** The auxiliary instance must be started for duplication. Also, check that you haven't shut down the database (or Windows database service) while connected to it in RMAN.

5. **RMAN-06136: ORACLE error from auxiliary database:**
   ORA-01503: CREATE CONTROLFILE failed
   ORA-01158: database already mounted
   RMAN-06097: text of failing SQL statement: CREATE CONTROLFILE REUSE SET DATABASE CLNE RESETLOGS ARCHIVELOG If the control file was created but you encountered a different failure prior to duplication completion, Windows may complain that the database has mounted the control files already. Shut down the Windows service, restart it, and make sure the CLNE instance is started but not mounted. Then rerun the duplication script again.

6. **RMAN-06023: no backup or copy of datafile 1 found to restore** If you used the set until value to specify a point-in-time recovery, the point specified is out of range for your current backups and database. For example, you may have set the stop point of the backup to a log sequence greater than the current value for the database. You also get this error if you have not performed a log switch on the primary since the backup of the primary used for duplication was taken.

Summary

Take a moment to compare this chapter to Chapter 6. User-managed database duplication is more work than letting RMAN perform the duplication. Both user- and server-managed duplication require that the database directories and supporting files be set up. A backup is used for database creation in both methods, but with server-managed duplication, RMAN does the work for you. Table 15-1 summarizes the difference between user-managed duplication and server-managed duplication.

In this chapter, you learned how to duplicate a database with RMAN. You learned how to control the location of datafiles and log files on the duplicated database and, I hope, you succeeded in creating a duplicate of the PRACTICE database. You'll also use an auxiliary database in Chapters 16 and 17. For more information on RMAN duplication, look at Chapter 7 in the RMAN *Oracle8i Recovery Manager User's Guide and Reference* entitled "Creating a Duplicate Database with Recovery Manager."

User-Managed Duplication	Server-Managed Duplication
Configure duplicate database (directories, parameter file, password file, Windows Services); Net8 configuration is optional.	Configure duplicate database (directories, parameter file, password file, Windows Services); Net8 configuration is required.
Back up primary database using user-managed open or closed backup. Backup takes as much disk or tape space as all the datafiles.	Back up target database using server-managed open or closed backup or image copies. Backup takes less disk or tape space than all the datafiles. Image copies take as much disk or tape space as all the datafiles.
Move backup files via operating system commands.	Move backup files via operating system commands only if duplicate database is on a different machine and the backups are stored on the primary disk or the tape system is not available on the duplicate server.
Create a control file script using backup control file to trace and edit the file. Run the script to create a new control file.	Issue the duplicate database command while connected to the target, catalog, and auxiliary.
Must perform manual incomplete recovery and open with RESETLOGS.	Incomplete recovery and open reset logs is performed by RMAN.
Complete recovery is possible.	Complete recovery is not possible.

TABLE 15-1. *Comparison between User-Managed and Server-Managed Duplication*

Chapter Questions

As a refresher, try answering these questions to reinforce the concepts and exercises in this chapter.

1. What RMAN command duplicates a database that has been backed appropriately via RMAN?

   A. clone target database

   B. duplicate target database

   C. clone auxiliary database

   D. duplicate auxiliary database

2. The backups of the auxiliary database are duplicated in the target database.

   A. True

   B. False

3. What work is accomplished by the RMAN duplicate database command? (Pick any that apply.)

   A. Restores datafiles from RMAN backups.

   B. Recovers datafiles using incremental backups and redo application.

   C. Creates a new control file.

   D. Creates new online redo log files.

4. During RMAN duplication, how can you control the location of datafiles? (Pick any that apply.)

   A. DB_FILE_NAME_CONVERT initialization parameter

   B. SET NEWNAME RMAN keyword

   C. SET AUXNAME RMAN command

   D. DUPLICATE … LOGFILE command

5. RMAN duplication can only perform incomplete recovery on the auxiliary database.

   A. True

   B. False

Answers to Chapter Questions

1. B.   The DUPLICATE TARGET DATABASE is the command that instructs RMAN to create a duplicate database from the target database backups to the auxiliary database.

2. False.   Though the target database is typically the focus of RMAN restore and recover operations, the duplicate command uses target as the source and auxiliary as the target.

3. A, B, C, D.   RMAN duplication does a lot of work, doesn't it?

4. A, B, C.   As RMAN duplication names a datafile, it looks first for a newname setting for that datafile. Next, it looks for an auxname setting for that datafile. If none is found, it looks for a conversion match in the auxiliary parameter file. If no name change is specified, the restored datafile will have the same name and directory as the target backup.

5. True.   RMAN duplication will not access the online logs of the primary/target database. Therefore, recovery must be incomplete on the duplicate/auxiliary database.

CHAPTER
16

RMAN Standby
Database

n Chapter 7, you learned how to implement a standby database using user-managed techniques. As you remember, a standby database is a copy of a primary database just like the duplicate database you learned about in the last chapter. The standby database is identical to the primary database, including the database name. When archive log files are generated on the primary, they are transferred and applied to the standby. If the primary database has a failure that cannot be resolved quickly, or there is a requirement to have an immediate failover solution, the standby database can be activated. When this happens, the standby becomes the primary database, all users now connect to this new primary, and there is an instant need to create a new standby database. If this is not done and the new primary fails, there is no failover solution to move all the users to.

Very similar to the way a duplicate database was created with RMAN in Chapter 15, RMAN can be used to create a standby database. In fact, the steps are almost identical, with a few important changes, which will soon become obvious when you perform this chapter's exercise. Once the standby database has been created, the maintenance of it (transferring and applying archive log files) is exactly the same as was discussed in Chapter 7. Creating a standby database using RMAN uses the DUPLICATE command, which first appeared in Oracle 8*i*. Therefore, it is not possible to create a standby database using RMAN with earlier releases than 8*i*.

The prerequisite for reading this chapter is to read all of Chapter 7, which provides all the basic information needed to understand the concepts and administration of standby databases. Throughout this chapter, I'll describe how you can create a standby

An Understudy for Your Database

Imagine yourself as the director of the local community play, *The Wizard of Oz*. After weeks of preparation, set construction, prop collection, rehearsals, and ticket sales, it's show time! During Act I, Scene 2, Dorothy (the lead actress) is just about to say, "Toto, I have a feeling we're not in Kansas anymore," when she passes out. Maybe its fear, or exhaustion that caused her to keel over. Whatever the reason, the play comes to a stop and everyone looks at you the director for...direction. That's OK. You prepared for this potential situation. Without batting an eye, you motion to the understudy to step in and take the lead role. The understudy picks up Toto the dog and chimes right in: "Toto, I have a feeling we're not in Kansas anymore," while the Dorothy who has fainted gets dragged offstage by the stagehands. During the rehearsals, the understudy prepared to substitute for the lead actress for an emergency like this. A standby database is much like an understudy in theater: always prepared to step in when an emergency arises.

database and back up that standby with RMAN. As with database duplication, the primary database is known as the target database. The standby database is known as the auxiliary database.

In this chapter, I'll only introduce you to a few new RMAN commands. Existing commands explained in previous chapters still apply.

- **INCLUDE CURRENT CONTROLFILE FOR STANDBY**   Includes a current standby control file within the backup command. RMAN must have a standby control file within its backup to create a standby database.

- **DUPLICATE TARGET DATABASE FOR STANDBY**   Creates a duplicate database as a standby of the target. This command is similar to the database cloning operation you learned about in Chapter 15.

- **DORECOVER**   Recovers the standby database using archive logs backups from the target database. Once the creation of the standby database completes, RMAN will apply all archive logs from the primary to the standby up to the last archived log that has been registered with RMAN.

During the RMAN duplication of a database for standby purposes, RMAN executes all the tasks required automatically. While connected to the target, auxiliary, and the optional catalog database, RMAN will:

1. Determine which baseline backups will be restored.

2. Determine where to place the datafiles on the auxiliary instance based on auxiliary database parameters or RMAN set commands and options.

3. Restore a standby control file for the auxiliary database.

4. Mount the standby database's control file.

5. Restore the datafiles from backup pieces or image copies as determined in step 1.

6. If the DORECOVER option is specified, apply any incremental backups to the restored datafiles based on the recovery stop point.

7. If the DORECOVER option is specified, apply any archived log files from disk or backups to the restored datafiles based on the recovery stop point.

Why would you use RMAN to create a standby database? You must use RMAN if your only backups are RMAN backups. If you have RMAN backups and user-managed backups, RMAN makes standby creation easier and more automated.

RMAN creates a new standby control file for you and handles the restoration and recovery of datafiles.

When you undertake the creation of a standby database using RMAN, keep in mind these important considerations:

- Specify NOCATALOG on the RMAN command line if you don't want to use the catalog during standby creation.

- The redo log that is current during the backup of the standby control file must be archived. (During recovery, the backup SCNs of the datafile headers will be needed during archive log file application.)

- You must have a backup, including a standby control file. Otherwise, you'll get an "RMAN-06024: no backup or copy of the control file found to restore" error when trying to create the standby database.

- You cannot perform a complete recovery during standby creation. This is always the case if the current online redo log is not available to the database. Using the DORECOVER option, RMAN will apply known archive log files.

- If the standby database resides on a different server and has the same directory structure as the primary server, you do not have to rename any of the files during standby creation. By default, the DUPLICATE command will not succeed and RMAN notifies you that the restored auxiliary file locations are the same as the original files when the target database files were backed up. This is done to prevent the DBA from accidentally overwriting existing datafiles. Override this check with the NOFILENAMECHECK option.

- The database name of the standby database must be the same as the primary. If the primary and the standby are on the same machine (as in the exercises in this chapter), use the LOCK_NAME_SPACE initialization parameter on the standby. This will allow two databases of the same name to reside on the same machine without interfering with each other.

- RMAN will only create the standby database and initially recover it at the point of creation. It will not manage the ongoing maintenance and recovery of the standby (transferring and applying archive redo log files).

During this chapter, you are going to create a standby database of the PRACTICE database using RMAN (see Figure 16-1). After you've created the standby, you'll use RMAN to back up the standby database, effectively backing up the primary database.

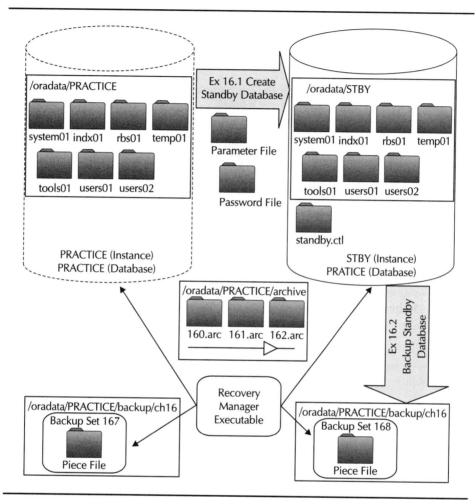

FIGURE 16-1. *Create and back up a standby database with RMAN*

Recovery Manager Standby

There are a number of steps that need to be followed when using RMAN to create a standby database. You will notice some of these are the same as when creating a duplicate database.

1. **Prepare the standby host.** A standby database can reside on the same machine as the primary database or on a different machine. If it's on the

same machine, the directory structures that house the datafiles, control files, and online redo logs must be different. Therefore, the directory structure that will contain the standby database must be created. This is similar to the steps carried out in Exercise 6.1 back in Chapter 6.

2. **Make an RMAN backup of the primary database.** In order for RMAN to create a standby database, a suitable backup must exist for RMAN to restore to the standby server. The backup can be taken when the primary database is open or closed and can be image copies, proxy copies, or backups. One extra thing that the standby database needs is a special standby control file. Before version 8.1.7, this control file backup had to be created using SQL command (ALTER DATABASE CREATE STANDBY CONTROLFILE AS) but now RMAN can also create such a control file.

3. **Configure the standby database parameter file.** A database initialization parameter file must be created for the standby database. Most of the parameters required for standby databases are related to the renaming of datafiles and log files automatically by Oracle. This prevents overwriting and manual intervention when a datafile needs to be moved from a different location. The parameter file used should be the same as the one in Chapter 7 (see Exercise 7.1, Task 3).

4. **Configure the standby database password file.** For DBA authentication a password file is needed for the standby database. This can be created following the steps in Chapter 6 (Exercise 6.1, Task 1).

5. **Configure the Net8 configuration files.** RMAN needs to connect to the primary database and the standby database at the same time. If both databases are located on different servers, use Net8 Assistant to configure the listener on the duplicate server and to configure the tnsnames file on the server that you are running RMAN from.

6. **Make the RMAN backups accessible to the server that will house the standby database.** If backups are created on disk, they can be transferred using binary mode ftp or by using a disk sharing scheme like NFS or mapping a shared drive in Windows. They must exist in the same directory on the standby as they were in on the primary to make sure RMAN knows where to retrieve them from. If tape backups are used, the duplicate server must have access to the Media Management Layer and tape library that the primary database uses to make its backups. If this is not possible, the backups can be restored to the primary server (make sure you specify a different location for the restored datafiles so you don't overwrite the production database) and then transferred to the standby database server. If the primary and standby databases will reside on the same machine, this step is not necessary.

7. **Start the standby instance.** Before RMAN can create the standby database, the standby instance needs to be started in NOMOUNT mode. The parameter file that was created in step 3 will be read at this time.

8. **Mount or open the primary database.** RMAN requires that the primary database is either mounted or open in order to create a standby database.

9. **Create the standby database.** Once RMAN is connected to the primary database and the standby instance, channels are created and you're ready to restore the backups. The DUPLICATE command creates the standby by restoring the standby control file and restores the datafiles from backup. Once the database has been restored, incremental backups and redo can be applied to roll it forward. Once the standby is created, the database will then stay in a mounted state waiting to be put into managed recovery mode or to manually apply redo.

A standby remains current with the primary via the application of archived redo log files. When the standby is created, RMAN can perform recovery for you. If you instruct RMAN to recover the standby during its creation, Oracle decides if it is best to apply incremental backups on top of the base-level backup just restored or to apply archive log files. RMAN will usually restore a base-level backup (full or incremental level 0) and then apply all subsequent incremental-level backups. Once the last incremental backup has been applied, archive redo logs will then be applied to roll the database further forward. Appending the DORECOVER keyword to the DUPLICATE command performs this automatic recovery at standby creation. When you do this, RMAN will automatically restore the most recent base-level backup, apply any subsequent incrementals, and then apply the archive redo logs. Unless a stop point for the recovery is given (using SET UNTIL), recovery will continue until the last archive log that RMAN knows about has been applied. This is the best way to create a standby database using RMAN as it reduces the amount of work that you have to do.

By default, when you tell RMAN to create the standby database, the base-level backup is restored and no recovery is carried out. This means that you must manually apply the archive log files since the restored backup was taken. If the last base-level backup was taken a long time ago, you have a lot of work ahead of you when applying all those archive logs, once you have made sure they are available on disk.

CAUTION
Placing a standby on the same machine as the primary is not a very sensible failover solution because if the machine has a failure, both primary and standby databases will be lost. I describe a single machine primary/standby configuration for training purposes only.

Exercise 16.1: Create a Standby Database with RMAN

In this exercise, you'll create a standby database using an RMAN backup that includes a standby database control file. Using this backup, you will create a standby database, recover it, and open it as read-only. In this chapter, the primary/target database is the PRACTICE database. The standby database is called STBY.

Task Description	Minutes
1. Prepare the Standby Database	5
2. Back Up the PRACTICE Database	5
3. Create the Standby Database	5
4. Verify Standby Creation	10
Total Time	25

The purpose of this exercise is to create a standby database with RMAN as you did using user-managed techniques back in Chapter 7. Managing and activating the standby is not an RMAN task; only the creation of it is. Therefore, I'm not going to repeat the management tasks in this exercise except to verify that the standby has been created properly.

Task 1: Prepare the Standby Database

The Standby database you are about to create needs to have the same supporting files set up as in Chapter 7. By now, you have had some practice setting up a database (in Chapters 6, 7, 9, and 15). In fact, all of these steps may have been accomplished when you set up your standby database back in Chapter 7. Set up these components for your standby database:

- **Directories**   Create all the administrative directories ($ORACLE_BASE /admin/STBY) and data directories (/oradata/STBY).

- **Parameter file**   Create a parameter file using a copy of the PRACTICE database and name it $ORACLE_BASE/admin/STBY/pfile/initSTBY.ora. Configure the standby database parameter file by changing every occurrence of the word 'PRACTICE' to 'STBY' with one exception: the database name (DB_NAME) must remain the same on the standby database as the original database. Add two conversion parameters so that file names will be translated during standby database creation. Also, add the LOCK_ NAME_SPACE parameter so that you can open the two databases of the same database name on the same machine at the same time:

```
db_file_name_convert        = ("PRACTICE", "STBY")
log_file_name_convert       = ("PRACTICE", "STBY")
lock_name_space             = "STBY"
standby_archive_dest        = /oradata/STBY/archive
```

■ **Password file**   Create a password file for the standby database so that
RMAN can connect to STBY database as SYSDBA.

■ **Windows service**   On Windows, create a new database service for the
STBY database named OracleServiceSTBY using the oradim utility.

■ **Configure Net8**   Finally, configure Net8 connectivity for the STBY
database. This was not necessary when you duplicated a database in
Chapter 7 because you did not have to connect to the STBY instance
while also being connected to the PRACTICE database. Using Net8
Assistant, add a database service for the STBY database and optionally
configure the listener for the STBY database.

If you created a standby database as described in Chapter 7, all of these steps
may not be necessary (with the exception of adding the two convert parameters to the
STBY parameter file). The database files may already be in the /oradata/STBY directory.
You can leave those previous database files (datafiles, log files, and control files)
created earlier, or you can remove them now if you'd like. To remove them, just
delete all the files from the /oradata/STBY directory.

Task 2: Back Up the PRACTICE Database
Creation of a standby requires a backup of a standby control file. You also need a
log switch after this standby control file backup. Add a log file parameter to the
command line so the output of the script will be written to a file:

```
LINUX> rman trace=b_standby.log
RMAN> connect target  sys/practice@practice
RMAN> connect catalog rman817/rman@rcat
RMAN> @b_standby.rcv
```

The backup shown next is similar to RMAN backups shown in previous chapters
with a few exceptions. This backup demonstrates how different parts of the database
can be backed up in a single backup run. Previously, backups of datafiles and
archive log files were run in separate scripts.

```
run {
  allocate channel d1 type disk;
  backup
    incremental level 0
```

```
    database
    format '/oradata/PRACTICE/backup/ch16/db_%d_%s_%p_%t'
    tag = 'STBY_INC0'
    include current controlfile for standby;
sql "alter system archive log current";
backup archivelog
    from time 'SYSDATE - 1/24'
    format '/oradata/PRACTICE/backup/ch16/ar_%d_%s_%p_%t';
}
```

Most of this backup script looks familiar to you by now. Some things to note about this backup:

■ **control file for standby**   While backing up the whole database, the control file is included automatically with the system tablespace. A special control file must be created for the creation of the standby. RMAN can store that special file in a datafile backup piece. This backup control file can also be used to restore the target database control file if needed.

■ **archive log current**   Recovery on the standby begins with the current log file when the standby control file was created. Therefore, this log file should be archived for recovery on the standby after it is created.

■ **from time 'SYSDATE - 1/24'**   The most recent archive log file in the archive log backup set. This command will back up archive logs containing the last hour's worth of redo.

Look through the output of the backup on the screen or in the RMAN log file and you'll see a message indicating that a standby control file has been included in the backup:

```
RMAN-08020: including standby controlfile in backupset
```

Before moving on to the next task, make a note of the current log sequence number in the PRACTICE database. Automatic recovery will begin with this log sequence:

```
SQL> connect sys/practice@practice
SQL> SELECT sequence# FROM v$log WHERE status = 'CURRENT';
```

In this exercise, let's say that the log sequence value returned from this query was 162. You can also see this in the sequence# backed up in the RMAN output messages.

How can you know if a backup set contains a standby control file? Query the catalog view named RC_BACKUP_CONTROLFILE for the registered database for control file type of 'S' (Standby). Normal control file backups will be a control file type of 'B' (Backup). The results from the first query shown below will show the backup that you just created. Compare the set count with the output from the backup output in the trace file name b_standby.log.

```
SQL> connect rman817/rman@rcat
SQL> SELECT set_count, checkpoint_change#, checkpoint_time,
  2           status, completion_time, controlfile_type
  3       FROM rc_backup_controlfile
  4      WHERE db_name = 'PRACTICE' AND controlfile_type = 'S'
```

Also, find the backup pieces and backup sets containing a standby control file with a query as just shown.

```
SELECT bs.bs_key, bs.set_count, bs.backup_type, bs.incremental_level,
     bs.completion_time, bs.elapsed_seconds, bp.handle, bp.status
  FROM rc_backup_set bs, rc_backup_piece bp
 WHERE bs.controlfile_included = 'STANDBY'
   AND bs.db_id = bp.db_id
   AND bs.bs_key = bp.bs_key
   AND bs.db_id IN
     (SELECT dbid FROM rc_database WHERE name = 'PRACTICE');
```

The output of this query will also correlate to the text displayed in the log file from the backup execution. Make sure the backup piece name in the log file is the same as the handle column from the query. The elapsed time of backup will be the same also.

Task 3: Create the Standby Database

The creation of the standby database will be accomplished with just a few commands. Simply start RMAN and connect to the target, catalog, and auxiliary databases. I've included a sample Linux setting of the NLS language environment variable. This variable may not need to be set if the target database has the same language characteristics as your default environment. Just be aware that standby creation will fail if your NLS_ LANG environment values are different from the target.

```
LINUX> export NLS_LANG=AMERICAN.WE8ISO8859P1
LINUX> rman trace=standby.log
RMAN> @standby.rcv
```

The work of standby creation carried out by RMAN can be done with just a few commands. The next listing shows the commands you can run that will create a standby using the backup created in the previous task.

```
connect target    sys/practice@practice
connect catalog   rman817/rman@rcat
```

```
connect auxiliary sys/stby@stby
run {
   set command id to 'Standby Creation';
   allocate auxiliary channel d1 type disk;
   duplicate target database for standby dorecover;
}
```

These few lines create a duplicate of the PRACTICE database using a backup of the database. This duplicate, however, is configured to be a STBY of the PRACTICE database. The standby database will be created to the auxiliary instance. Though the commands in this script are few, RMAN accomplishes a great deal of work:

■ **set command id**   This optional setting causes RMAN to populate the client_info column of the v$session view. Therefore, while the STBY database is being created, you can query the v$session table where client_info has a value of 'Standby Creation' and watch session activity.

■ **duplicate target database for standby**   The bulk of the work in standby creation happens because of this command. First, a standby control is replicated in the location defined by the auxiliary database init.ora CONTROL_FILES parameter. Next, the datafiles are restored from the target database backup to the auxiliary database restoration location.

■ **dorecover**   After the target database is duplicated, the standby is recovered using incremental RMAN backups and archived redo logs. Recovery continues until the stop point is reached.

How does the RMAN duplicate command know where to create the duplicated datafiles? Since the standby database is on the same server as the primary database, it cannot use the same file name and location. The duplicate command looks in three places for instructions on where to put each datafile in this order:

■ **set newname**   Specify a new datafile name for a specific duplicate command. Within a run block, define a file name with this parameter. This setting is a temporary setting for a specific duplication command. There is no persistence outside of the run block.

■ **set auxname**   Specify a new datafile name for any auxiliary operations until otherwise specified. This is executed outside of the run block and has persistence between RMAN sessions.

■ **db_file_name_convert**   Specify a translation string within a database parameter file for that database only. This setting applies to all datafiles for its database.

The log files can be specified one of two ways:

- In the duplicate command
- In the auxiliary database parameter file: log_file_name_convert

Task 4: Verify Standby Creation

Check, once again, that the database files for the standby database are in the correct directory (/oradata/STBY). You can also connect to the standby and select from v$database, v$datafile, v$logfile, or v$controlfile to confirm that all the database files are where you expect them to be.

Now that you have created a standby, I want you to verify that the STBY database is actually a standby of the PRACTICE database. How can you verify that STBY is a standby? Check that it performs the functions of the standby by changing data on the primary database, propagating that change to the standby, opening the standby in read-only mode, and checking for the changed data.

Change Data on Primary Database   To check that STBY is performing the functions of a standby, change some data on the primary database. First, remove any future rows in our trusty TINA.DATE_LOG table. Then, insert a row 16 years in the future that you'll later be able to see on the standby. After committing these changes, check the current redo log sequence number and switch the log file. The changes you just made to TINA's table will be contained in the redo records of the recently archived log file. If the log sequence during this change was 162, the log switch will cause an archive log file named 162.arc to be created in the /oradata/PRACTICE/archive directory:

```
SQL> connect sys/practice@practice
SQL> DELETE FROM tina.date_log WHERE create_date > SYSDATE;
SQL> INSERT INTO tina.date_log VALUES (SYSDATE+365*16);
SQL> SELECT sequence# FROM v$log WHERE status = 'CURRENT';
SQL> COMMIT;
SQL> ALTER SYSTEM SWITCH LOGFILE;
```

Transfer Data via Archive Log   Some data changes have occurred on the primary database that have not been applied to the standby. Those changes are contained in an archive log file named /oradata/PRACTICE/archive/162.arc. To propagate these changes to the standby, the newly created archive log file must be applied to the standby. Connect to the standby and apply the archive log file. Because the databases are on the same machine, you don't have to transfer the log file. Just tell the recover command to look in the directory where the file already exists. Then recover the standby choosing the auto option on the recover command.

```
SQL> connect sys/stby@stby as sysdba
SQL> set logsource /oradata/PRACTICE/archive
SQL> recover standby database;
```

Recover the log file containing the change to TINA's table.

Read New Data on the Standby   Check that the data changes created on the PRACTICE database have been propagated to the STBY database. Open the database in read-only mode. Select rows from the TINA.DATE_LOG table. You should see a date 16 years in the future. Then close the standby and return it to standby mode.

```
SQL> ALTER DATABASE OPEN READ ONLY;
SQL> SELECT create_date FROM tina.date_log WHERE create_date > SYSDATE;
SQL> SHUTDOWN IMMEDIATE;
SQL> STARTUP NOMOUNT;
SQL> ALTER DATABASE MOUNT STANDBY DATABASE;
```

If you are confused about any work done in this task, refer back to Chapter 7 for more details on how to verify standby database changes.

Way to go! You and RMAN created a standby database.

Recovery Manager Standby Backup

Once a standby database has been created, you can back up the standby with RMAN. When you back up the standby, you are actually backing up the primary database. This will also work with user-managed backups, but it is a lot simpler and easier to manage when using RMAN. Now that you have an exact copy of the primary database, which will be located on a different machine in a real production environment, you can take your backups from there. When backups are taken from the standby server instead of the primary, it reduces the resource overhead on the primary server that backups use when reading datafiles and archive log files before passing the data to the Media Management Layer.

Back in Chapter 11, you learned that each database registered in the RMAN catalog is registered using the DBID as a unique database identifier. This DBID is provided to a database by Oracle when it is first created and is sometimes changed under a number of other circumstances. One of these circumstances is when you create a duplicate database using RMAN. If you wish to take RMAN backups of a newly created duplicate database using an RMAN catalog, it must first be registered in the catalog (instructions on how to do this are in Exercise 11.1, Task 3 in Chapter 11). RMAN automatically forces the duplicate database to have a new DBID, which will be different from the database that was copied. With a standby database, while it has yet not been activated as a primary, RMAN can take backups of it as if it were the original primary database that this is created from. Because it is an exact copy of a primary database, the DBID is the same. The standby database is kept up-to-date with the primary by reading the archive redo logs transferred from the primary database. The datafile content differences between the primary and standby databases will depend on how many archive logs have not yet been transferred and applied. To take a backup of the standby database, you need to stop recovery, shut it down, and start it up in nomount mode. Use RMAN to connect to the standby database and the recovery catalog, and take a cold backup of the datafiles. You could even take a backup of all the archive log files that have been transferred from the primary database. This saves on CPU, memory, and disk resources that would normally be taken from the primary server. You cannot take a backup of the standby control file using RMAN for use in a restoration of the primary database; you must take a control file backup from the primary database. A standby control file can only be used for a standby database. You must also make sure that both the primary and standby servers are able to communicate with the MML and tape library. You will write data from the standby database and then restore data to the primary server. With this backup method, it is possible to restore a file taken from the primary database to be used in the standby database, or you can restore a datafile taken from a standby backup and restore it into the primary database.

Exercise 16.2: Back Up a Standby Database with RMAN

Now that you have created a standby, let's back up the standby using RMAN. You'll see how easy it is to back up the standby database by simply connecting to it instead of the primary.

Task Description	Minutes
1. Back Up the Standby Database	10
Total Time	10

The standby database and the primary database have the same DBID. You can try to connect to the standby database with RMAN and register it with the catalog, but you'll get this error: RMAN-20002: target database already registered in recovery catalog. Therefore, when RMAN backs up the standby, it thinks it is backing up the primary.

Task 1: Back Up the Standby Database
Create a backup script similar to the one used for an incremental level 0 backup in Chapter 12. You can use the exact same script, but change the tag and the directory

location of the backup so that you can easily distinguish this backup from others taken before. Create a script of RMAN commands as shown in here.

```
connect target sys/stby@stby
connect catalog rman817/rman@rcat
run {
    allocate channel d1 type disk;
    backup incremental level = 0 cumulative database
        format '/oradata/PRACTICE/backup/ch16/db_%d_%s_%p_%t'
        tag = 'WHOLE_STANDBY_INC0';
}
```

Back up the standby database with RMAN (b_whole_standby_ inc0.rcv). This script will create a backup of the target database. Note the tag for this backup will be WHOLE_STANDBY_INC0. Also note that the backup piece file will be placed in the ch16 directory. This way you can easily find the backup set and backup piece file.

Run the backup of the standby database and trap the output in a trace file like this:

```
LINUX> rman trace=b_whole_standby_inc0.log
RMAN> @b_whole_standby_inc0.log
```

When you run the backup of the standby database, the output will look similar to the previous output. Note the location of the datafiles being backed up, however. They are not in the PRACTICE database directory. Instead, you'll see output in the log file (and on the screen) like this:

```
RMAN-08010: channel d1: specifying datafile(s) in backupset
RMAN-08522: input datafile fno=00001 name=/oradata/STBY/system01.dbf
RMAN-08522: input datafile fno=00002 name=/oradata/STBY/rbs01.dbf
RMAN-08522: input datafile fno=00004 name=/oradata/STBY/temp01.dbf
RMAN-08522: input datafile fno=00005 name=/oradata/STBY/tools01.dbf
RMAN-08522: input datafile fno=00006 name=/oradata/STBY/indx01.dbf
RMAN-08522: input datafile fno=00003 name=/oradata/STBY/users01.dbf
RMAN-08522: input datafile fno=00007 name=/oradata/STBY/dnew07.dbf
RMAN-08013: channel d1: piece 1 created
RMAN-08503: piece
handle=/oradata/PRACTICE/backup/ch16/db_PRACTICE_11_1_450481477
```

Task 2: List Backup Contents

Now that the backup is complete, list its contents by identifying it via its tag. This list will show the same information about the backup as is recorded in the log file from the backup (b_whole_standby_inc0.log). Confirm that the backup set count is the same and the backup piece names concur:

```
RMAN> list backup tag 'WHOLE_STANDBY_INC0';
```

Something interesting to note: the datafiles listed in the backup are the locations of the primary PRACTICE datafile locations:

```
List of Datafiles Included
File Name                                    LV Type Ckp SCN   Ckp Time
---- --------------------------------------- -- ---- ---------- ---------
1    /oradata/PRACTICE/system01.dbf          0  Full 201752     16-JAN-02
2    /oradata/PRACTICE/rbs01.dbf             0  Full 201752     16-JAN-02
3    /oradata/PRACTICE/users01.dbf           0  Full 201752     16-JAN-02
4    /oradata/PRACTICE/temp01.dbf            0  Full 201752     16-JAN-02
5    /oradata/PRACTICE/tools01.dbf           0  Full 201752     16-JAN-02
6    /oradata/PRACTICE/indx01.dbf            0  Full 201752     16-JAN-02
7    /oradata/PRACTICE/users02.dbf           0  Full 201752     16-JAN-02
```

Though the backup of the standby copied blocks for datafiles in the /oradata/STBY directory, the catalog and control file think the files are in the /oradata/PRACTICE directory. Therefore, a restore will automatically put the datafiles in the correct place on the primary server.

One last thing to do: connect again to the primary database as the target and, using the same list command, see if the backup exists. The knowledge of the standby backup is contained in the standby control file and in the catalog.

```
LINUX> rman
RMAN> connect target sys/practice@practice
RMAN> connect catalog rman817/rman@rcat
RMAN> list backup tag 'WHOLE_STANDBY_INC0';
```

As the list command executes, the catalog and primary control file synchronize automatically. RMAN is clever enough to detect a change in server-managed content between the PRACTICE database control file and the catalog. The catalog now has information about a backup that the target control file doesn't have.

```
RMAN-03022: compiling command: list
RMAN-03024: performing implicit full resync of recovery catalog
```

Once the resynchronization completes, you'll see the backup listing connected to the PRACTICE database exactly as it was displayed while connected to the STBY database as the target. Therefore, RMAN sees the backup of the STBY standby database as a backup of the PRACTICE primary database.

Troubleshooting

If you run into problems creating a standby database with RMAN, you might encounter one of these errors. These notes may point you in the right direction to solve the issue.

1. **RMAN-06024: no backup or copy of the control file found to restore**
   While creating the standby, RMAN requires a backup of a standby control file. Either a backup of the standby control file has not been taken *or* the stop point set for the standby restore and recover occurred before that backup was taken.

2. **RMAN-05500: the auxiliary database must not be mounted when issuing a DUPLICATE command**   If the standby creation failed, the auxiliary database (STBY) may still have the newly created control file mounted. Make sure the STBY database is started in nomount mode.

3. **You created a standby but the datafiles were not named and located where you thought they'd be**   Set auxname from a previous RMAN session remains in effect until the datafile set is unset. For example, if you set datafile 1 to be /oradata/STBY/datafile01.dbf, on the next duplicate command, that name will be used again. If you use the run option set newname, the auxname will not be used in that run block only. The set auxname can be reset by using the set auxname # to null command.

4. **RMAN-05507: standby control file checkpoint (180959) is more recent than duplication point in time (180957)**   The backup containing the standby control file was performed within the current online redo log file.

Summary

In this chapter, you learned how much easier it is to create a standby database using RMAN than it is to do it manually. You do not have to spend much of your time restoring and applying archive logs from the restored backup to bring it up to the current point in time. Instead, RMAN will restore the base-level backup and then apply incremental backups and archive log files. You also learned how to take backups of the standby database, which can then be restored to the primary database. This is allowed because both databases have the same name and the same DBID. Performing backups on the standby can reduce the workload from taking backups from the primary server. Table 16-1 shows the main differences between creating a standby database using user-managed and server-managed techniques.

User Managed Duplication	Server Managed Duplication
Configure standby database (directories, parameter file, password file, Windows Services); Net8 configuration is optional.	Configure standby database (directories, parameter file, password file, Windows Services); Net8 configuration is required.
Back up primary database using user-managed open or closed backup. Backup takes as much disk or tape space as all the datafiles.	Back up target database using server-managed open or closed backup or image copies. Backup takes less disk or tape space than all the datafiles. Image copies take as much disk or tape space as all the datafiles.
Create a standby control file on the primary and copy it to the primary.	A backup of the database must contain a copy of the standby control file.
Move backup files via operating system commands.	Move backup files via operating system commands only if standby database is on a different server machine or the tape system is not available on the standby server.
The standby control file is created using a command from SQL*Plus.	Issue the duplicate database command while connected to the target, catalog, and auxiliary.
Recovery of the standby from the time of the backup has to be applied by restoring the archive log files and applying them.	RMAN handles the application of incremental backups and archive redo log files.

TABLE 16-1. *Comparison Between User-Managed and Server-Managed Standby Creation*

Consult the *Oracle 8i Standby Database Concepts and Administration Guide* for all the details on successfully implementing an Oracle standby database. You can find more information in the Oracle 8*i* Documentation Addendum on creating a standby database using RMAN. You can also find helpful notes on the Oracle Metalink website about standby creation with RMAN.

Chapter Questions

Test yourself with these questions about standby creation to reinforce the topics covered in this chapter.

1. What RMAN command creates a standby database from an RMAN backup?

   A. duplicate target database for standby

   B. create standby database

   C. duplicate standby database on auxiliary

   D. duplicate standby

2. What tasks are accomplished by RMAN in the DUPLICATE TARGET DATABASE FOR STANDBY command? (Pick any that apply.)

   A. Restores a standby control file from RMAN backup

   B. Restores datafiles from RMAN backup

   C. Optionally recovers the restored datafiles

   D. Restores the online redo log files

3. RMAN can create the standby database from an RMAN backup and perform initial standby recovery but cannot carry on the maintenance of the standby database.

   A. True

   B. False

4. By default, RMAN standby creation does not recover the standby from the target/primary RMAN incremental backups and archive log backups. What optional parameter can be added to the duplicate command to accomplish this?

   A. recover

   B. propagate

    C. dorecover

    D. apply

5. You can back up a standby database with RMAN and use those backups for recovery of the primary.

    A. True

    B. False

Answers to Chapter Questions

1. A.   The duplicate command creates a standby using backups that contain a standby control file.

2. A, B, C.   RMAN restores a standby control and all the datafiles and can optionally recover the database up to the last archived log file. Online redo log files are not restored: they don't even exist for a standby until the standby is activated.

3. True.   RMAN can create a datafile, but it's up to you to manage the transfer of archive log files from the primary to the standby after initial creation.

4. C.   The dorecover option instructs RMAN to apply redo to the standby from RMAN backups and archive log files. Those backups can be incremental-level 1–4 backups or archive log files. Incrementals are applied first; then archive log files. If the archive log files are already found on disk, they are used first.

5. True.   A standby is an exact copy of a primary. They even have the same DBID. RMAN can back up a standby. Those backups can be used to recover the primary.

CHAPTER
17

RMAN Tablespace
Recovery

ack in Chapter 9, you learned how to recover the database from failures such as a dropped table without having to take the whole database back to the time before the error occurred. Oracle allows you to recover a partial set of the database consisting of a number of tablespaces. The tablespace datafiles are restored and then recovered using archive log files up until the point of the failure or error. The tablespaces containing the objects needing recovery are then transported to the primary database using the 8*i* Transportable Tablespace feature. This type of recovery is called tablespace point-in-time recovery (TSPITR).

In the previous two chapters, you learned how much easier it is to carry out recovery tasks using RMAN. A duplicate database can be created with a couple of commands, and the standby database can also be created with little fuss. TSPITR can also be handled by RMAN in a much more hassle-free manner than doing it all yourself. If you only take RMAN backups of your primary databases, then RMAN is the only choice you have to restore and recovery from such a problem. If you have a mixture of user-managed backups, exports and RMAN backups, then RMAN is still usually much quicker and easier to manage.

The benefit of TSPITR is that you can recover one or more tablespaces to a previous state while leaving the rest of the database as is. The downside of TSPITR occurs when recovering a subset of your database pertains to the integrity of logical data relations between the recovered subset and the remaining database. If your data relationships are being managed by an application instead of database referential integrity, you need to make sure all related data objects are recovered consistently. Inconsistent data across tablespaces can produce some interesting surprises. If related data is spread across a number of tablespaces, you have to increase the number of tablespaces that you wish to recover to ensure all related objects are included.

Just as in previous chapters, a number of terms that are used in this chapter need to be defined. Though these terms were discussed in Chapter 9, I think they need to be repeated here. (You may want to refer back to Chapter 9 before tackling this chapter.)

- **Auxiliary instance**   The background processes and memory structures that recover specific tablespaces. This instance will open the auxiliary database and will be called AUXY in this chapter.

- **Auxiliary database**   A subset of the primary/target database for the temporary purpose of tablespace recovery. In this chapter, the AUXY instance will open a subset of the database named PRACTICE. This PRACTICE database will be a restored backup, including some of the datafiles and control files from your primary PRACTICE database.

- **Primary database**   The database in need of TSPITR. In this chapter, it's the PRACTICE database whose USERS tablespace will be recovered to a different time from all other tablespaces in the primary database.

- **Recovery set** Datafiles comprising the tablespace(s) to be recovered to a previous point in time. The SYSTEM tablespace datafiles cannot be part of the recovery set. In this chapter, the recovery set is the two backup datafiles in the USERS tablespace.

- **Auxiliary set** Any database files required for tablespace recovery. In this chapter, the auxiliary set is the primary PRACTICE database backup control file, backup datafiles of the SYSTEM and RBS tablespaces, the auxiliary database parameter file, and the primary PRACTICE database archived log files.

During the TSPITR, RMAN accomplishes a number of tasks. While connected to the target, auxiliary, and the optional catalog database, RMAN will do the following:

1. Determine which baseline backups will be used to restore the required database subset based on the most recent backup taken or the recovery stop point you provide.

2. Create a new control file for the auxiliary database from an RMAN backup.

3. Determine where to place the datafiles on the auxiliary instance based on auxiliary database parameters or RMAN set commands and options.

4. Restore the datafiles from backup pieces or image copies as found in step 1. This is exactly the same function RMAN uses when you normally carry out a database restoration. *Only files in the recovery set and the auxiliary set are restored and recovered.*

5. Apply any incremental backups to the restored datafiles based on the recovery stop point. This works in the same way it does when you issue a recover database command within RMAN.

6. Apply any archived log files from disk or backups to the restored datafiles based on the recovery stop point. Just like a normal recovery using RMAN, the archives are the last things to be applied to the restored database.

7. Open the auxiliary database while resetting the online redo log files. The new online redo log files are created as specified via the translation from the auxiliary parameter file.

8. Export the dictionary metadata pertaining to objects in the recovered (not the auxiliary) tablespaces using the Transportable Tablespace feature and close the auxiliary database.

9. Switch the location of the datafiles in the recovered tablespace to the new datafile location in the target control file.

10. Import the dictionary metadata of the recovered tablespaces to the primary/target database. The objects in the recovered tablespaces can be accessed by the database now.

At the conclusion of TSPITR, the recovered tablespace(s) are offline. They are kept offline to bring to your attention the fact that those tablespaces should now be backed up. Once a tablespace has taken part in TSPITR, none of the previous backups and archive log files can be used to recover this tablespace through the TSPITR time. Taking a new backup will provide a new baseline for future recoveries.

When you consider the RMAN TSPITR, keep in mind several important considerations that Oracle provides in their documentation. Some of these restrictions are the same as user-managed TSPITR:

- The auxiliary and primary databases must stay on the same machine (they can be on different nodes in an OPS cluster). If your machine is short on disk space or other resources, this limitation can present a tough problem.

- Running TSPITR without a catalog can have more limitations still. Just like all other RMAN recovery scenarios, you can only restore and recover datafiles that are currently stored in the target database control file. If you have only configured the database to store 7 days' worth of RMAN backup information, it may not be possible to recover a tablespace from 21 days ago if there have been no newer backups taken of it.

- You can't recover dropped tablespaces or recover a tablespace that has been dropped and then re-created with the same tablespace name.

- You can't use TSPITR to remove a datafile that has been added to a tablespace.

- You can't perform data changes on the auxiliary database; the auxiliary database performs a temporary function only.

- Some objects can't be in the recovery set, including replicated master tables, tables with VARRAY columns, tables with nested tables, tables with external files, snapshot logs, snapshot tables, objects owned by SYS, and rollback segments.

CAUTION
RMAN TSPITR is bound by the same constraints and research that must be carried out before doing TSPITR to make sure you don't make a mess of data dependencies and integrity. See Chapter 9, Exercise 9.1 for all the gory details.

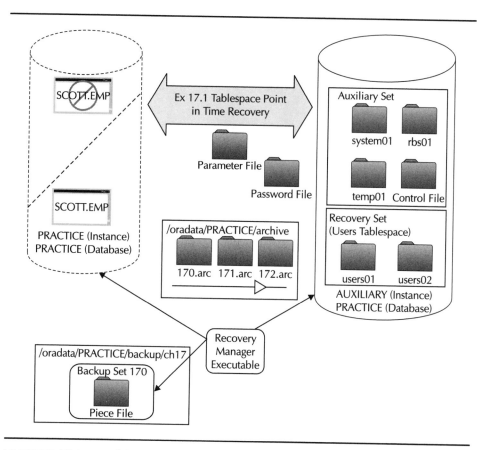

FIGURE 17-1.   *Tablespace point-in-time recovery with RMAN*

In this chapter, you'll use RMAN to perform the user-managed recovery exercise you performed in Chapter 9. This will be useful because the differences will stand out, and you can reinforce what you learned previously. Therefore, be sure to review Chapter 9 before tackling this chapter's exercise.

Recovery Manager TSPITR

How do you do RMAN TSPITR? The steps required are almost identical to the first few steps of duplicating a database and creating a standby database:

1. **Make an RMAN backup of the primary database.**   For RMAN to perform TSPITR, a suitable backup must exist for RMAN to restore and recover an

auxiliary database. The backup can be taken when the primary database is open or closed and can be image copies, proxy copies, or backups. Because the auxiliary instance must reside on the same machine as the primary database, it is not necessary to make the tapes available to a second machine as it was when duplicating or creating a standby database on a different host.

2. **Configure the auxiliary database parameter file.** A database initialization parameter file must be created for the auxiliary database. Most of the parameters required for auxiliary databases are related to the renaming of datafiles and log files automatically by Oracle. This prevents overwriting and manual intervention when a datafile needs to be moved from a different location. Important parameters include lock_name_space (creates a unique memory space for an instance using the same database name as another on the same machine), db_file_name_convert, and log_file_name_convert (automatically relocates the datafiles and log files).

3. **Configure the auxiliary database password file.** For DBA authentication, a password file is needed for the auxiliary database.

4. **Configure the Net8 configuration files.** RMAN needs to connect to the target database and the auxiliary database at the same time. One of the connections can be local as defined by the ORACLE_SID environment variable, but the other connection must be made via Net8. To also connect to a catalog database, another Net8 connection will be made.

5. **Start the auxiliary instance.** Before RMAN can perform TSPITR on the auxiliary, the auxiliary instance must be started in NOMOUNT mode. The parameter file that was created in step 2 will be read at this time.

6. **Open the primary database.** RMAN requires that the target database be open during TSPITR. The import of the recovery set dictionary data requires that the target database be open.

7. **Instigate TSPITR while connected to target, auxiliary, and optional catalog.** When you tell RMAN to recover a tablespace while connected to an auxiliary instance, it will perform TSPITR. Allocate a disk channel to the auxiliary and set the stop point for the recovery. Specify the tablespace(s) to recover, and RMAN takes care of the rest.

RMAN determines the best base-level backups to restore and then works out which incrementals and archive redo logs are required. At the completion of auxiliary recovery, RMAN will automatically open the auxiliary database with a RESETLOGS because you are doing incomplete recovery. Also, the auxiliary database needs the log files to be re-created. Once the auxiliary database is open,

RMAN will export the metadata about all objects contained in the recovered tablespaces, in the same way data is exported when you manually transport a tablespace from one database to another. After the metadata has been exported and the auxiliary instance had been closed, the target database control file is changed to point to the new datafiles just recovered. This is automatically done using RMAN switch commands. Finally, the metadata is imported into the primary database and the tablespaces remains offline. It is important to now take a backup of these tablespaces, as previous tablespace backups of these can no longer be used to roll the database forward through this TSPITR period. Once a backup has been taken, bring the tablespaces back online; they're ready for use.

CAUTION
You must make sure you are using a different redo log directory for the auxiliary database so as not to harm the primary database.

Exercise 17.1: Tablespace Point-in-Time Recovery+

This chapter has only one exercise. The goal is to accomplish a very simple TSPITR operation with no complications. This way, you'll witness the work done for you by RMAN to recover a single tablespace containing two datafiles.

Task Description	Minutes
1. Drop Table SCOTT.EMP	5
2. Prepare the Auxiliary Database	10
3. Perfom RMAN TSPITR	10
4. Confirm Recovery	5
5. Clean Up after TSPITR	10
Total Time	40

In this exercise, the target database will be PRACTICE and the auxiliary database will be AUXY (short for auxiliary). The following tasks will guide you through the successful recovery of a tablespace after a table is mistakenly dropped. You'll continue to make object changes before and after the drop table command to show how tablespace recovery will affect other objects. Once the recovery completes, you'll be able to confirm the dropped table has been recovered while other tablespace data has remained unchanged. To keep things simple, I picked a tablespace that is self-contained, and I won't change the schema as I did in Chapter 9. No object-dependency investigation should be necessary for this exercise.

Task 1: Drop Table SCOTT.EMP

Once again, drop SCOTT's employee table. You will recover this table using TSPITR. Mark the time before the table drop occurs. Later, you'll recover the users' tablespace up to this time and SCOTT's employee table will be recovered, along with all other objects contained in the tablespace.

```
SQL> CONNECT sys/practice@practice;
SQL> SET TIME ON;
10:57:13 SQL> DELETE FROM tina.date_log WHERE create_date > SYSDATE;
10:57:35 SQL> DROP TABLE SCOTT.EMP;
10:57:46 SQL> SET TIME OFF;
```

You can see that the drop table occurred at 10:57:35. For our example, the exercise takes place on January 17, 2002. This time will be used again in Task 3 during TPSPITR on the AUXY instance. To help confirm that TSPITR worked as intended, create an object in the USERS tablespace after the drop table command occurs. Also, insert a row into a table contained in the USERS tablespace. Finally, insert a row into a table in a different tablespace from USERS:

```
SQL> CREATE TABLE scott.dept_copy TABLESPACE users AS
  2    SELECT * FROM scott.dept;
SQL> INSERT INTO scott.dept (deptno, dname, loc)
  2    VALUES ('50','SUPPORT','DENVER');
SQL> INSERT INTO tina.date_log VALUES (SYSDATE+365*17);
SQL> COMMIT;
SQL> ALTER SYSTEM SWITCH LOGFILE;
```

After you perform TSPITR, the SCOTT.DEPT_COPY table will not exist in the USERS tablespace on the primary PRACTICE database. Since any data changes made to objects in the USERS tablespace after TSPITR will not be recovered, the support department will not be found in the department table. Finally, the data in TINA. DATE_LOG will remain untouched after TSPITR. You should see a date 17 years in the future after TSPITR. You will see that all nonrecovered tablespaces lose no data or objects. Objects in nonrecovered tablespaces can still be affected if there are direct associations with objects in the recovered tablespace, such as indexes, triggers, and constraints. Finally, switch the log files so all these changes made to the PRACTICE database will be stored in an archived log file.

Task 2: Prepare the Auxiliary Database

The preparation of the auxiliary database named AUXY is identical to the preparation you went through in the last chapter, with one exception: use the word AUXY instead of STBY for all the directories, parameters, and file names. All these files may already be in place because of your work in Chapter 9:

- **Directories**   Create all the administrative directories ($ORACLE_BASE /admin/AUXY) and data directories (/oradata/AUXY).

- **Parameter file**   Create a parameter file using a copy of the PRACTICE database and name it $ORACLE_BASE/admin/AUXY/pfile/initAUXY.ora. Add these parameters and change all occurrences of PRACTICE to AUXY (except for DB_NAME).

```
db_file_name_convert      = ("PRACTICE", "AUXY")
log_file_name_convert     = ("PRACTICE", "AUXY")
lock_name_space           = "AUXY"
```

- **Password file**   Create a password file for the standby database so that RMAN can connect to AUXY database as SYSDBA.

- **Windows service**   On Windows, create a new database service for the AUXY database named OracleServiceAUXY using the oradim utility.

Task 3: Perform RMAN TSPITR

One last time, you need to get SCOTT's employee table back. Instruct RMAN to perform TSPITR on the USERS tablespace. The actual command listing is quite small, as shown here:

```
connect target    sys/practice@practice
connect catalog   rman817/rman@rcat
connect auxiliary sys/auxy@auxy
run {
   set command id to 'Performing TSPITR';
   set until time "11-JAN-2002 10:57:35";
   allocate auxiliary channel d1 type disk;
   recover tablespace users;
}
```

This script file opens a connection to the target database (PRACTICE), the catalog database (RCAT), and the auxiliary database (AUXY). A channel is allocated for the auxiliary instance, and the V$SESSION.CLIENT_INFO dynamic view column is updated with the text "Performing TSPITR." Then, in just one recover tablespace command, RMAN takes over!

Run the script and examine the output in a trace file:

```
LINUX> rman trace=tspitr.log
RMAN> @tspitr.rcv
```

I'll point out some of the more interesting output that gives you indication of all the things RMAN is accomplishing. Remember that RMAN is restoring and recovering a subset of the target database to the auxiliary database first. Once the auxiliary is recovered, the recovery set tablespace is transported back into the target database:

```
RMAN-08021: channel d1: restoring controlfile
RMAN-08505: output filename=/oradata/AUXY/control01.ctl
```

The first file created is the auxiliary database control file. A backup of the PRACTICE database control file is restored to the location specified by the auxiliary parameter file. The backup piece where the control file is restored from shows up in the output messages. Remember that RMAN creates the auxiliary instance from the backups of the PRACTICE database, not from the database itself.

```
# set a destination filename for restore
set newname for datafile  1 to
 "/oradata/AUXY/system01.dbf";
# set a destination filename for restore
set newname for datafile  2 to
 "/oradata/AUXY/rbs01.dbf";
# set a destination filename for restore
set newname for datafile  3 to
 "/oradata/PRACTICE/users01.dbf";
# set a destination filename for restore
set newname for datafile  7 to
 "/oradata/PRACTICE/users02.dbf";
# restore the tablespaces in the recovery set plus the auxiliary tablespaces
```

To recover the USERS tablespace, RMAN knows that it must restore the datafiles in the recovery set of tablespaces, *and* it must also restore the required tablespaces and datafiles for the upcoming recovery. The users01.dbf and users02.dbf belong to the USERS tablespace and must be restored. These two datafiles are the datafiles that comprise the recovery set in this example. The system01.dbf and rbs01.dbf must also be restored (they comprise the auxiliary datafile set in this example).

```
sql clone "alter database datafile  1 online";
#online the datafiles restored or flipped
sql clone "alter database datafile  2 online";
#online the datafiles restored or flipped
sql clone "alter database datafile  3 online";
#online the datafiles restored or flipped
sql clone "alter database datafile  7 online";
# make the controlfile point at the restored datafiles, then recover them
recover clone database tablespace  USERS, SYSTEM, RBS;
alter clone database open resetlogs;
```

These commands will recover the three tablespaces in the auxiliary database required to deliver the USERS tablespace back to the target practice database. These commands are not the recovery; they are the scripts generated by RMAN in memory for the recovery that will occur. Thus, RMAN is creating scripts that it will run to accomplish the work you asked it to do. After recovery, the auxiliary database must be opened so that the USERS tablespace can have its dictionary metadata exported.

```
RMAN-06162: sql statement: alter tablespace  USERS offline for recover
...
RMAN-08089: channel d1: specifying datafile(s) to restore from backup set
RMAN-08523: restoring datafile 00001 to /oradata/AUXY/system01.dbf
RMAN-08523: restoring datafile 00002 to /oradata/AUXY/rbs01.dbf
RMAN-08523: restoring datafile 00003 to /oradata/PRACTICE/users01.dbf
RMAN-08523: restoring datafile 00007 to /oradata/PRACTICE/users02.dbf
RMAN-08023: channel d1: restored backup piece 1
...
RMAN-08024: channel d1: restore complete
```

This output ought to look familiar by now (considering all the practice you've been getting). These lines show the output from RMAN actually restoring baseline backups. Notice that the auxiliary set datafiles are being placed in the /oradata/AUXY directory, but the recovery set datafiles are being copied over the target datafile locations. The target database USERS tablespace is offlined prior to the restoration of the datafiles.

```
RMAN-08054: starting media recovery
...
RMAN-03023: executing command: recover(4)
RMAN-08515: archivelog filename=/oradata/PRACTICE/archive/170.arc thread=1
sequence=170
...
RMAN-08055: media recovery complete
RMAN-03022: compiling command: alter db
RMAN-06400: database opened
```

After restoration, the online tablespaces in the auxiliary database are recovered up to the stop point. Incremental backups are applied to the restored datafiles (no incrementals are shown here). Then redo from archive log files is applied to the auxiliary database. After recovery, the database is opened for the export:

```
host 'exp userid =\"sys/auxy@auxy as sysdba\"
point_in_time_recover=y tablespaces= USERS file=tspitr_a.dmp';
...
host 'imp userid =\"sys/practice@practice as sysdba\"
point_in_time_recover=y file=tspitr_a.dmp';
```

RMAN generates the export/import command to transport the newly recovered USERS tablespace from the AUXY database to the PRACTICE database.

If the script runs to completion without an error, TSPITR succeeded. At the conclusion of TSPITR, the auxiliary database (AUXY) is shut down, the target database (PRACTICE) is open, and the recovered tablespace(s) (USERS) is offline.

Task 4: Confirm Recovery

Confirm that the USERS tablespace recovery worked as desired by checking the state of tables in the database after placing the USERS tablespace online.

- Check that the objects and data in the USERS tablespace exist as they did just before the SCOTT.EMP table was dropped.

- Check that the SCOTT.EMP table exists and the SCOTT.DEPT_COPY table does not exist.

- Check to see if the SUPPORT department can be found in the SCOTT.DEPT table.

- Check to confirm that you don't have the DEPT_COPY table or the SUPPORT department in the SCOTT.DEPT table.

- Check that data in other tablespaces contains data that was changed after the recovery time of the users tablespace.

- Check that the TINA.DATE_LOG table has an insert date 17 years in the future.

All these checks can be performed with the SQL below:

```
SQL> connect sys/practice@practice;
SQL> ALTER TABLESPACE USERS ONLINE;
SQL> describe scott.emp;
SQL> describe scott.dept_copy;
SQL> SELECT * FROM scott.dept;
SQL> SELECT max(create_date) FROM tina.date_log;
```

Using RMAN TSPITR is easier than doing it yourself, isn't it?

Task 5: Clean Up after TSPITR

Once you've performed TSPITR, you must back up the datafiles in the primary database. You won't be able to recover the tablespace(s) using the pre-TSPITR datafile backups because the archived logs from that backup do not correspond to the newly recovered tablespace(s). Though a whole database backup will certainly work to protect the newly recovered USERS tablespace, you may just back up one tablespace with commands like these:

```
RMAN> run {
2        allocate channel d1 type disk;
3        backup tablespace USERS
4        format '/oradata/PRACTICE/backup/ch17/db_%d_%s_%p_%t';
5    }
```

One last matter of business: you don't need the auxiliary database files hanging around on disk any more. They've served their purpose. Remove the files from the /oradata/AUXY directory. This will get rid of the datafiles, control files, redo log files, and export file temporarily used by RMAN for TSPITR. You can also get rid of the database initialization file, password file, and other directories created for the auxiliary instance.

Troubleshooting

If you run into problems with this RMAN exercise, you might have encountered one of these errors. Look over this list for possible solutions.

1. **RMAN-11003: failure during parse/execution of SQL statement: alter system archive log current**
   RMAN-11001: Oracle Error: ORA-01109: database not open The target database (PRACTICE) must be open during TSPITR. The target switches logs and will have metadata in it. Open the PRACTICE database and restart TSPITR.

2. **ORA-27086: skgfglk: unable to lock file - already in use** Check that the file being created during TSPITR is the right one. If the file that RMAN cannot obtain a lock on is in a control file, confirm that you started the AUXY instance with the correct parameter file and have changed the control file parameter. If the file that RMAN cannot obtain a lock on is a datafile, verify that you set DB_NAME_FILE_CONVERT_FILE appropriately in the AUXY parameter file. If the problem file is an online redo log file, double-check the LOG_FILE_NAME_CONVERT parameter is set correctly.

3. **RMAN-11001: Oracle Error: ORA-01190: controlfile or data file 3 is from before the last RESETLOGS**
   ORA-01110: data file 3: 'd:/oradata/PRACTICE/users01.dbf' If you set the stop point time value incorrectly, you may get this error. Change the value and restart TSPITR. The datafile being restored or the control file being used are from different times and before the time of the last RESETLOGS opening.

4. **ORA-01124: cannot recover data file 7 - file is in use or recovery ORA-01110: data file 7: '/oradata/PRACTICE/users02.dbf'** You did not set a stop point or set it too far in the future. TSPITR must be an incomplete recovery. Use the set until option for recovery or add an until keyword after the recover tablespace command.

Summary

Take a few moments to compare Chapter 9 with this chapter. User-managed TSPITR is more work than the server-managed TSPITR covered in this chapter. Although user- and server-managed TSPITR both require that the database directories and supporting files be set up and a backup is used for database creation in both methods, RMAN does most of the database tasks for you. Table 17-1 summarizes the difference between user-managed and server-managed TSPITR.

User-Managed TSPITR	Server-Managed TSPITR
Configures duplicate database (directories, parameter file, password file, Windows Services); Net8 configuration is *optional*.	Configures duplicate database (directories, parameter file, password file, Windows Services); Net8 configuration is *required*.
Backs up primary database auxiliary and recovery set datafiles using user-managed open or closed backup. Backup takes as much disk or tape space as the required datafiles.	Backs up target database auxiliary and recovery set datafiles using server-managed open or closed backup or image copies. Backup takes less disk or tape space than all the datafiles. Image copies takes as much disk or tape space as all the datafiles.
Moves backup files via operating system commands.	Restores auxiliary database datafiles.
Creates a copy of the primary control file to the auxiliary location.	Restores a backup of the control file to the auxiliary control file location.
Performs manual incomplete recovery and open with RESETLOGS.	Performs manual incomplete recovery and open with RESETLOGS.

TABLE 17-1. *Comparison Between User-Managed and Server-Managed Tablespace Recovery*

User-Managed TSPITR	Server-Managed TSPITR
Exports/imports recovery set tablespace(s).	Handles export/import of recovery set tablespace(s).
Either renames datafiles to the recovered datafiles or copies the files at the operating system.	Switches the target database to use the recovered datafiles.
Drops the recovered tablespaces from the primary prior to TSPITR.	Switches the datafiles for you so the tablespace doesn't need to be dropped.
Target and auxiliary databases can be on different servers.	Target and auxiliary databases must be on the server.

TABLE 17-1.   *Comparison Between User-Managed and Server-Managed Tablespace Recovery* (continued)

In this chapter, you learned how to perform TSPITR with RMAN. You learned how to use an auxiliary database with RMAN to recover a tablespace and then plug that tablespace back into the primary database. For more information on RMAN TSPITR, look at Chapter 8 in the *RMAN Oracle8i Recovery Manager User's Guide and Reference.*

Chapter Questions

Here is your very last battery of questions (in this book, anyway). See how well you've gathered up the information in this chapter on RMAN TSPITR.

1. Use the RMAN duplicate command to perform tablespace point-in-time recovery.

   A. True

   B. False

2. During RMAN TSPITR, what parameter do you set in the auxiliary database parameter file to control the location of the online redo log files for the auxiliary database?

   A. db_file_name_convert

   B. log_file_name_convert

   C. The auxiliary database doesn't use online log files

   D. log_archive_dest

3. In this chapter's exercise, the recovered tablespace was the USERS tablespace. What other tablespaces must be recovered along with the data tablespaces? (Pick any that apply.)

   A. SYSTEM

   B. RBS

   C. TEMPORARY

   D. INDEXES

4. When considering RMAN TSPITR, you must address and resolve potential database dependencies and objects as you would with user-managed TSPITR.

   A. True

   B. False

5. Which of these tasks does RMAN TSPITR perform?

   A. Restores necessary target datafiles to the auxiliary database

   B. Recovers the restored database datafiles on the auxiliary database

   C. Switches target database to use the recovered datafiles

   D. Removes auxiliary database files after TSPITR completes

Answers to Chapter Questions

1. False. Though RMAN performs some duplication activities, the combination of the connection to an auxiliary database and the recover tablespace command team up to dictate TSPITR.

2. B. Once the auxiliary set and recovery set are restored, the auxiliary database is opened with the resetlogs option. During recovery of the auxiliary, the newly created online redo logs are not required (because of this, resetlogs creates them). Use the log_file_name_convert to create the new online redo logs into a different directory when the auxiliary database is opened with RESETLOGS.

3. A, B. During TSPITR, the system tablespace and nonsystem rollback segments are included as the auxiliary set.

4. True. RMAN TSPITR will fail as user-managed TSPITR if objects exist in the recovery set that cannot be transported via Export/Import. Also, dependencies between tablespaces in and out of the recovery set will cause RMAN TSPITR to fail.

5. A, B, C. RMAN does not remove the auxiliary database files (control files, datafiles of the recovery and auxiliary set, redo logs, and the export dump file).

PART
IV

Appendixes

APPENDIX
A

Glossary

isted here are the definitions of relevant keywords presented in this book.

- **alert log**   A text file that Oracle continuously writes important messages to. Events that are recorded in this file include database shutdowns, database startups, addition or removal of tablespaces or datafiles, and some database error messages. This file is located in the directory defined by the initialization parameter BACKGROUND_DUMP_DEST.

- **archiver process (ARCH or ARCn)**   An Oracle background process that copies the contents of the online redo log files into archived redo log files.

- **archive redo log file**   A copy of an online redo log file created by the archiver process (whenever a log switch occurs) or when a user requests a log to be archived. The archive log is used to recover the database from a backup.

- **auxiliary database/instance**   When certain features are used within RMAN (duplicate database, standby database, and tablespace point-in-time recovery), a second instance/database, called the auxiliary database, is created as a new or temporary database.

- **auxiliary set**   When carrying out tablespace point-in-time recovery, a number of datafiles must be restored which are not part of the recovery set. These files include the control file, the system datafiles, any datafiles containing rollback segments and, optionally, the temporary tablespace datafiles.

- **background process**   An Oracle process that carries out tasks in the background for all connected users. Background processes include database writer (DBWR or DBWn), System Monitor (SMON), Process Monitor (PMON), archiver (ARCH or ARCn), log writer (LGWR), and the checkpoint process (CKPT).

- **backup**   A copy of the whole database or partial set of the database. The backup can consist of the control file, tablespaces, datafiles, database objects, or archived redo log files.

- **backup piece**   A physical file that RMAN creates, using a format only known to RMAN, when you create a backup. This file is stored on disk or on tape.

- **backup set** A logical grouping of RMAN backup pieces. When RMAN takes a backup, it creates one or more backup sets comprising one or more backup pieces. A backup set contains control files and datafiles or archive log files. A backup set will not contain a mixture of datafiles and archive log files.

- **buffer cache** An area within the System Global Area that stores data retrieved from the database datafiles. Data blocks are read from disk and are stored in the buffer cache before they can be viewed or modified.

- **channel** A communication pathway between RMAN and the target database. A channel is used to query the target database and pass that data to the selected backup media (disk or tape) during a restore and recovery operations.

- **change vector** Makes a single change to a data block to move it from one state to another. Change vectors, sometimes referred to as redo vectors, are applied directly to data blocks during recovery and are created before the actual data block change is made in the buffer cache.

- **checkpoint** A structure stored in the control file and datafiles to indicate that all changes up to a given SCN have been written to the datafiles. During a checkpoint, redo records in the log buffer get written to the current online redo log before modified blocks in the buffer cache are written to the datafiles.

- **checkpoint (CKPT) process** An Oracle background process that writes the checkpoint information to the control file and the file headers. This process also signals database writer to flush dirty blocks from the buffer cache to disk. Starting in Oracle 8*i*, a checkpoint is recorded in the control file every three seconds.

- **clone** A copy of a database that takes on a new name.

- **closed/cold backup** A backup taken of the datafiles or control file when the database is closed. This is also referred to as a consistent backup.

- **complete recovery** When a database or subset of a database is restored from a backup and all archive log files and online log files are applied to it. All data block changes have been applied to the restored datafiles. During RMAN recovery, incremental backups might also get applied.

- **control file** A database file that is part of the database and stores all the key structural information. Information stored includes datafiles, online and archived redo log files, and checkpoint information. If RMAN is being used to take backups, backup information is also stored in the control file.

■ **corruption**   When a data block has changed from its correct state or some Oracle internal structure is incorrect. To resolve this, file recovery is often needed, or the new 9*i* block media recovery feature can be used.

■ **crash recovery**   When an instance crashes unexpectedly, crash recovery will automatically apply all redo contained in the online redo log files during the next database startup. The archived redo log files are not needed during crash recovery. This is also referred to as *instance recovery.*

■ **database writer (DBWR or DBWn)**   An Oracle background process that writes modified blocks from the buffer cache to the datafiles. Database writer does not write data from the buffer cache when a transaction commits; it mostly writes out dirty buffers when space is needed in the buffer cache for new blocks or if a checkpoint is issued.

■ **data block**   The smallest unit of space within an Oracle database, the size of which is determined by the initialization parameter DB_BLOCK_SIZE.

■ **data block address (DBA)**   The address of each data block within the database. It is an encoded representation of the file number and the block number within the file.

■ **datafile**   A physical file created by Oracle comprising a number of data blocks. A datafile can only belong to one tablespace within a single database.

■ **Data Guard**   The new and improved version of the standby database released on certain platforms with 8.1.7 and made generally available with 9*i*. Significant enhancements to the standby database have been added in the areas of shipping and application of the archive log files.

■ **data definition language (DDL)**   SQL statements that define, create, drop, and maintain schema objects. An example of such a statement is the CREATE TABLE command.

■ **data manipulation language (DML)**   SQL statements that manipulate the data stored in the database. Such statements include INSERT, UPDATE, and DELETE.

■ **duplicate database**   A copy of a database that can have the same name or a different name as the original copied database.

■ **export**   An Oracle utility that can extract the contents of your database or a subset of your database into a binary formatted file. This file can then be used to transfer objects and data to other databases.

■ **image copy** RMAN is able to make exact image copies of datafiles, archive log files or archive log files. This is similar to a file copy created by using operating system copy commands.

■ **import** An Oracle utility that will insert the objects into a database that are contained within an Oracle binary export file.

■ **incomplete recovery** When a database or subset of a database is restored from a backup and an incomplete amount of redo information is applied, some changes have not been applied to the database. Therefore, some previous database changes stored in redo files will not be recovered in the database. To open a database after incomplete recovery, the online redo logs must be reset.

■ **instance** The combination of the Oracle background processes and the System Global Area (SGA) created when the database is first started up.

■ **log buffer** A memory area within the SGA that contains the redo records when changes to data blocks are made. The information from the log buffer is flushed out to the current online redo log file when the log buffer is one-third full, when a commit is issued, when 1MB of redo is generated, or when a log switch is requested.

■ **logical backup** When a backup is generated by creating the database contents without physically copying the database file. The Oracle tool called Export can be used to take a logical backup of the database or a subset of the database.

■ **LogMiner** A tool that allows you to read the redo log files from an Oracle database and reconstruct the SQL used to generate the data block changes and the SQL to undo those changes. This tool was introduced in Oracle 8*i* but can be used to view log files from Oracle 8.0 databases.

■ **log sequence number** A number that uniquely identifies a single redo log file. When the database is first created, the first redo log will have a log sequence number of 1. When a log switch occurs, the log sequence number is incremented by 1 to 2.

■ **log switch** When the log writer process stops writing to one online redo log file and begins writing to the next one. This can happen when the current online redo log file is full or a user issues an ALTER SYSTEM SWITCH LOGFILE command.

■ **log writer (LGWR)** An Oracle background process that is responsible for writing the redo information from the log buffer to the current online redo logs.

- **Media Management Layer (MML)** A third-party piece of software that handles the movement of data to and from sequential media, such as magnetic tapes.

- **NOLOGGING** A mode of logging redo when carrying out direct-load insert operations. The amount of redo generated is significantly reduced when using NOLOGGING, but you must back up the affected object after the insert is complete to recover in the event of a failure. Potential direct-load operations include CREATE TABLE ... AS SELECT, CREATE INDEX, ALTER TABLE MOVE/SPLIT PARTITION, and ALTER INDEX ... REBUILD/SPLIT PARTITION.

- **online redo log file** The set of two or more log files that are continuously being written to by LGWR when flushing out the contents of the log buffer. These files are used in a circular fashion. For example, if you have two online redo log file groups, after the second one has been written to, the first one will be written to, overwriting its contents.

- **open/hot backup** A backup taken when the database is open and available for use. This type of backup can only be taken if the database is running in ARCHIVELOG mode. This is also referred to as an inconsistent backup.

- **physical backup** When the database files are physically copied from one location to another. This can be done using operating system utilities or by using the RMAN image copy feature.

- **primary database** The original or source database that gets copied during database duplication or standby creation. During tablespace point-in-time recovery, the primary database is partially duplicated and recovered.

- **process global area (PGA)** Private memory area allocated for a server process when it connects to the database. This memory area is used for such things as sorting, session information, and LogMiner.

- **Process Monitor (PMON)** A background process that handles the recovery of user process failure. It will clean up and free any resources that the failed process was holding.

- **proxy copy** A type of backup method that gives the control of managing and backing and restoration up the database files to the Media Management Layer.

- **recovery** The process of applying incremental backups (if using RMAN) and redo information to reconstruct changes made to data blocks.

- **recovery catalog** A repository of information used by RMAN to record information about Oracle databases and the backups that have been taken for those databases. This is an optional part of the RMAN architecture. Some of this information is also recorded in the target database control file.

- **Recovery Manager (RMAN)** An Oracle utility that backs up, restores, and recovers Oracle databases.

- **recovery set** During tablespace point in time recovery, the set of datafiles that undergo incomplete recovery to retrieve desired data or data objects. The recovery set cannot include any system datafiles or any datafiles that contain rollback segments.

- **redo record** A group of redo vectors that make an atomic change to the database. Redo vectors are grouped up into records that are applied to the database during recovery. If one redo vector is applied during recovery, all vectors within the same redo record are also applied.

- **Remote File Server (RFS)** An Oracle background process that is created on a standby database and creates the archive log files received from the primary database over Net8 during standby managed recovery.

- **RESETLOGS** A mode of opening the database after incomplete recovery has been performed that re-creates or reformats the current online redo log files, removing any of their contents. A new incarnation of the database is created, and a backup should be performed immediately. Recovery through a RESETLOGS operation is nearly impossible after the database has been opened and data has been changed.

- **restore** The replacement from a backup of lost or damaged database files. Once the files have been restored, they can be recovered to reconstruct the data block changes.

- **resync** The process of updating the recovery catalog with the information stored in the target database control file. This is carried out automatically by RMAN before certain operations like BACKUP, COPY, RESTORE, and RECOVER. It can also be done manually by issuing the RESYNC CATALOG command to RMAN.

- **rollback** When the rollback segments are used to undo any uncommitted data changes. This is carried out automatically by Oracle after the database has been rolled forward using redo logs, or when a user manually issues a ROLLBACK command before their transaction has been committed.

- **rollback segment** Contains data values from data blocks as they appeared before they were changed. Rollback segments are used to roll back uncommitted transactions and allow a consistent read image of the database so that a user will always see data as it was when their transaction started, whether or not the data changed since the beginning of their transaction.

- **ROWID**   A structure that is used to reference rows within an object. The ROWID identifies the object identifier, the file number, the data block number in the file, and the row location in the data block.

- **segment**   A set of one or more extents that are logically grouped together within a single tablespace. Segments are categorized into four types: data segments, index segments, rollback segments, and temporary segments. When a table is created, one or more extents are allocated to form a data segment.

- **server-managed recovery**   The backup, restore, and recovery methods that are managed by the Oracle RMAN utility.

- **shared pool**   A memory area within the System Global Area that is divided up into the library cache (which contains shared SQL areas) and the dictionary or row cache (which contains data dictionary).

- **standby database**   An exact copy of a database used in case of failure to the primary database. The standby database is kept up-to-date by applying the archive redo log files transferred from the primary database. In the event of a failure to the primary database, the standby can be activated as the new primary database.

- **standby managed recovery**   When a standby database automatically applies the archive redo logs transferred from the primary database.

- **standby manual recovery**   When you must manually apply the archive redo logs to the standby database that have been transferred from the primary database.

- **system change number (SCN)**   A number that represents a consistent committed version of the database at a single point in time; it can be thought of as the database equivalent to a clock. Each committed transaction receives a unique SCN.

- **System Global Area (SGA)**   A shared area of memory that is accessed by all users connected to the database. The System Global Area consists of the buffer cache, the shared pool, and the log buffer, as well as many memory structures that the Oracle RDBMS uses to function.

- **System Monitor (SMON)** An Oracle background process that carries out many jobs in the database, including crash recovery on database startup, cleanup of temporary segments that are no longer in use, coalescing of free extents for dictionary managed tablespaces, and cleanup of dropped objects from the data dictionary.

- **tablespace** A logical storage area for related objects. Every database object is stored in a tablespace, which is comprised of one or more datafiles.

- **tablespace point-in-time recovery (TSPITR)** The process of recovering one or more nonsystem tablespaces to a point in time that is different from the rest of the database. This is achieved by restoring a recovery and auxiliary set of datafiles using user-managed or server-managed recovery techniques.

- **target database** The main database that is being backed up, restored, or recovered. It must be queried by RMAN when creating a duplicate database, standby database, or auxiliary database for carrying out tablespace point-in-time recovery.

- **transportable tablespace** A feature of Oracle that allows a tablespace to be moved or copied from one database to another on the same hardware architecture and operating system. It uses the Export utility to transfer the metadata for the objects contained in the tablespaces being transported. The export file is transported along with the tablespace datafiles to another database. The Import utility is used to import the metadata, making the newly transported tablespace accessible to the destination database.

- **user-managed recovery** The backup, restore, and recovery methods that are managed by the DBA. RMAN is not used during these methods. Instead, operating system utilities are relied upon to back up and restore your database, and the DBA must manually apply the redo log files and open the database.

APPENDIX
B

RMAN in Oracle 9i

hroughout this book, I chose to use Oracle 8*i* as the version for the exercises and discussions since most readers are still using a version 8 database. However, many Oracle customers have already migrated to Oracle 9*i* or are planning to do so soon. Most of the details in this book are as valid for 9*i* as they are for 8i. However, Recovery Manager (RMAN) has improved significantly with Oracle's 9*i* release. In several RMAN chapters, I've discussed some of the new 9*i* new features. In addition, this appendix describes how you can use the new 9*i* features in contrast to the discussions in Chapters 11, 12, 13, and 14. This appendix is not comprehensive, but it will provide an illustration of some of the improvements in 9*i*.

RMAN Configuration

Configuring the catalog with RMAN is very similar in both versions. In Oracle 8*i* RMAN, you must either provide nocatalog as a command line option, or connect to the catalog within the script. In 9*i*, nocatalog is assumed by default (whether or not you supply this parameter at the command line).

A very useful configuration feature to take advantage of in 9*i* is the ability to configure persistent channels for backup operations. In the backup scripts in Chapter 12, each backup had to allocate a channel and provide a format for that channel. The format either specified a directory and filename on disk or a filename on tape. In 9*i*, you can define the characteristics for default channels on both disk and tape. This way, backup, restore, and recovery executions can use the preconfigured channel definitions. These default channel definitions can be overridden by explicitly allocating a channel during a backup script in the same way as demonstrated in this book. To illustrate, I'll use the examples from Chapter 12.

In Chapter 12, each backup script wrote the backups to the /oradata/PRACTICE/backup/ch12 directory, and each script in the chapter had to allocate a channel of type disk and define the format for each backup. In 9*i*, you can use RMAN's configure command to tell RMAN that your default device for backups will be type disk and the location for those backups will be a specific directory. Use these commands to accomplish this:

```
LINUX> rman
RMAN> connect target sys/practice@practice9i
RMAN> connect catalog rman901/rman@rcat
RMAN> configure default device type to disk;
RMAN> configure channel device type disk format =
  2        '/oradata/PRACTICE/backup/ch12/db_%d_%s_%p_%t';
```

To use the configure parameter, you must be connected to the target database and, optionally, the recovery catalog. You must connect to the target database because the configuration details are stored in the target control file. This information is also stored in the recovery catalog.

You can define other channel definitions, like the maximum size for the backup pieces. RMAN can back up parts of the database in parallel. Therefore, you can also define the default degree of parallelism for your backups. Say you have two file systems set aside for RMAN backups where the maximum file size on those file systems is 2GB. Tell RMAN that, unless otherwise specified, it should create backups to the /u01 and the /u02 file systems and should not let any backup pieces get larger than 2GB. Once connected to the target database and the optional recovery catalog, issue the following:

```
RMAN> configure device type disk parallelism 2;
RMAN> configure channel 1 device type disk
2>      format = '/u01/oracle/backup/disk1/db_%d_%s_%p_%t'
3>      maxpiecesize 2G;
RMAN> configure channel 2 device type disk
2>      format = '/u02/oracle/backup/disk1/db_%d_%s_%p_%t'
3>      maxpiecesize 2G;
```

During backups, RMAN will use the two defined channels and call them ORA_DISK1 and ORA_DISK2. They will write to /u01 and /u02, respectively. Tape configuration can be done in much the same way.

You can configure RMAN to create a backup of a control file each time a backup command is issued. The backup control file created will not be contained in a backup set. Instead, it will be a binary file copy ready for use during a restore and recovery when the recovery catalog and the current target control file have been lost. This can be done using these commands (once you've connected to the target database and the optional recovery catalog):

```
RMAN> configure controlfile autobackup on;
RMAN> configure controlfile autobackup format for device type
2>      disk to '/u01/oracle/backup/disk1/cf_%f';
```

Also, use the configure command to relocate the snapshot control file used by RMAN during backup operations:

```
RMAN> configure snapshot controlfile name
2>      to '/u01/oracle/backup/disk1/snap.f';
```

It is possible to view all of the RMAN configurations for each database by using RMAN or by connecting the recovery catalog and issuing some SQL. Below is an example of the RMAN method:

```
LINUX> rman
RMAN> connect target sys/practice@practice9i
RMAN> connect catalog rman901/rman@rcat
RMAN> show all;
```

And here is an example of the SQL method:

```
LINUX> sqlplus /nolog
SQL> connect rman901/rman@rcat
SQL> SELECT dbid, dbinc_key, d.name, c.name, c.value
2      FROM rc_database d, rc_rman_configuration c
3      WHERE d.db_key = c.db_key
4      ORDER BY d.name, d.dbinc_key, c.conf#;
```

Using either RMAN or SQL, you can review your current RMAN configuration settings.

RMAN Backup

In 9*i*, the backup scripts can be much simpler because of the new configuration features available. Also, the backup command (and others) don't have to be included within a run block. For example, in Chapter 12, you learned how to make a whole database incremental level 0 baseline backup. The commands for that script in 8*i* contained text like you see below. You had to allocate a channel before you could run the backup. Since you want to store the backup pieces in a different directory than the one RMAN will place them in by default ($ORACLE_HOME/dbs), you had to define a format for the channel or for the backup command.

```
run {
    allocate channel d1 type disk;
    backup
      incremental level = 0
      database
      format '/oradata/PRACTICE/backup/ch12/db_%d_%s_%p_%t'
      tag = 'WHOLE_INC0';
}
```

In Oracle 9*i*, the same backup script is much neater and easier, assuming that the default channels have been preconfigured using the steps just outlined. You must still be connected to the target database and the optional recovery catalog before running these commands.

```
RMAN> backup incremental level 0 database tag = 'WHOLE_INC0';
```

The backup command will use the preconfigured channels to locate the placement of the backup pieces. A cumulative level 1 incremental backup can be accomplished with this one command:

```
RMAN> backup incremental level 1 database tag = 'WHOLE_INC1';
```

Oracle recommends that you back up key components of your database whenever you add a datafile. Such components would include the control file and the newly created datafile. The NOT BACKED UP keyword to the backup command provides an easy way to do this in 9*i*:

```
RMAN> backup incremental level 0 database NOT BACKED UP;
```

Running this command will tell RMAN to back up all datafiles that have not been backed up since they were created. If you have configured the automatic control file backup, the control file will also be backed up for you.

What if your long-running backup fails half way through? In Oracle 8*i*, you have to start the backup again. In Oracle 9*i*, you can tell RMAN to restart the backup but back up only those files that were not backed up the first time (assuming that you perform a backup daily):

```
RMAN> backup incremental level 1 cumulative database
2>     NOT BACKED UP since 'SYSDATE - 1';
```

In Oracle 8*i*, you have to run a separate backup command to make backups of your archive log files after the datafiles are backed up. This is made easier in 9*i* using the PLUS ARCHIVELOG option to the backup command. When RMAN sees this, it will automatically issue a BACKUP ARCHIVELOG ALL command after it has issued an ALTER SYSTEM SWITCH LOGFILE to ensure the current online log file is archived. The archive logs are backed up within their own backup set, separate from the datafiles being backed up before the datafiles. After the datafiles have been backed up, RMAN will issue another ALTER SYSTEM SWITCH LOGFILE and then back up any more archive log files that have been produced during the datafile backup. Use this example to create an incremental backup with all of the archive logs:

```
RMAN> backup database incremental level 1 cumulative plus archivelog;
```

RMAN has also added some other functionality to the back up of archive logs:

- Automatic deletion of archive log files on disk from all archive log destinations once they have been backed up. Before 9*i*, you had to manually make sure all the archive logs were backed up and removed from all destination directories.

- Automatic archiving of the current online redo log file before backing up the archive log files. This ensures that each backup has the most recent log files created by the database.

- An automatic search of all other archive log destinations for a correct version of the file when an archive log file is missing or found to be corrupt.

- An additional column, BACKUP_COUNT, in the V$ARCHIVED_LOG view that keeps track of the number of times RMAN has backed up each archive log file. This makes it far easier to monitor the current backup situation of the archive log files.

RMAN Catalog Maintenance

In 9*i*, Oracle has improved the list options. With Oracle 8*i*, you have to wade through all the details displayed to you by RMAN. It can be grueling to work your way through so much output to find a small part of the backup that you want to confirm is there. One major improvement with Oracle 9*i* is that you can see the highlights of your backups. Follow these examples to see how much better the output has become:

```
RMAN> list backup summary;
RMAN> list backup by file;
RMAN> list backup of datafile 1 summary;
```

Many Oracle users keep some backups on disk and some on tape. Suppose you wanted to keep last week's backups on disk and put older disk backups on tape. In 9*i*, you can create backups to tape of the current RMAN disk backups. When you carry out a restore and recovery using RMAN, it will try and restore the disk backup, but if it is not available, the backup from tape will be restored. This command will accomplish just that:

```
RMAN> backup device type sbt backupset
2>      created before 'sysdate-7' delete input;
```

Removing old backups from the MML and from the recovery catalog requires attention with Oracle 8*i*. In 9*i*, you can instruct RMAN to make use of a retention policy similar to typical tape management software retention policies. While RMAN is taking backups, it is also applying the retention policy constraints that you have assigned with the configure command to determine which backups or copies are no longer needed. Backups that are no longer needed are automatically marked as obsolete in the recovery catalog. You are then able to report that backups are obsolete and delete them. RMAN will not automatically delete obsolete backups; you must issue the command to do it. The retention policy that you can define is based on either the number of days you wish to recover from or the number of redundant backups you have. This period of time is called the Recovery Window. For example, if you want RMAN to automatically delete backups that are no longer needed to recover the database before the last 21 days, tell it so with this command:

```
RMAN> configure retention policy to recovery window of 21 days;
```

To report the obsolete backups and then delete them from the recovery catalog and media, issue the following:

```
RMAN> report obsolete;    # will use the configured retention policy
RMAN> allocate channel for maintenance device type disk;
RMAN> delete obsolete;
RMAN> release channel;
```

RMAN Restore and Recovery

RMAN has also changed the way in which backups can be restored using a more optimized approach. Before 9*i*, RMAN automatically restored the datafiles that it requires to carry out recovery of all or part of the database. If the datafile already existed on disk from a previous restoration, RMAN would overwrite it with the restored file. In 9*i*, RMAN is clever enough to use an existing file for recovery rather than restoring a file from backup.

In Oracle 9*i*, you can perform block media recovery. RMAN has always performed operations at the Oracle data block level for datafiles. RMAN reads each block, decides if it should be backed up (according to the incremental backup strategy), and writes it into a backup piece. Up until 9*i*, the smallest level of restoration and recovery that RMAN could perform was a single datafile. With 9*i*, it is now possible to restore and recover a single data block. One reason you might want to do this would be if you had a small number of data block corruptions in a 2GB datafile: it would be far quicker to restore just the affected blocks and roll them forward using the archive and online redo log files than it would be to restore the whole 2GB datafile and apply redo to it. The other main advantage to using this feature is that all data in the affected tablespace and datafiles remain available. The only data not available to the user during recovery is the data within the corrupted blocks.

RMAN requires that a full backup of the blocks being recovered be in place, and complete recovery must also be carried out. Just like recovering a single datafile while the database remains open, all redo up to the current redo information must be applied to the recovering data blocks. To carry out block media recovery, use this example:

```
RMAN> BLOCKRECOVER DATAFILE 4 BLOCK 7 DATAFILE 4 BLOCK 15;
```

Summary

That's a little taste of the new and improved features available with RMAN in Oracle 9*i*. I hope this will get you started when you migrate your 8*i* RMAN deployment to 9*i*. To find out more about RMAN in 9*i*, look at the Oracle 9i manuals: *Oracle9i Recovery Manager User's Guide Release 1* (9.0.1) and *Oracle9i Recovery Manager Reference Release 1* (9.0.1). An especially helpful place to begin is the "What's New in Recovery Manager?" section in the beginning of the *Oracle9i Recovery Manager User's Guide*.

Index

C

M

U

INTERNATIONAL CONTACT INFORMATION

AUSTRALIA
McGraw-Hill Book Company Australia Pty. Ltd.
TEL +61-2-9417-9899
FAX +61-2-9417-5687
http://www.mcgraw-hill.com.au
books-it_sydney@mcgraw-hill.com

CANADA
McGraw-Hill Ryerson Ltd.
TEL +905-430-5000
FAX +905-430-5020
http://www.mcgrawhill.ca

GREECE, MIDDLE EAST,
NORTHERN AFRICA
McGraw-Hill Hellas
TEL +30-1-656-0990-3-4
FAX +30-1-654-5525

MEXICO (Also serving Latin America)
McGraw-Hill Interamericana Editores S.A. de C.V.
TEL +525-117-1583
FAX +525-117-1589
http://www.mcgraw-hill.com.mx
fernando_castellanos@mcgraw-hill.com

SINGAPORE (Serving Asia)
McGraw-Hill Book Company
TEL +65-863-1580
FAX +65-862-3354
http://www.mcgraw-hill.com.sg
mghasia@mcgraw-hill.com

SOUTH AFRICA
McGraw-Hill South Africa
TEL +27-11-622-7512
FAX +27-11-622-9045
robyn_swanepoel@mcgraw-hill.com

UNITED KINGDOM & EUROPE
(Excluding Southern Europe)
McGraw-Hill Education Europe
TEL +44-1-628-502500
FAX +44-1-628-770224
http://www.mcgraw-hill.co.uk
computing_neurope@mcgraw-hill.com

ALL OTHER INQUIRIES Contact:
Osborne/McGraw-Hill
TEL +1-510-549-6600
FAX +1-510-883-7600
http://www.osborne.com
omg_international@mcgraw-hill.com